Contents

vi

Articles on

Witchcraft, Magic and Demonology

A Twelve Volume Anthology
of Scholarly Articles

Edited with introductions by

Brian P. Levack
University of Texas

A Garland Series

Contents of Series

Introduction

The prosecution of witches was accompanied by the production of a large volume of learned writing on the subject. This literature, which was written for the most part by theologians and judges, was a product of the trials and one of the forces that led to their continuation and geographical expansion. The earliest treatises were originally written in manuscript form and, in that capacity, had only limited value in providing guidance to judges and magistrates regarding the crime of witchcraft. With the introduction of printing in the late fifteenth century, however, these treatises gained a much larger audience and became available throughout Europe. Some of the more famous treatises, such as the *Malleus Maleficarum* (1486), went into multiple editions and were translated into the main vernacular languages. By the middle of the sixteenth century a clergyman, judge or educated layman had access to a large and varied literature on the subject of witchcraft. This material often had the effect of intensifying his fear of witchcraft and strengthening his determination to take action against individuals suspected of practicing it. And since this literature spread easily and quickly throughout the European continent, it helped to introduce learned beliefs in areas which had not yet received them. In this way the dissemination of witchcraft treatises became one of the driving forces of the great European witch-hunt.

The literature of witchcraft possesses immense value for scholars. First, it provides detailed evidence regarding the content of learned witch beliefs. The ideas of educated clerics and laymen about witchcraft differed from those of poorly educated villagers who were usually the original source of witchcraft accusations. While popular beliefs were concerned mainly with the alleged practice of *maleficium* or harmful magic, learned beliefs emphasized the diabolical nature of the crime. Witchcraft treatises discussed at length such matters as the pact with the Devil and the collective worship of him at the Sabbath. Some learned witch beliefs can be found in the recorded confessions of witches, since those confessions, having been adduced under torture or other forms of judicial pressure, often reflect the ideas of their interrogators. But the treatises themselves, which sometimes incorporated the content of these confessions, give us a more complete picture of learned or "elite" beliefs. Indeed, the treatises actually helped to fuse the various elements that comprise the cumulative concept of witchcraft, the set of ideas regarding all the alleged activities of witches. By the time the *Malleus Maleficarum* was published, this concept was already in large part formed, but later treatises by the Belgian Jesuit Martin Del Rio, the Italian monk Francesco Guazzo, and the French Protestant Lambert Daneau added important elements to it.

This literature also provides evidence about the judicial mechanisms used to bring witches to justice and the attitudes of judges toward the entire process. Often intended as manuals for inquisitors, the treatises give detailed information about the ways witches should be treated in the courtroom as well as why it was necessary to pursue and try them successfully.

Finally, this literature gives us an awareness of the differences of opinion within the intellectual community regarding the nature and reality of witchcraft. Although the cumulative concept of witchcraft commanded widespread support by the middle of the sixteenth century, it did encounter some skeptical challenges. The most famous of these came from Johann Weyer, a physician who in his *De Praestigiis Daemonum* (1563) attributed the confessions of witches to female melancholia, and Reginald Scot, an English gentleman whose *Discovery of Witchcraft* (1584) openly attacked the credulousness of the *Malleus Maleficarum*. The arguments of these skeptics elicited determined and effective responses from the French judge and political theorist Jean Bodin, the Swiss theologian and professor of medicine Thomas Erastus, and King James VI of Scotland.

Although the defenders of orthodoxy were able to blunt the attack of the skeptics in the late sixteenth century, the skeptics ultimately triumphed in the late seventeenth century, when new intellectual currents, especially Cartesianism, began to influence European education. After a series of late seventeenth-century debates, some of which are discussed in this and subsequent volumes, European elites gave up their beliefs in magic and diabolism and refused to bring accused witches to justice. After that time witch beliefs remained a part of popular culture but virtually disappeared from learned culture.

The articles reproduced here represent scholarly commentaries on some of the witchcraft treatises and the debates they inspired. Most of the articles deal with specific witchcraft treatises, including some that are relatively unknown. One of them actually reproduces an early Spanish treatise by Martin De Casteñega. A few of the articles deal with the controversies between the credulous and the skeptical in the late sixteenth century. The article by Erik Midelfort discusses the growth of a distinctly Catholic theory of witchcraft in late sixteenth-century Germany, one which arose in response to Protestant pressure. The final article by Stuart Clark raises some interesting questions regarding the "scientific" character of many demonological treatises. Taken together, these essays provide us with

Volume 4

The Literature
of Witchcraft

edited with introductions by
Brian P. Levack

Garland Publishing, Inc.
New York & London 1992

Library of Congress Cataloging-in-publication Data

The Literature of witchcraft / edited by Brian P. Levack
     p.   cm. — (Articles on witchcraft, magic and demonology ; v. 4)
    Reprint of works originally published 1907–1984.
    Includes bibliographical references.
    ISBN 0-8153-1026-9 (alk. paper)
    1. Witchcraft—History—Sources. I. Levack, Brian P. II. Series.
BF1563.A77   1992 vol. 4
133.4'09 s—dc20
[133.4'3'09]   92-21029
                                             CIP

#26132672

Printed on acid-free, 250-year-life paper
Manufactured in the United States of America

some valuable insights into the way witchcraft was viewed by the men who occupied positions of power within Church and state.

Further Reading

Bekker, Balthasar. *The World Bewitch'd*. London, 1695.

Binsfield, Peter. *Tractatus de confessionibus maleficarum et sagarum*. Trier, 1591.

Bodin, Jean. *Démonomanie des sorciers*. Paris, 1580.

Boguet, Henri. *An Exam of Witches*, ed. Montague Summers. London, 1929.

De Lance, Pierre. *Tableau de l'inconstance des mauvais anges et démons*. Paris, 1982.

Del Rio, Martin A. *Disquisitionum Magicarum*. Louvain, 1599.

Daneau, Lambert. *A Dialogue of Witches*. London, 1575.

Gifford, George. *A Dialogue Concerning Witches and Witchcraft*. London, 1593.

Glanville, Joseph. *Saducismus Triumphatus*. London, 1681.

Guazzo, Francesco M. *Compendium Maleficarum*, ed. M. Summers. London, 1929.

Hopkins, Matthew. *The Discovery of Witches,* ed. M. Summers. London, 1928

Kramer, Heinrich and James Sprenger. *Malleus Maleficarum*, ed. M. Summers. New York, 1928.

Leutenbauer, S. *Hexerei- und Zaubereidelikt in der Literatur von 1450 bis 1550*. Berlin, 1972.

Remy, Nicolas. *Demonolatry*, ed. M. Summers. London, 1930.

Sinclair, George. *Satan's Invisible World Discovered*. London, 1685.

Scot, Reginald. *The Discoverie of Witchcraft*. London, 1930.

Weyer, Johann. *Witches, Devils, and Doctors in the Renaissance: Johann Weyer: De Praestigiis Daemonum*, George Mora, ed. Binghamton, NY, 1991.

Series Introduction

The main purpose of this collection is to bring together a large number of scholarly articles on the subject of witchcraft, magic and demonology. These articles are drawn from a broad selection of journals in many different disciplines. They reflect the sustained interest of historians, anthropologists, legal scholars, psychologists, sociologists, art historians, and literary scholars on the subject. In one way or another they all deal with man's belief in and fear of supernatural evil.

In early modern Europe a witch was believed to be a person who not only practiced harmful magic but who also made a pact with the Devil and sometimes worshipped him in nocturnal assemblies. The magical powers of the witch were generally the concern of her neighbors, who accused her of causing physical harm or bringing about some kind of misfortune. The witch's commerce with the Devil, however, remained the main concern of the clergy and the educated elite, who believed that she was a heretic and apostate involved in a vast conspiracy to undermine Christianity and destroy the moral order. As a scholarly subject, witchcraft involves an investigation of both aspects of the witch's alleged crime. On the one hand it studies magic, which is the human exercise of some preternatural, supernatural, or occult power to produce empirical effects, and on the other hand it is concerned with demonology, the study of evil spirits and its alleged activities. Most of the articles in this collection are concerned with witchcraft in the full early modern European sense of the word, but some focus exclusively on magic, while others are concerned mainly with demonic spirits and their relations with humans.

The majority of the articles in this collection deal with the historical process of witch-hunting in Europe and America between 1450 and 1750. During these years the prosecution of more than 100,000 persons, mostly women, has led scholars to investigate the development of learned and popular beliefs regarding witchcraft, the social and religious tensions which resulted in accusations, the legal processes that were used to bring witches to trial, and the ultimate end of witchcraft prosecutions. Six of the twelve volumes deal with different aspects of this massive judicial assault on witchcraft. Volume 3 includes a variety of interpretations of the entire process of witch-hunting in Europe, while volumes 5, 6, 7, and 8 deal successively with local and regional witchcraft prosecutions in continental Europe, England, Scotland, and Colonial America. Volume 4 explores the large body of printed treatises on witchcraft that helped to spread learned witch beliefs throughout Europe and thus inspired and reinforced the prosecutions.

Three volumes treat themes that are closely related to the great European witch-hunt. Volume 2 studies the various beliefs regarding magic and the Devil that originated in the classical and medieval periods and eventually came together in the cumulative concept of witchcraft in the fifteenth and sixteenth centuries. Volume 9 is devoted to the subject of demonic possession and exorcism. Possession did not always involve the agency of a witch, but a number of witchcraft trials in the sixteenth and seventeenth centuries resulted from allegations that witches had commanded demons to take physical possession of other persons. Volume 10 addresses the question: why do witches, both in Europe during the early modern period and in other cultures at other periods of time, tend to be women? A further objective of that volume is to examine the social and economic context in which witchcraft accusations and prosecutions arose.

The remaining three volumes deal with topics that are only indirectly related to the witchcraft prosecutions of the early modern period. Volume 1 is devoted to anthropological studies of witchcraft and magic among non-literate peoples. This literature has had a strong influence on historical scholarship during the past twenty-five years, and it has contributed to a deeper understanding of the nature of witchcraft, magic and religion. Because of the theoretical value of this literature, the volume serves as an introduction to the entire collection. Volume 11 discusses the learned magic that was practiced during the Renaissance. Although this magic is not directly connected to witchcraft, it possesses enormous importance to the intellectual history of the early modern period and even made a contribution to the development of modern science. The final volume explores the ways in which witchcraft and demonology have served as themes in both art and literature.

The articles reproduced in these volumes were selected on the basis of many different criteria. Some were chosen because of the wealth of information they provide regarding particular witch-hunts or witch beliefs, while others were included because of the cogency of their arguments or the importance of their approaches to the problem of witchcraft. The great majority of the articles were written in the past thirty years, during which time the most valuable scholarship in the field has been done. A few articles, however, date from the late nineteenth and early twentieth centuries, when some of the pioneering work in this field was undertaken.

I

EVIDENT AUTHORITY AND AUTHORITATIVE EVIDENCE: THE *MALLEUS MALEFICARUM*

Sydney Anglo

It is astonishing that there should still be found today people who do not
believe that there are witches. For my part I suspect that the truth is
that such people really believe in their hearts, but will not admit it;
for the Pagans have a lesson for them in this matter; they are refuted by
the Canon and Civil Laws; Holy Scripture gives them the lie; the
voluntary and repeated confessions of witches prove them wrong; and
the sentences passed in various places against the accused must shut
their mouths.[1]

It is thus that Henri Boguet introduces his *Examen of Witches* (1602): a
manual based upon his own experiences as a judge concerned with the trial,
torture, and burning of numerous victims of the witch scare in Burgundy
towards the end of the sixteenth century. Boguet knows that witches exist
because he can cite both learned authority and factual evidence to prove his
case conclusively.

The study of witchcraft has recently enjoyed a boom at all levels, extending
from the popular and merely sensational to the erudite and technical.[2] The
majority of serious modern studies have concerned themselves with a
number of difficult problems. They have considered the extent to which
witchcraft practices at the folk level really existed in the Middle Ages and
the Renaissance, and how these might be illuminated by comparison with
the beliefs of modern primitive societies. They have pondered the relationship, or irrelation, between popular and learned magic. Or they have
attempted to explore and to elucidate the popular mentality of past societies.
Attention has accordingly been focused upon witch trial records rather than
upon literary sources; and when such studies have attempted to explain
the witch craze they talk about social tensions, economic pressures, and

I

alienation; endeavour to psychoanalyse the past; and even seek to quantify the development of persecution. The temptation of such impossibilities is considerable; and their undertaking may be of value, though all attempts to reconstruct the inchoate prejudices of the illiterate multitude are hampered by the fact that they leave so few written records. However unfashionable, it is sometimes worthwhile to consider the beliefs of educated men who actually took the trouble to argue their case to posterity: and it is not unreasonable to address oneself to questions which admit of answers, and to study evidence which is clearly written on, rather than between, the lines.

It appears to be tacitly assumed by many scholars that discursive arguments by the learned have little relevance to the reality of witch persecution. It is usual to pass over long, and often elaborate, treatises with a few casual remarks; to summarise their intricacies within a single paragraph; or to cope with their obscurities by ignoring them. Many of these books are well known and frequently cited; yet there has been little analysis of their structure, arguments, language, and interrelation. For example, every student of witchcraft knows of the *Malleus Maleficarum*: but, in England, there is not a single study devoted to this text. Weyer and Scot were famous opponents of the witchcraft persecution in the late sixteenth century, and are constantly referred to; but significant work on the former is exclusively German and Dutch, while the substance of Scot's arguments has received no attention whatever. Perhaps the most distinguished name in the literature of witch persecution is that of Jean Bodin: but there has been only desultory study of his *Démonomanie* in relation to his other writings. The *Daemonologie* of King James I is a familiar text: yet it is only very recently that historians have troubled to read it in the light of James's political works. De Lancre's account of the sabbat is often plundered for lurid detail, but his work, as a whole, has scarcely been considered within its historical and literary context. From such indifference to some of the most notable texts in the witchcraft debate, it is not difficult to deduce the treatment accorded to less famous tracts. The fact that these works were published, and do not lie buried in archives; that they are discursive arguments, and not fragmentary records; that they are literary rather than *ad hoc* documentation, does not render further comment superfluous. The content of books is not absorbed by some process of historical osmosis. Books have to be read and pondered; and, just as their arguments demand closer analysis and elucidation than the endless sordidities of trial records and the trivia of folk beliefs, so do they offer considerably richer rewards to the historian of ideas.

The present volume, therefore, approaches witchcraft and demonology on the basis of their literary remains: treatises which deal, in various ways,

2

with the theories underlying persecution. The majority of the following essays treat works specifically devoted to establishing the reality of a demono-logical system, to the elaboration of witchcraft beliefs, and to establishing the need for retribution. The others deal with authors who were trying to sub-vert such theories: but even their arguments illustrate both the limitations of sixteenth-century scepticism, and the compelling nature of the material ranged against them.

The principal purpose of this first essay is to comment upon the *Malleus Maleficarum*. But, by way of introduction, I wish to develop the ideas raised in the brief opening quotation from Boguet: for, though it is customary to treat witchcraft as a separate study, it does not constitute a self-sufficient body of doctrine. Quite the contrary, for it is firmly rooted in a complex of interrelated magical ideas which informs many aspects of medieval and Renaissance thought. How were these ideas treated by trained thinkers? Why were educated professional men such as Boguet so convinced about the reality and the horrors of witchcraft? In other words, what constituted a conclusive argument in the period between the fifteenth and late seventeenth centuries? Certainly, for the most part, it was something very different from what scholars now regard as valid argument: that is the deliberate attempt at objectivity; inductive reasoning; the evaluation of evidence rather than its mere accumulation; conscious scepticism of received authorities; and, above all else, the process of constantly testing hypotheses by controlled experiment.

The application of such critical techniques to the fabric of magical belief has tended to shred it asunder. But such techniques were scarcely known in the Middle Ages; only slowly developed in the Renaissance; and can hardly be deemed general in modern times. That magic, as an explanation for everything, has been largely set aside is due more to fashion than to a com-prehension of any alternative theory of causation. Ernest Jones long ago suggested that the average modern man unhesitatingly rejects 'the same evidence of witchcraft that was so convincing to the man of three centuries ago, though he usually knows no more about the true explanation than the latter did'. And Keith Thomas, who cites this observation, himself goes on to remark that 'most of those millions of people who today would laugh at the idea of magic and miracles would have difficulty in explaining why'. They are, he says, 'victims of society's constant pressure towards intellectual conformity'.[3] To this one could add what are perhaps even more funda-mental observations: the first being the limited capacity of the human intel-lect. Given the vast multiplicity of information increasingly available—and the paradox that the further knowledge is advanced, and the more avenues

3

opened up for exploration, so the greater becomes the distance between actual and potential knowledge—the more assertions we are obliged to take on trust. In addition there remains the human need to reduce the infinite to finity; the divine to the anthropomorphic; the incalculable to the mensurable; and the unknowable to the comprehensible. Hence the creation of deter' ministic historical systems enabling man to foretell the future from his past. Hence the creation of number mysticisms empowering adepts to become prophets. Astrology may be rejected as untenable, and numerology dis' missed as an arcane absurdity. Yet modern states do not hesitate to implement the recommendations of statistical prognosticators, despite the existence of the very factors which undermined earlier divinatory superstitions: the fact that the figures are susceptible to as many conflicting interpretations as there are experts; and that the predictions are frequently wrong. If we remain abject before our own seers, it is not difficult to comprehend the force of those beliefs with which this volume is concerned: beliefs which fashioned a world where magic was not merely possible but normal; and where witchcraft was simply its most lurid manifestation.

Scholarship has tended to separate the witch from the magician, and to treat, as discrete, low magic and higher magic. But witchcraft beliefs arose from the blurring of such distinctions and from a cosmic vision which saw witch and magus operating within a single system.[4] At its lowest level magic could be expected to operate through love potions, charms, secret cures and harms, as employed by 'cunning folk' and 'wise women'; but a problem arose when any attempt was made to explain how such cures and harms actually functioned, for such explanations could only be propounded by professional thinkers who provided a system of occult relationships which subsumed the witch. Few doubted that it was possible for someone to bring about transitive effects upon other people, beasts, or inanimate objects; and various methods of achieving these ends were recognised and commented upon. Macrocosmic and microcosmic imagery was commonplace, and it was generally accepted that the entire universe was composed of a vast system of correspondences and harmonies, so that anything carried out on one level must inevitably affect other levels of existence. Astral influences were postulated, where the spirits or essences of the planets held sway over lower levels of creation; and the cosmos was filled with demonic and angelic intelligences, all capable of affecting human affairs. Correspondences and harmonies, astral influences, demonic and angelic activity: all offered explanations as to the functioning of the universe. Given such explanations, it was also possible to suppose that knowledge of these functionings might, in turn, lead to their manipulation. Harmonies might be sympathetically

4

exploited; the power of the stars might be attracted and harnessed; angels might be persuaded to lend their aid; and demons might be exhorted and even compelled. In short, the magician might be able to utilise superhuman powers for his own ends.[5]

Such a conviction was strengthened by another closely related magical mode which depended upon the innate properties of material things. Such properties might be easily comprehended as, for example, was the case with certain herbs and minerals possessing curative or harmful powers. On other occasions they might be less readily apparent as, for instance, the alleged efficacy of the emerald in restraining sexual passion, where the virtue was said to be occult.[6] Nevertheless, all such innate properties could be described as natural; and their exploitation was categorised as natural magic. As we shall see, natural magic could be a powerful intellectual weapon; and in the hands of Pomponazzi it became a distinct threat to all other magic, including religion. Pomponazzi explains every kind of magical effect and marvellous event by 'natural' causes, and thereby eliminates direct divine, demonic, or angelic agency.[7]

In the main, however, natural magic reinforced rather than undermined other magic. The efficacy of talismans provides an obvious example. Since stones were held to receive their innate qualities from the planetary influences, it was theoretically possible to attract the power of a particular celestial body by engraving the correct image at the correct time on the appropriate gem— a recondite skill which could only appertain to the learned magus. But what of the witch? She, too, was deemed to operate largely through the exploitation of natural magic and was commonly accused of employing drugs to procure effects such as love and the recovery of health, or, conversely, poisoning and death. How did she master knowledge which cost the magus a lifetime of arduous study? Such abilities could not be innate. Instead they were attributed to demonic pacts; and this arrangement, in effect, opened up all magical arts to the terrestrial partner since the devil and his demons know infinitely more than even the most learned mortal. Boguet, for instance, having established the authorities for the reality of witchcraft, goes on to say that, although the stories told of witches are very strange and seem supernatural and miraculous,

Do we not know how great is the knowledge and experience of demons?
It is certain that they have a deep knowledge of all things. For there
is no Theologian who can interpret the Holy Scripture better than
they; there is no Lawyer with a profounder knowledge of Testaments,
Contracts and Actions; there is no physician or philosopher who better

5

understands the composition of the human body, and the virtue of the Heavens, the Stars, Birds, and Fishes, of trees and herbs and metals and stones. Furthermore, since they are of the same nature as the Angels, all bodies must obey them in respect of local motion. Again, do we not know how great is the power which God in express words has given them upon earth. The Book of Job teaches us this so plainly that there is no need of other proofs; for God even says that there is no power upon earth which may be compared with that of Behemoth.[8]

Evident authority and authoritative evidence

Views such as those expressed by Boguet were typical of many erudite thinkers who were so certain about maleficent demonic activity that they were prepared to advocate the systematic torture and capital punishment of those accused and convicted of trafficking with the devil. These views were not vague apprehensions and superstitions. They were intellectual convictions arrived at on the basis of seemingly unassailable authorities and authenticated evidence. Throughout the Middle Ages and the Renaissance, arguments in virtually every field of human enquiry proceeded upon the basis of accumulated authority. The more authorities one could cite, the greater their names, and the more ancient they were deemed, the more cogent seemed one's argument. And the authorities supporting a system of magic in general, and the reality of witchcraft in particular, were overwhelming.

Within a Christian society both the first and the final authority in any debate must be the Holy Scriptures, despite the difficulty—when manipulating such mystical and allusive writings—of establishing precisely what words mean. Indeed, this difficulty became crucial in the case of Weyer and Scot, for their attempt to overthrow witchcraft beliefs, because it was possible so to reinterpret the Scriptures that the existence of witches in biblical times was eliminated. Nonetheless, the Bible seemed unequivocal on the general issue: it established conclusively (for those to whom scriptural evidence was *ipso facto* conclusive) that all the magical arts were real and that, without exception, they were to be condemned when practised by anybody other than an accredited prophet of God. The biblical universe teemed with spiritual intermediaries between God and man: angels, good and bad, were constantly appearing to, interfering with, and aiding mere mortals. The devil, too, as the principal of evil, though scarcely formed in the older Hebraic books, developed his powers throughout the biblical narrative;

6

assumed alarming menace in the pseudepigraphical Jewish literature; and became the direct adversary of Christ in the New Testament. His career, it was prophesied in the Apocalyptic vision of St John, would end in total defeat at the hands of the heavenly hosts. That battle is still eagerly awaited; and, in the meantime, the devil has apparently been more than holding his own.[9]

Human associates of the devil and of his minions were explicitly condemned in passages which themselves assumed almost magical potency in any argument. 'Thou shalt not suffer a witch to live' (Exodus, XXII. 18) was the most powerful text of all, though its validity depended upon an interpretation of the word *maleficos*, which came increasingly to be challenged. Were Exodus deemed insufficient, however, there was always Leviticus (XX. 27): 'A man also or woman that hath a familiar spirit, or that is a wizard, shall surely be put to death: they shall stone them with stones: their blood shall be upon them.' Most comprehensive was Deuteronomy (XVIII. 10–12):

> There shall not be found among you any one that maketh his son or
> his daughter to pass through the fire, or that useth divination, or an
> observer of times, or an enchanter, or a witch. Or a charmer, or a con-
> sulter with familiar spirits, or a wizard, or a necromancer. For all that
> do these things are an abomination unto the Lord: and because of
> these abominations the Lord thy God doth drive them out from before
> thee.

Such injunctions could not have been issued in vain. 'God has again and again forbidden us to sacrifice to devils or to idols which are of devils', wrote Noel Taillepied; 'now he would not have commanded this if there were no devils.'[10] Furthermore, the Bible provided historical examples as well as moral imperatives and prohibitions. Did not Pharaoh's magicians engage in a contest with Moses when, though undeniably inferior to their Hebrew adversary, they were able with the devil's aid, to work seeming miracles? Was not the conjuration of dead spirits—or, at the least, demonic simulation of the dead—attested by the woman of Endor, who apparently conjured up the two-year-dead Samuel to prophesy King Saul's impending doom?[11] Were not Balaam's curses against the Children of Israel deemed worthy of purchase by King Balak, and of intervention by an angel of the Lord? Did not Joseph practise hydromancy? Did not Jacob cause Laban's cattle to conceive spotted offspring by means of sympathetic magic? Did not Jesus himself cast out devils which had possessed people? Did he not himself accord this same power to his disciples? And did this not in turn indicate

7

that evil spirits could and did take possession of human bodies? All this was clear from a purely literal reading of the Scriptures: but there were other passages which, in the light of a pre-existent belief in witchcraft, could be interpreted as further evidence of its reality. In short, to doubt the existence of demons and their activities, 'as do the epicurean Atheists', was to deny the very existence of God.[12]

Upon these foundations was erected a towering edifice of exegetical writings. The early Christian Fathers—many of whom, in desert solitariness, were able to add materials from their own hallucinatory experiences and from their knowledge of pagan sources—developed increasingly elaborate views concerning spirits and demons, witches and wizards. Endlessly they commented upon the key passages in the Scriptures. In the opinion of Justin Martyr and Origen, for instance, the woman of Endor really did conjure up dead Samuel before King Saul; Tertullian, Eustathius of Antioch, and Gregory of Nyssa, all argued that the vision was merely a demon impersonating the prophet; while Augustine, admitting that Samuel himself could have appeared only by divine dispensation, also inclines to the theory of diabolic impersonation.[13] Pharaoh's magicians, according to Tertullian, Origen and Eustathius, accomplished their miracles with direct demonic aid. Augustine pushes this belief even further by arguing the existence of a pact whereby demons give instruction in efficacious magical rites, so that magicians are subsequently able to work by themselves.[14] One thing, above all else, stood out in the patristic corpus. Evil spirits abounded and, under the malign leadership of Satan, they were constantly at work polluting man who was, in turn, always ready to deal with his tempters.[15]

Nor did such exposure of their wicked schemes deter the hosts of darkness, whose activities were documented in the work of every theologian from the days of the Christian Church's youth to those of its dotage. That dotage, according to the sceptical Pomponazzi, had already arrived in his lifetime: and certainly sixteenth-century religious writers were as obsessed by demons and by magic as their predecessors. The stock exemplars—Pharaoh's magicians, the woman of Endor, and all the rest—were as earnestly debated by the Reformers as by Catholic theologians. It is true that those to whom the word of God had been recently and exclusively revealed poured scorn on Catholic miracles, blasphemous rites, and magical relics: 'In the beginning and gathering of the Church, many things were necessary which now be needless. Miracles were used then, which outwardly be denied now.'[16] The truth had been established in apostolic times, and it was fruitless, the Reformers argued, to seek fresh signs and miracles which, 'in these latter

8

days, have been ofter wrought by power of the devil than by Spirit of God'. Wicked spirits, wrote Calfhill,

> do lurk in shrines, in Roods, in Crosses, in Images: and first of all pervert the Priests, which are easiest to be caught with bait of a little gain. Then work they miracles. They appear to men in divers shapes; disquiet them when they are awake; trouble them in their sleeps; dis-tort their members; take away their health; afflict them with diseases; only to bring them to some Idolatry.[17]

But this attribution to the devil of virtually all post-apostolic miracles increased, rather than diminished, the scope of diabolic interference in human affairs; and the Reformers' devil seemed even more immanent than in the works of their adversaries whom they were happy both to castigate and to plagiarise.[18] The devil was a very necessary fellow; and Luther, for one, would have been lost without his company.[19]

The anger of the Reformers against Catholicism is readily understandable. The Catholic Church itself practised magic: by producing effects on inanimate objects; inducing psychosomatic symptoms; and, above all, working miracles in the Mass with its music, words of consecration, incense, wine, and transubstantiation. It had long been recognised that grave difficulties confronted those who might attempt to show how such practices differed fundamentally from other magical activities—a problem illuminated by Jean Gerson's discussion of the authenticity of the visions of St Brigitta. He felt that too many people were being canonised, and was deeply con-cerned that there was no certain method of distinguishing between true and false visions, and no way of looking into people's inner experiences.[20] Subsequently, anti-Catholic theologians solved this problem by rejecting the greater part of modern miracles, and by simply attributing them to the devil. But a problem yet remained. Christianity was itself a religion founded upon, and authenticated by, miraculous occurrences; and intricate were the attempts to establish objective criteria whereby one might distinguish godly miracles from diabolic marvels. Three things, however, were generally agreed: true miracles had taken place; false marvels were still occurring; and it was impossible not to declare allegiance to one side or the other. As Henry Holland wrote, in his *Treatise against Witchcraft* (1590):

> There are two spirituall kingdomes in this world, which have continual hatred and bloody wars, without hope of truce for ever. The Lord and King of the one is our Lord Jesus, the tyrannical usurper of the other, is Sathan. Again, this also we are as clearly taught, that all men living,

9

without exception, are either true subjects of the one, or slaves unto the other. For albeit, the Neuters of this worlde dreame that they may indifferentlie view the scarres and woundes of other men, and never approach neere those bloody skirmishes; yet the truth is they are fowlie deceived: for the great Lord and King hath said with his own mouth, *Hee that is not with me, is against me.*[21]

The theological authorities seemed conclusive; but Christian writers had yet other sources to support their belief in magic and maleficence. Pagan literature was full of the deeds of witches, magicians, and aerial spirits; and the works of demonologists abound in references to Homer, Virgil, and Ovid, despite the fact that much of this material had been rejected as fantastic rubbish by many of those very Fathers whose views were otherwise considered definitive. This abuse of poetry was one of many feeblenesses discerned by Reginald Scot in Bodin's *Démonomanie*; but his withering contempt did not prevent others from continuing to regard the poets as solid evidence. Even in the seventeenth century such sources were still employed as though they had historical validity. William Perkins, for example, in his *Discourse of the Damned Art of Witchcraft* (1608), rejects any suggestion that the witches of his own age were unknown in the days of Moses or Christ. Ancient writings, he claimed, proved that, about 1,200 years before Christ's birth, and shortly after the Trojan War (itself over a century prior to the building of the temple of Solomon), there were 'the like witches that are now, as the *Circes* and *Syrenes*, and such like, mentioned in the narration of that warre, as is manifest to them that know the storie'. The *storie*, to which Perkins so confidently refers, is that unimpeachable source, Homer's *Odyssey*.[22]

There were other more significant traditions which added ancient authority to the system of magic. Plato, especially as interpreted by the Neoplatonists, was a tower of strength; while the way in which the anti-demonic Aristotle was pressed into service by the demonologists represents one of the triumphs of medieval ingenuity. But not even ingenuity was required to derive support for the reality of magic from the *Prisci Theologi*. There abounded, in the Roman Empire, a great variety of writings purporting to be either of divine origin and authorship, or at least to be the work of ancient founders of religion, men reputedly descended from the gods and themselves divinely inspired. Such oracular and mystic writings pretend to immense antiquity, often claiming origin in ancient Egypt and Chaldea. Texts such as these claimed to disclose the secrets of the most ancient priesthoods, and were replete with magic and mystic theologies expressed in inextricable ambi-

10

guities. The very existence of such material encouraged authors of astrological and alchemical works to pass off their own productions as part of the
same venerable and cryptic tradition, so that there grew up a considerable
body of mystical writings compelling attention by virtue of its antiquity and
the unparalleled eminence of its originators: Orpheus the Theologian;
Zoroaster the first magician; and Hermes Trismegistus whose fragmentary
and spurious canon expounds the occult virtues of natural substances,
magical procedures, and the intimate relationship between nature, stars, and
spirits. 'Philosophy and magic', said Hermes, 'nourish the soul.'[23]

This farrago enjoyed a wide diffusion; and the acceptance of such texts
as genuinely antique—in the case of Hermes, only a little less ancient than
Moses and far more venerable than Plato—ensured their continuing authority
throughout the Middle Ages and the Renaissance. Lactantius, as Frances
Yates has pointed out, respected Hermes as a pagan prophet of the true God;
whereas Augustine considered his work to have been demonically inspired.[24]
Nonetheless, both Lactantius and Augustine, and the other Fathers of the
Church, accepted that, for good or ill, this material was genuine; and thus a
passage such as the following, from the *Asclepius*, was of importance for all
who needed to establish the reality of demonic magic. The discussion concerned the way in which the ancient Egyptians invented the art of making
gods on earth by creating idols with magical powers, and Asclepius
demands to know the nature of these terrestrial gods. Hermes replies that it
consists of

> herbs, stones, and aromas, which have in them a natural divine power.
> And it is for the following reason that people delight them with fre-
> quent sacrifices, with hymns and praises and sweet sounds concerted
> like the harmony of the heavens: that this heavenly thing, which has
> been attracted into the idol by repeated heavenly rites, may bear joy-
> ously with men and stay with them long.[25]

This passage had been cited by Augustine, and was always well known to
demonologists; but it gained fresh significance when, in 1489, Ficino
employed it to support his own theory of magically influencing the human
spirit so that it might become receptive to celestial forces. It is a useful
passage, too, for our enquiry: for it brings us back full circle to the fundamental authority of the Scriptures. Hermes tells us how the ancients invoked
spirits, put them into images, and worshipped them. And does not David
say—as all demonologists well knew—that the 'Gods of the Gentiles are
devils'?[26]

For centuries all of this would have seemed irrefutable authority to a

11

majority of thinking men; but it was not the only material available to silence scepticism. In recent years, distinctions between magic and experimental science have been increasingly blurred as historians have come to recognise the importance not only of intellectual traditions which continue to evolve, but also of those which proved ultimately to be dead-ends. There was in fact an enormous weight of medieval and Renaissance scientific writing which served to confirm magical correspondences, occult innate virtues, astral influences, talismanic magic, and the operation of aerial spirits both good and bad. Many writers condemned astrology for its impiety, and some attacked the exaggerated claims of its practitioners; but few disputed the reality of celestial influence over terrestrial affairs. The immense vogue of almanacs and prognostications, the scope and volume of serious astrological debate, the notice taken of astrologers by princes, and the number of serious panics caused by knowledge of unfavourable planetary circumstances, all testify to the grip in which the astrologers held both popular and erudite imagination. Much the same may be said of amulets, talismans, and images, the efficacy of which was maintained, explained, and elaborated by scientific writers from pagan antiquity to the Renaissance. It is impossible here even to summarise this complex of ideas: but one example may serve to illustrate the relation between magic and science within a demonological context. Albertus Magnus, discussing the differences between magical marvels and divine miracles, explains that, whereas the latter occur instantaneously, feats of magic are really normal natural processes enormously accelerated. Demons, harnessing astral influences, perform these lightning operations so that, to take the classic example, the rods which Pharaoh's magicians turned into serpents were merely undergoing, at immense speed, the process by which worms generate in decaying trees.[27] Here we have a perfect focus. Scriptural exemplar, demonic activity, astral influence, and natural process, combine to produce a feat of magic; and all this in the work of one of the greatest names in medieval intellectual history. Medieval erudition offered rich fare for the demonologist with an appetite for scientific corroboration.

All these varied authorities offer assertions that magic was done, together with explanations of how it was done. To illustrate precisely what was done, writers could draw upon an inexhaustible thesaurus of examples. This was partly provided by the literature devoted to prodigies, portents, and marvels (of which the *Dialogue on Miracles* by Caesarius of Heisterbach is an outstanding example), and partly by an army of chroniclers who set down extraordinary occurrences in the midst of their historical narratives.[28] Thus, since for most readers history was simply a storehouse of moral, immoral, and political exemplars, the miraculous episode had complete historical validity.

12

Finally, most dramatic and irrefutable of all, were the countless instances where evil-doers betrayed themselves. As Boguet pointed out, the demonologists could cite 'voluntary and repeated confessions of witches', and the 'sentences passed against them in various places'. Here was the factual evidence to destroy those sceptics who demanded more objective evidence than a battery of great names and authorities. A massive tradition of belief in the power of local witches to work harms and cures seemed to point to a continuity of witch activity from scriptural and classical times to the present. Various sorts of folk practices had long been identified with, and persecuted as, heresy; and there was thus a body of material deriving from trials all over Europe, which gave what seemed to be an empirical basis for witchcraft beliefs. As Bodin put it: the truth had been laid bare by thousand upon thousand 'presomptions violentes, accusations, tesmoignages, recollemens, confrontations, convictions, recognoissances, repentances, et confessions volontaires jusques á la mort'.[29] It was, above all, these voluntary confessions which seemed proof incontrovertible; and, although they came to be explained away as the result of social pressures, mental disease, or covert torment, there was still a substantial residue of cases where magic was knowingly employed to obtain some particular end.[30] And it is at this point that we return to the confusion between high and low magic. It was the flatulent claims of learned magicians such as Ficino which confirmed demonologists in their belief that diabolic magic was a present reality. Ficino might claim that he was dealing only with good spirits. His adversaries knew that there was no way in which he could be certain that this was so; that he was, indeed, deluded; and that such trafficking was almost certainly only possible with demons who delighted above all else in so deceiving mankind. How could there be any doubt when, in addition to all the scriptural, patristic, philosophical, and scientific authorities, they had not only the circumstantial confessions of vulgar low magicians, but also the eloquent and damnable testimony of divers books of ceremonial magic and pacts, the pretentious claims of astrologers, and the ambiguous ravings of alchemists, cabbalists, and a heterogeneous assortment of unlicensed visionaries and mystics. In due course, other savants added their incoherencies to the swelling volume of magical writings, and further horrified the demonologists. Henry Cornelius Agrippa, for whom religion and superstition were the two supports of ceremonial magic, defined magic itself as a very powerful faculty, full of the most elevated mysteries,

and which comprises a very profound knowledge of the most secret matters, their nature, their power, their quality, their substance, their

13

effects, their difference, and their relation: whence it produces its marvellous effect by the union and application of the different virtues of the
superior beings with those of the inferior. This is the true, the most
elevated, and the most mysterious science—in a word the perfection
and fulfilment of all the natural sciences.[31]

Agrippa doubtless deemed himself an erudite magus: but for the witch-
hunters his writings merely confirmed the possibility of human dealings with
the devil; and for Bodin he was 'le plus grand sorcier qui fut onques de son
aage'.[32] Agrippa himself tells how he once intervened to save the life of a
poor old woman accused of witchcraft; but his own magical proclivities and
publications helped to justify the witchcraft persecution which swept Europe
late in the sixteenth century.

Malleus Maleficarum

In the latter half of the fifteenth century there was a marked proliferation of
treatises specifically devoted to witchcraft, employing the great corpus of
authority to establish the reality of a perverted magical conspiracy.[33] The
most important of these manuals, both in scope and practicality, was the
Malleus Maleficarum, one of those rare works written—in the opinion of its
most ardent modern admirer—'sub specie aeternitatis'.[34] This claim is, I
believe, true: although not for any intrinsic merit the work possesses. The
fact is that the *Malleus* affords a comprehensive summary of arguments for
persecution, together with a persecution method, which has precisely that
combination of unoriginality, popularity, and influence so valuable to the
historian of ideas seeking to discover conventional, rather than atypical,
modes of thought.

The book was written by two prominent Dominican inquisitors, Jakob
Sprenger and Heinrich Kramer, and first published in 1486/87. This
couple had been empowered by Pope Innocent VIII, in December 1484, to
deal with those who 'unmindful of their own salvation and straying from
the Catholic Faith, have abandoned themselves to devils, incubi and
succubi', and who, by incantations, spells, conjurations, and other forms of
magic have caused the death of unborn babies, destroyed crops, afflicted
live-stock, caused dreadful sickness to both men and beasts, and hindered
both the sexual act in men and conception in women.[35] Much of the
Malleus's early bibliographical history remains obscure; though its immediate
success is attested by at least eight editions before the close of the fifteenth

14

century.[36] The authors' purpose was clear. Witchcraft was a vast and vile conspiracy against the Faith; it was on the increase; witches were depopulating the whole of Christendom; and, through the impotence of the secular courts, these creatures remained unpunished. The *Malleus* was written to demonstrate precisely what witches were doing, and how they could be stopped. It first establishes the truth of the existence of witchcraft and its heretical nature; then elucidates the principal evils practised by witches and demons; and finally lays down formal rules for initiating legal action against witches, securing their conviction, and passing sentence upon them (pp. 20, 68, 104).

Underlying the entire structure of the *Malleus* are three beliefs: that witchcraft is real and that it is heresy to maintain the opposite; that demonic interference in human affairs is incessant; and that both witchcraft and demonic activity are permitted by God for his own purposes. The first two beliefs can be established by the authorities and by evidence: but the last can only be an inference from these—that is, since they are real, God must have permitted them. This is scarcely a satisfactory position, but its implications are alarming when one considers that, in the course of the *Malleus*, virtually every species of misery and misfortune is attributed to demonic agency. It seems that God, despite occasional assertions to the contrary, has given the devil *carte blanche* in terrestrial affairs. The *Malleus* admits the existence of natural disasters. Yet, overwhelmingly, the functioning of the universe is depicted as demonic and devilish. Even the stars play only a minor role in human affairs, and certainly cannot coerce demons to perform any actions against their will. Indeed, demons deliberately choose to appear when summoned by magicians at certain astrologically significant moments, because they thereby deceive men and lead them into idolatry. The stars, it is conceded, have a conditional influence upon human affairs, and it is thus possible for astrologers to have some success in their predictions. Nevertheless, anyone who argues more extensive celestial influence is undermining free will, and cannot be tolerated (pp. 11, 32–4). Kramer and Sprenger, however, never do satisfactorily explain why their own total commitment to demonic interference does not inhibit free will.

Catastrophes of the weather, failing crops, and diseases amongst livestock, are all generally regarded as demonic in origin; and, although both physical and mental ailments are possible within purely natural terms, these too are principally caused by demons. There are six ways in which witches, with the devil's aid, can injure humanity (p. 115). They can cause evil love; inspire hatred or jealousy; and interfere with the sexual act and childbirth. They can also cause disease 'in any of the human organs'; take away life; and deprive men of reason. There is nothing wonderful in demons' ability to cause

15

delusions and frenzies, 'when even a natural defect is able to effect the same result', as is shown in the case of frantic men, melancholics, maniacs, and drunkards, all of whom see things which are not really there (p. 120). The *Malleus* gives a circumstantial account of the manner in which demons cause mental sickness: though it is noteworthy that—according to contemporary theories of the localisation of brain function—the authors place reason in the wrong ventricle.[37] Having entered our bodies, the demons 'make impressions on the inner faculties corresponding to the bodily organs', for the devil can

> draw out some image retained in a faculty corresponding to one of the senses; as he draws from the memory, which is in the back part of the head, an image of a horse, and locally moves that phantasm to the middle part of the head, where are the cells of imaginative power; and finally to the sense of reason, which is in the front of the head. And he causes such a sudden change and confusion, that such objects are necessarily thought to be actual things seen with the eyes. This can be clearly exemplified by the natural defect in frantic men and other maniacs (p. 125).

The *Malleus* thus employs natural disease to establish the reality of demonically induced sickness; and the authors' attempts to distinguish between the two afford infinitely greater scope to the latter.[38]

The entire range of these injuries is within the competence of the devil working by himself. He has no need of human agents to accomplish his designs. Nevertheless, he prefers to work through witches because

> he thus gives greater offence to God, by usurping to himself a creature dedicated to Him. Secondly, because when God is the more offended, He gives him the more power of injuring men. And thirdly, for his own gain, which he places in the perdition of souls (p. 122).

The majority of witches are women; and the monkish misogyny of the *Malleus* is blatant. Its explanations for female susceptibility are in themselves conventional and, like most such attacks, its arguments are confused. On the one hand, woman, having been formed from a bent rib, is an imperfect animal and is always a deceiver. Her very name, *Femina*, derives from *Fe* and *Minus*, 'since she is ever weaker to hold and preserve the faith': and this is the very root of witchcraft. Women are more given to carnal lust than men; more credulous and slippery tongued; 'intellectually like children'; feeble in memory; and easily provoked to hatred. On the other hand, there have been many examples of virtuous women; and above all in the New Testament we find the 'whole sin of Eve taken away by the benediction of MARY'—a pious

16

reminder which is immediately followed by an affirmation that, in these times, the perfidy of witchcraft is more often found in women than in men 'since they are feebler both in mind and body' (pp. 41-7).

Women's insatiable lust is of crucial significance because witchcraft is spread, and its power augmented, through the venereal act. God allows the devil special powers to interfere in sexual intercourse, not only because of its 'natural nastiness', but also because it was this act 'that caused the corruption of our first parents and, by its contagion, brought the inheritance of original sin upon the whole human race' (pp. 93, 169). The devil has a thousand ways of doing harm, but his power is principally confined to the 'privy parts and the navel', because in men 'the source of wantonness lies in the privy parts, since it is from them that the semen falls, just as in women it falls from the navel' (pp. 23-4). So the devil spends his time gathering semen from concupiscent men by pretending to be a woman and then, masquerading as a man, he injects it into his witch partners during further acts of demonic intercourse. The semen is specially selected and is kept fresh and fertile because the devil is able to move it at lightning speed (p. 28). It is thus that demonic offspring are engendered; and this, together with his general encouragement to lechery, appears to be the main purpose of the devil's sexual machinations. Pleasure, we are told, cannot be the demons' aim, since they are not flesh and blood—a view contradicted within a few pages when the Scriptures are adduced to show how incubi and succubi lust after women (pp. 29-30).

The various ways in which the devil can render the penis totally useless are discussed in great and ingenious detail, as are the naughty tricks witches play with the same vulnerable member. Witches even collect the male organs, twenty or thirty at a time, and put them in a 'bird's nest, or shut them up in a box, where they move themselves like living members, and eat oats and corn, as has been seen by many and is a matter of common report' (p. 121). There is little that the forces of evil will not get up to when the sexual act is involved. Yet, anomalously, even demons draw the line at 'vices against nature', and refuse to engage in acts 'wrongfully performed outside the rightful channel' (p. 30).

None of this scholastic pornography is original; but it was of great importance to the witch-hunters because, in their view, not only did witches satisfy their own 'filthy lusts'; they also pandered to the desires of great men. And it was through such men, whom the witches protect from other harm, that 'there arises the great danger of the time, namely, the extermination of the Faith' (p. 48). Here we see the whole conspiracy laid bare. Men of the noblest birth, governors, the rich and the powerful, are all in thrall to their

17

demonically dedicated lovers. Thus witches are themselves protected. Thus they increase in power.

No less unoriginal, and equally important, is the *Malleus*'s insistence on the reality of a pact between the devil and his human partners. This pact is no tacit or symbolic arrangement (pp. 81–2), but is 'exactly defined and expressed', blaspheming God and pledging harm to God's creatures (p. 20). The whole formal process is detailed in the text and concludes with an agreement for the witch to make unguents from the bones and limbs of children, especially those unbaptised, by which means she will be able to fulfil all her wishes. In return, the witch pledges to abjure the Christian Faith; to give herself to the devil, body and soul; to do her utmost to bring others into his power; and to leave behind her a survivor, carefully instructed, so that the number of witches may be increased (pp. 99–100, 144). This contract is designed to anger God more than either purely demonic evil or straightforward human malice can ever do. For witchcraft is no ordinary heresy. It is 'high treason against God's Majesty', and it must be treated accordingly (p. 6).

Anybody reading the *Malleus Maleficarum*—its authors confidently assert—will find therein 'nothing contrary to sound reason, nothing which differs from the words of Scripture and the tradition of the Fathers' (p. 21). Their arguments are constantly said to be 'proved by reason and authority'; and indeed the whole work is a perfect illustration of the appeal to established authority and time-honoured evidence. Reason is comprised simply in making that appeal, and—where authority and evidence are concordant—in drawing the inevitable conclusions. A considerable number of authorities are cited in the course of the work, and even include tags from Cicero, Seneca, Cato, Terence, Valerius Maximus, and Theophrastus. Dionysius the Pseudo-Areopagite, Jerome, Chrysostom, Lactantius, Gregorius Magnus, Origen, and Isidore, loom very large; and a host of historians, lawyers, and philosophers are drawn upon. Four principal authorities, however, dominate the *Malleus*: Aristotle, who provides both natural explanations and the logical structure of each proposition; the Scriptures, which form the basis for all theological, miraculous, and moral arguments; St Augustine, whose assertions concerning magic and demonology are scattered broadcast throughout the text; and St Thomas Aquinas, who furnishes a synthesis of the other three major sources. The handling of such writers is not over-scrupulous, and they are all employed selectively; so that single observations, sentences, and even mere phrases, are ripped out of context and used as if they have universal validity. This method enables its practitioners to prove anything they wish; though, Aristotle apart, the

18

authorities valued by Kramer and Sprenger required little twisting to serve their turn.

Use and experience, says the *Malleus*, are of more value to judges in witch-craft cases 'than any art or text-book' (pp. 226, 244), and the authors certainly cite numerous examples in the course of their discussion. Some of their stories are taken from Nider, the principal specialist writer against witchcraft prior to their own work; but many are derived from their own experiences as inquisitors. Indeed, they claim to have collected enough evidence from the town of Innsbruck alone to make a book of them (p. 139). They constantly adduce 'examples that have been personally seen or heard, or are accepted at the word of credible witnesses' (p. 89); and they could turn the minds of their readers if they related all their experiences, were it not 'sordid and mean' to praise oneself (p. 90). There is truly no lack of evidence in the *Malleus*. The only problem is the attitude of its authors, epitomised in the chapters dealing with incubi and succubi. These extraordinary activities are denied by some but attested by many other witnesses: and, according to Aristotle, 'that which appears true to many cannot be altogether false' (pp. 25, 27). Thus, much that we would deem merely hearsay is admitted as proof; and, in this respect, the *Malleus* reads very much like earlier collections of miracles and prodigies.

It is, however, in its dialectical procedures that the *Malleus* is simultaneously at its most feeble and most devastating. Indeed, it is the very weakness of its logic that results in its terrifying conclusions: for, despite appearances to the contrary, this work is not an argument but rather a series of assertions masked by an accumulation of authorities and exemplars assembled in disputation form. Any methodology may be well or ill used, and—cumbrousness apart—there is little intrinsically amiss with the scholastic procedure of propositions, objections, and rejoinders. The method had achieved some notable triumphs of subtlety and ingenuity. But not in the hands of Kramer and Sprenger. They rarely succeed in overcoming the objections they themselves raise to their own propositions; sometimes an argument is left in mid-air; sometimes a proposition is assumed to have been proven when it patently has not; examples are frequently inadequate to support a conclusion advanced; and very often a position assumed at one point in the text is contradicted elsewhere as occasion demands.

Some of these weaknesses are inherent in the very process of arguing on the basis of authority. This technique operates rather like the law of diminishing fleas: each writer citing his predecessors and becoming, in turn, an authority worthy of citation. The *Malleus* is itself an example of this process; and its own pronouncements were cited as definitive throughout the following

19

century and even beyond. Another problem arising when authority weighs so heavily is a tendency to incorporate conflicting ideas, a habit frequently deemed typically medieval, but just as typical of the Renaissance. And we find this inability to recognise or to resolve contradictions in historians, in writers on magic and science, and even in so practical a field as mechanics where one might imagine that necessity would eliminate totally discrepant theorems.[39]

The normal shape of the argument in the *Malleus* is circular. Everything is built upon the assumption that God permits the devil to perpetrate evil through human agents. In other words, the whole argument for persecution rests upon a monstrous paradox, since witches are merely serving God's mysterious purposes and might, on that account, be deemed more worthy of praise than of blame.[40] God, we are told, frequently allows devils to act as His ministers and servants (p. 8). Were the devil completely unrestricted he would destroy the works of God. But he cannot destroy the works of God (p. 11). Therefore whatever he does can only be with divine permission. Should one attempt to break this circle by demanding why God goes to such trouble, Kramer and Sprenger have an abundance of authorised arguments, if not to convince, at least to stupefy any critic. Not only does God punish by the power of evil angels, but He also allows the devil to work willy-nilly entirely for His own glory, for the commendation of the Faith, for the purgation of the elect, and for the acquisition of merit (pp. 16, 23, 85). So we see the devil tormented very greatly, for

> it is certain that nothing can be more galling to the pride of the devil, which he always rears up against God . . . than that God should con- vert his evil machinations to His own glory. Therefore God justly permits all these things.

God allows evil so that He can draw good therefrom; and he will not prevent all evil because otherwise 'the universe should lack the cause of much good' (pp. 29, 69). Evil exists to perfect the universe, and God is 'glorified in sin, when He pardons in mercy and when He punishes in justice; there- fore it behoves Him not to hinder sin'. It is, nonetheless, difficult for us to see how God is 'glorified in sin' when he permits the innocent to suffer with the guilty; allows child-eating witches to accomplish almost everything they wish; and tolerates diabolical changelings (pp. 77, 99, 128, 192). Nor does it seem either merciful or just when—although the devil can do nothing without divine permission—God is still so offended when witches use image magic that He allows plagues to fall upon the earth 'in punishment of their misdeeds' (p. 20). Similarly it is strange that God takes special offence when

20

witches pay homage to the devil (p. 101); and that, because demons do most of their evil on holy days, He is so angry that He 'allows them greater power of injuring even innocent men by punishing them either in their affairs or their bodies' (p. 113). It thus appears that because the devil employs the power allowed him by God, God is increasingly vexed and, as a result, grants further powers to His enemy—a truly 'incomprehensible judgment' (p. 129).

Even stranger is the contradictory behaviour of the devil. We are told at one point that he assails good people more bitterly than he does the wicked because, whereas he already possesses the latter, he is eager to draw the just into his power by tribulation (pp. 86, 97). Yet we are subsequently assured not only that God allows demons more power against the wicked than against the just, and that when God does permit injury to the good it is only to increase their merit, but also that demons know this full well and are therefore 'the less eager to injure them' (p. 136). All of this makes one wonder why demons arrange for the murder of unbaptised children and dedicate them to the devil. The theory is that, since such children are debarred from the Kingdom of Heaven, 'by this means the Last Judgment is delayed, when the devils will be condemned to eternal torture; since the number of the elect is more slowly completed, on the fulfilment of which the world will be consumed' (p. 141). But the fulfilment of the number of the elect, the Day of Judgment, and the end of the world, must all be for God's decision alone. It is impossible to see either how demons can delay such matters even for a fraction of a second, or (since their maleficence depends solely upon divine permission) why they bother.

The phrase, 'with the permission of God', recurs throughout the *Malleus*, and every similar witch-hunting manual, like an involuntary mental spasm afflicting authors whenever inconsistent, nonsensical, or impossible assertions are made. It is employed like some invincible chess piece empowered, in moments of emergency, to remove all the opposing pieces from the board. It is an argument favoured by Catholic theologians and Reformers alike; and it reveals a colossal arrogance on the part of those who believe that their vapid subtleties really do elucidate the most intimate divine purposes which they alone fully comprehend. It is impossible to argue rationally against those who have been taken entirely into God's confidence.

Privileged though they are, Kramer and Sprenger encounter difficulties over the knotty problem of free will, which they are unable to resolve. Man has the choice between good and ill: but the devil's will is 'made up for evil', and he causes evil will in men, and especially in witches (p. 32). The latter 'do enjoy absolute liberty' when they make their compact with the devil

21

(p. 16), despite the fact that divine providence and knowledge extend to all created things, 'not in the mass generally, but also in the individual particularly' (p. 69). Thus evil—as we have seen—must be part of God's purpose; and He does indeed extract good from evil. On the other hand, we are told that God will not bestow the quality of impeccability, not because of any imperfection in His power 'but because of the imperfection of the creature: and this imperfection lies chiefly in the fact that no creature, man or angel, is capable of receiving this quality' (p. 70). This is as strange as it is unfortunate, since all creatures including witches were made by God in the first place.

Divine permission and free will had troubled and perplexed Christians long before the *Malleus Maleficarum*, and it is scarcely surprising that its authors remain confused on these issues. But their work is full of other feeblenesses, too. Circular arguments are rolled out ceaselessly; *non sequiturs* follow hard upon each other; and questions are begged without embarrassment. Incomprehensibilities are sometimes almost inspired as, for example, the assertion that it is not the least surprising that an innocent man should be demonically possessed for the slight fault of another person, 'when men are possessed by devils for their own light fault, or for another's heavy sin, or for their own heavy sin, and some also at the instance of witches' (p. 130)—or, the authors might have added in the same vein, for any reason (or no reason) whatsoever. Kramer and Sprenger are able to combine fallacies within a single argument. They affirm that even virtuous people can be deceived by the devil, and their imagination perverted by his fiendish wiles. Yet they also maintain with equal certainty that the devil can in no way enter the mind or body of any person, nor has the power 'to penetrate into the thoughts of anybody, unless such a person has first become destitute of all holy thoughts, and is quite bereft and denuded of spiritual contemplation' (p. 120). It follows, *ipso facto*, that all who are so deluded must be lacking in the gift of divine grace, and that the virtuous can never be taken in by the devil.

An interesting minor instance of the authors' major failure to pursue the logic of their own argument may be seen in their approval of a story concerning a certain holy man who once found the devil, in the form of a devout priest, preaching in a church. The pseudo-priest was irreproachable in his attack on sin; so the holy man approached him after the sermon to demand the reason for this. And the devil answered, 'I preach the truth, knowing that because they are hearers of the word only, and not doers, God is the more offended and my gain is increased' (p. 128). The logical consequence of this must be that any preacher who inveighs against sin, and utters the truth, is offending God and aiding the devil. Kramer and Sprenger do not see this; and, even if they did, it would matter little since they are capable of

22

contradicting themselves within the space of a short chapter or even on the same page. A particularly striking instance occurs in a discussion of a problem which constantly disturbed writers against witchcraft: how far should they go into details concerning the enemies' practices?[41] Some critics, says the *Malleus*, have argued that to preach and write about such matters is very dangerous, because people might thereby acquire evil knowledge. But this, claim the authors, is not possible. No matter how much folk might wish to do evil, and however much they invoke the devil in order to accom, plish this, it can be of no avail unless they have paid homage to him and have abjured the Faith: 'it is impossible for anyone to learn from a preacher how to perform any of the things that have been mentioned' (p. 145). This seems decisive until we read, three short paragraphs later, that the very act of seeking the devil's help is apostasy: for 'if invocations, conjurations, fumi, gations and adorations are used, then an open pact is formed with the devil, even if there has been no surrender of body and soul together with an explicit abjuration of the Faith either wholly or in part. For by the mere invocation of the devil a man commits open verbal apostasy' (pp. 145–6).

Another contradiction which continued to baffle thinkers concerned the power of witches to harm those appointed as judges over them. Amongst the classes of men blessed by God, whom witches cannot harm, 'the first are those who administer public justice against them, or prosecute them in any public official capacity'. This is proved by 'actual experience' when witches have admitted that, 'merely because they have been taken by officials of public justice, they have immediately lost all their power of witchcraft' (pp. 89–90). Kramer and Sprenger forget this reassuring fact, and later they warn their readers against witches who can 'bewitch their judges by a mere look or glance from their eyes, and publicly boast that they cannot be punished' (p. 139); while others are able 'with the help of the devil to bewitch the Judge by the mere sound of the words which they utter'. There, fore judges must take every kind of precaution, including having the witch led in backwards so that he may see her before she can see him (p. 228). But if judges are immune from witchcraft, why take this trouble?

Such instances are typical of the *Malleus* and could be illustrated from every chapter throughout the text. However, by far the most serious logical flaws—because of their far, reaching practical consequences—relate to the accusation, torture, and punishment of witches. The authors seem, for much of the time, convinced that witch spells are extremely difficult, and frequently impossible, to cure; and they devote much space to discussing whether or not it is lawful to oppose witchcraft with witchcraft, or vanity with vanity. Their authorities are here in disagreement; and for once Kramer and

23

Sprenger recognise this fact explicitly and even promise to reconcile dis-
crepancies. They never do so, but content themselves by quibbling that
certain superstitious remedies may be safely employed—though their attempt
to distinguish between lawful and unlawful cures results in total confusion
(pp. 157, 268-9). They also produce a whole armoury of pious and religious
magic which is sometimes effective against witchcraft: pilgrimages to holy
shrines, true confession and contrition, 'the plentiful use of the sign of the
Cross', devout prayer, and lawful exorcism by solemn words (p. 170).
Judges, in particular, are advised to wear around the neck 'consecrated salt
and other matters, with the Seven Words which Christ uttered on the Cross
written in a schedule, and all bound together'. If possible this material
should be made up 'into the length of Christ's stature', and worn against the
naked flesh, 'for it is shown by experience that witches are greatly troubled
by these things' (p. 231). Again one demands, why is all this necessary if
judges are immune from witchcraft? But the fact is that ultimately, in
Kramer's and Sprenger's view, nothing is really effective against witches.
Much less conviction is carried by their lists of holy magical remedies than
by their heartfelt exasperation at the way people persist in consulting witches
for cures, and their exclamation:

> But alas! O Lord God . . . who shall deliver the poor who are bewitched
> and cry out in their ceaseless pains? For our sins are so great, and the
> enemy is so strong; and where are they who can undo the works of the
> devil by lawful exorcisms? (p. 160)

The only effective remedy lies in the hands of the judges. Witches must be
checked by relentless punishment; and there can be no doubt that, above all
the criminals in the world, such creatures merit the most severe penalties. They
are not merely heretics but apostates; and indeed in their apostasy they not
only deny the Faith but pay homage to the devil, and afflict men and beasts
with temporal injuries (p. 77). Counterfeiters of coin which is nothing more
than a prop to the life of the body are sentenced to death by the secular
courts; so how much heavier is the sin of the witch who corrupts the Faith
which is the life of the soul (p. 153)? Exodus XXII is cited with approval
(p. 193); and it is suggested that even where a witch is shown mercy by the
spirituality on account of a last-minute confession (a proceeding not seriously
envisaged), she is still liable to punishment by the civil authorities for the
temporal crimes she has committed (p. 261).

Death is the only penalty for witches seriously considered in the *Malleus
Maleficarum*. The authors are at pains to demonstrate precisely how convictions
may be secured and, following the precedents established in heresy prosecu-

24

tions, they produce the most one-sided judicial procedure it would be possible to devise. So great a crime, they say, cannot be proceeded against 'with no other warrant than a vague charge or a grave suspicion' (p. 164); and they maintain that no person ought to be condemned 'unless he has been convicted by his own confession, or by the evidence of three trust-worthy witnesses'. The drawback here is that, within a single sentence, we slip from initiating a witchcraft accusation to the problem of condemning the accused. The procedure advocated by the *Malleus* is of the utmost simplicity: trustworthy witnesses comprehend all who are prepared to come forward, secretly and without fear of consequences, to make any wild accusation they choose; and confession may be extorted by duplicity or torture.

The single-minded one-sidedness of the argument is laid bare in a dis-cussion of the three methods of beginning a witchcraft process (pp. 205–7). The first of these is when an accuser comes forward offering to 'submit him-self to the penalty of talion if he fails to prove it'—that is to suffer the same penalty as would be inflicted on the accused if the charges could be sub-stantiated. The second method is for someone to come forward 'not as an accuser but as an informer'; so that, should the accusation fail, he will not be liable to a penalty. The third method is where there is no accuser or informer, but simply 'a general report that there are witches in some town or place; and then the Judge must proceed, not at the instance of any party, but simply by virtue of his office'. Solemnly the *Malleus* assures us that the third method is the most usual, 'because it is secret'; and judges are enjoined to avoid the first method of direct accusation, for 'the deeds of witches in conjunction with devils are done in secret, and the accuser cannot in this case, as in others, have definite evidence by which he can make his statements good'. The accuser must therefore be advised to drop the formal method and to offer himself simply as an informer (p. 211). The argument is truly extraordinary. It is too dangerous to proceed on an accusation where the plaintiff is obliged to prove his case; and preferable to proceed on mere information or rumour. That it is easier, in the latter case, for both judges, informers, and witnesses, to be thoroughly irresponsible and malicious, is evident. But it can certainly be no easier to prove the accusations objectively since, presumably, gossip-mongers can have no more reliable access to facts than a genuine complainant. Indeed, as the *Malleus* points out, since witches never threaten their intended victims in the presence of a third party, there never can be witnesses to such matters (p. 213).

Personal enemies, especially mortal enemies, cannot—we are assured—be allowed as witnesses. But this caution is soon eroded by a reminder that

25

the judge should not greatly heed such a plea on behalf of the accused: 'for in these cases it is very seldom that anyone bears witness without enmity, because witches are always hated by everybody' (p. 220). In effect, therefore, mortal enemies are allowed as witnesses in witch trials, along with everybody else. As in heresy proceedings, even people under sentence of excommunication, criminal associates and accomplices, notorious evil-doers and criminals, servants, family, and kindred—all are permitted to give evidence in these trials, although their identity must not be revealed unless perfect safety can be guaranteed. And such a guarantee is deemed virtually impossible (pp. 209, 216–17).

With this array of anonymous informers against her, the witch's chance of proving her innocence was already slender; but there were additional ways to prejudice her case. She was to be allowed an advocate only if she specifically requested one; and he was to be formally admonished not to incur the charge of defending heresy, which would render him liable to excommunication. Since the trial proceedings must be 'plain and summary', he must not introduce any complications or appeals; and if he 'unduly defends a person already suspect of heresy, he makes himself as it were a patron of that heresy' (p. 218). If, after such warnings, an advocate does accept the brief, then he finds himself going into battle with his hands firmly tied behind his back. He may see everything contained in the depositions against his client: but on no account may he have the names of the witnesses. It is thus extremely difficult for him to attempt the obvious defence of personal enmity on the part of the accusers; and even if he does try this, the judge is advised to ignore it. A second line of defence might be to suggest that there was no causal connection between a threat uttered by his client and some subsequent sickness. To this the judge must reply that 'if the illness is due to natural causes, then the excuse is good. But the evidence indicates the contrary' (p. 220). And what is that *evidence*? Simply if the disease cannot be cured by natural remedies; if the physicians themselves believe that it is due to witchcraft; if other witches are so convinced; or if the illness came on suddenly without warning. Since medieval medical science was likely to aggravate rather than to alleviate the symptoms of almost any ailment known to afflict mankind; since physicians were unlikely to admit that their ministrations had failed to cure a natural disease; since other witches would be convinced that most diseases were of demonic origin; and since many illnesses do manifest themselves without discernible warning—the implications of these criteria are obvious.

Supported by a reluctant and impotent advocate, and with her two most likely defences theoretically feasible but practically impossible, the witch was

26

not likely to give a convincing answer to the charges against her. None the less 'common justice demands that a witch should not be condemned to death unless she is convicted by her own confession' (pp. 222–3), and this was to be obtained, where necessary, by deceit or by force. The deceit resides in using every kind of equivocation, false promise, spies and lies, to trap the accused into an admission of guilt: 'and finally let the Judge come in and promise that he will be merciful, with a mental reservation that he means he will be merciful to himself or the State; for whatever is done for the safety of the State is merciful' (p. 231). If, however, the traps fail, recourse must be had to less subtle means such as detaining the accused 'in case perhaps, being depressed after a year of the squalor of prison, she may confess her crimes' (p. 214). But, if 'after keeping the accused in suspense', with constant postponements and exhortations, she still denies the truth, then the judge should order his officers to proceed to the torture. 'Then let them obey at once', says the *Malleus*, 'but not joyfully' (p. 225). Thus the enthusiastic sadism of the tormenters is involuntarily betrayed. At first torture should be light, bearing in mind that such treatment is often 'fallacious and ineffective'. Some victims are so 'soft-hearted and feeble-minded' that, at the least pain, they will confess anything 'whether it be true or not'; whereas others are so stubborn that they will confess to nothing, however much they are tormented. Some, having suffered previously, are better able to endure the ordeal, 'since their arms have been accommodated to the stretchings and twistings involved'; while others, weakened by previous tribulations, confess too readily. Finally, there are some who, being bewitched, are able to support any pain and die rather than confess anything (p. 243).

This indictment of the inefficacy of torture is complete and convincing. What is the point of these cruelties, since those with nothing to confess are the likeliest to make confession; while the genuinely wicked have a good chance of confessing nothing whatever? The two Dominican authors' acquaintance with God enables them to resolve this difficulty. A witch may confess due to a 'divine impulse conveyed through a holy angel'; or she may confess when the devil withdraws his protection, thus fulfilling God's mysterious purposes (p. 102). So we are left with confessions elicited by torture, which condemn the accused out of her own mouth; and refusal to confess which is equally damning because it reveals demonic assistance. In the former case there is no problem; in the latter, after a suitable time has elapsed, the accused is to be declared an impenitent heretic and handed over to the secular powers for punishment (p. 214).

Even in those wholly hypothetical cases when, due to disagreement amongst witnesses, the accused is 'found to be entirely innocent', she is still

27

not to be so declared. 'Let care be taken', admonish Kramer and Sprenger, 'not to put anywhere in the sentence that the accused is innocent or immune, but that it was not legally proved against him; for if after a little time he should again be brought to trial, and it should be legally proved, he can, notwithstanding the previous sentence of absolution, then be condemned' (p. 241). This is the treatment accorded to the entirely innocent. Others are to be shown commensurate consideration. Even if nothing but ill repute can be established, the accused must submit to a canonical purgation; and if she cannot find the requisite number of supporters she is held to be guilty, and duly convicted (p. 242). Anything worse than ill repute is granted no mercy whatever.

Cases concerning the Faith are to be conducted in a simple and summary fashion, and admit of no appeal. Inconsistently, however, the *Malleus* does envisage the possibility of an appeal to Rome. Should this happen, and should the judges be summoned to appear there, they must avoid fatigue, misery, labour, and expense, 'for by this means much damage is caused to the Church, and heretics are greatly encouraged'. Judges will be less respected and less feared; and other heretics, seeing the judges wearied and detained at Rome, 'will exalt their horns, and despise and malign them, and more boldly proclaim their heresies'. Worse still, when accused they will appeal in the same way, and judges will become less zealous through fear of being involved in similarly protracted proceedings. All this is most 'prejudicial to the Faith of the Holy Church of God; wherefore may the spouse of that Church in mercy preserve her from all such injuries' (p. 275). This awful prospect of endless litigation closes the *Malleus Maleficarum*. But the danger was not really imminent because the authors had already demonstrated how, in practice, appeals could be delayed, shelved, and ultimately denied.

The judicial process advocated in the *Malleus* is inexorable; its inquisitorial procedures were, theoretically, implacable; and technically there would appear to have been no escape once a witchcraft accusation had been initiated. Yet all was well. The devil simply could not defame innocent persons of witchcraft to the extent that they would be condemned to death. 'Here we are dealing with actual events; and it has never yet been known that an innocent person has been punished on suspicion of witchcraft, and there is no doubt that God will never permit such a thing to happen' (p. 136). And that was a comfort: not, perhaps, to the numberless multitudes accused, convicted, and executed for witchcraft; but certainly to the infallible authors, Heinrich Kramer and Jakob Sprenger. Their consciences—like those of Bodin, Rémy, Boguet, Del Rio, De Lancre, and all the other advocates of witch persecution, who followed in their footsteps—were clear. Who could

28

doubt the truth of their case? Were not their authorities evident, and their evidence authoritative?

Notes

1 Henri Boguet, *An Examen of Witches*, trans. E. Allan Ashwin (London, 1929), p. xxxix.
2 The following books all differ in approach, are all open to challenge, but offer serious contributions to the general history of witchcraft. J. C. Baroja, *The World of Witches*, trans. N. Glendinning (London, 1964); R. Mandrou, *Magistrats et Sorciers en France au XVIIᵉ siècle* (Paris, 1968); A. Macfarlane, *Witchcraft in Tudor and Stuart England* (London, 1970); K. V. Thomas, *Religion and the Decline of Magic* (London, 1971), repr. with corrections and additions (London, 1973); J. B. Russell, *Witchcraft in the Middle Ages* (Cornell University Press, 1972); H. C. Erik Midelfort, *Witch Hunting in Southwestern Germany 1562–1684: The Social and Intellectual Foundations* (Stanford University Press, 1972); N. Cohn, *Europe's Inner Demons* (London, 1975).
3 Thomas, *op. cit.* (1973), p. 774.
4 On this problem see Robert-Léon Wagner, *'Sorcier' et 'Magicien': Contribution à l'histoire du vocabulaire de la magie* (Paris, 1939).
5 For valuable general comments on the functioning of magic, see D. P. Walker, *Spiritual and Demonic Magic from Ficino to Campanella* (London, 1958); Frances A. Yates, *Giordano Bruno and the Hermetic Tradition* (London, 1964). On macrocosmology, see Rudolf Allers, 'Microcosmus: From Anaximandros to Paracelsus', *Traditio*, II (1944), pp. 319–407.
6 Lynn Thorndike, *A History of Magic and Experimental Science* (Columbia University Press, New York, 1923–58), II, p. 553.
7 Walker, *op. cit.*, pp. 107–11. See also below, pp. 132–4.
8 Boguet, *op. cit.*, pp. xli–xlii.
9 On demonology in general, see W. C. van Dam, *Dämonen und besessene. Die Dämonen in Geschichte und Gegenwart und ihre Austreibung* (Aschaffenburg, 1970). On aspects of scriptural demonology, see Johannes Smit, *De Daemoniacis in Historia Evangelica* (Rome, 1913); S. Eitrem, *Some Notes on the Demonology in the New Testament*, 2nd ed. (Oslo, 1966); R. S. Kluger, *Satan in the Old Testament* (Northwestern University Press, Evanston, 1967).
10 Noel Taillepied, *A Treatise of Ghosts*, trans. M. Summers (London, n.d.), p. 10.
11 M. Summers, *The History of Witchcraft and Demonology* (London, 1926), pp. 176–81, discusses this episode, and supports the view that it was, indeed, Samuel who appeared before Saul.
12 Jean Bodin, *De la Démonomanie des Sorciers* (Paris, 1580), fol. 1ᵛ. Cf. Summers, *op. cit.*, pp. 191, 203–6. A good example of the extension of witchcraft ideas to passages in the Bible not specifically connected with them may be seen in the

29

treatment accorded to the First and Third Commandments in John Hooper, *Declaration of the Ten Commandments* in *The Early Writings of John Hooper*, ed. S. Carr (Parker Society, 1843), pp. 307–15, 326–34.

13 Thorndike, *op. cit.*, I, pp. 469–71, 509–10.

14 *Ibid.*, pp. 446, 464, 470, 506–9.

15 See F. X. Gokey, *The Terminology for the Devil and Evil Spirits in the Apostolic Fathers* (Catholic University of America Press, Washington DC, 1961). See also E. Schneweis, *Angels and Demons according to Lactantius* (Catholic University of America Press, Washington DC, 1944).

16 James Calfhill, *Answer to John Martiall's Treatise of the Cross*, ed. R. Gibbings (Parker Society, 1846), pp. 332–3.

17 *Ibid.*, pp. 316–18.

18 See, for example, Johann Bullinger, *The Decades*, trans. and ed. T. Harding (Parker Society, 1849–52), III, pp. 356–63.

19 See H. Obendiek, *Der Teufel bei Martin Luther: eine theologische Untersuchung* (Berlin, 1931).

20 Thorndike, *op. cit.*, IV, p. 129.

21 Henry Holland, *Treatise against Witchcraft* (Cambridge, 1590), sig. A2[r].

22 William Perkins, *Discourse of the Damned Art of Witchcraft* (Cambridge, 1608), p. 197.

23 Thorndike, *op. cit.*, I, pp. 287–97; Yates, *op. cit.*, pp. 1–61; D. P. Walker, 'Orpheus the Theologian and the Renaissance Platonists', *Journal of the Warburg and Courtauld Institutes*, XVI (1953), pp. 100–20.

24 Yates, *op. cit.*, pp. 6–12.

25 Walker, *Spiritual and Demonic Magic*, pp. 40–1.

26 'Dii gentium daemonia sunt' (Psalm 96, Vulgate version). See below, p. 128.

27 Thorndike, *op. cit.*, II, pp. 552–3.

28 *Die Wundergeschichte des Caesarius von Heisterbach*, ed. A. Hilka (Bonn, 1933–7); Caesarius of Heisterbach, *The Dialogue on Miracles*, trans. H. von E. Scott and C. C. Swinton Bland (London, 1929).

29 Bodin, *op. cit.*, fol. 251[r–v].

30 Bodin, *op. cit.*, fol. 1[r], opens his argument by defining *Sorcier* as 'celuy qui par moyens Diaboliques sciemment s'efforce de parvenir à quelque chose'.

31 Agrippa, *De occulta philosophia*, I, ii.

32 Bodin, *op. cit.*, fol. 219[v].

33 The most convenient, though too cursory, discussion of this material is in the two great works by Joseph Hansen: *Zauberwahn, Inquisition und Hexenprozesse im Mittelalter und die Entstehung der grossen Hexenverfolgung* (Munich, 1900); *Quellen und Untersuchungen zur Geschichte des Hexenwahns und der Hexenverfolgung im Mittelalter* (Bonn, 1901). H. C. Lea, *Materials Toward a History of Witchcraft*, ed. A. C. Howland (University of Pennsylvania Press, 1939; repr. New York, 1957), I, pp. 260–353, provides interesting though often inaccurate summaries and selection from a variety of fifteenth-century texts.

30

34 This was Montague Summers's characterisation in the Introduction to the 1946 reprint of his translation of the text. All my references in this chapter are to the first edition of Summers's translation, published by John Rodker (London, 1928).

35 Bull of Pope Innocent VIII, dated 9 December 1484, trans. M. Summers, *Malleus Maleficarum*, pp. xliii–xlv.

36 It now seems to be becoming fashionable to suggest that the *Malleus Maleficarum* has been accorded an exaggerated importance. This may well be true, for the influence of most books tends to be exaggerated by historians. On the other hand, it was reissued more frequently than any other major witch-hunting manual; it was long the most commonly cited; and it remained one of the works which the opponents of persecution sought especially to refute. But perhaps none of this matters.

37 For a concise account of theories concerning the brain, see E. Clarke and K. Dewhurst, *An Illustrated History of Brain Function* (Sandford Publications, Oxford, 1972). See also E. Ruth Harvey, *The Inward Wits: Psychological Theory in the Middle Ages and the Renaissance* (Warburg Institute Surveys, VI, London, 1975).

38 *Malleus Maleficarum*, pp. 87, 134–7, 178, 220.

39 A good example is given by Stillman Drake, 'Renaissance Music and Experimental Science', *Journal of the History of Ideas*, XXXI (1970), pp. 486–7.

40 Lea, *Materials*, I, pp. 264–5, has a brief but highly pertinent comment on the 'permission of God' theory.

41 It was this giving of details concerning infernal conjurations and the like, which so angered Bodin against Weyer. Scot went even further in spelling out such absurdities: and was subsequently used as a magical source book for his pains.

DR. JOHN WEYER AND THE WITCH MANIA

By E. T. WITHINGTON

THE value of every new truth or discovery is relative, and depends upon the state of ideas or knowledge prevalent at the time. Should it go greatly beyond this, it may lose much in practical effect, like good seed falling on unprepared soil ; but the discoverer is no less worthy of praise though he be so far in advance of his fellows that they refuse to accept his teaching, and persecute instead of honouring him. Posterity, however, often ignores former conditions, especially in an era of rapid progress, for the quicker the advance the sooner will the early stages be forgotten, however important and difficult they may have been.

Among those who were so far beyond their age that the truths they proclaimed not only were rejected by the majority but brought them into danger was Dr. John Weyer, the first serious opponent of the witch mania. He stood almost alone. His attack on the witch-hunters, though it marks the turn of the tide, was followed by more than a century of cruelty, injustice, and superstition ; yet our ideas on the subject are now so entirely altered that it is hard to imagine the value and danger of the service he performed, and his name was almost forgotten even by members of his own profession, when his biography was published by Dr. K. Binz in 1885.[1]

[1] *Dr. Johann Weyer, der erster Bekämpfer des Hexenwahns*, Bonn, 1885, 2nd ed., Berlin, 1896. Also J. Geffcken, 'Dr. Johann Weyer' in *Monatshefte der Comenius*

Let us try to get some idea of the nature of the witch mania, that we may better appreciate the courage and intelligence of this ancient physician.

In the second half of the fifteenth century a new age began in Western Europe. The revival of Greek, the invention of printing, and the discovery of America gave fresh ideas and new prospects to mankind. But, as the sun's rays were believed to breed serpents in fermenting matter, so amid this ferment of new life and light rose a hideous monster, more terrible than any fabled dragon of romance or superstition of the darkest ages, which for generations satiated itself on the tears and blood of the innocent and helpless. This was the witch mania. For two centuries the majority of theologians and jurists in Western Europe were convinced that vast numbers of their fellow creatures, especially women, were in league with the devil, that they had sexual intercourse with him or his imps, and that he bestowed on them in exchange for their souls the power of injuring their neighbours in person or property. They thought it their duty to search out these witches, to force from them, by the most terrible tortures they could devise, not only confessions of their own guilt, but also denunciations of their associates, and finally to put them to death, preferably by burning. In consequence, many thousands of innocent persons of all ages and ranks, but especially poor women, were judicially murdered, after being first compelled by unspeakable torments to commit moral suicide by declaring themselves guilty of unmentionable crimes, and to involve their dearest friends and relations in a similar fate. There is no sadder scene in the whole tragicomedy of human history.

There had been nothing like it in the darkest of the dark ages, there was nothing like it among the far more ignorant and superstitious adherents of the Eastern Church. The witch mania in its extreme form has been manifested only by the Catholics and Protestants of the sixteenth and seventeenth centuries and by some tribes of African savages.

In early Christian times, witchcraft was recognized as a relic of paganism, but it was not feared. Christ had overcome the powers of darkness, and His true followers need fear no harm from them. A canon of the Church, at least as early as the ninth

Gesellschaft 3, 1904; J. Janssen and L. Pastor, *Geschichte des deutschen Volkes*, 8 vols., Freiburg im Breisgau, 1898–1903, viii. 600 ff.

century, declared that women who thought they rode through the air with Diana or Herodias were only deluded by the devil, and that those who believed human beings could create anything, or change themselves or others into animal forms, were infidels and worse than heathens ; and confessors were instructed to inquire into and inflict penance for the belief that witches could enter closed doors, make hail-storms, or kill persons without visible means.[1]

In the enlightened sixteenth century, any one who professed his disbelief that witches could ride through the air, change themselves into cats, or make caterpillars and thunder-storms, would have had an excellent chance of being burnt as a heretic or concealed sorcerer. St. Boniface (680–755) classed belief in witches and were-wolves among the works of the devil, and St. Agobard of Lyons (779–840) declared the idea that witches caused hail and thunder-storms to be impious and absurd.[2] The laws of Charlemagne made it murder to put any one to death on charge of witchcraft, and in the eleventh century King Coloman of Hungary asserted briefly, ' Let no one speak of witches, seeing there are none '.[3] Few, indeed, were quite so sceptical as this ; still witchcraft was in the Middle Ages looked upon by the educated in a half-contemptuous fashion, and even those who openly professed sorcery frequently escaped with no worse punishment than penance, banishment, or an ecclesiastical scourging.

This may be well illustrated by a story told in the life of the learned Dominican, St. Vincent of Beauvais. An old woman once (1190–1264) came to a priest in his church and demanded money from him, saying she had done him a great service, for that, when she and her companions, who were witches, had entered his bed-room the previous night, she had prevented them from injuring him. ' But how ', asked the priest, ' could you enter my chamber, seeing that the door was locked ? ' ' Oh,' said the witch, ' that matters naught to us, for we go through keyholes as easily as through open doors.' ' If what you say is true,' replied the holy man, ' you shall not lack a reward, but I must first have proof of it.' With these words, he locked the church door, and began

---

[1] Jean Hardouin (Harduinus), *Collectio regia maxima conciliorum graecorum et latinorum*, 12 vols., Paris, 1715, i. 1506 ; H. C. Lea, *History of the Inquisition of the Middle Ages*, 2nd ed., 3 vols., London, 1906, iii. 494 ; W. G. Soldan and H. Heppe, *Geschichte der Hexenprocesse*, 2 vols., Stuttgart, 1880, i. 132.

[2] Lea, loc. cit., iii. 414.   [3] Soldan and Heppe, loc. cit., i. 128, 139.

vigorously to beat the old woman with the handle of the crucifix he carried, asking her, when she complained, why she did not escape through the keyhole.[1]

The great Pope Nicholas I (died 867) strongly condemned the use of torture to induce confessions, and Gregory VII (died 1085) forbade inquisition to be made for witches and sorcerers on occasions of plague or bad weather.[2] Later, the inquisitorial process, combined with torture to enforce denunciations, became the chief agent in spreading and maintaining the witch mania.

The Eastern Church remained in this mediaeval stage, and never developed a witch mania. In the West the change seems to have been brought about mainly by two causes, the development of heresies and the increasing prominence of the devil.

There is no doubt that the Albigensian and other heresies of the twelfth and thirteenth centuries contained Manichean elements. It was taught that there were two divinities—one perfectly good, the creator of the invisible spiritual world, the other the creator of the material world, the Demiurgus, a being capable of evil passions, wrath, jealousy, &c., who was identified with the Jehovah of the Old Testament.[3] It required very little to confound this Demiurgus with Satan, the Prince of this world; after which it was easy to look upon Satan as a being not entirely evil, as Lucifer, son of the morning, the disinherited son or brother of God, a natural object of worship for the oppressed and discontented.[4]

The serfs, equally tyrannized over by bishop and noble, the relics of the persecuted sects Waldenses and Cathari,[5] sought refuge, like Saul of old, in forbidden arts, and thus sects of Luciferans, or devil-worshippers, arose (especially in Germany and France) whose numbers were exaggerated by the fear and horror of the orthodox.[6]

---

[1] See also Lea, loc. cit., iii. 434, on this mildness of the Church up to the fourteenth century.

[2] Soldan and Heppe, loc. cit., i. 136.   [3] Lea, loc. cit., i. 91.

[4] The Paulicians were accused of teaching that the devil created this world, but seem merely to have taken such texts as John xii. 31, xiv. 30 ; 2 Cor. iv. 4 'in their plain and obvious sense'. F. C. Conybeare, *Key of Truth, A Manual of the Paulician Church of Armenia*, Oxford, 1898, 46.

[5] The term 'Cathari' was said to come 'from their kissing Lucifer under the tail in the shape of a cat'. Lea, loc. cit., iii. 495.

[6] Lea, loc. cit., i. 105, ii. 334, &c. The main evidence is Conrad of Marburg's report to Pope Gregory XI, 1233 : 'A tissue of inventions', but 'apparently doubted by no one'.

36

At the same time the devil acquired more importance in other ways. That fearful calamity, the Black Death, seemed to display his power over both the just and the unjust; while the Great Schism in which each pope excommunicated the other, handing him and his adherents over to Satan, put every one not absolutely certain of being on the right side in reasonable fear of the powers of darkness.

The belief in the great activity and power of the devil and his servants the sorcerers was further supported by the vast authority of St. Thomas Aquinas (1225–74), whose ingenuity enabled him to explain away those ancient canons which seemed opposed to the more extreme views. Thus the synod of Bracara (A. D. 563) had declared the doctrine that the devil can produce drought or thunder-storms to be heresy; to which the Doctor Angelicus replied that though it is doubtless heresy to believe the devil can make natural thunder-storms, it is by no means contrary to the Catholic faith to hold that he may, by the permission of God, make artificial ones.[1]

For these and other reasons, the devil assumed greater prominence during the fourteenth and fifteenth centuries than ever before. Men believed that he might appear to them from behind every hedge or ruin, that his action was to be seen in almost all pains and diseases, but that he was to be dreaded most of all when he entered into a league with some man or woman. Thus everything was ready for the outbreak of witch mania when, in 1484, Pope Innocent VIII by his bull *Summis desiderantes* gave the sanction of the Church to the popular beliefs concerning witches, such as sexual intercourse with devils, destruction of crops, and infliction of sterility and disease on man and beast.

The charge of sorcery had usually been employed in earlier times either to check learned men who seemed to be going too far, or tending to heresy in their researches, as in the case of the physicians Arnold of Villanova (1240–1312) and Peter of Abano (1250–1320), or to crush individuals and societies who were politically dangerous, as with Joan of Arc, the Duchess of Gloucester, and the Templars—the Church being called in to aid the civil power. Now it was the Church which called upon the civil power to assist in a crusade against witches and sorcerers as being the worst and most dangerous of heretics.

[1] Quodlibet, xi. 10 ; Soldan and Heppe, loc. cit., i. 143 ; Lea, loc. cit., iii. 415.

In the Middle Ages it was held that a man who called up the devil, knowing it to be wrong, was not a heretic but merely a sinner.   But if he thought it was not wrong, or that the devil would tell him the truth, or that the devil could do anything without God's permission, he was also a heretic, since these beliefs are contrary to Church doctrine.   In the fifteenth century it was taught that all sorcerers are heretics, *maleficus* being, according to the learned authors of the *Malleus Maleficarum*, a contraction of *male de fide sentiens* or heretic.[1]

Nor was the identification of heresy and witchcraft illogical, whatever we may think of the etymology.   The Church is the kingdom of God, heretics form the kingdom of the devil, and just as the Church possesses saints who see visions, work miracles, and commune with Christ face to face, so there are specially eminent heretics, saints of the devil's church, who work miracles and have obscene intercourse with their master.   All true Christians are potential saints, all heretics potential sorcerers, for all have committed treason against the divine Majesty, though only some may have entered into a definite compact with the enemy.   The former, if they repent, may hope for perpetual imprisonment ; the latter are to be put to death whether they repent or not.

This view was also of advantage to the Church, for it increased the horror of heresy and facilitated its suppression.   The laity had never entirely reconciled themselves to the sight of their apparently harmless neighbours being tortured and burnt for differences in abstract belief, but almost every one was ready to torture and burn a sorcerer, and local outbreaks of witch-hunting were frequently started by mob violence.   In 1555 it was declared by the Peace of Augsburg that no one should suffer in life and property for his religion ; but to take a Lutheran, call him a sorcerer, confiscate his goods, and force him by torture to confess that he was led into his errors by the devil himself, seems to have been too great a temptation for the prince-bishops who headed the 'counter-reformation' in South Germany to resist.   That this was partly the cause of the great witch-burnings in the bishoprics of Würzburg, Bamberg, Fulda, and Trèves is evidenced by the large proportion of male victims, and by the frequent and signi-

---

[1] H. Institoris and J. Sprenger, *Malleus Maleficarum*, editio princeps, Cologne, 1486, and frequently reprinted until the end of the seventeenth century. See especially pars 1, quaestio 2.

ficant appearance of the phrase 'is also Lutheran' in the official reports.

As soon as the Reformation was established, Protestants vied with Catholics as witch-hunters. Eager to show that they were in no way inferior to their opponents in zeal for the Lord and enmity against Satan and his servants, they had the advantage of being able to follow the scriptural injunction, 'Thou shalt not suffer a witch to live', without previously explaining away ancient canons and decrees of Church synods which seemed to throw doubt on the very existence of the more typical forms of witchcraft. Nor did they hesitate to attack their rivals with similar weapons. If Protestants were burnt as sorcerers at Würzburg, we find the first Danish Lutheran bishop, Peter Palladius, recommending the zealous members of his flock to seek out the so-called wise women of their neighbourhoods on pretence of having some disease. If then the latter use paternosters, holy water, or invocations of saints, they are probably not only Catholics but witches, and should be treated accordingly.[1]

Almost all the victims of the witch mania were executed on their own confession, extorted in the vast majority of instances by torture or the fear of torture. In England, where torture was theoretically illegal, confessions were comparatively rare, and nearly all died protesting their innocence. The few exceptions prove the rule; thus Elinor Shaw and Mary Philips, almost the last witches legally executed in England, 1705, confessed because they were threatened with death if they refused, and promised release if they pleaded guilty,[2] while others were induced to admit their guilt by being kept awake several nights, and forced to run up and down their cells till utterly exhausted, methods almost as effectual in producing 'a readiness to confess' as the rack or the thumbscrew.[3]

Nearly all the confessions were to a similar effect. From Lisbon to Liegnitz, from Calabria to Caithness, the central point of the story was the 'sabbat', an assembly of witches and sorcerers in some barren spot where they adored a visible devil, indulged in

[1] J. Diefenbach, *Der Hexenwahn*, Mainz, 1886, p. 299.

[2] The story of Elinor Shaw and Mary Philips, as well as many other accounts of witchcraft, may be read in two volumes entitled *Rare and Curious Tracts illustrative of the History of Northamptonshire*, Northampton, 1876 and 1881.

[3] F. Hutchinson, *Historical Essay*, London, 1718, cap. iv.

o 2

feasts, dances, and sexual orgies, reported what evil they had done and plotted more.

A few examples will therefore suffice, and they may be best taken from the *Daemonolatria* [1] of Nicholas Remy, Inquisitor of Lorraine, who burned nearly 900 witches and sorcerers in fifteen years, 1575–90.

He proves the reality of the witch dances as follows : A boy named John of Haimbach confessed that his mother took him to a sabbat to play the flute.   He was told to climb up into a tree that he might be heard the better, and was so amazed by what he saw that he exclaimed : ' Good God ! where did this crowd of fools and lunatics come from ? ' Thereupon he fell from the tree and found himself alone with a dislocated shoulder.   Otillia Velvers, who was arrested soon after, confirmed the whole story, as did also Eysarty Augnel, who was burnt the following year.   So too, Nicholas Langbernard, while going home in the early morning of July 21, 1590, saw in full daylight a number of men and women dancing back to back, some of them with cloven hoofs.   He cried out ' Jesus ' and crossed himself, upon which all vanished except a woman called Pelter, whose broomstick dropped, and who was then carried off by a whirlwind.   The grass was afterwards found to be beaten down in a circle with marks of hoof-prints.   Pelter and two other women were arrested and confessed they were present, as also did John Michael, who said he was playing the flute in a tree, and fell down when Nicholas crossed himself, but was carried off in a whirlwind, his broomstick not being at hand.

' What further evidence', asks the inquisitor, ' can any one require ? ' The only possible objection, viz. that they were phantoms or spirits of people whose bodies were asleep in their beds, is worthless, ' it being the pious and Christian belief that soul and body when once parted do not reunite till the day of judgement'.

The food at these sabbats usually included the flesh of unbaptized children, and was always abominable.   A certain Morel said he was obliged to spit it out, at which the demon was much enraged.   ' Dancing opens a large window to wickedness,' and is therefore specially encouraged by the devil, but the dances cause great exhaustion, just as his feasts cause loathing, and his money changes to dung or potsherds.   ' Barberina Rahel, and nearly all others, declared they had to lie in bed two days after a witch dance,

---

[1] *Daemonolatriae libri tres*, Lyons, 1595.

but even the oldest cannot excuse themselves, and the devil beats them if they are lazy.' The music is horrible; every one sings or plays what he likes, a favourite method being to drum on horse skulls or trees. Sometimes the devil gives a concert of his own, at which all are required to applaud and show pleasure ; those who do not are beaten so that they are sore for two days, as Joanna Gransandeau confessed.

All are compelled to attend and give an account of their evil deeds under heavy penalties. C. G. said 'he was beaten till he nearly died for failing to attend a sabbat, and for curing a girl whom he had been told to poison. The devil also carried him up into the air over the river Moselle, and threatened to drop him unless he swore to poison a certain person.' The witch Belhoria was attacked by dropsy because she refused to poison her husband. If they failed in their attempts on others, they were compelled to poison their own children, or destroy their own property.

Antonius Welch was asked to lend his garden for a witch dance. He refused, and found it full of snails and caterpillars. Men of little faith have objected that only God can create, for ' without Him nothing is made that was made '; but why should not demons collect vast numbers of insects in a moment ? Look at the well-known rain of frogs, blood, &c. This is doubtless done by devils out of mere sport: how much more would they do for love of harm ? The making of thunder-storms is harder to believe, but has been admitted by more than 200 condemned witches and sorcerers. Almost all confessed that they could creep into locked rooms and houses in the form of small animals, and resuming their natural shape commit all sorts of crimes, showing, says Remy, what a peril they are to mankind.

A worthy comrade of Remy was Peter Binsfeld, suffragan Bishop of Trèves and foremost opponent of John Weyer. He is said to have burnt no fewer than 6,500 persons and to have so desolated his diocese that in many villages round Trèves there was scarcely a woman left. His *Tractatus de confessionibus maleficorum* [1] begins with the following case, which with those mentioned above affords a complete view of the usual witch confessions. John Kuno Meisenbein, a youth about eighteen years old, was studying ' poetry and the humaner letters ' at the High School in Trèves, when he confessed to the authorities that his mother,

[1] Trèves, 1595.

41

brother, sister, and self were all in league with the devil. He said
that in his ninth year his mother had initiated him as a sorcerer,
and had carried him up the chimney on a goat to a heath near
Trèves, where he took part in the usual sabbat and had intercourse
with a female demon named Capribarba. The mother, Anna
Meisenbein, a woman of good position, had already escaped to
Cologne, but a son and daughter were arrested, strangled, and
burned. 'They died with much sorrow and penitence.' The
eldest son, John Kuno, thereupon urged the judges to use all means
to capture his mother, ' that by punishment and momentary death
in this world she might escape eternal damnation '.

Moved by this most creditable and merciful petition (*honestis-
sima et plenissima misericordiae petitione excitatus*), the prior wrote
to his friends at Cologne, and the unhappy woman was arrested and
taken back to Trèves. At first she protested her innocence, ' but
when more severe tortures were employed ' she made the usual
admissions. Having lost a baby, she had, for a moment, doubted
the goodness of God. Whereupon a man in black raiment appeared at the side of the bed, and promised if she would renounce
God and serve him he would give her peace of mind. She did so,
and he became her lover, and gave her money, which however
vanished. He called himself Fedderhans, and had asses' feet.
Then follows the usual story of the sabbat. 'This woman', concludes the bishop, 'was burnt alive October 20, 1590, and had a
good end.' They offered to behead John Kuno as a reward for his
filial piety and repentance, but he said he was unworthy of such
a favour and was therefore strangled and burnt. ' He had a most
edifying end,' says the bishop, who proceeds to comment upon
sexual intercourse between witches, sorcerers, and demons, ' which
is so certain that it is an impudence to deny it, as St. Augustine
saith,[1] being supported by the confessions of learned and unlearned,
and by all the doctors of the Church, though a few medical men,
advocates of the devil's kingdom [an obvious reference to Weyer,
whom he abuses in the preface], have dared to deny it'.[2]

It is not our purpose to try and discover what amount of truth
is contained in the immense farrago of absurdities comprised in the

[1] *Civ. Dei*, xv. 23.
[2] Peter Binsfeld, *Tractatus de confessionibus maleficorum*, Trèves, 1595, pp. 37–
44, 230, &c. Binsfeld often refers to this case as proving the reality of disputed
forms of witchcraft and the soul-saving work of the witch-hunters.

witch confessions.   Actual nocturnal meetings of peasants, either
to celebrate heathen rites or to plot against their oppressors, or
merely to enjoy rude dances and music, as the negro in the Southern
States was supposed to play the banjo nightly after his labours on
the plantation, may or may not have assisted in spreading and
confirming the belief in the sabbat, but they were not necessary.
The whole story of child murder, obscene worship of a demon,
dances and sexual orgies, was ready to hand long before.   It had
been applied in classic times to the worshippers of Isis and Bacchus,
by the pagans to the early Christians, by the orthodox to the first
heretics, to the Jews, to the Templars, and in our own day we have
seen very similar charges brought against the Freemasons.   All
these sets of people had known meeting-places—the witches had
none ; they must therefore meet on some barren moor or mountain
and be carried there supernaturally.   Once started, the belief
spread rapidly.   Indeed we know from contemporary writers that
it was a common subject of village gossip, and if any wretched
victim had any doubt as to what she was expected to confess,
the gaoler and judges were always ready with hints or leading
questions.

One learned German [1] has attributed the whole witch mania to
the *Datura Stramonium*, or thorn-apple, a plant introduced into
Europe about this time.   Women dosed themselves with this drug,
or applied it in ointments, and forthwith had hallucinations of
broomstick rides and witch dances.   Others look upon belladonna
as the principal agent, and one ardent investigator took dangerous
doses of it in the hope of experiencing the adventures of a mediaeval
sorcerer, but without definite effect.   A similar experiment has
recently been made by Kiesewetter the historian of 'Spiritualism'.
He used the witch ointments described by Baptista Porta and
others, but could produce nothing more diabolical than dreams of
travelling in an express train.[2]   Others, again, have supposed that
the badly baked rye bread of the period must have produced an
immense amount of nightmare among the poorer classes.   The
power of suggestion, doubtless, had a very real influence both on
the victims and their judges, and with the aid of narcotics may not
infrequently have produced vivid dreams of dancing and other
intercourse with demons.

[1] L. Meyer, *Die Periode der Hexenprocesse*, Hannover, 1882.
[2] K. Kiesewetter, *Die Geheimwissenschaften*, Leipzig, 1895, p. 579 f.

No doubt many persons were quite ready to become witches or sorcerers, and some really believed they had acquired such powers. Cases are recorded in which formal agreements, duly signed in blood, and awaiting the devil's acceptance, were discovered, and resulted in the arrest and burning of the would-be wizard. Others took pleasure in the terror the reputed powers inspired, and may have sometimes caused or increased it by the use of actual poisons.

But these formed but a small minority of the vast army of victims ; and even when some real criminal was arrested or some half-insane person voluntarily ' confessed ', she was encouraged or compelled to denounce her supposed associates, and thus often involved scores of innocent acquaintances in her own awful fate.

The witch-hunters are not to be blamed for believing in witch-craft, or even for carrying out the scriptural injunction ' Thou shalt not suffer a witch to live '. It is the methods they employed, compared with which the procedure of a Jeffreys or a Caiaphas was just and merciful, which cannot be excused by any talk about the spirit of the age, which brought agony and death to many thousands of innocent men, women and little children, and which excited the fiery and righteous indignation of Dr. John Weyer.

According to Pascal, men never do wrong so thoroughly and so cheerfully as when they are obeying the promptings of a false principle of conscience. To which we may add that men are never more cruel and unjust than when they are in a fright. The witch-hunters, most of them at least, were pious and conscientious men. They appeal to God, the Church, and the Bible at every step. Nicholas Remy, for instance, after torturing and burning over 800 of his fellow creatures, retired from work thinking he had done God and man good service. But one thing troubled his conscience. He had spared the lives of certain young children, and merely ordered them to be scourged naked three times round the place where their parents were burning. He is convinced that this was wrong, and that they will all grow up into witches and sorcerers. Besides, if God sent two she-bears to slay the forty and two children who mocked Elisha, of how much greater punishment are those worthy who have done despite to God, His Mother, the saints, and the Catholic religion ?[1] He hopes his sinful clemency will not become a precedent—a fear which was quite unnecessary, for scores

[1] Op. cit., ii. 2 (p. 200).

44

of children under twelve were burnt for witchcraft; and the one plea which even then respited the most atrocious murderess did not always avail a witch, since it was believed that her future child, if not the actual offspring of the devil, would infallibly belong to his kingdom.

But the witch-hunters were urged on by fear as well as by piety, for not only did they think themselves exposed to personal attacks from the devil and his allies, but they believed there was a vast and increasing society of men and women in league with the evil one, and that the fate of the world depended on its suppression.

All the machinery, therefore, which the Roman emperors had devised for their protection against treason and the Church for the suppression of heresy was brought into action against the witches, for witchcraft was the acme of treason and heresy, a *crimen laesae maiestatis divinae*.[1]

For a description of the methods employed we cannot do better than go to the *Malleus Maleficarum*,[2] the guide and handbook of the witch-hunters.

All proceedings in cases of witchcraft, say the reverend authors, must be on the plan recommended by Popes Clement V and Boniface VIII, ' summarie, simpliciter, et de plano, ac sine strepitu ac figura iudicii ', a harmless looking phrase which swept away at a stroke all the safeguards which the lawyers of pagan Rome and the ruder justice of ancient Gaul and Germany had placed around accused persons. There are, says the *Malleus*,[3] two forms of criminal procedure: (1) the old legal or *accusatorial* form where the prosecutor offers to prove his charge and to accept the consequences of failure, which must be carefully avoided as being dangerous and litigious; and (2) the *inquisitorial*, where a man denounces another either from zeal for the faith, or because called upon to do so, but takes no further part nor offers to prove his charge, or where a man is suspected by common report and the judge makes inquiry, and this method must always be preferred. The inquisitors, on entering a new district, should issue a proclamation calling on all persons to give information against

---

[1] *Malleus*, pars i, quaestio 1, p. 6, edit. 1596.

[2] By H. Institoris and J. Sprenger. Between 1486 and 1596 several editions were printed in specially small form ' that inquisitors might carry it in their pockets and read it under the table '.

[3] iii. 1 (p. 337 f.).

suspected witches on pain of excommunication and temporal penalties. Any one may be compelled, by torture if necessary, to give evidence, and if he refuses must be punished as an obstinate heretic. Other sorcerers, or the man's wife and family, are lawful witnesses against, but not for, the accused. Criminals and perjured persons, if they show zeal for the faith, may be admitted to give evidence. Priests, nobles, graduates of universities, and others legally exempt from torture are not exempt in the case of witch trials.[1]

'Delation,' the scandal of imperial Rome, was not only encouraged but enforced, and in some places, as at Milan, boxes were put in the churches, into which any one might drop an anonymous denunciation of his neighbour.

Names of informers are not to be revealed under penalty of excommunication; the advocate, if there is one, need be told the charges only. This advocate must not be chosen by the accused but by the inquisitor, and he must refuse the case if it seems to him unjust or hopeless. He must not use legal quibbles or make delays or appeals, and is to be specially warned that if he be found a protector of heretics or a hinderer of the inquisition, he will incur the usual penalties for those heinous crimes. If he reply that he defends the person, not the error, this avails not, for he must make no defence which interferes with proceeding *summarie, simpliciter, et de plano*.[2] After this it is not surprising to find that those accused of witchcraft were rarely defended by an advocate.

Faith need be kept with heretics and sorcerers 'for a time only'.[3] Therefore an inquisitor may promise not to condemn a person if he confesses, and then pass sentence after a few days, or if of very tender conscience by the mouth of another. It is also lawful to introduce persons, *etiam mulieres honestae*, to the accused who promise to find means for their escape if they will teach them some form of witchcraft. This, say the authors, is a most successful method for getting convictions.[4]

Torture, though it may not be repeated on the same charge, may be continued as long as necessary, and any fresh evidence justifies a repetition. Finally the accused may be burnt without confession if the evidence is strong enough, or he may be kept

---

[1] *Malleus*, iii. 4, p. 344. [2] iii. 10.
[3] iii. 14. [4] iii. 16.

in prison for months or years, when the *squalor carceris* may induce him to confess his crimes.[1]

Such are the proceedings recommended against persons suspected of or denounced for witchcraft, and they conclude appropriately with the hideously hypocritical formula with which they were delivered over to be burnt : ' Relinquimus te potestati curiae secularis, deprecantes tamen illam ut erga te citra sanguinis effusionem et mortis periculum suam sententiam moderetur ',[2] which means, according to the *Malleus*, that sorcerers are to be burned even though they repent, while repentant heretics may be imprisoned for life.

What was meant by the *squalor carceris* may be seen from the following description by an eye-witness, Pretorius :[3]

' Some [of the dungeons] are holes like cellars or wells, fifteen to thirty fathoms (?) deep with openings above, through which they let down the prisoners with ropes and draw them up when they will. Such prisons I have seen myself. Some sit in great cold, so that their feet are frost-bitten or frozen off, and afterwards, if they escape, they are crippled for life. Some lie in continual darkness, so that they never see a ray of sunlight, and know not whether it be night or day. All of them have their limbs confined so that they can hardly move, and are in continual unrest, and lie in their own refuse, far more filthy and wretched than cattle. They are badly fed, cannot sleep in peace, have much anxiety, heavy thoughts, bad dreams. And since they cannot move hands or feet, they are plagued and bitten by lice, rats, and other vermin, besides being daily abused and threatened by gaolers and executioners. And since all this sometimes lasts months or years, such persons, though at first they be courageous, rational, strong, and patient, at length become weak, timid, hopeless, and if not quite, at least half idiotic and desperate.'

Yet all this was not considered torture, and if some poor wretch, after a year of it, went mad, or preferred a quick death to a slow one, her confession was described as being ' entirely voluntary and without torture '.

As to the torture itself, it combined all that the ferocity of savages and the ingenuity of civilized man had till then invented. Besides the ordinary rack, thumb-screws, and leg-crushers or Spanish boots, there were spiked wheels over which the victims were drawn with weights on their feet; boiling oil was poured on

---

[1] iii. 14.   [2] iii. 29–31, repeated with slight variations.
[3] *Von Zauberei und Zauberern*, p. 211 ; Soldan and Heppe, i. 347.

their legs, burning sulphur dropped on their bodies, and lighted candles held beneath their armpits. At Bamberg they were fed on salt fish and allowed no water, and then bathed in scalding water and quicklime. At Lindheim they were fixed to a revolving table and whirled round till they vomited and became unconscious, and on recovery remained in so dazed a state that they were ready to confess anything.[1] At Neisse they were fastened naked in a chair ' with 150 finger-long spikes in it ' and kept there for hours. And so effective were these tortures that nine out of ten innocent persons preferred to die as confessed sorcerers rather than undergo a repetition of them.

The Jesuit Father Spee, a worthy successor of John Weyer, accompanied nearly two hundred victims to the stake at Würzburg in less than two years. At the end of this time his hair had turned grey and he seemed twenty years older, and on being questioned as to the cause, declared that he was convinced that all these persons were innocent. They had, he said, at first repeated the usual confession, but on being tenderly dealt with had one and all protested their innocence, adjuring him at the same time not to reveal this, for they would much rather die than be tortured again. He added that he had received similar reports from other father confessors.[2] A few years later, 1631, he plucked up courage to publish anonymously his *Cautio Criminalis*, in which he exclaims :

' Why do we search so diligently for sorcerers ? I will show you at once where they are. Take the Capuchins, the Jesuits, all the religious orders, and torture them—they will confess. If some deny, repeat it a few times—they will confess. Should a few still be obstinate, exorcise them, shave them : they use sorcery, the devil hardens them, only keep on torturing—they will give in. If you want more, take the Canons, the Doctors, the Bishops of the Church—they will confess. How should the poor delicate creatures hold out ? If you want still more, I will torture you and then you me. I will confess the crimes you will have confessed, and so we shall all be sorcerers together.'[3]

---

[1] The Lindheim cases are recorded by G. C. Horst, afterwards pastor of the place, in his *Dämonomagie*, 2 vols., Frankfort, 1818, and *Zauberbibliothek*, 6 vols., Mainz, 1821-6. See also O. Glaubrecht, *Die Schreckensjahre von Lindheim*, 1886.

[2] *Cautio Criminalis*, Rinteln, 1631, Dubium xix (p. 128). He calls himself ' Sacerdos quidam '.

[3] Dubium xx (p. 153).

In the most notorious of judicial murders, we read that the judges had some difficulty owing to a disagreement between the witnesses. This rarely troubled the witch-hunters. At Lindheim a woman was accused of having dug up and carried off the body of an infant, which, under torture, she admitted, denouncing four others as her accomplices. But on the grave being opened, the body was found uninjured. The inquisitors at once decided that this must be a delusion of the devil, and all five women were burned. A man confessed, under torture, that he was a werewolf, and in that form had killed a calf belonging to a neighbour; the latter, however, said he had never lost a calf, though two or three years ago two hens had disappeared, he believed through witchcraft. The accused was burnt, for what need had they of witnesses ? Had they not heard his confession ? [1]

It was even laid down as a principle that doubtful points must be decided 'in favour of the faith '—in other words, against the accused. 'If a sorcerer retracts his denunciations at the stake, it is not void, for he may have been corrupted by friends of the accused. Also when witnesses vary, as they often do, the positive assertion is always to be believed,' says Bishop Covarivias, a prominent member of the Council of Trent. In which he is supported by the jurist Menochius of Padua, ' ne tam horrendum crimen occultum sit '.

Anything might start a witch-hunting, and once started it increased like an avalanche. If an old woman happened to be out of doors in a thunder-storm; if the winter was prolonged; if there was a more than usual number of flies and caterpillars; if a woman had a spite against her neighbour, some one might be denounced and forced in turn to denounce others. The prolonged winter of 1586 in Savoy, for instance, resulted in the burning of 113 women and two men, who confessed, after torture, that it was due to their incantations.

It is thus not difficult to understand how, in the diocese of Como, witches were burnt for many years at an average rate of 100 per annum; how in that of Strassburg 5,000 were burnt in twenty years, 1615–35; how in the small diocese of Neisse 1,000 suffered between 1640–50, insomuch that they gave up the stake and pile as being too costly, and roasted them in a specially prepared oven; and how the Protestant jurist Benedict Carpzov could boast not

[1] Horst, *Zauberbibliothek*, ii. 374, and *Dämonomagie*, ii. 412.

only of having read the Bible through fifty-three times, but also of having passed 20,000 death sentences, chiefly on witches and sorcerers.[1]

One of Carpzov's victims is specially interesting to medical men, the Saxon physician, Dr. Veit Pratzel, who on one occasion (1660) produced twenty mice by sleight of hand in a public-house, probably for the sake of advertisement. He was denounced as a sorcerer, tortured and burnt, while his children were bled to death in a warm bath by the executioner, lest they should acquire similar diabolical powers.[2]

A like fate befell the servant of a travelling dentist at Schwersenz in Poland. The dentist, John Plan, left his assistant in the town to attract attention by conjuring tricks, while he went to sell his infallible toothache tinctures in the neighbouring villages. On his return next evening, he was horrified to see the body of the unfortunate man hanging on the town gallows, and was told on inquiry that he was an evident sorcerer who had made eggs, birds, and plants before everybody in the market-place. He had therefore been arrested, scourged, put on the rack, and otherwise tortured till he confessed he was in league with the devil. Whereupon the town council, ' out of special grace and to save expense', had, instead of burning him, mercifully condemned him to be hanged. The dentist fled in terror to Breslau.[3]

But it was by no means necessary to be so foolhardy as this to fall into the hands of the witch-hunters. A woman at Lindheim was noticed to run into her barn as the inquisitorial officials came down the street. She had never been accused or even suspected of witchcraft, but was nevertheless immediately arrested, and brought more dead than alive to the chief inquisitor, Geiss,[4] who declared her flight justified the strongest suspicion. Exposed to the most extreme torture, she confessed nothing, but at length, at the question whether she had made a compact with the devil, one of the inquisitors declared he saw her nod her head. This was enough ; she was burnt ; probably a happy fate under the circumstances, for she thus escaped being forced by further tortures to give details of her imaginary crime and to denounce her neighbours.

[1] Soldan and Heppe, ii. 209.   [2] Soldan and Heppe, ii. 130.
[3] J. H. Böhmer, *Ius ecclesiasticum*, 5 vols., Halle, 1738–43, v. 35.
[4] Horst, *Dämonomagie*, ii. 377.

Once in the clutches of the witch-hunters, the unfortunate victim was confronted by a series of dilemmas from which few escaped. A favourite beginning was to ask whether he believed in witchcraft. If he said ' Yes ', he evidently knew more of the subject; if ' No ', he was *ipso facto* a heretic and slanderer of the inquisition ; if in confusion he tried to distinguish, he was *varius in confessionibus*,[1] and a fit subject for immediate torture. If he confessed under torture, the matter was, of course, settled ; if he endured manfully, it was evident that the devil must be aiding him. If a mark could be found on his body which was insensible and did not bleed when pricked, it was the devil's seal and a sure sign of guilt ; but if there was none, his case was no better, for it was held that the devil only marked those whose fidelity he doubted, so that a suspected person who had no such mark was in all probability a specially eminent sorcerer.[2]

Then came the water test, of which there is no better account than the report sent by W. A. Scribonius, Professor of Philosophy at Marburg, to the town council of Lemgo in 1583 :

' When I came to you, most prudent and learned consules, 26th September, there were, two days later on St. Michael's eve, three witches burnt alive for divers and horrible crimes. The same day three others, denounced by those aforesaid, were arrested, and on the following day about 2 p.m. for further proving of the truth were thrown into water to see whether they would swim or not. Their clothes were removed and they were bound by the right thumb to the left big toe and vice versa, so that they could not move in the least. They were then cast three times into the water in the presence of some thousands of spectators, and floated like logs of wood, nor did one of them sink. And it is also remarkable that almost at the moment they touched the water a shower of rain then falling ceased, and the sun shone, but when they were taken out it started raining as before.'

On request of the burgomaster, he investigated ' the philosophy' of this, and, though he could find nothing definite, had no doubt of its value as a test of witchcraft. ' The physician Weyer rejects it as absurd and fallacious, but he can produce no good arguments or examples against it, and may therefore be ignored.' Perhaps witches are made lighter because possessed by demons who are ' powers of the air ' and often carry them

[1] *Malleus*, iii. 14 (p. 370).
[2] Father Spee gives a long list of these dilemmas, *Cautio Criminalis*, Dubium li.

through the air. All who float have afterwards confessed, there-fore though not scriptural nor of itself sufficient to convict, the swimming test is not to be despised.[1]

With regard to the number of victims, even sober historians, such as Soldan, speak of millions, but if we take three-quarters of a million for the two centuries 1500–1700, it will give a rate of ten executions daily, at least eight of which were judicial murders.

Even more pathetic than the notice of 800 condemned in one body by the senate of Savoy[2] are the long lists of yearly execu-tions preserved in the fragmentary records of small towns and villages. Thus at Meiningen, between 1610–31 and 1656–85, 106 suffered—in 1610 three, 1611 twenty-two, 1612 four, &c. &c., the intervening records being omitted owing to war. Similar notices have survived at Waldsee, Thun in Alsace, and many other ham-lets, where through a long series of years we read of one to twenty persons burnt annually, some of them being previously ' torn with red-hot pincers '.[3]

At Würzburg the Prince-bishop, Philip of Ehrenberg, is said to have burnt 900 in five years (1627–31), and we have terrible lists of twenty-nine of the burnings, almost all of which include young children. Here are two of them :

' In the thirteenth burning, four persons : the old court smith, an old woman, a little girl of nine or ten years, a younger girl her sister.'

' In the twentieth burning, six persons : Babelin Goebel, the prettiest girl in Würzburg; a student in the fifth form who knew many languages and was an excellent musician, instrumental and vocal; two boys from the new minster, twelve years old; Babel Stepper's daughter; the caretaker on the bridge.' [4]

At Bamberg the Prince-bishop, John George, 1625–30, burnt at least 600 persons, and his predecessors had been hardly less vigorous witch-hunters. He was ably seconded by his suffragan, Bishop Förner, and two doctors of law, Braun and Kötzendörffer, who besides the ordinary torture implements, salt fish and quick-lime baths, found a so-called prayer stool or bench covered with

---

[1] *De sagarum natura et potestate, deque his recte cognoscendis et puniendis deque purgatione earum per aquam frigidam epistola*, Lemgo, 1583. Also in Sawr, *Thea-trum de Veneficiis*, 1856.

[2] Lea, iii. 549.   [3] Haas, *Die Hexenprocesse*, Tübingen, 1865.

[4] Soldan and Heppe, ii. 46, and elsewhere.

spikes, on which the victim was forced to kneel, and a cage with a sharp ridged floor on which he could not stand, sit, or lie without torment, of great value in extorting confessions. The record of their deeds has been published by Dr. F. Leitschuh,[1] librarian of Bamberg, and contains, among other cases, that of the Burgomaster, John Junius, which throws more light on the nature of the witch trials than do volumes of second-hand history.[2]

John Junius, a man universally respected, had been five times Burgomaster of Bamberg, and held that office in June 1628, when he was arrested on a charge of sorcery. He protested his innocence though six witnesses declared, under torture, that they had seen him at the witch dances. On June 30 he endured the torment of the thumb-screws and leg-crushers (Spanish boots) without confession. Then they stuck pins in him and found a ' devil's mark ', and finally drew him up with his arms twisted backwards, but he would admit nothing. Next day, however, when threatened with a repetition of the torture, he broke down, made the usual confession (including intercourse with a female demon who turned into a he-goat), and denounced twenty-seven persons whose names and addresses are given.[3] He was condemned to be beheaded and burnt, but before his death wrote the following letter to his daughter :

' Many hundred thousand good-nights, my dearest daughter Veronica ! Guiltless was I taken to prison, guiltless have I been tortured, guiltless I must die. For whoever comes here must either be a sorcerer, or is tortured until (God pity him) he makes up a confession of sorcery out of his head. I'll tell you how I fared. When I was questioned the first time, there were present Dr. Braun, Dr. Kötzendörffer, and two strangers. Dr. Braun asked me, "Friend, how came you hither?" I answered, "Through lies and misfortune." "Hear you," said he, "you're a sorcerer. Confess it willingly or we'll bring witnesses and the executioner to you." I said, "I am no sorcerer. I have a clear conscience on this matter, and care not for a thousand witnesses, but am ready to hear them." Then the chancellor's son, Dr. Haan, was brought out. I asked, "Herr Doctor, what do you know of me? I never had anything to do with you, good or bad." He answered, "Sir, it is a judgement matter, excuse me for witnessing against you. I saw you at the dances." "Yes, but how?" He did not know. Then I asked the commissioners to put him on oath, and examine him properly.

---

[1] Beiträge zur Geschichte des Hexenwesens in Franken, Bamberg, 1883.
[2] 48 ff.   [3] Official report, given by Leitschuh in appendix.

P

"The thing is not to be arranged as you want it," said Dr. Braun; "it is enough that he saw you." I said, "What sort of witness is that? If things are so managed, you are as little safe as I or any other honourable person." Next came the chancellor and said the same as his son. He had seen me, but had not looked carefully to see who I was. Then Elsa Hopffen. She had seen me dancing on Haupt's moor. Then came the executioner and put on the thumb-screws, my hands being tied together, so that the blood spurted from under the nails, and I cannot use my hands these four weeks, as you may see by this writing. Then they tied my hands behind and drew me up. I thought heaven and earth were disappearing. Eight times they drew me up and let me fall so that I suffered horrible agony. All which time I was stark naked, for they had me stripped.

'But our Lord God helped me, and I said to them, "God forgive you for treating an innocent man like this; you want not only to destroy body and soul, but also to get the goods and chattels." [At Bamberg, two-thirds of the property of convicted sorcerers went to the bishop, and the rest to the inquisitors.] "You're a rascal," said Dr. Braun. I replied, "I am no rascal, but as respectable as any of you ; but if things go on like this, no respectable man in Bamberg will be safe, you as little as I or another." The doctor said he had no dealings with the devil. I said, " Nor have I. Your false witnesses are the devils, your horrible tortures. You let no one go, even though he has endured all your torments."

'It was Friday, 30th June, that, with God's help, I endured these tortures. I have ever since been unable to put my clothes on or use my hands, besides the other pains I had to suffer innocently.

' When the executioner took me back to prison, he said to me, " Sir, for God's sake confess something, whether true or not. Think a little. You can't stand the tortures they'll inflict on you, and even if you could you wouldn't escape, though you were a count, but they'll go through them again and again and never leave you till you say you are a sorcerer, as may be seen by all their judgements, for all end alike." Another came and said the bishop had determined to make an example of me which would astonish people, and begged me for God's sake to make up something, for I should not escape even though I were innocent, and so said Neudecker and others.

' Then I asked to see a priest, but could not get one. . . . And then this is my confession as follows, but all of it lies.

' Here follows, dearest child, what I confessed that I might escape the great torments and agonies, for I could not have endured them any longer. This is my confession, nothing but lies, that I had to make on threat of still greater tortures, and for which I must die.

54

'"I went into my field, and sat down there in great melancholy, when a peasant girl came to me and said, 'Sir, what is the matter? Why are you so sorrowful?' I said I did not know, and then she sat down close to me, and suddenly changed into a he-goat and said, 'Now you know with whom you have to do.' He took me by the throat and said, 'You must be mine, or I'll kill you.' Then I said, 'God forbid.' Then he vanished and came back with two women and three men; bade me deny God, and I did so, denied God and the heavenly host. Then he baptized me and the two women were sponsors; gave me a ducat, which turned into a potsherd."

'Now I thought I had got it over, but they brought in the executioner, and asked where I went to the witch dances. I did not know what to say, but remembered that the chancellor and his son and Elsa Hopffen had mentioned Haupt's moor and other places, so I said the same. Then I was asked whom I had seen there. Replied I did not recognize any. "You old rascal, I must get the executioner to you. Was the chancellor there?" Said "Yes." "Who else?" "I recognized none." Then he said, "Take street by street, beginning from the market." Then I had to name some persons. Then Long Street. I knew nobody; had to name eight persons. . . . Did I know any one in the castle? I must speak out boldly whoever it was. So they took me through all the streets till I could and would say no more. Then they gave me to the executioner to strip, shave off my hair, and torture me again. "The rascal knows a man in the market-place, goes about with him daily, and won't name him." They meant Dietmeyer, so I had to name him.

'Next they asked what evil I had done. I replied, "None." The devil bade me to, and beat me when I refused. "Put the rascal on the rack." So I said I was told to murder my children but killed a horse instead. That wasn't enough for them. ·I had also taken a sacramental wafer and buried it. When I said this they left me in peace.

'There, dearest child, you have all my confession, for which I must die, and it is nothing but lies and made-up things, so God help me. For I had to say all this for fear of the tortures threatened me, besides all those I had gone through. For they go on torturing till one confesses something; be he as pious as he will, he must be a sorcerer. No one escapes, though he were a count. And if God does not interfere, all our friends and relations will be burnt, for each has to confess as I had.

'Dearest child, I know you are pious as I, but you have already had some trouble, and if I may advise, you had better take what money there is and go on a pilgrimage for six months, or somewhere where you can stay for a time outside the diocese till one sees what will happen.   Many honourable men and women in Bamberg go to church and about their business, do no evil, and have clear consciences as I hitherto, as you know, yet they come to the witch prison, and if they have a tongue to confess, confess they must, true or not.

' Neudecker, the chancellor, his son, Candelgiesser, Hofmeister's daughter, and Elsa Hopffen all denounced me at once.   I had no chance.   Many are in the same case, and many more will be, unless God intervenes.

' Dear child, keep this letter secret so that nobody sees it, or I shall be horribly tortured and the gaoler will lose his head, so strict is the rule against it.   You may let Cousin Stamer read it quickly in private.   He will keep it secret.   Dear child, give this man a thaler.

' I have taken some days to write this.   Both my hands are lamed.   I am in a sad state altogether.   I entreat you by the last judgement, keep this letter secret, and pray for me after my death as for your martyred father . . . but take care no one hears of this letter.   Tell Anna Maria to pray for me too.   You may take oath for me that I am no sorcerer, but a martyr.

' Good-night, for your father, John Junius, will see you never more.

24th July, 1628.'

On the margin is written :

' Dear child, six denounced me : the chancellor, his son, Neudecker, Zaner, Ursula Hoffmaister, and Elsa Hopffen, all falsely and on compulsion as they all confessed.   They begged my pardon for God's sake before they were executed.   They said they knew nothing of me but what was good and loving.   They were obliged to name me, as I should find out myself.   I cannot have a priest, so take heed of what I have written, and keep this letter secret.'

The letter is still preserved, with its crippled handwriting, in the library at Bamberg.   This case is beyond comment.   It is like the trial of Faithful at Vanity Fair, but with rack and thumb-screw in place of a jury.   Yet it is but a moderate sample of those outrages on justice and humanity called witch trials.   Men rarely held out long, but, did space permit, we might tell stories of many heroic women who endured ten, twenty, even fifty repetitions of torture, till they died on the rack or in the dungeon rather than falsely accuse themselves or their neighbours.[1]

---

[1] Maria Hollin at Nördlingen (1593) withstood fifty-six repetitions of torture, and was finally ' dismissed ' on the terms mentioned (Janssen, op. cit., viii. 719).

56

For when once arrested, the victim had small hope of acquittal, and in the most favourable cases, when there was no external evidence, and no amount of torture could induce a 'confession', the accused was sent back friendless and crippled to her home, which she was forbidden to leave, having first sworn to have no more dealings with the devil, and to take no proceedings against her accusers.   To acquit her would imply that an innocent person had been tortured, a thing naturally repugnant to the tender consciences of the inquisitors.

Nor was the mania confined to any special class.   Protestants vied with Catholics, and town councils with bishops in cruelty and injustice.   At Nördlingen they had a special set of torture instruments which the Protestant town council lent to neighbouring district authorities, with the pious observation that 'by these means, and more especially by the thumb-screw, God has often been graciously pleased to reveal the truth, if not at first, at any rate at the last '.[1]

It is obvious from the above cases that the main cause of the continuance of the witch-burnings, and of the number of the victims, was the use of torture to obtain denunciations.   The instances in which insane persons accused themselves or others seem to have been fewer than we might have expected.

Then, as now, there were melancholics who thought they had committed the unpardonable sin, and in those days the unpardonable sin might be represented by an imaginary compact with the devil.   Then, as now, the 'mania of persecution' was a prominent symptom in some forms of insanity, and the idea of being bewitched by some old woman corresponded to the modern dread of detectives, electric batteries, or telephones.

Some of the supposed signs of witchcraft resemble those of mania and melancholia.   Thus maniacs sometimes collect dirt for money, and witches often confessed that the devil's money changed to dirt.   Melancholics mutter to themselves, look on the ground, and avoid society, all of which were considered signs of witchcraft. But then red hair and left-handedness were no less infallible indications.

Insanity and crime were indeed present at the witch trials, but they were at least as obvious in the accusers and judges as in the

---

[1] The Nördlingen authorities acquired an evil eminence in this frightfulness, which they termed 'eine heilsame Tortur' (Soldan, ii. 470).

victims, and the first man who was bold enough to say so was Dr. John Weyer. Though a few feeble protests may have been made by others, it was from the medical profession that the first determined opposition came. Mystics like Paracelsus and Cardan might encourage the superstition ; pious and able members of the profession like Ambroise Paré and Sir Thomas Brown might give it their sanction, but it was the physician Cornelius Agrippa who first successfully defended a witch at the risk of his own life,[1] and it was his pupil John Weyer who first declared open war against the witch-hunters and invoked the vengeance of heaven upon their atrocities.

' The fearful abounding at this time in this countrie of those detestable slaves of the divell, the witches or enchanters hath moved me (beloved reader) to dispatch in post the following treatise of mine, not in any wise (as I protest) to serve for a shewe of my learning and ingine, but only (moved of conscience to preasse thereby) so far as I can, to resolve the doubting hearts of manie both that such assaults of Satan are most certainly practised, and that the instruments thereof merit most severely to be punished, against the damnable opinions of two principally in our age, whereof the one called Scot, an Englishman, is not ashamed in public print to denie that there can be such a thing as witchcraft and so maintains the old error of the Sadduces in denying of spirits, the other called Wierus, a German physition sets out a publike apologie for all these crafts-folks, whereby procuring for their impunity, he plainly bewrayes himself to have been of that profession.'

Thus did our ' British Solomon ', James I, commence his *Daemonologia* (1598), a work directed against the two men who alone up to that time had made a bold and open protest against the witch mania and its abominations. Reginald Scot in his *Discovery of Witchcraft* (1584) took the view of a modern common-sense Englishman, that the whole thing is absurd, a mixture of roguery and false accusations. Weyer, on the other hand, his predecessor by twenty years, is a firm believer in the activity of the devil, whose object, however, is not to get possession of the souls of crazy old women, but by deluding them, to convert pious and learned lawyers and theologians into torturers and murderers.

Born about 1516 at Grave in Brabant, the son of a dealer in hops and faggots, Weyer was acquainted with the supernatural

---

[1] Lea, iii. 545, and references there given.

from his earliest years, for they had a domestic ' house cobold ' or
Poltergeist, who was heard tumbling the hop-sacks about whenever a customer was expected. At seventeen years of age the
boy was sent to study medicine as apprentice to Cornelius Agrippa,
an extraordinary man, long held to be a sorcerer, who had recently
incurred yet stronger suspicion by his heroic and successful defence
of a woman accused of witchcraft at Metz, and by his fondness for
a black dog called ' Monsieur ' which scarcely ever left him. The
young Weyer used to take this animal out on a string, and soon
became convinced, to use his own words, that it was ' a perfectly
natural male dog '.[1] He next went to Paris and thence to Orleans,
a university then famous for its medical school, where he took the
degree of M.D. in 1537. He commenced practice in Brabant,
became public medical officer at Arnheim in 1545, and in 1550
physician to Duke William of Cleves. In 1563 he published his
great work *De praestigiis daemonum et incantationibus ac veneficiis*,[2]
the object of which is to show that so-called witchcraft is usually
due to delusions of demons, who take advantage of the weaknesses
and diseases of women to bring about impious and absurd superstitions, hatreds, cruelties, and a vast outpouring of innocent blood,
things in which they naturally delight.

He proposes to treat the subject under four heads corresponding
to the four faculties, theology, philosophy, medicine, and law. In
the first section he attempts to show that the Hebrew word *Kasaph*
does not mean ' witch' but ' poisoner', or at any rate that Greek,
Latin, and Rabbinical interpreters so vary, that no reliance can
be placed upon them. Moreover the law of Moses was given to the
Jews ' for the hardness of their hearts ', and is by no means always
to be used by Christians.[3] Magicians and sorcerers do indeed still
exist, as in ancient Egypt, but these are always men, and usually
rogues and swindlers, such as was Faust, of whom Weyer gives us
one of the earliest and most authentic notices. Faust, he says, was
once arrested by Baron Hermann of Batoburg, and given in charge
of his chaplain, J. Dursten, who hoping to see some sign or wonder,
treated him with much kindness, giving him the best of wine. But
all he got out of him was a magic ointment to enable him to shave
without a razor, containing arsenic, and so strong that it brought

---

[1] *De praestigiis, &c.*, ii. 5.
[2] The privilege for publication is dated November 4, 1562; three editions
appeared before the end of 1564, and a sixth in 1583.   [3] *Op. cit.*, ii. 1.

not only the hair but the skin from the reverend gentleman's cheeks.
' The which he has told me more than once with much indignation.' [1]

Weyer, however, firmly believes that the devil may assist sorcerers, such as Faust, in some of their feats, though he does this
chiefly by deluding the eyes of the spectators.   He may also delude
women into the belief that they have been at witch dances and
caused thunder-storms, &c., but his greatest deception is to make
men believe in the reality of witchcraft and so torture and murder
the innocent.[2]   Women are more liable to his deceptions owing to
their greater instability both of mind and body, and the delusion
may be favoured by the use of drugs and ointments, especially
those containing belladonna, lolium, henbane, opium, and even more
by herbs recently introduced from east and west, such as Indian
hemp, datura, ' and the plant called by the Indians " tabacco ",
by the Portuguese " peto ", and by the French " nicotiana " '.[3]

As for the supposed compact with the devil, it is an absurdity
only surpassed by the belief in sexual intercourse with demons.
This delusion, Weyer points out, may be explained medically by the
phenomena of nightmare and the effects of certain drugs, and is
not sanctioned by Scripture.   For, though holy men such as
Lactantius, Justin Martyr, and Tertullian have maintained that
the ' sons of God' mentioned in Genesis vi. 2 were spirits, this
interpretation is opposed by still more eminent theologians, such
as Saints Jerome, Gregory Nazianzen, and Chrysostom, though he
is obliged to admit that St. Augustine believed in *incubi* and
succubae,[4] and that distinguished living theologians hold that
Luther's father was literally the devil.   This, however, says
Weyer, is an unfair and prejudiced way of attacking the Lutheran
heresy.[5]

People who fancy themselves bewitched are really possessed or
assaulted by the devil, as were Job and the demoniacs of the New
Testament.   If these demoniacs had lived in our days, he remarks,
they would probably have each cost the lives of numerous old
women.[6]   The strange objects vomited by such persons are either
deceptions or put into the person's mouth by the devil, as is shown
by there being no admixture of food, and the absence of pain or
injury in spite of the size of the objects.[7]

[1] Op. cit., ii. 4.   [2] iii. 6.   [3] iii. 18.   [4] iii. 21.
          [5] iii. 23.   [6] iv. 1.   [7] iv. 2.

A girl near Cleves fell into convulsions with clenched hands and teeth which, according to her father, could only be opened by making the sign of the cross. She also complained of pains for which it was necessary to buy a bottle of holy water from a priest at Amersfort, on drinking which she proceeded to vomit pins, needles, scraps of iron, and pieces of cloth. She spoke in an altered boyish voice, intended for that of a demon, and declared the whole was caused by an 'in my opinion honest matron', who was imprisoned with her mother and two other women.

Weyer undertook the case, 'whereupon she said in her boy's voice she would have nothing to do with me, and that I was a cunning fellow. "Look what sharp eyes he has."' Weyer opened her hands and mouth, without making the sign of the cross, 'not that I would in any way speak irreverently thereof'. He also showed that the objects produced, even soon after eating, were free from admixture of food, and had therefore never been farther than the mouth; and he thus obtained the release of the four women after a month's imprisonment.[1]

As for the stories of men changed into animals, they are partly poetic and moral allegories, as the sailors of Ulysses, and partly a form of insanity long recognized by physicians, and termed lycanthropy.[2]

Many think they are possessed when they are only melancholic, and others pretend to be so to excite interest and obtain money. Those who fancy themselves attacked by devils should, instead of accusing their neighbours, take to themselves the armour of God as described by St. Paul. Unfortunately, spiritual pastors, in their ignorance and greed, teach that not only diabolical possession, but even ordinary diseases are to be cured by charms, incantations, palm branches, consecrated candles, and an execrable abuse of scriptural words. Cures are, indeed, sometimes so produced, but are really due to the imagination.

Persons supposed to be possessed should first be taken to an intelligent physician, who should investigate and treat any bodily disorder. Should spiritual disorders be also present he may then send the patient to a pious minister of the Church, but this will often be unnecessary. The devil is especially fond of attacking nuns, who should be separated from the rest, and, if possible, sent home to their relations.[3]

[1] iv. 3.   [2] iv. 23.   [3] iv. 10.

Here Weyer inserts several instances in his own experience.

Philip Wesselich, a monk of Knechtenstein near Cologne, an honest, simple-minded man, was miserably afflicted by a spirit about the year 1550. Sometimes he was carried up to the roof, at others thrust in among the beams of the belfry, often carried unexpectedly through the wall (*plerumque per murum transfere-batur inopinato*) and knocked about generally. At length the spirit declared he was Matthew Duren, a former abbot, condemned to penance for having paid an artist insufficiently for a painting of the Blessed Virgin, so that the poor man went bankrupt and committed suicide, 'which was true'. He could only be released if the monk went to Trèves and Aix and recited three masses in the respective cathedrals. The theological faculty of Cologne advised that he should do so, but the abbot Gerard, a man of firmness and intelligence, told the possessed man that he was a victim of diabolical deceptions, and that unless he put his trust in God, and pulled himself together, he should be publicly whipped. Whereupon the monk did so, and the devil left him and went elsewhere.[1]

A similar case was that of a young woman known to Weyer, who had convulsions in church whenever the ' Gloria in excelsis ' was sung in German, and said she was possessed. It was observed, however, that she looked about for a soft place to fall on. She was therefore sent for by Weyer's friend the Countess Anna of Virmont, who said she was about to sing the chant, and that if the demon attacked her she would soon drive him out. The young woman fell in the usual fit, on which the countess, *prudens et cordata matrona*, with the aid of her daughter pulled up her dress and gave her a good whipping. ' She confessed to me afterwards that it completely cured her.' Extreme diseases, adds Weyer, require, according to Hippocrates, extreme remedies, but care should be taken to distinguish suitable cases.[2]

The last and most important section of the book treats of the punishment of witches, who are to be carefully distinguished from poisoners and magicians, such as Faust, who are often wealthy men and spend much money in travel, books, &c., to learn diabolic arts ; or deceivers, such as the mason who buried wolves' dung in a cattle stall, and when the animals showed great excitement, said they were bewitched, and offered to cure them for a consideration. Such men, when proved to have done serious harm, are to be severely

[1] Op. cit., v. 34.   [2] v. 35.

punished.   The less guilty should be admonished, and among them are those who spread superstitious practices and persuade sick people that they are bewitched by some old woman.

This is all that the laws of Church or State require, and is a very different thing from seizing poor women possessed by diabolic delusions, or on the malicious accusations or foolish suspicions of the ignorant vulgar, and casting them into horrible dungeons, whence they are dragged to be torn and crushed by every imaginable instrument of torture, till, however guiltless they are, they confess to sorcery, since it is better to give their souls to God in innocence, even through flame, than longer endure the hideous torments of bloodthirsty tyrants.   And should they die under torture or in prison, the accusers and judges cry out triumphantly that they have committed suicide, or that the devil has broken their necks.

Here follows a burst of indignant eloquence which would have cost Weyer dear had he fallen into the clutches of the witch-hunters, and which may be given in the terse vigour of the original :

'Sed ubi tandem is apparuerit quem nihil latet, Scrutator cordium et renum, ipsius abstrusissimae etiam veritatis Cognitor et Iudex, vestri actus palam fient, O vos praefracti tyranni, O iudices sanguinarii, hominem exuti et caecitate ab omni misericordia procul remoti.   Ad ipsius extremi iudicii tribunal iustissimum vos provoco, qui inter vos et me decernet ubi sepulta et culcata Veritas resurget vobisque in faciem resistet latrociniorum ultionem exactura.' [1]

Their credulity almost equals their cruelty, as shown by the belief that a certain old woman caused the excessive cold of the preceding winter, and by the absurd swimming test.   What effect can denial of faith, evil intentions, or a corrupt fantasy have upon a person's specific gravity, on which floating depends ?   Moreover, women usually float, since their specific gravity is less than that of men, as Hippocrates pointed out.[2]   But nothing is too absurd for a witch inquisitor.   Some fishermen at Rotterdam drew up their nets full of stones but fishless.   This was clearly witchcraft, so they seized an unfortunate woman who confessed in her terror that she had flown out of the window through a hole the size of a finger-end, dived under the sea in a mussel-shell,[3] and there terrified the fishes

---

[1] vi. 4.   [2] vi. 9.
[3] 'Mossel-scolp nostratibus dicitur.'

and put stones in the nets. The woman, says Weyer, was evidently mad or deluded by the devil, but they burnt her all the same. Treachery and cruelty go together. A priest, having failed to make a witch confess, promised that if she would admit some small act of sorcery, he would see that she was released after some slight penance. Thereupon she confessed and was burnt alive.[1]

In contrast to this, Weyer describes the method of dealing with witchcraft in the duchy of Cleves. In 1563 a farmer, finding his cows gave less milk than usual, consulted a witch-finder, who told him that one of his own daughters had bewitched them. The girl, deluded by the devil, admitted this and accused sixteen other women of being her accomplices. The magistrate wrote to the duke proposing to imprison them all, but the latter, probably at Weyer's instigation, replied that the witch-finder was to be imprisoned, the girl to be instructed by a priest and warned against the delusions of demons, and the sixteen women in no way to be molested.[2]

An old woman of eighty was arrested at Mons on charge of witchcraft, the chief evidence being that her mother had long ago been tortured to death on a similar charge. To make her confess they poured boiling oil over her legs, which produced blisters and ulcers, and her son hearing of it sent her a roll of lint to put round them. This was supposed to make magic bandages by the aid of which the woman might escape, and the son was promptly arrested. The mother was to be burnt in a few days, and her son would probably have followed, when Weyer, by permission of the Duke of Cleves, visited Count William of Mons and explained his views on witchcraft. He also examined the old woman, who was so broken down that she fainted several times, and finally obtained the release of both.[3]

Theologians (says Weyer in conclusion) may object that he is only a physician and bid him keep to his last. He can only reply that St. Luke was a physician, and that he is one of those who hope by the mercy of God and grace of Christ to attain that royal priesthood of which St. Paul and St. John speak. Finally he is ready to submit all he has said to the judgement of the Church, and to recant any errors of which he may be convicted.

The Church answered by putting his name on the *Index* as an *auctor primae classis*, that is, one whose opinions are so

[1] Op. cit., vi. 15.   [2] vi. 16.   [3] vi. 16.

dangerous that none of his works may be read by the faithful
without special permission, while his book was solemnly burnt
by the Protestant University of Marburg.[1] The Duke of Alva,
then engaged in his notorious work in the Netherlands, used his
influence to get Weyer removed from his position at the court
of Cleves. In this he was aided by the duke's increasing melancholia and ill health, which were considered by many a judgement
upon him for his protection of Weyer and neglect of witch-burn-
ing. In 1578 Weyer resigned his post to his son Galen, and in
1581 witch-hunting commenced in the duchy of Cleves. Weyer,
however, as befitted the chivalrous defender of outraged womanhood, enjoyed the friendship and protection of Countess Anna of
Techlenburg, at whose residence he died, 1588, aged seventy-two.

The work on *The Deceptions of Demons* has been aptly compared
to a torch thrown out into the darkness, which for a moment
brightly illumes a small space and then disappears. It made
a temporary sensation, and was welcomed by a few of the more
enlightened spirits of the time; it saved the lives of some unfortunate women (being successfully quoted the very year after
publication in defence of a young woman at Frankfort, who confessed she had flown through the air and had intercourse with
the devil), and it marks the beginning of an open and persistent
opposition to the witch mania. Spee also has a curious story
showing the influence of Weyer's book :

' A great prince invited two priests to his table, both men of
learning and piety. He asked one of them whether he thought
it right to arrest and torture persons on the evidence of 10 or
12 witches. Might not the devil have deceived them in order
to make rulers shed innocent blood, as certain learned men had
lately argued, "thereby causing us pangs of conscience" ? The
priest stoutly maintained that these pangs were needless, for God
would never allow the devil to bring innocent men to a shameful
and horrible death in this way ; and so he (the prince) might
continue the witch trials as usual. He persisted in this, till the
prince said, " I am sorry, my father, you have condemned yourself and cannot complain were I to order your immediate arrest,
for no less than 15 persons have sworn you were with them at
the witch dances ", and he produced the records of their trials in
proof. Then the good man stood like butter in the sun in the
dog-days, and had nothing more to say for himself.' [2]

---

[1] Diefenbach, p. 241.   [2] *Cautio Criminalis*, Dubium xlviii.

But it had little effect on the superstition itself, which reached its height during the following half-century ; and the author is compelled by his religious beliefs to admit so much that his position is hardly tenable. Indeed, his premisses had already been granted by the witch-hunters themselves. The jurist Molitor, for instance, admits that much witchcraft is imaginary and due to the deceptions of demons, but while the physician argues that these deceptions are rendered possible by disease, and are themselves largely of the nature of disease, so that the victims deserve pity and medical treatment rather than burning, the lawyer asserts that a person can only be so deceived by his free will, and therefore a woman who believes she has made a compact or had intercourse with the devil is as deserving of punishment as if she had actually done so.[1]

Just over a century after the appearance of Weyer's book (1664)

' Sir Thomas Brown of Norwich, the famous physician of his time, was desired by my Lord Chief Baron [Hale] to give his judgement [in a case of witchcraft]. And he declared that he was clearly of opinion That the Fits were natural, but heightened by the devil co-operating with the malice of the witches at whose instance he did the villanies. And he added, That in Denmark there had been lately a great Discovery of Witches, who used the very same way of afflicting persons by conveying pins into them.'

The jury ' having Sir Thomas Brown's Declaration about Denmark for their encouragement, in half an hour brought them in guilty. . . . They were hanged maintaining their innocence.'[2]

Had Brown been better acquainted with *The Deceptions of Demons* he might have hesitated to make that ' Declaration about Denmark ', but Weyer's early opponent, Bishop Binsfeld, has no difficulties. Quoting Origen (in Matt. xvii. 15) he exclaims, ' Physicians may say what they like, we who believe the Gospel hold that devils cause lunacy ' and many other diseases.[3] But for a demon to cause disease or do other harm, two things are requisite, the permission of God and the free will of some malicious person, witch, or sorcerer. The physician, Weyer, has denied the possibility of a compact with the devil, but is easily refuted by

[1] U. Molitor, *Tractatus de lamiis*, 1561, p. 27.
[2] Hutchinson, *Historical Essay concerning Witchcraft*, London, 1718, pp. 40, 118, 120.   [3] Op. cit., Preludium, i.

Scripture and Church authority. Did not the devil try to make a compact with Christ Himself ? [1] Similarly he has no difficulty in showing that the Hebrew word for witch means much more than ' poisoner ', and, given the almost universal beliefs of the age, it must be admitted that Brown and the bishop have the best of the argument.

In the opening chapter of his well-known work on rationalism, Lecky says that the decline of the belief in witchcraft ' presents a spectacle not of argument and conflict, but of silent evanescence and decay '; it was ' unargumentative and insensible '. Scot's work ' exercised no appreciable influence ', and, so far as the result was concerned, he, Weyer, and their like might as well have kept quiet and waited for the change to be effected by ' what is called the spirit of the age ', that is, ' a gradual insensible yet profound modification of the habits of thought ' due to ' the progress of civilization '. This theory has been ably criticized elsewhere.[2] The truth it contains seems to be that argument would not have sufficed to change public opinion about witchcraft, without the aid of changes in other matters, and especially the development and success of scientific investigation. Such discoveries as the motion of the earth and circulation of the blood, when generally accepted (which was not till late in the seventeenth century), showed that the learned as well as the vulgar might be utterly mistaken in important beliefs supported by apparently good evidence, and that scientific methods of attaining truth differed widely from those of the witch-hunters.

The progress of civilization by practically abolishing the use of torture would alone have immensely diminished the number of victims, and of those ' confessions ' on which the belief was fed. To use military language, the witch mania was an ugly and formidable redoubt connected with other forts and entrenchments. It suffered somewhat from the bombardment by Weyer and Scot, but could only be finally demolished by a general advance of the forces of science and civilization. But if every one had trusted to ' the spirit of the age ' rather than disturb his neighbours' beliefs, we might still be burning our grandmothers.

Though born in what is now Holland and educated in France, German writers claim Weyer as their countryman and compare

---

[1] Preludium, vi.

[2] J. M. Robertson, *Letters on Reasoning*, London, 1905, cap. vi.

him with Martin Luther. The monk of Wittenberg is indeed a fine figure with his ' Here stand I ; I cannot otherwise, God help me ! ' But he had half Germany behind him ; both princes and populace were ready to protect him. Weyer stood practically alone, and if he escaped being burnt by jurists and theologians, had a fair chance of being lynched by an enraged mob as a sorcerer and protector of witches. There was little to save him from torture and death but the strength of mind of Duke William of Cleves, who came of an insane family and already showed signs of melancholia.

Weyer was happily spared such a trial of his fortitude, but none the less does he deserve our admiration as the chivalrous champion of womanhood, who first, with vizor up and lance in rest, greeted, alas! not, like the knights of legend, by prayers and blessings but by threats and imprecations, went forth to do open battle with the hideous monster which had so long tortured and slain the innocent and helpless.

7
LAMBERT DANEAU
1530–1595
OLIVIER FATIO
Translated by Jill Raitt

LIFE Little is known about the childhood and the education of Lambert Daneau (Lambertus Danaeus).[1] He was born around 1530 at Beaugency-sur-Loire into a family of the lesser nobility. After attending the schools of Orléans, Lambert was sent to Paris around 1547 or 1548 where he studied with the hellenist Adrien Turnèbe. One may surmise that he also attended the courses of other royal lecturers and there acquired the humanist knowledge and methods in grammar, logic, rhetoric, physics, history, and geography of which he would make such extensive and pertinent use in his work as a theologian.

From 1553 to 1557 Daneau undertook legal studies at Orléans, where he obtained his license in civil law. After two unsuccessful efforts to become a professor of law there, he left for Bourges, where he remained until 1559; it was probably at Bourges that he obtained his degree of doctor of law. He was particularly impressed by two professors: François Hotman, whom he would meet again in Geneva after the Massacre of St. Bartholomew, and Anne du Bourg, whose martyrdom would determine Daneau's religious vocation.

As a lawyer in Orléans, Daneau frequented the literary circle of jurists and of humanists, whose preoccupations were juridical as well as philological, rhetorical, historical, ethical, and religious. From this period there exists an unedited treatise by Daneau dated 1560: *De Jurisdictione omnium judicum dialogus*.[2] In it Daneau employed the dialectical method so characteristic of his theological works.

---

1. For the few documents that yield some information about Daneau's early years see Paul de Félice, *Lambert Daneau, pasteur et professeur en théologie, 1530–1595. Sa vie, ses ouvrages, ses lettres inédites* (Paris: Fischbacher, 1882), pp. 1–23; and Olivier Fatio, *Méthode et théologie. Lambert Daneau. Les débuts de la scolastique réformée* (Genève: Droz, 1976), pp. 1–3.

2. (Bern: Burgerbibliothek), Cod. Bern. 284.

Almost nothing is known about Daneau's religious convictions before his arrival in Geneva. It is probable that he grew up in an Evangelical environment. Among his friends at Orléans, in following the courses of the royal lecturers at Paris, and then at the Universities of Orléans and Bourges, he must have been in contact with Evangelical ideas. In any case, if one is to believe the autobiography contained in his 1576 dedication of his commentary on Augustine's *De haeresibus ad Quodvultdeum*,[3] Daneau was only faintly attracted toward the Evangelical movement. It was the martyrdom of Anne du Bourg, burned at the stake in Paris on December 23, 1559, that inflamed Daneau and determined him to go to Geneva, where he arrived in 1560. In fact, this tardy dedication dramatizes and telescopes events by presenting as a kind of conversion what may have been in reality a desire to deepen his knowledge of theology—a desire common to many humanists at that time—quickly followed by a total consecration to theology.

In Geneva the thirty-year-old laywer began to follow the sermons and classes of Calvin. As a result, he decided to give up his legal career and to dedicate himself to theology. He was conquered not only by Calvin's doctrine, but also by the ecclesiastical and civil order that this very doctrine had engendered in Geneva. He would become the instrument and advocate of this ideal "model."[4]

Daneau would willingly have remained in Geneva where, it seems, he taught philosophy for a time. But the company of pastors decided otherwise, and he was one of the many pastors sent into France to "shape up" the Reformed church.[5] Daneau became minister of the church at Gien from 1562 to 1572.[6] During these ten years the Wars of Religion troubled all of France, and Daneau had to take refuge at Orléans from September 1562 to April 1563 and again at Sancerre in 1568. On his return to Gien, he was imprisoned. Twice his library was confiscated.[7] But in spite of the extent and harshness of his ministerial tasks at Gien, his intellectual ardor began to bear fruit. It is during this period that Daneau acquired a good part of his astonishing patristic learning and knowledge of St. Augustine in particular. It is equally during his stay at Gien that Daneau conceived the first project of his *Isagoge*, an introduction to the commonplaces of theology treated according to the dialectical method.[8] His other works published between 1564 and 1566 consist of translations of the polemical and moral treatises of Tertullian and

---

3. Lambert Daneau (hereafter abbreviated as LD), *Augustini liber de haeresibus ad Quodvultdeum commentariis illustratus* (Geneva, 1576), fol. a ii verso.

4. Fatio, *Méthode*, pp. 5–6.

5. LD, *Augustini liber de haeresibus*, fol. a iii and verso.

6. Félice, *Daneau*, pp. 43–69; Fatio, *Méthode*, pp. 7–14.

7. Cf. Daneau's letter to J. Simler, Mar. 23, 1576, in Felice, *Daneau*, p. 314.

8. Cf. Daneau's letter to P. Daniel, Sept. 8, 1564, in Félice, *Daneau*, p. 266. See also pp. 268, 272–73, 288–89.

Cyprian on the dress of women and on idolatry.[9] In these works Daneau's taste for patristics and philosophy was joined with his pastoral concern for morality and the practical application of the Word of God.

Among the Reformed churches in France Daneau acquired such a reputation that the Synod of La Rochelle, on April 17, 1571, designated him as one of the ministers charged with drawing up a response to the books of the "adversaries."[10] Thus his name was included with the best-known pastors of the kingdom. This period of activity, so full of promise, was brutally terminated by the St. Bartholomew's Day Massacre in 1572. He returned to Geneva and there grew from a pastor who occasionally had time to attend to the study of theology, morals, and apologetics, into an internationally recognized theologian.

Daneau arrived in Geneva at the end of September 1572[11] and was given the parish of Vandoeuvres in November.[12] He was also given the post of "lector in theology" at the academy, a position created to give some assistance to Theodore Beza.[13] On the following June 25, Daneau was named pastor of St. Pierre, the fine old church in the heart of Geneva.[14] But in spite of his important pastoral and professorial functions, Daneau did not play a primary role in the Genevan church, which was effectively directed by Theodore Beza and Jean Trembley. This is partly explained by Daneau's position as a refugee. A good number of the French refugees remained withdrawn from the life of the church and state of Geneva. Nevertheless, Daneau counted among his friends Theodore Beza, whom he respected as his teacher, the lawyer François Hotman, and the pastors Antoine de Chandieu, Simon Goulart and Jean François Salvard, with whom he collaborated on the 1581 edition of the *Harmonia confessionum fidei.*

When in July 1576, doubtless because of the Edict of Beaulieu, the church of Gien asked Daneau to return, he refused on account of ill health.[15] In fact, poor health forced him to relinquish his pastoral charge and to reduce his

9. During this period Daneau translated *Traité de Tertullian touchant l'Idolâtrie* (Orléans, 1565); *Deux Traictez de Tertullian. L'un des Parures. L'autre des Habits des femmes Chrestiennes.* (Paris, 1565); *Deux traittez de S. Cyprian. L'un contre les Ieux. L'autre par lequel il monstre que l'homme chrestien ne doit voir spectacles publics* (La Rochelle, 1566); *Traité de S. Cyprian du mal qu'apporte l'Envie et Jalousie. Item, un autre traité touchant la discipline et les habits des filles* (Orléans, 1566). Cf. Fatio, *Méthode*, bibliography 1, 2, 4, 5.

10. Jean Aymon, *Tous les synodes nationaux des Eglises réformées de France*, 2 vols. (The Hague, 1710), 1, p. 108; and John Quick, *Synodicon in Gallia reformata or the Acts of those famous national councils in France*, 2 vols. (London, 1692), 1, p. 99.

11. Paul Geisendorf, ed., *Le livre des habitants de Genève*, 2 vols. (Geneva: Librairie Droz, 1963), 2, p. 29: Sept. 29, 1572.

12. *Registres de la Compagnie des Pasteurs de Genève*, 5 vols. ed. O. Fatio and O. Labarthe (Geneva: Librairie Droz, 1969), 3, p. 90.

13. *Registres*, vol. 3, pp. 90, 93, 94.

14. *Registres*, vol. 3, p. 138.

15. *Registres*, vol. 4, ed. O. Labarthe (Geneva: Librairie Droz, 1974), pp. 59–60.

teaching.[16] But his difficulties did not impede the intensive labor to which a prodigious literary production bears witness. Daneau, encouraged by Beza, who was anxious to find well-qualified champions of Calvinism, published in less than eight years (1573–81) some twenty-seven works, nearly all of which are important volumes.[17] Among them are the moral treatises: *Les Sorciers, Briève remonstrance sur les jeux de sort* (1574); editions of St. Augustine's works, with abundant commentary;[18] a commentary on Peter Lombard's first book of the *Sentences* (1580); works on methodology like *Elenchi haereticorum* (1573) or *Methodus tractandae sacrae scripturae* (1573); a commentary on 1 Timothy (1577); a *Physica Christiana* (1576) and an *Ethice Christiana* (1577); and a series of polemical works against the ubiquitarians[19] and the papists.[20]

This intensive activity brought Daneau into the network of Reformed theologians whose principal centers were Geneva, Zürich, Basel, Heidelberg, and, temporarily, Neustadt-an-der-Hardt. From 1576 on, Daneau became equally well known as the implacable pursuer of the ubiquitarians. From this date until 1584 he responded, in eight works, to all the great Lutheran theologians: Nikolaus Selnecker, Lucas Osiander, Stefan Gerlach, Jakob Andreae and Martin Chemnitz. Raised to the first rank of Calvinist polemicists, he showed himself to be firm and persevering, capable of tenacious enmities and of a vehement and violent oratory that was truly awesome.

Through his publications, his contacts, and his polemical activity, Daneau made a name for himself at Geneva. It is not, therefore, surprising that in May 1579, on the advice of Jerome Zanchi and Daniel Toussaint, he was considered as a candidate for the chair of theology at the University of Leiden, a chair left vacant by the departure of William Feugueray. But neither the government of Geneva nor Beza, who was ill, wished to let him go. Nevertheless, the magistrates of Leiden returned to the charge at the end of 1580, and this time Daneau received authorization to leave Geneva in spite of the profound regret of Beza. Daneau was given Genevan citizenship on January 16, 1581, and left the city on the following February 10.[21]

The Genevan years had been decisive for Daneau: they had allowed him to acquire control of his extraordinarily extensive knowledge and to bring his theological thought to maturity. He had arrived with a certain limited

16. Olivier Fatio, *Nihil pulchrius ordine. Contribution à l'étude de l'établissement de la discipline ecclésiastique aux Pays-Bas (1581–1583)* (Leiden: Brill, 1971), p. 15.

17. Fatio, *Méthode*, bibliography 8–80.

18. *Augustini Enchiridion commentariis illustratus.* (Geneva, 1575); *Augustini de haeresibus; Paratitla in Augustini tomos duos praecipuos* (Geneva, 1578).

19. Among these pamphlets are *Antiosiander* (Geneva, 1580); *Examen libri de duabus in Christo Naturis a Martino Kemnitio conscripti* (Geneva, 1581).

20. *Response chrestienne à Matthieu de Launoy et Henry Pennetier* (Geneva, 1578) and *Ad novas Genebrardi calumnias responsio* (Geneva, 1578).

21. See Fatio, *Nihil pulchrius*, pp. 15–22, for the sources for this period of Daneau's life.

reputation and he left after being elevated to the rank of a renowned Calvinist theologian.

In calling Daneau, the curators of the University of Leiden and the burgomasters of the town hoped to contribute to the reputation of their new university. In fact, they would receive a doctor of the Reformed church, who conceived of his teaching duties as a ministry and subordinated them to ecclesiastical needs. The confrontation would not be long in coming between a magistracy with caesaro-papist tendencies and a professor trained in a presbytero-synodal form of the church such as Calvin had conceived for France.

In May and June of 1581 Daneau participated in the national Synod of Middelburg and took part in the interrogations of Pastor Gaspard Coolhaas, declared adversary of Reformed ecclesiastical discipline, who was firmly supported by the magistracy of Leiden. In a work showing the necessity of a visible church, Daneau confronted the magistracy of Leiden and Dirck Coornhert, its ideologue and partisan of an individualistic Christianity constituted as such in its very institutions.[22]

In July of 1581 Daneau was engaged in a test of strength with the magistracy of Leiden over the appointment of elders and deacons to form a consistory in the French-speaking community for which he was preacher. He appointed them without consulting the civic authority, in spite of the latter's recognized rights.[23] The conflict reached its peak in February of 1582, when the magistracy of Leiden, after having compared the Genevan discipline favored by Daneau to the Spanish Inquisition, accused him of wanting to place upon the churches a new yoke as insupportable as that of the papacy. Daneau, cut to the quick, offered his resignation on February 28, 1582.[24]

Nothing could retain him, neither the affection of his students nor the support of the prince of Orange, who affirmed in March that "without Daneau, the theology faculty would be empty."[25]

His sojourn at Leiden seemed to be a failure. Could he have acted otherwise? He did not understand Dutch and held in little esteem the country's intellectual development. In addition he had been taken up in the

---

22. See Fatio, *Nihil pulchrius*, for the details of this crisis, which resulted on the one hand in the excommunication of Coolhaas (1534–1615), pastor of Leiden from 1574, by the provincial synod of Haarlem, and on the other hand in the dismissal of Daneau. In the same volume, one will also find an analysis of Daneau's response to the famous Dirck Coornhert (1522–90), moralist, politician, latitudinarian, and man of tolerance. LD, *Ad Libellum ab anonymo quodam libertino recens editum, hoc titulo, de externa seu visibili Dei Ecclesia, ubi illa reperiri possit, et quaenam vera sit etc. seu potius, adversus externam et visibilem ecclesiam* (Geneva, 1582). Cf. Fatio, *Méthode*, bibliography 90.

23. Cf. Leiden, Gemeentearchief, Gerechtsdagboek A (Secretariearchief no. 9248), fol. 145, July 11, 1581, published in Fatio, *Nihil pulchrius*, p. 171, n. 1.

24. P. C. Molhuysen, *Bronnen tot de geschiedenis der Leidsche Universiteit*, vol. 1 (The Hague, 1913), pp. 27–28; and Fatio, *Nihil pulchrius*, pp. 83–89.

25. William of Orange to the University of Leiden, Mar. 10, 1582, in Molhuysen, *Bronnen*, d. 86, p. 99.

larger issue of the establishment of the Reformed church, which, although authorized and rooted in the Low Countries, was far from being understood according to Daneau's conception of the whole church. This conflict between two conceptions of the church and its relations with the state, in fact between two conceptions of society, continued after Daneau's departure.

These troubled circumstances, however, did not interfere with Daneau's unwearying intellectual activity. He found time at Leiden to prepare, and probably to teach, the beginnings of his great theological work, the *Isagoge de Deo*, which was published in 1583 by Vignon in Geneva.[26] It should be noted also that among his students was the celebrated Arminius, whose gifts Daneau praised publicly.[27]

Daneau left Leiden for Gand where, enjoying the excellent atmosphere of this Reformed haven, he taught in the Calvinist academy from May 1582 to May 1583.[28] He then answered a call to southern France to teach theology at Orthez. In 1583 he occupied the principal chair of theology in the academy, which had nearly 600 students. At the same time, he performed ministerial duties and seemed to enjoy the tranquility of Orthez after his embattled stay at Leiden.[29] During the seven years at Orthez, Daneau was able to finish his *Isagoge*, publishing *De salutaribus Dei donis erga Ecclesiam* in 1586 and *De homine* in 1588.[30] In addition, he published a commentary on the minor prophets in 1586[31] and an explanation of the Apostles' Creed in 1587.[32] Through correspondence he maintained his bonds of friendship with his teachers and friends such as Beza in Geneva and Rudolf Gwalter in Zürich. In 1591 Daneau moved the university to its new home at Lescar. One year later he left Béarn to become pastor at Castres.[33] There he wrote a refutation of Bellarmine's work, which was published posthumously in 1596 and 1598,[34] and a work on Christian politics that appeared in 1596.[35] The year of his death, 1595, Daneau synthesized his thought for the last time in *Compendium sacrae theologiae*, published at Montpellier.[36]

26. LD, *Christianae Isagoges ad Christianorum Theologorum locos communes libri II* (Geneva, 1583). (Fatio, *Méthode*, bibliography 106). Cf. Fatio, *Nihil pulchrius*, p. 95.

27. P. Bertius, *Oratio in obitum D. Iac. Arminii*, (1609), cited in Fatio, *Nihil pulchrius*, p. 186, n. 12.

28. On Daneau's years at Gand, see Fatio, *Nihil pulchrius*, pp. 98–102.

29. Félice, *Daneau*, pp. 118–133. Cf. Daneau's letter to Gwalter, Dec. 11, 1584, published in Fatio, *Méthode*, pp. 122*–123*.

30. Fatio, *Méthode*, bibliography 116 and 122.

31. LD, *Commentarii in Prophetas Minores* (Geneva, 1586). Fatio, *Méthode*, bibliography 118.

32. LD, *Symbolici Apostolici explicatio* (Geneva, 1587). Fatio, *Méthode*, bibliography 120.

33. Félice, *Daneau*, pp. 126–27.

34. LD, *Ad Bellarmini disputationes theologicas responsio* (Geneva, 1596), and *Ad tomum secundum controversiarum Bellarmini responsio* (Geneva, 1598). Fatio, *Méthode*, bibliography 132 and 135.

35. LD, *Politices christianae libri septem* (Geneva, 1596). Fatio, *Méthode*, bibliography 133.

36. LD, *Compendium sacrae theologiae* (Montpellier, 1595). Fatio, *Méthode*, bibliography 128.

THEOLOGY The reader of Daneau's works is less struck by the originality of his thought than by the range of his interests and erudition, by the diversity of his points of view, by the order and elegance of his reasoning. Daneau is a universal mind. Inspired by a vast encyclopedic plan, he undertook to found on Holy Scripture a number of recognized areas of knowledge, in order to integrate secular influences into the Reformed churches and academies. He added thereby to his theological and polemical works a *Physica christiana* (Geneva, 1576 and 1580); an *Ethice christiana* (Geneva, 1577); a Christian history, *Vetustissimarum primi mundi antiquitatum libri IIII* (Geneva, 1590); and a *Politice christiana* (Geneva, 1596). In doing this, Daneau is typical of scholars of the developing Reformed academies, who tried to extend to every aspect of knowledge the specific mark of Calvinism.

In Calvin and Beza, Daneau recognized his masters. But by the multiplicity of his interests and above all by his plan to base all knowledge on Scripture, he ventured into territory toward which his masters themselves had not turned. In more than one case, he was obliged to supplement their silence by direct borrowings from the Fathers, from Augustine through the middle ages to contemporaries such as Melanchthon, Peter Martyr Vermigli, Zanchi, Pierre Viret, and Chandieu. In order to synthesize his thought and to enlarge his points of view, he looked to a theologian who influenced his thought almost as much as Calvin and Beza, Andreas Hyperius.[37] To this name must also be added those of Niels Hemmingsen, the Danish crypto-Calvinist, and Johann Jakob Grynaeus of Basel. In short, Daneau's theology was eclectic. Nevertheless this man at the crossroads had succeeded in giving to his thought an order that is the expression of an intellectual energy and of an activity that never weakened to the end of his days. More than the term "orthodox," which brings with it a notion of rigidity and absence of imagination, the term "scholastic" applies to Daneau's work. In fact, he tried to present to his students in the most synthetic and accommodating manner both a theological understanding, which he considered admirably developed by Calvin and Beza, and the extension of this understanding to other areas of study. Why, then, should scholars criticize the rational framework to which he resorted as a corruption of the existential discoveries of the Reform?[38] It would be better to recognize it as a pedagogical support favoring the presentation of ideas easily put to use and corresponding to the process of scholarly transmission and the establishment of the Reform.

37. Note, for example, the influence of Hyperius's *De Theologo, seu de ratione studii theologici libri IIII*, 3rd ed. (Strasbourg, 1562) on Daneau's *Methodus sacrae scripturae tractandae*, (Geneva, 1579). Cf. Fatio, *Méthode*, pp. 64ff.

38. Ernst Bizer, "Frühorthodoxie und Rationalismus," in *Theologische Studien*, no. 71, Zürich, 1963, pp. 6, 15, 60–63.

Instead of describing some of Daneau's theological positions, it seems more useful to show the constitutive elements of his thought.

Before being a commentator on Scripture, Daneau was a man gifted at presenting a systematic construction. He was a professor who presented a summation of a problem in the briefest and most comprehensible manner, and at the same time exposed the roots of heresies. To accomplish this double objective, which corresponded, he thought, to the true method of teaching theology, that is, to affirm a doctrine and to refute its contrary (compare 2 Timothy 3:16 and Titus 1:9), Daneau needed an instrument that would assure both rigor and rationality. He found it in dialectic, the science of argumentation and reasoning, which provided him with the basis of his method.[39]

This dialectic is the Ciceronian Aristotelianism of Johannes Caesarius, of Johann Sturm, and, above all, of Philip Melanchthon. It points out that the most direct way to present the matter is to advance by posing questions (an sit, quid sit, quis sit, etc.) the responses to which are contained in the different dialectical loci, such as, for example, definition, gender, species, difference, cause. The first important work that Daneau published, Elenchi haereticorum (1573), provided a method intended to refute the arguments of heretics. This entire work was inspired by the Topica theologica (1564) of Hyperius.

Inspired by the refutations of Aristotle, Daneau taught that one passed through the discovery, analysis, and refutation of sophistries, that is to say, those places where erroneous arguments result in erroneous conclusions. Thanks to this dialectic, Daneau presented a universal method for exposing the corruptions inflicted by heretics on theological teaching and reestablishing it in its true form. He intended to furnish an instrument that would be valid against all heretics, by attacking the construction of their paralogisms without having to know each point of their doctrines.[40] He justified his method by the fact that Revelation itself utilizes logical categories. Is there, he asked, a dialectician more rigorous in argumentation or more keen in refutation than Paul?[41] To Daneau, prophets and apostles, under the direction of the Holy Spirit, are the greatest rhetoricians and dialecticians. The heretic, by contradicting the Gospel, commits therefore faults of logic and of rhetoric; his language is made up of confused propositions reducible to paralogisms. At the very instant that the heretic thinks he has overthrown the faith, he is constrained by logic. Dialectic comes therefore to support the confession of faith.

39. LD, Elenchi haereticorum (Geneva, 1573), p. 1, and Methodus sacrae scripturae tractandae, pp. 4 and 33.

40. LD, Elenchi, pp. 2, 3, and 5.

41. LD, Elenchi, p. 10.

In the face of the reluctance of certain theologians, those of Zürich, for example, to use dialectic in theology,[42] Daneau responded carefully utilizing the distinction between matter and form: dialectic does not give the substance of the faith to teaching; only Scripture contains true doctrine. On the other hand, the form of theology, that is to say, "the method and the manner of teaching and defending the faith," can be aided by the art of Aristotle and the dialecticians. Following Melanchthon and Beza, Daneau affirmed that dialectic is a gift of God; it must be used as a servant, as an instrument facilitating reasoning.[43] In his treatise *Transubstantiation* (La Rochelle, 1589), Daneau wrote: "As thus the true God is the author of the nature possessed by each thing, and notably of that reason by which man differs from brute beasts, and by which he discourses, argues and concludes from premises which are afforded him, he sees the consequences of things and separates the true from the false, certainly it must be said that anyone who rejects this conclusive reason, rejects also the wisdom of God of which the reason of man is a spark, a small flame, or a ray or streamlet."[44]

This taste for methodology is found again in the manner in which Daneau approaches biblical exegesis. *Methodus tractandae scripturae* (1579) proposes to the pastor and to the professor the way to explain Scripture. For each verse, Daneau proposes to begin with the rhetorical, dialectical, and theological *loci*. [45] The rhetorical locus makes apparent the type of liaison that unites a passage to its context and, at the same time, the frame of the theological explanation. The dialectical locus searches out the type of argument used by the author of the scriptural passage. As for the theological locus, it allows one to express the theological content of the text, and it comprises many stages: *summa, divisio membrorum, collatio locorum similium et dissimilium, explicatio verborum.*[46] In a manner that foreshadows Puritanism, Daneau's method insists finally on practical application and moral exhortation which ought to follow the exposition of a theological locus. In practical terms the exposition of the theological locus does not suffice to teach that which is necessary for the instruction, edification, correction, and consolation of the Christian.[47]

Daneau's method holds to a strict plan patently drawn from the popular and learned methods of teaching proposed by Hyperius in *De Theologo*.[48] The plan does not provide a key to interpretation but proposes a way to move

42. Bullinger's letter to Beza, Dec. 1, 1568, in *Correspondance de Théodore de Bèze*, (9 vols.) (Geneva: Librairie Droz, 1978), 9, p. 197.

43. LD, *Elenchi*, pp. 9–11.

44. LD, *Deux traitez. L'un de la Messe et de ses parties. L'autre, de la transsubstantiation du pain et vin de la Messe* (La Rochelle, 1589), p. 197.

45. LD, *Methodus sacrae scripturae tractandae*, p. 12.

46. Ibid., pp. 30–34.

47. Ibid., p. 35.

48. Hyperius, *De Theologo*, p. 398.

through the explication of a text. It indicates the steps of this path without saying anything about the content of the exegesis, a task that belongs to theology. Its end is to formalize the project expressed in the preface of Calvin's commentary on Romans: to explain the biblical text in a continuous manner without skipping anything.[49]

The content of Daneau's exegesis is found in the few commentaries that he published: In *Priorem Epistolam ad Timotheum commentarius* (Geneva, 1577), a veritable treatise on ecclesiastical discipline (to which we will return); *Orationis Dominicae Explicatio* (Geneva, 1582); *In Ev. secundum Matthaeum commentarii brevissimi* (Geneva, 1583); *In tres Joannis et unicam Judae Epistolam* (Geneva, 1585); *In prophetas minores commentarii* (Geneva, 1586); *Quaestionum in Ev. secundum Marcum liber unus* (Geneva, 1594).[50] Daneau followed Calvin's exegesis in general, while paying considerable attention to Beza's *Annotationes*. Nor did he neglect Hemmingsen, Melanchthon, or Erasmus. But the formal framework in which his commentaries were written prevented his exegesis from being a repetition of those authors just cited. It should be noted that the hermeneutic that dominates the commentary on the minor prophets is very close to that of Calvin, in the sense that it allows the text of the Old Testament to retain its historical density. Attentive to the development of the history of salvation and to the paradigmatic signification that each of its moments could take for the present situation, Daneau refused to move at once to a Christological interpretation of the prophetic texts.[51]

Another characteristic of the thought of Daneau is that reference to the fundamental authority, Scripture, is accompanied by numerous references to diverse authorities. These certainly do not constitute a second source of revelation, but they illustrate, or even prove, theological affirmations.

Daneau was a connoisseur of the Greek and Latin classics, from whom he drew an encyclopedic knowledge of geography, physics, schemes of logical thought, ethics, and politics. Certainly he affirmed that the word of God surpassed infinitely these pagan luminaries, and it is on this basis that he intended to build his *Ethice christiana*, his *Physica christiana*, and his *Politice christiana* in order to grasp the influence on Christians of the *Nicomachean Ethics*, the *Physics*, and the *Politics* of Aristotle.[52] But it is evident that these works of Daneau owed much to the structures of those of his illustrious predecessor.

The Church Fathers retained his attention, in particular Augustine, whose *Enchiridion* he edited and commented upon (Geneva, 1575), followed

---

49. John Calvin, dedicatory letter to S. Grynaeus in the "Commentaire aux Romains," in *Calvini Opera*, vol. 10, (*C.R.* 38) 2, cols. 402–06.

50. Fatio, *Méthode*, bibliography 55, 85, 105, 115, 118, 127.

51. Compare the exegesis of Mic. 2:13 in Calvin (*Calvini Opera*, vol. 43, [*C.R.* 71] cols. 315–318) and in LD, *Commentarii in prophetas minores*, pp. 538–540.

52. See, for example, LD, *Physica christiana pars altera* (Geneva, 1580), fol. q. ii–iii verso, dedicatory epistle to Peter de Sborow, palatine of Cracovia.

by *De haeresibus ad Quodvultdeum* (Geneva, 1576).[53] Contrary to the reformers of the first generation, Daneau did not first seek in Augustine an anti-Pelagian and anti-Donatist theologian. His personal preoccupations caused him to see first in Augustine the man of theological method and the systematician, then as the adversary of heresies, and finally as the exegete.[54] Daneau gave, therefore, in the *Enchiridion*, a systematic work par excellence, a commentary that is the first expression of a theology in which the influence of Calvin and Beza appears. Thus chapters 33 to 35 of Augustine, dedicated to the incarnation and the work of the mediator, furnished Daneau with the occasion to treat the hypostatic union in a manner that reflected the theology developed by Beza in his battle against the ubiquitarian Lutherans.[55]

Daneau distinguished himself from his contemporaries by his interest in scholasticism, for which he felt, at the same time, aversion and fascination. One is aware of these two attitudes in his commentary on the first book of the *Sentences* of Peter Lombard, *In Petri Lombardi librum primum sententiarum commentarius* (Geneva, 1580).[56] He expressed aversion for a theology that is contained in tedious questions and that, by distancing itself from Scripture, allows itself to be invaded by Aristotelian philosophy. But he is fascinated by a method whose application resulted in clear and rational constructions; he has admiration also for some of the elements of truth still present in this theology justified by numerous proofs drawn from St. Thomas, Durand de Saint-Pourçain, from canon law, or from Nicholas of Lyra.[57]

These multiple influences were brought together and carefully ordered in the *Isagoge*, Daneau's great theological work. The witness par excellence to his eclecticism and his dedication to system, it presents an original synthesis, while at the same time it covers all the theological loci, from the doctrine of God to that of eternal life. The *Isagoge* ought to be considered as an introduction to theology, prepared by a professor for his students.[58] It also helped to stabilize Reformed academies, many of which had, at this time, a precarious existence. In many of them, professors remained only a short time. Daneau's career is itself an excellent example of this instability. The *Isagoge* appeared then as a manual that presented, at a high level of popularization, a means of learning theology outside of an academic setting. As a Reformed version of the *Sentences*, it allowed ministers or doctors who had already finished their formal education a means of refreshing their understanding of theological principles.

---

53. Fatio, *Méthode*, bibliography 28 and 40.

54. See "De methodo librorum Augustini, et de eorum evoluendorum ratione" in LD, *Augustini Enchiridion*, fol. **i verso–** iii.

55. Fatio, *Méthode*, pp. 113–116.

56. Ibid., bibliography 75.

57. LD, *In Petri Lombardi librum primum sententiarum commentarius* (Geneva, 1580), fol. ** i verso–fol. ** iiii. Cf. Fatio, *Méthode*, pp. 129–130.

58. In this regard, see Daneau's prolegomena in *Compendium sacrae theologiae*, fol. i recto and verso.

From 1564 to its publication between 1583 and 1588, Daneau labored over this work. It has five parts—*De Deo, de angelis, de homine, de Ecclesia, de salutaribus Dei donis erga Ecclesiam*—which Daneau, as usual, had visualized in a great diagram. The last part is constructed according to Beza's diagram of the *Summa totius christianismi* (1555),[59] which "geometrically" organized the stages of the history of salvation and of reprobation as functions of the divine decree.

In order to treat each theological locus, Daneau utilized the dialectical questions: *an sit, quid sit, qualis sit, etc.*[60] This dialectical structure led him to present a description of God *in se* in order to answer the question *quid sit.*[61] Calvin had eschewed describing the essence of God (*Institutes* I, 13, 1) so Daneau borrowed from the Calvinist Zanchi his plan for describing the divine essence according to its attributes. More distantly, he followed the *Summa theologica* of St. Thomas and *The Orthodox Faith* of John Damascene. He remained, nevertheless, more reserved than Zanchi with regard to metaphysics and in particular to the Thomist definition of God as *ens simplicissimum.*[62] Zanchi began his own doctrine of God with definitions in the light of which he understood Scripture. Never did he see the least opposition between metaphysics and exegesis. Daneau, on the other hand, presented a less speculative theology in spite of its method and its rationalizing character. He made a point of beginning with Scripture and then aligning his points with certain metaphysical elements. Nor did he always find it easy to bring about such a conciliation. Pulled between Calvin and the new school of someone like Zanchi, he opted for prudence and worked out a theology with a remarkable formality, but he was very hesitating and ill at ease to be thus at the juncture of two worlds.

But in the final part of *Isagoge, De salutaribus Dei erga Ecclesiam*, there is no trace of uncertainty. Daneau could base himself here on both Calvin and Beza in speaking of the decree of God, of its realization either through justification and sanctification or though reprobation and hardening. In the *De homine*, a rich anthropological chapter, Daneau utilizes a multiplicity of sources from St. Thomas and Aristotle, passing through Beza, Martyr, and Melanchthon to Grynaeus.[63] As an eclectic work, *Isagoge* echoes some of the diverse points of view of Calvinist theologians in the second half of the sixteenth century.

59. Frédéric Gardy, *Bibliographie des oeuvres de Théodore de Bèze* (Geneva: Librairie Droz, 1960), pp. 47–53.

60. On the genesis, the plan, and the dogmatic method of the *Isagoge*, see Fatio, *Méthode*, pp. 147–150.

61. LD, *Christianae Isagoges, libri II (De Deo)* chaps. 1–8. Cf. Fatio, *Méthode*, pp. 154–165.

62. Compare LD, *Christianes Isagoges, libri II*, fol. 2 verso, 10; and Girolamo Zanchi, *De natura dei*, in *Opera theologica*, 2 vols., (Geneva, 1613), 2, cols. 63–73.

63. Johann Jakob Grynaeus, *Synopsis historiae hominis: seu, de prima hominis origine, eiusdemque corruptione, reconciliatione cum Deo, et aeterna salute, theses ducentae* (Basel, 1579), cited in LD, *Isagoges Christianae pars quinta quae est de homine* (Geneva, 1588), fol. 47–48, 69.

Daneau would summarize the *Isagoge* in 1595 in his *Compendium Sacrae Theologiae.*

To Daneau the Word of God is the foundation, not only of theology, but also, as we have said, of many other sciences, such as physics, ethics, or politics. In fact, Scripture not only contains Truth but all truths. This attempt by Daneau to found the profane sciences on Scripture brings to mind the great medieval syntheses. Daneau's method is subtle and he risks losing a hurried reader. In the *Ethic christiana* (Geneva, 1577), he employs classical terms as heavily loaded with meaning as that of *habitus.* Must one say then that he introduces into Protestant territory an ethic that is dependent on natural law or on scholastic anthropology? In fact he does not at all intend to yield to human nature a capacity to initiate moral actions or the task of fixing norms. In an authentically Calvinist sense, he constantly recalls that it is the Holy Spirit who gives the good *habitus*, then transforms it. Every moral action depends on the will of God, and man has no quality that he has not received.[64] Daneau therefore employs some classical or medieval notions without at the same time espousing their ideologies; he draws them rather into a Calvinist framework, which demands that one recall the consequences of original sin and sends the reader back to God and Scripture as the source of all moral conduct.

Daneau's work is without doubt one of the most representative in its exaltation of Scripture in all areas of knowledge and human conduct. Built for eternity, his work was nevertheless transitory. Its design and its universal pretensions could not be taken up by theologians of the following generation in an age of the more and more autonomous development of the sciences. But it endures as an exciting and unique piece of work through its attempt, sometimes equivocal or hesitating, to synthesize the Calvinist *sola scriptura* and the humanist methodology.

ROLE IN THE CHURCH   Documents are too few to measure Daneau's pastoral contribution in Gien, Geneva, Leiden, Gand, and the south of France. On the other hand, certainly his contribution strengthened ecclesiastical discipline. In 1577, he underlined the importance of discipline in a letter dedicating to William of Orange his commentary on the first epistle to Timothy, *Nihil pulchrius ordine.*[65] In the life of the church, discipline expresses the same search for method and order that Daneau exhibited in his theology. Following Antoine de Chandieu and

---

64. LD, *Ethices Christianae Libri III* (Geneva, 1577), fol. 101, 102, 106, 109.

65. LD, *In priorem Epistolam ad Timotheum commentarius* (Geneva, 1577), fol. q ii–iv. This letter to William of Orange has been published in English: *The Judgement of Lambert Danaeus, touching certaine points now in controversie, contained in his preface before his commentary upon the first Epistle to Timothie.* According to the British Museum catalogue, the work was published by R. Waldgrave, Edinburgh, 1590.

his *Confirmation de la discipline ecclesiastique, observée es eglises reformees du royaume de France*, published in 1566 in response to Jean Morely,[66] Daneau affirms the revealed character of discipline.[67] Daneau's work is made up of four long chapters, which in fact are based upon the principal parts of the *Ecclesiastical Ordinances* of Geneva of 1541, and re-edited in 1576: the election of ministers, pastors, elders, and deacons, as well as their duties; the moral censures applied to sinners by the consistory; and finally the reconciliation of sinners with the church, whether through excommunication or suspension from the Lord's Supper.[68]

In distinguishing (with the help of Aristotle) between the essential and the accidental, Daneau made precise the limits of the revealed character of the ecclesiastical order.[69] If one pretends, for example, that it is not necessary to examine the life and doctrine of a candidate for the ministry before electing him, an essential part of that election is vitiated. On the other hand, if one wishes to know when, where, and how one passes that examination, one touches only an accidental aspect of the election. The essential elements of discipline are intangible.[70] They ought to be the same in all the evangelical churches, from the beginning and perpetually. Thus in every time and place, the government of the church ought to be aristocratic and not monarchical; in each church there should be a consistory of elders elected by the community.[71]

By affirming the intangible character of the essence of discipline, Daneau was able to prevent the magistracy from changing anything whatever. In effect, the end of discipline is to establish the legitimacy of ministerial vocations and to bring church members to do penance and so return to God. But God, who gives vocations and directs consciences, is the only one who knows what laws to promulgate in these areas. Neither church nor king ought to tamper with vocation or conscience. Daneau thus safeguarded the full liberty of the ecclesiastical minister from any intrusion by civil authority.[72]

Preaching the Gospel is surely primary in the building of the church, but this primacy did not prevent Daneau from affirming that a church without sacraments and without discipline is bankrupt. By neglecting discipline, the church risks straying from God and true doctrine. Discipline protects doctrine, reforms conduct, and hold Christians in the fear and service of God. It is, in fact, the rampart and the remedy against heresies.[73]

66. On the problems with Jean Morely, whose Congregationalist tendencies were opposed by the Reformed churches, see the documents gathered in *Correspondance de Théodore de Bèze*, (9 vols.) vols. 7 and 8 (Geneva: Librairie Droz, 1973 and 1976).

67. LD, *In priorem Epistolam ad Timotheum commentarius*, fol. q vii verso–q viii.

68. Ibid., fol. qv and verso.

69. Ibid., fol. qv verso–qvi; pp. 169, 288–289.

70. Ibid., fol. qv verso–qvi.

71. Ibid., fol. qvi verso–qvii verso.

72. Ibid., fol. qviii and verso.

73. Ibid., fol. qq i verso, qq iiii and verso.

What has preceded should help one to understand the severity of the conflict between Daneau and the magistracy at Leiden, which intended to bring the church into submission to the state by dismantling the presbyterio-synodal organization confirmed by the Synods of Dordrecht (1578) and Middelburg (1581).

By contributing to the church's reflection on ecclesiastical discipline, Daneau gave the Calvinist churches the theological basis for their assertion of autonomy over against civil authority. He thus contributed to the determining manner and the specificity of the Calvinist Reform.

INFLATION AND WITCHCRAFT:
THE CASE OF JEAN BODIN

E. WILLIAM MONTER

MANY problems becloud the scholarly evaluation of Jean Bodin, who was surely one of the finest and most original thinkers of the late sixteenth century. He has always been something of a puzzle to subsequent generations. The opinion that Bodin's genius displayed itself unequally in his works—that the *République* was an undoubted masterpiece but that some of his other works ought to be consigned to decent oblivion—was expressed only a generation after his death by such erudite libertines as Guy Patin and Gabriel Naudé.[1] Bayle's *Dictionnaire historique et critique* expressed similar judgments in its article on Bodin, and in a general way these opinions about the unevenness of Bodin's works have been shared by nineteenth- and twentieth-century scholars. The modern version of Bodin's fame was crystallized over a century ago by Henri Baudrillart, who praised him as a philosopher of history, of law, and of political economy but passed impatiently and with obvious embarrassment over his other writings.[2]

Today most important students of Bodin continue to concentrate on his political theories and on their connections to his essays in history and jurisprudence. Fifty years ago there appeared a Sorbonne thesis, which remains the fullest biography of Bodin: Roger Chauviré's *Jean Bodin, auteur de la République*. Since then the leading Bodinist has been Pierre Mesnard, who is justly famous for his work in the history of political philosophy.[3]

[1] Naudé is given primary responsibility for this opinion by Harold Mantz, "Jean Bodin and the Sorcerers," *Romanic Review*, XV (1924), 155, n. 7; Platin, by F. von Bezold, "Jean Bodin als Okkultist und seine *Démonomanie*," *Historische Zeitschrift*, CV (1910), 3.

[2] See his *Jean Bodin et son temps* (Paris, 1853), pp. v-viii. Baudrillart introduces a brief discussion of the *Démonomanie* and the *Theatrum* by remarking (p. 183), "Voici un bizarre et ridicule chapitre qui vient s'ajouter à l'histoire des contradictions de l'esprit humain."

[3] Mesnard has written several articles on Bodin and has naturally discussed him at length in his chief work, *L'essor de la philosophie politique au XVIe siècle*, 2nd edn. (Paris, 1951). His most recent general appraisal may be found in *Jean Bodin en la storia del pensamiento* (Madrid, 1962). The newest study in English, Julian Franklin's *Jean Bodin and the Sixteenth-Century Revolution*

371

85

The reasons behind this modern consensus are not hard to find. Bodin was a prolific author, and his immortal *République* of 1576 is only the bulkiest of his many published works. However, Bodin's other writings are less remarkable for their number than for the variety of their subject matter. He composed a *Methodus* "for the easy understanding of history" in 1565; the *Response à M. de Malestroit*, explaining the recent rise in prices, in 1568; the *Démonomanie des sorciers*, a guide to witchcraft, in 1580; the *Heptaplomeres*, an essay (long unpublished) on the comparative merits of seven major religions and philosophies, in 1593; and the *Theatrum Naturale Universarum*, a guide to the physical universe, in 1596. Bodin wrote many other things, including a short treatise on the nature of universal jurisprudence (1578), an annotated Latin edition of an ancient treatise on hunting (1555), and minor polemics during the days of the Holy League. In other words, Bodin's total corpus is a potpourri which rebuffs efforts at simple classification or arrangement from a single common denominator.

In the eyes of the twentieth century, there are flagrant contradictions between the Bodin of some treatises and the Bodin of others. Not long ago a historian of sixteenth-century rationalism observed that "there are two men in Bodin," one a conventional lawyer and the other a boldly skeptical religious relativist, an "achriste":[4] Jekyll-Bodin, the author of the *République* and Hyde-Bodin, the author of the *Heptaplomeres*. A different variation on this theme has been offered by a distinguished historian of science. This time the opposition is between the Bodin of the *République* and the Bodin of the *Démonomanie*, one a remarkably shrewd analyst of human society and the other a naive fool as an investigator of physical phenomena. Bodin, he grumbled, deserved to be as infamous for the latter as he was famous for the former. This most renowned of lawyers, master of evidence and organization, produced a treatise on witchcraft which "may be described as a formless screed and a dribbling mess."[5]

A good contemporary summary of opinions about Bodin was offered in 1951 by M. Mesnard. While eschewing the more flagrant paradoxes

---

in the Methodology of Law and History (New York, 1964), is broadly in the same vein.

[4] Henri Busson, *Le rationalisme dans la littérature française de la Renaissance*, 2nd edn. (Paris, 1957), pp. 541ff.

[5] Lynn Thorndike, *A History of Magic and Experimental Science*, 8 vols. (New York, 1923-1958), VI, 525f.

372

of the type described above, he does recognize several important diffi-culties in the path toward a comprehensive evaluation of Bodin's thought. Documentary evidence about Bodin is scanty, confusing, and ambiguous. Much ink has been shed, pro and con, on whether or not he lived in Calvin's Geneva in the early 1550's and whether or not he supported the Holy League against the French monarchy (and thus against his own theory of sovereignty) after 1590. Mesnard concludes his survey of Bodin's career in politics and literature by describing him as a "brilliant example of a generation seeking a synthesis of law, litera-ture, government, and religion."[6] What has been omitted from this summary, and also from the first thick quarto of Bodin's *Oeuvres philosophiques* which it introduces, is mention of Bodin's interest in natural science, which increasingly occupied him in his later years. Even here it seems that Bodin is a difficult subject to synthesize and to explain satisfactorily to a contemporary audience.

Yet, despite the wide variety of his subjects and despite the apparent paradoxes or inconsistencies in his treatment of these subjects, there is an obvious fact which any serious student of Bodin must immediately recognize: this man was a remarkably organic thinker. His works overlap—or rather interlock—with each other at several points, and sometimes Bodin himself will supply his reader with the appropriate cross-reference. The *République* is partly an expanded recapitulation of his earlier works, especially the *Methodus*. In particular, the sixth book of the *Methodus* ("The Type of Government in States," which fills over two-fifths of the entire treatise) serves as the point of depar-ture for Bodin's masterpiece of political theory.[7] The sixth book of the *République* repeats and expands the ideas on economics first developed in the *Response à M. de Malestroit*.[8] A short digression in the *Ré-publique* on state control of education repeats the phrases of Bodin's first public oration at the University of Toulouse in 1559.[9] Similar arguments, which frequently extend down to fine points of detail,[10] link the *République* to Bodin's earlier writings.

[6] P. Mesnard, ed., *Oeuvres philosophiques de Jean Bodin*, I (Paris, 1951), xv.

[7] All major students of Bodin (Baudrillart, Chauviré, Mesnard, Franklin) have recognized this fact, and the connections have been studied at length.

[8] This point is admirably discussed by Henri Hauser in his very complete introduction to *La response de Jean Bodin à M. de Malestroit* (Paris, 1932), pp. lix-lx. The *Response* looks backward as well as forward, for at one point (p. 25) it cites the *Methodus*.

[9] R. Chauviré, *Jean Bodin, auteur de la République* (Paris, 1914), p. 113.

[10] See, e.g., Bodin's description of the aristocracy of the Republic of Ragusa

373

Turning in the opposite direction, one sees that Bodin continued to repeat ideas from the *République* in his later works. General theories about the influence of climate on human behavior and on the ideal form of government can be found in later works. His refutation of some theories of Copernicus reappears in the *Theatrum*, virtually unchanged from the *République*.[11] In the *Démonomanie* Bodin refutes a minor contention of Aristotle by referring his reader to the sixth book of the *Methodus*.[12] In the *Heptaplomeres* he refutes the arguments of the Manichaeans with the same reasoning he has used in the *République*.[13] Not only are Bodin's works on witchcraft, religion, and physics consistent with the *République*, but they are also consistent with each other. The argument that witches can only cure evils which are of demoniacal rather than natural origin appears in the *Heptaplomeres*, summarized from the *Démonomanie*.[14] Bodin uses the phenomenon of ecstasy in both the *Theatrum* and the *Démonomanie* to show how the spirit can leave the body without causing death.[15] He tells the same story in the *Heptaplomeres* and in the *Démonomanie* about the god Mopsus and diabolical advice of oracles,[16] and he gives the same explanations for the physical substance of demons in the *Theatrum* that he gives in the *Démonomanie*.[17] The most thorough student of Bodin's thought has underlined the "almost immobile fixity of his mind across thirty years" and has observed that one of Bodin's

in the *Methodus*, tr. B. Reynolds (New York, 1945), p. 245, and in the *République*, Bk. II, ch. 7 (*The Six Bookes of a Commonweale*, ed. K. D. McRae [Cambridge, 1962], pp. 235f.); or his preference for "harmonic" over either arithmetic or geometric justice (*Methodus*, 286f.; *Rép.*, Bk. VI, ch. 6 [McRae, pp. 756f.]).

[11] See Chauviré, *Bodin*, p. 113.

[12] *Démonomanie des sorciers* (Paris: J. Dupuys, 1580), Bk. I, ch. 5, fol. 29ᵛ. All page numbers are cited from the earliest editions.

[13] Cf. R. Chauviré, *Le colloque de Jean Bodin des secrets cachez des choses sublimes entre sept scavans qui sont de differens sentimens* (Paris, 1914), p. 30 (all further notes refer to the book and folio number of Bibliothèque Nationale, MS fr. 1923, from which Chauviré translated and summarized the *Heptaplomeres*: as, in this case, *Hept.*, Bk. III, foll. 156-159), with *Rép.*, Bk. II, ch. 2 (McRae, *Six Bookes*, p. 199).

[14] Cf. *Hept.* Bk. II, fol. 66, with *Dém.*, Bk. III, ch. 2, foll. 127ᵛ-132.

[15] Cf. *Theatrum*, Bk. IV, ch. 15, with *Dém.*, Bk. II, ch. 5.

[16] Noticed by Chauviré, *Bodin*, p. 113 (*Hept.*, Bk. IV, fol. 259, and *Dém.*, Bk. I, ch. 5, in the later editions after 1587).

[17] Cf. *Theatrum*, Bk. IV, ch. 14, and *Dém.*, Bk. I, ch. 1, fol. 6ᵛ.

374

characteristics "seems to be an invariable fixity in his ideas."[18] With his mind well trained by the philosophers of Paris and the jurists of Toulouse and with his memory thoroughly stocked by continuous and varied reading (including a remarkable quantity of Jewish and Protestant authors), Bodin confronts us as an intellectual monolith. His interests may have shifted slightly as he grew older, but he seldom changed his opinions. The paradox of two or more Bodins—political scientist and witch-hunter, pioneer economist and reactionary physicist, religious skeptic and earnest calculator of the speed of angels whirling through the eighth heaven, a Bodin of dazzling inconsistencies— is a paradox created by us and not by him.

In his own eyes Bodin was not only consistent; he was also methodical. Considering the extent to which his works overlap, is it possible to discern some master plan, some grandiose structure in which each treatise would have its appointed place? If there is an answer to these questions, it should be sought from the clues provided in the introduction to his first important work, written at the age of thirty-five:[19]

Of history, that is, the true narration of things, there are three kinds: human, natural, and divine. The first concerns man; the second, nature; the third, the Father of nature. One depicts the acts of man while leading his life in the midst of society. The second reveals causes hidden in nature and explains their development from earliest beginnings. The last records the strength and power of Almighty God and of the immortal souls, set apart from all else. . . . It shall come about that from thinking first about ourselves, then about our family, then about our society, we are led to examine nature, and finally to the true history of Immortal God.

If anyone does not wish to include mathematics with the natural sciences, then he will make four divisions of history: human, of course, uncertain and confused; natural, which is definite, but sometimes uncertain on account of contact with matter or an evil deity, and therefore inconsistent; mathematical, more certain, because it is free from the admixture of matter . . . ; finally, divine, most uncertain and by its very nature changeless.

A certain simple, three-level program may be constructed from this outline. Long ago Chauviré suggested a schema in which Bodin was

---

[18] Chauviré, *Bodin*, pp. 112, 113.
[19] *Methodus*, Bk. I (Reynolds, pp. 15, 16, 19).

375

regarded as having revealed his general goals in the *Methodus*, accomplished the first part in the *République*, accomplished the second part with the *Theatrum*, and began the final part with his unpublished dialogue, the *Heptaplomeres*.[20] If the whole of human wisdom consists of knowledge of man, nature, and God, then Bodin explored them all in a truly encyclopedic program of a sort rarely undertaken in his troubled age.

Yet something is wrong with this schema. Chauviré himself admitted that "J'excepte le *Démonomanie des sorciers*, parce qu'elle gêne mon propos sans doute,"[21] although it is certain that this was one of Bodin's more important books. Except for the *République*, it was the most popular and widely read of his works. It was his only other full-length book to be composed in the vernacular, and it was the only other book to be translated into a foreign vernacular.[22] It seems that his discourse on witchcraft is the most important stumbling block in the road to a unified and systematic interpretation of Bodin's writings and thought. This is the ultimate pill which his numerous admirers cannot swallow and which they cannot ignore. This is the principal reason for the ambiguity of Bodin's posthumous reputation from the seventeenth to the twentieth century—from Guy Patin, who considered it hypocritical, to the late Lynn Thorndike, who considered it detestable.

Is it possible to remove these logical (and psychological) difficulties and to integrate the *Démonomanie* with Bodin's other works? We already know that several ideas found in it are repeated elsewhere in Bodin's writings, that it bears the authentic stamp of his inflexible mind. We know that the *Démonomanie* was a popular book, that its author regarded it as an important and timely book. Perhaps the first clue toward a correct evaluation of this book comes from the circumstances which prompted its publication. In large measure the *Démonomanie* was a polemic directed against a clear and present danger: the skepticism in regard to witchcraft expressed by prominent jurists like Alciati and, more recently, in the notorious books of the Rhine-

---

[20] Chauviré, *Bodin*, p. 114-115.   [21] *Ibid.*, p. 114, n. 2.

[22] The best bibliography of the *République* (McRae, *Six Bookes*, pp. A 78-83) lists nineteen French editions by 1608, plus five Latin editions and Italian, Spanish, German, and English translations. The *Démonomanie* (Chauviré, *Bodin*, pp. 518-519) saw nine French editions by 1604, plus three Latin editions and an Italian translation (Venice: Aldus, 1587). Both books were originally printed by the same *libraire*, Jacques Dupuys of Paris. None of Bodin's other books went through more than five editions before 1604.

376

land physician Johann Weyer. In all editions of the *Démonomanie* there is a lengthy appendix of at least seventy pages which refutes Weyer's opinions. This polemic with a single opponent was a sport in which Bodin, unlike many other authors of his age, seldom engaged. I know of only one other case in all his writings where a single opponent is refuted at such length and with such devastating skill (for Bodin never felt the need to answer his rivals or their spokesmen more than once). The lone parallel is the *Response à M. de Malestroit*, composed twelve years earlier.

The parallel between these two polemics may seem at first glance to be superficial and capricious, but they do have other common features. Of course, it must be noted that the historical fate of Bodin's polemic with Malestroit about inflation was exactly the reverse of his polemic with Weyer about witchcraft. Three centuries later Bodin had become a precursor of the quantity theory of money and a precursor of historical research in economics from his first polemic; but he had become an opponent of justice and reason, as well as a gullible consumer of the worst kind of old wives' tales, from his second polemic. Yet, after a bit of reflection, one begins to see a common pattern of concern underlying both polemics, endowing them with a common purpose and even at times with a common method. To Bodin, the respective errors of Malestroit and Weyer sprang from their common love of artificial and illusory paradoxes which went against the grain of common sense. Each man attempted to demonstrate, by a form of sophistry which Bodin found infuriating, that what was so was not. One man denied the reality of inflation, the other the reality of witchcraft. And both could be refuted, earnestly and convincingly, by common and reliable weapons. Bodin preferred to smother his opponents under the accumulated weight of ancient and modern evidence, of personal and recorded experience. Then, after lining up his authorities, he proceeded to reveal the hollowness of his opponents' reasoning by skillful and precise analysis.

Let us consider Bodin's means of persuasion, point by point. In both polemics he undergirds his arguments at each and every point with a wealth of ancient and modern evidence which he draws from a huge fund of sources, including unpublished financial and legal records and testimony from many different countries, both past and present. Bodin seems to have tried to strike some rough balance between ancient and modern testimony in his arrangement of evidence, so that his case rested precisely on their agreement. We know that he generally oc-

377

cupied a position of neutrality with regard to the relative merits of the ancients and the moderns. If, at thirty-five, he had said that "they are mistaken who think that the race of men always deteriorates; when old men err in this respect, it is understandable," by the time he was sixty-three he had changed his mind; he observed then that the world was becoming decrepit, slowly but surely, and bemoaned that the men of old were giants compared with the men of his day.[23] But the important point was not who was superior to whom as a witness: it was whether or not they agreed. Bodin skillfully selected a cosmopolitan array of evidence which he draped like a protective shield around each of his assertions. The *Response à M. de Malestroit* is, in fact, so stuffed with evidence that it has little space for assertions. Throughout this pamphlet runs a basic parallel between the rapid Roman conquest of the ancient world and the equally rapid Spanish conquest of the New World, both of which brought a sudden sharp rise in prices.[24] Bodin compares the price of pearls in the age of Cleopatra with the price in Francis I's time to support his hypothesis that an abundant supply of anything leads to a fall in its price.[25] He compares the rapid depreciation of Rome's coinage after the Punic wars with that of France's money after the Hundred Years' War to show the catastrophic effects of tampering.[26]

The most curious case of Bodin's use of ancient and modern evidence, however, comes in a fascinating and little-noticed passage near the end of the *Response*. Here he marshals bits of evidence from Herodotus, Livy, Pliny, and contemporary Europe to show that the value of gold relative to silver had never varied farther than from 1:10 to 1:15 and that their ratio naturally stabilized around a "just price" of 1:12. Money, concludes Bodin in a typical piece of his reasoning, is literally a law unto itself: "even the Greeks called money and law by the same word, as we say *loy* and *aloy*. And just as the law is a sacred thing, which should not be violated, so money is a holy thing which should not be altered, once given its just weight and worth."[27] The

[23] Cf. *Methodus*, Bk. VII (Reynolds, p. 302), with *Hept.*, Bk. II, fol. 51. Because Hans Baron misses Bodin's change of opinion, his discussion of this point in "The Querelle of the Ancients and the Moderns as a Problem for Renaissance Scholarship," *Journal of the History of Ideas*, XX (1959), pp. 10-11, is misleading.

[24] *La response à M. de Malestroit*, pp. 10, 13, 22-25.

[25] *Ibid.*, p. 19.   [26] *Ibid.*, p. 47.

[27] *Ibid.*, p. 52f. When Bodin discusses this point in the *République*, Bk. VI, ch. 3 (McRae, *Six Bookes*, p. 691f.), he does not refer to money as "une chose sainte."

378

essentially sacred nature of money and the peculiarity of the nearly constant ratio of gold to silver have been noticed by some modern authors, who connect their relative values to the 1:12+ ratio between the cycles of the golden sun and the silvery moon around the earth.[28] One wonders what Bodin would have thought of this theory; I feel sure he would have welcomed it as one more proof of the harmonies of the universe.

The same balance and concordance between ancient and modern evidence is equally obvious in the *Démonomanie*. Bodin's preface[29] notes that, according to St. Augustine, all ancient sects except the Epicureans punished sorcery. The Pythagoreans, he adds, wondered if there had ever existed a man who had *not* seen a demon. He gives a lengthy review of the history of necromancy and witchcraft in Homer and Orpheus, in early Jewish history, and in Greco-Roman antiquity down to St. Augustine, who reported in the *City of God* that demons surely did copulate with women. Bodin continues with an array of modern witnesses, including Pico della Mirandola, who once saw two sorcerers (disguised as priests) meeting with several demons (disguised as women). Bodin himself, of course, had seen confessed sorcerers on several occasions. He points out the remarkable unanimity between ancient and modern witnesses on the subject of witchcraft: for example, everyone agrees that demons are black and that they are either giants or dwarfs, but never normal-sized. We have known about sorcerers and their *maleficia* for three thousand years, he concludes, and our sources have told us substantially the same story. To doubt it is to doubt ancient and modern history and Holy Scripture—hence, to doubt God himself.

In the refutation of Weyer which concludes the *Démonomanie* Bodin repeats part of this array of evidence, occasionally to expose Weyer's shallow scholarship, his obvious twisting of scriptural texts, or his fraudulent confusion of sorcery with poisoning in antiquity (they were distinct, argues Bodin, and it most assuredly was sorcery which the laws punished).[30] Later he amasses ancient and modern evidence on the unnatural and evil deeds wrought by sorcerers. Bodin cleverly cites Weyer himself in this list, for his opponent admitted to having seen a case of triple levitation exactly like those reported by

---

[28] See N. O. Brown, *Life Against Death*, paper edn. (New York, 1964), p. 247, esp. nn. 39, 40.

[29] Unpaginated in all editions. Bodin resumes many of these arguments at the start of Book III of the *Démonomanie*.

[30] *Dém.*, foll. 220-224ᵛ.

379

confessed witches.[31] Bodin also deals with one important piece of evidence used by Weyer: the *Canon Episcopi*, a clerical forgery, supposedly from the fourth century, which denied that sorcerers had any real power. Here Bodin simply notes that none of the Fathers of the Church mentioned the *Canon*, and he compiles a list of the "very best theologians" (Augustine, Aquinas, Bonaventure) who affirmed the contrary.[32] History was on Bodin's side in both polemics, and he used his well-stocked arsenal of unimpeachable authorities with devastating effect. No one dared use a historical argument against him for a very long time. Even in regard to witchcraft, the ultimate refutation of Bodin's arguments had to come from new *a priori* reasoning, from a will to disbelieve, rather than from *a posteriori* appeals to "the facts."[33]

Having disposed of the facts, Bodin proceeded to the second part of his polemic, namely, his insistence on precise reasoning. To a modern observer, this appears to be the weaker part of Bodin's strategy, partly because it tends to slide into mere quibbling about Aristotle's definitions and logic. It has recently been suggested that this "carping and often unfair criticism of Aristotle which runs like a continuous thread through the whole of Bodin's writings" should be understood in the light of his Ramist background.[34] Yet this quibbling with Aristotle, although frequently encountered in the *République*, is of minor importance in Bodin's polemics on witchcraft and inflation. The explanation is simple. Aristotle wrote a treatise on *Oeconomica*, but his subject was household management rather than gold and silver coinage, which was the object of dispute between Bodin and Malestroit. Aristotle also wrote nothing about witchcraft, yet Bodin could not let the matter rest. He argues in the preface to the *Démonomanie* that Aristotle's silence about demons and things supernatural proves nothing, because "most natural things were not known by him either." Weyer had been rash enough to make use of Aristotle's silence in his treatises, and Bodin returns to this point in his refutation, explaining why Aris-

[31] *Ibid.*, fol. 241ᵛ. Weyer had also seen wild beasts stopped by a mere word (fol. 239).

[32] *Ibid.*, fol. 249; Bodin had already made this point in his text (Bk. II, ch. 4, fol. 81).

[33] This point was made a century ago by one of the great champions of Victorian rationalism, who was no friend to the witch-hunters. See W.E.H. Lecky, *History of the Rise and Progress of Rationalism in Europe* (London, 1865), I, 34-37, 88.

[34] K. D. McRae, "Ramist Tendencies in the Thought of Jean Bodin," *Journal of the History of Ideas*, XVI (1955), p. 320.

380

totle never wrote about spirits and why his arguments about incorporeal things were contradictory.[35]

In general, we can see a clear difference with regard to this question of reasoning between Bodin's earlier and later polemics. Malestroit's paradoxes were inductively demonstrated, based on fact alone; a clearer and broader array of facts, which Bodin provided in his *Response*, sufficed to dissolve them. Weyer's arguments, on the other hand, were based both on incorrect facts and on flawed reasoning, and Bodin's refutation needed to be both inductive and deductive. Consider the problem of defining witchcraft. Bodin lampoons Weyer's attempt to define a *lamia* as a person "who is believed to be in league with Demons, and by their aid to do that which she cannot do." This definition is dialectically poor, says Bodin, because it contains no fewer than six disjunctions and because it describes something which is supposed to be but is not. A good definition would "point right at the thing and show at a glance its true essence."[36] He, Bodin, had begun his treatise with the first clear definition of a witch (reprinted with admiration by the late Montague Summers at the start of his *History of Witchcraft*): "A witch is a person who knowingly tries to accomplish something by Diabolical methods."[37]

Weyer's shabby definition, however, was among his lesser sins. Bodin was more angered by his opponent's contradictions. For example, Weyer admitted that in antiquity a sorcerer like Simon Magus could fly through the air but denied that modern sorcerers had this ability—a contradiction which showed his "extreme folly."[38] Bodin fills whole pages listing supernatural occurrences whose reality Weyer did admit, both in ancient and modern times. Weyer merely maintained that such deeds were due solely to demons and never to the witches who invoked the demons. This, said Bodin, was to deny the whole relation-

[35] *Dém.*, foll. 246-246ᵛ. Bodin was much less ingenious in this matter than the famous Italian naturalist Cesalpino, who in 1580 constructed an "Aristotelian" explanation for the physical reality of demons (see Thorndike, *History of Magic and Science*, VI, 335ff.).

[36] *Dém.*, fol. 229.

[37] *Ibid.*, Bk. I, ch. 1 ("Sorcier est celuy qui par moyens Diaboliques sciemment s'efforce de parvenir à quelque chose"). Summers's *History of Witchcraft*, reprint (New York, 1956), observes (p. 1) that "it would be, I imagine, hardly possible to discover a more concise, exact, comprehensive, and intelligent definition of a Witch." Bodin thought so too; he refers to his definition at several different places in the *Démonomanie*.

[38] *Dém.*, fol. 238.

381

ship between cause and effect in a "capricious and sophistic" attempt to absolve witches of responsibility for their *maleficia*.[39]

Weyer's whole line of reasoning, Bodin observes, must have come either from wickedness or from ignorance. Obviously Weyer was not ignorant. How else could he have learned all the words and diagrams used by practitioners of black magic in order to summon demons? How else could he have learned the constitutional structure of the Diabolic Monarchy, with its 72 princes (each with his own special attributes) and its legions of 6,666 lesser demons, adding up to 7,405,926 demons "sauf erreur de calcul"?[40] Worse yet, what reason did he have to reveal all those incantations and all those names and attributes in print? Even Weyer's master, Cornelius Agrippa, "the greatest sorcerer of his age," never dared go this far in the fourth book of his *De Occulta Philosophia*, as Bodin had already noted.[41] Since Weyer was not ignorant, his actions could only be explained on the hypothesis that he was trying to *teach* black magic while claiming to combat it and that he was truly in league with the devil. This line of reasoning, I believe, best explains the towering wrath which Bodin displayed toward his opponent, particularly at the end of his refutation.

Bodin made many other attacks upon Weyer, including one interesting foray into his rival's professional corner to demonstrate that he was a poor physician. Weyer had explained that most women accused of witchcraft were really suffering from melancholia. Bodin, relying on Galen, said that this was a disease peculiar to men (at least in its acute form) and prevalent in warmer climates than Germany.[42] His refutation of Weyer, whose sophistries sprang from wickedness rather than ignorance (which was the source of Malestroit's errors), was appropriately thorough and pulverizing. His answer to Malestroit had been based on fuller evidence and on personal experience;[43] ultimately Bodin ringed his facts around a few simply hypotheses, of which the most important was that a greatly increased supply of gold and silver automatically caused a rapid rise in prices. In his later quarrel with

[39] *Ibid.*, fol. 218ᵛ.   [40] *Ibid.*, fol. 219.   [41] *Ibid.*, Bk. II, ch. 1, foll. 54-54ᵛ.

[42] *Ibid.*, foll. 225ᵛ-226ᵛ; same point made earlier (Bk. II, ch. 5, fol. 90ᵛ).

[43] In the *Response* (p. 44) Bodin refers to his personal experience in diminishing gold in a furnace, which freed him from a common error. He had also experimented with dissolving silver by aquafortis. Later, in the *Theatrum* (Bk. II, ch. 9), Bodin called experience "the master of all certitude." There is a good discussion of his empiricism in Chauviré, *Bodin*, pp. 118ff. Of course, the *Démonomanie* is stuffed with the fruit of Bodin's personal experiences.

382

Weyer the facts were not in doubt so much as their explanation; here the argument really turned on matters of cause and effect, since both sides agreed that supernatural effects exist. As Bodin said in his preface to the *Démonomanie*, skeptics "should not obstinately deny the truth if they can perceive only the effects but not the cause." In these polemics, as in all his writings, Bodin imagines himself as a man who knows both theory and practice, who has acquired all the important evidence and has at the same time unraveled its network of causes and effects. It should also be noted that Bodin presents himself as a layman in both polemics. He has, he says, no intimate acquaintance with the royal treasury (as had Malestroit), nor is he a merchant like many other writers on monetary questions; moreover, he has been only marginally involved in witchcraft trials, never engineering giant witch-hunts like many other demonologists, and he is not a magician like Weyer. In other words, he has no immediate personal interest, beyond that of the concerned citizen, in either inflation or witchcraft.

In our study of Bodin's polemical procedures, his massive use of diversified evidence and his criticism of his opponent's logic, we have left aside some of his more curious attitudes. The most interesting of these is Bodin's fascination with mathematical relationships in nature. This loyal follower of Pythagoras had proclaimed in his *Methodus* that "Immortal God arranged all things in numbers, order, and marvellous measure," and demonstrations of these harmonious relationships appear in all his important works. Not only was Bodin intrigued by the importance of numbers in human and natural affairs, but he was also highly interested by the possibility of a reformed and purified astrology—a hope which he shared with such other prominent neo-Pythagoreans as Kepler.[44] Yet Bodin's fascination with numbers plays only a marginal role in his polemics. Only elementary calculations are involved in his answer to Malestroit, on such questions as the rate of inflation during the past sixty years in France, or on Guillaume Budé's evaluation of Roman weights and measures.[45] In the *Démonomanie* Bodin's calculations are primarily decorative and digressive. There is one passage in which he discusses the relative speeds of celestial

[44] *Methodus*, Bk. VI (Reynolds, p. 223). The importance of numbers fills a long chapter of the *République* (Bk. IV, ch. 2). Remarks on the purification of astrology, similar to those in the *République* but somewhat fuller, occur in *Dém.*, Bk. I, ch. 5 (foll. 30ʳ-34ʳ). Cf. Kepler's remarks on the reformation of astrology, summarized by Max Caspar, *Kepler*, tr. C. D. Hellman, paper edn. (New York, 1962), pp. 190ff.

[45] *Response*, pp. 9, 30f., 49f.

383

and demonic motion in order to prove that angels guiding the eighth sphere of heaven move much faster than demons transporting witches,[46] but this demonstration is not central to his purpose. If Bodin really did agree with the ancients who considered mathematics to be "the bridge between physics and metaphysics,"[47] he postponed its most extensive use for his most important syntheses, such as the *République* or the *Theatrum*.

After discussing the strength and variety of Bodin's polemical techniques, we should not be surprised to find that he generally did convince his readers that the skeptics who doubted the reality of inflation and witchcraft were wrong. This is not to suggest that Bodin's solutions to these problems were universally accepted; they were not. But discussions of these issues in the early 1600's had to begin where Bodin had left the problems, not where Malestroit or Weyer had left them. Pamphlets dealing with inflation were not terribly numerous between 1580 and 1620, perhaps because the problem itself was not quite so acute as it had been earlier. Bodin's conclusions were sometimes repeated or refuted by important pamphleteers, especially by Malynes in England in 1603.[48] But, in general, inflation was a far less lively issue for the next generation than witchcraft, and it is here that Bodin's analysis of his subject received the most attention.

Because the history of witchcraft theory is a great deal less well known and less well organized than the history of monetary theory, it may be helpful to review the former as it developed after 1580. Within thirty years of the publication of the *Démonomanie*, a sizable number of important tracts on witchcraft were composed by lawyers and theologians in many European countries. The largest single contingent came from the Germans, who tended to agree with some of Bodin's main contentions (and almost none of Weyer's) but to disagree with him on matters of detail. The famous Bishop Peter Binsfeld, whose *De confessionibus maleficarum et sagarum* appeared in 1589, offers a good example of such learned German comment.[49] Demonologists in other

---

[46] *Dém.*, foll. 248-248ᵛ. Bodin calculated 1,706,155 leagues per minute for the angels vs. 200 leagues "in a short time" for the demons.

[47] *Dém.*, Preface.

[48] Bodin's influence is carefully discussed by Hauser, *Response*, pp. lxviii-lxxv. One French pamphleteer, who wrote from 1609-1614, totally ignored Bodin's quantity theory and apparently considered Malestroit's theories to be unrefuted (pp. lxxi-lxxii).

[49] Thorndike, *History of Magic and Science*, VI, 538. See pp. 534f., 539, 240, for other German discussions of Bodin.

384

lands—such as the transplanted Spanish Jesuit Martin Delrio, whose *Disquisitionum magicarum* appeared at Louvain in 1599, the Italian Francesco Maria Guazzo, whose *Compendium maleficarum* appeared in 1608, or King James VI of Scotland, whose *Demonologie* appeared in 1597—seldom discussed Bodin's opinions as carefully as Binsfeld.

The French-speaking world also saw a rapid increase in demonologies after 1580. "By a typical paradox of history," writes the most recent and intelligent historian of witchcraft, "France, the home of reason and critical sense, seems to have been plagued more than the rest of Europe by this kind of book, often written by secular judges, and even by men who in other spheres of life were very distinguished. ... Thanks to men such as Bodin, Grégoire, Remy, Boguet, DeLancre, and others less well known, the crime of witchcraft was taking on a more uniform appearance."[50] Like Bodin, the other French demonologists were lawyers; but, unlike him, they were generally men who had personally instigated large-scale witch-hunts in lands on the periphery of French civilization (Bodin lived and worked after 1576 in the Île-de-France). Remy based his *Demonolatry* of 1595 on his experiences as a judge in the imperial and bilingual territory of Lorraine; Boguet based his *Discours des sorciers* of 1602 on experiences in the Hapsburg Free County of Burgundy; DeLancre, judge of the Parlement of Bordeaux and husband of Montaigne's grand-niece, hunted the witches he described in the *Tableau de l'inconstance des mauvaises anges et démons* of 1612 in the Basque lands. All three were famous and useful legal guides in their day. Boguet's work was particularly valuable for its appendix, which codified existing statutes and court practices in witchcraft cases, but the others were more erudite.

Although Bodin's *Démonomanie* clearly belongs with this latter group insofar as it is a lawyer's approach to witchcraft, it is different from them in some important ways. Bodin had never had practical experience in uprooting whole communities of witches. He was, of course, aware that witches gathered in assemblies called Sabbats and that demons carried them through the air to such assemblies;[51] but he was not obsessed with the fine points of the Sabbat, as were the three other demonologists. In other words, he was less concerned with

[50] Julio Caro Baroja, *The World of the Witches*, tr. O.N.V. Glendenning (Chicago, 1964), p. 112; see also Robert Mandrou, *Magistrats et sorciers en France au XVIIᵉ siècle* (Paris, 1968), pp. 137-143.

[51] *Dém.*, Bk. I, ch. 6, fol. 47; Bk. II, ch. 4, foll. 81ff. Remy, Boguet, and DeLancre all devote at least seven chapters to the minutiae of the Sabbat.

385

99

witches as an organized sect of devil-worshippers. But he was more concerned than they were with occult phenomena in general, and the whole first book of the *Démonomanie* is directed toward such questions as separating angelic from demonic advice and useful from harmful magic.[52]

Whereas both these features separate Bodin's work from that of many of the later French demonologists, other features help link it to an earlier demonology which he may have been trying to modernize and update. The similarities between the *Démonomanie* and the *Malleus Maleficarum*, composed almost a full century earlier, are striking. Except for their first sections, these books share a common organization. Bodin's second book consists of eight long chapters on the *maleficia* of witches, and his third book consists of six chapters telling how to combat their magic. The second book of the *Malleus* is split into two parts which treat these two problems in the same order and almost in the same proportions as Bodin's work. The fourth and final book of the *Démonomanie* corresponds especially closely, both in form and in spirit, with the third and final book of the *Malleus*; both deal with the legal problems raised by witch-trials. Although other demonologies obviously treat many of these same questions, they do not have the same neat and symmetrically organized discussion as the *Démonomanie* and the *Malleus*.[53]

It seems probable that Bodin in his *Démonomanie* was constructing a new handbook—partly a philosophical examination of the subject, partly a practical guide to the detection and punishment of witches—to replace the *Malleus*. In an age when the investigation and punishment of witchcraft had long since been transferred from the Inquisition to lay judges, Bodin's book filled a real need. By the late sixteenth century the scholastic shell of *quaestiones* in which the *Malleus* en-

[52] See an excellent discussion by F. von Bezold, "Jean Bodin als Okkultist und seine *Démonomanie*," *Historische Zeitschrift*, CV (1910), pp. 1-64; also D. P. Walker, *Spiritual and Demonic Magic from Ficino to Campanella* (London, 1958), pp. 171-177.

[53] In other words, precisely because the *Démonomanie* is *not* a "formless screed and a dribbling mess," as Thorndike described it (*supra*, p. 372), it is superior to such later rivals as the works of Remy or Boguet. A thorough comparison between the *Démonomanie* and the *Malleus* would be a highly useful effort. Bodin cites the *Malleus*, of course (see Bk. II, ch. 5, fol. 93; Bk. III, ch. 2, foll. 129, 130ᵛ; Bk. III, ch. 4, fol. 141ᵛ; Bk. III, ch. 5, foll. 146ᵛ, 151ᵛ; Bk. III, ch. 6, foll. 155, 155ᵛ, 157, 160; Bk. IV, ch. 1, fol. 171; etc.), but no more than some other eminent authorities, such as Pico, Grillandus, or Daneau.

386

cased its discussion of witchcraft was badly antiquated. The whole subject needed to be updated. Yet the *Malleus renovatus* which Bodin constructed in 1580 still had to serve the same dual purpose for the secular court which its predecessor had filled for the ecclesiastical court. It had to refute skeptics who scoffed at the deeds of witches or objected to the severity of the prosecution (for witchcraft was *crimen exceptum* in both kinds of courts), and it had to instruct the judge as fully as possible concerning his duties in such cases. The measure of Bodin's success was the popularity of the *Démonomanie*, which soon spawned several inferior rivals (none of which, with the possible exception of Boguet's work, was as successful). If imitation truly is the sincerest form of flattery, then the fact that the *Démonomanie* virtually began a literary genre speaks eloquently for its timeliness. These considerations may also help explain why this was Bodin's only major literary effort, except for the *République*, to be composed in French. Like its illustrious predecessor, the *Démonomanie* discussed a clear and present danger, and its author had particular cause to address it to the widest possible audience.

Let us now return to the question asked much earlier and see if we can arrange the *Démonomanie* within the total corpus of Bodin's writings, so that it need not "gêner mon propos" as it did Chauviré's. To begin with, we can consider the *Démonomanie* as the first indication of Bodin's shift of interest from human history to natural history—from a type of history which the *Methodus* called "uncertain and confused" to one which was "definite, but sometimes uncertain on account of contact with matter on an evil deity." It was his first step[54] after the great synthesis of human history in the *République* toward the great synthesis of natural history in the *Theatrum*, which he completed on his deathbed in 1596. Admittedly, the *Démonomanie* is a halting and halfway transition between human and natural history. Its subject matter is unusual precisely insofar as it involves elements of both kinds of history. This makes it a particularly interesting topic for a professional lawyer who was also widely read in the occult and natural sciences. Continuing this line of thought, we can suggest that the role which the *Démonomanie* played in Bodin's later syntheses corresponds very roughly to the role which a lengthy pamphlet like the *Response* of 1568 eventually played in his grand synthesis of human history. Of

---

[54] If we except the *Juris universi distributio*, published in 1578 but written at least twelve years earlier (see McRae, "Ramist Tendencies in Bodin," p. 310).

387

course, demons and witches play a somewhat greater role in natural and divine history than do monetary factors in human history. But Bodin's polemic on witchcraft could be gracefully absorbed into his later treatment of a larger subject in much the same way as his polemic on inflation was absorbed into the *République*. It seems, upon preliminary investigation, that Bodin's use of his information about witches was more important in divine than in natural history; it is the second book of the *Heptaplomeres*, his "notoriously radical" essay in comparative religion, which most fully incorporates the results of the *Démonomanie*, rather than the more "reactionary" *Theatrum*.[55]

A provisional arrangement of this sort has several advantages. It is not offered as a desperate attempt to make order out of chaos in the wide variety of writings which Bodin offered to the world. Neither is it offered as an attempt to whitewash Bodin on the issues of witchcraft. Its main assets are that it will remove a few of the artificial paradoxes about Jean Bodin. It will reestablish a minimum of consistency and logic in our evaluation of this man of inflexible and virtually unchanging opinions. Bodin believed he was logical—even if his logic was often that of Petrus Ramus, difficult to understand today and not always followed by Bodin himself, who was incurably fond of digressions.[56] One must therefore examine his thought as a unit, in which the subject matter changes often, while the methods and prejudices remain fixed. In the *Démonomanie*, as in his other writings, whether polemics or encyclopedic syntheses, Bodin utilized the same basic procedures. He was always fundamentally empirical, fascinated by the problem of collecting and comparing bits of evidence from widely scattered authorities. His empiricism was very crude, because his critical apparatus was superficial. He could never distinguish hearsay from genuine eyewitness reporting, either among the ancients or among the moderns; this shortcoming led him to accept tales which told of men with skin like cows and men who had eyes like owls, being able to see better by night than by day.[57] But, though Bodin was gullible, he tried hard; whenever possible, he tried to experience things himself, to see strange

[55] I repeat that this is a preliminary observation. It seems that *Hept.*, Bk. II, esp. foll. 58-67, 88-91, 114-117, contains more material on witchcraft than all of the *Theatrum*. Demons, of course, are very important in both books, though here, too, Books II and III of the *Hept.* seem to contain more material than the *Theatrum*, IV and V.

[56] McRae, "Ramist Tendencies in Bodin," esp. pp. 316, 319f.

[57] *Rép.*, Bk. V. ch. 1 (McRae, *Six Bookes*, p. 548).

388

beasts like crocodiles and ostriches.[58] If we conceive of Bodin as an empiricist, albeit a blindfolded empiricist, we can dissolve many of the paradoxes surrounding him, such as that between Bodin the "pragmatic" economic historian and Bodin the "gullible" demonologist. In his lifetime nobody possessed any truly accurate guide for separating fact from fiction.[59]

The only other immortal figure among the lawyers and *politiques* of Bodin's generation, Michel de Montaigne, is often set up as his rival, particularly in such questions of gross superstitution as witchcraft. Yet Montaigne's systematic skepticism, as displayed in the *Essais*, was in no way superior to Bodin's systematic credulity in the *Démonomanie*; it was merely its reverse. Montaigne was once confronted with a dozen confessed witches, all medically examined and found to be possessed with the devil's mark, by a well-meaning nobleman who intended to cure his doubts about witchcraft—but to no avail.[60] The man who refuses to believe what he has seen is no better off than the man who all too readily believes what he has not seen, and the first position is psychologically much harder to sustain.

[58] *Theatrum*, Bk. III, chs. 11, 14.

[59] Cf. the remarks in Robert Mandrou, *Introduction à la France moderne (1500-1640): essai de psychologie historique* (Paris, 1961), pp. 258-260: the later 1500's saw "men of experience—but of few experiments—and of tradition. . . . Experience, at this time, must be understood not as the art of demonstrating a fact by repeating it, but as a fact purely and simply noted down, or carefully observed; an apparition, a flaming star in the sky, a dream which proved prophetic are facts of experience."

[60] Busson, *Rationalisme dans la littérature française*, pp. 452ff.; see also A. M. Boase, "Montaigne et la sorcellerie," *Humanisme et renaissance*, no. 2 (1935), pp. 402-421.

NICOLAS REMY

ET LA

SORCELLERIE EN LORRAINE A LA FIN DU XVIᵉ SIÈCLE

La fin du xvıᵉ siècle est la période de l'histoire où furent brûlés le plus grand nombre de sorciers. Les bûchers s'allumèrent
dans tous les États de l'Europe, dans les pays protestants comme
dans les pays catholiques. Il est malaisé de dire pour quelles
raisons le mal sévit avec tant d'intensité en cette période. Miche-
let a écrit : « D'où vient la sorcière? Je dis sans hésiter : Des
temps du désespoir. » Mais cette époque était une époque relati-
vement prospère. L'Europe sortait des guerres de religion. Le
règne de Henri IV en France est un règne réparateur ; le commerce et l'industrie renaissent ; l'Angleterre, sous Élisabeth,
devient une nation riche ; l'Allemagne elle-même respire après
la paix d'Augsbourg et avant la guerre de Trente ans. En
Lorraine, aucune époque n'est aussi féconde que celle du duc
Charles III. Une nouvelle ville de Nancy sort du sol comme par
enchantement à côté de la Ville-Vieille ; des industries de luxe y
sont créées et attirent de nombreux artisans. C'est en des pays
heureux que sévit la sorcellerie. Et sans doute on peut dire que,
pendant les guerres religieuses, les hommes s'étaient habitués
aux bûchers ; leur cœur s'était endurci et ils passaient, indiffé-
rents ou hostiles, devant les flammes qui consumaient les préten-
dues sorcières. Mais peut-être est-on obligé de reconnaître qu'il
y a des épidémies morales comme des épidémies physiques. Les
idées funestes circulent insaisissables, gagnent de proche en
proche et répandent la contagion. A la fin du xvıᵉ siècle, catholiques et protestants étaient hantés par l'idée du Démon, être
personnel, doué d'un immense pouvoir, cherchant à nuire aux
hommes de toutes manières. Ils le voyaient partout, dans les
phénomènes naturels et dans les événements les plus fortuits. De

cette croyance, qui est sans doute au fond de christianisme, mais qui, à cette époque, passe au premier plan, tirez toutes ses conséquences; les procès de sorcellerie sont au bout.

Or, au moment où les bûchers s'allumaient, il se trouva des théoriciens pour les justifier et les exalter; et leurs livres, lus avec avidité[1], propagèrent le mal. Un publiciste qu'on représente souvent comme un esprit très libre, qu'on a appelé parfois le Montesquieu du XVIe siècle[2], Jean Bodin, publie en 1580 son *Traité de la Démonomanie des sorciers*[3] où il étale un zèle indiscret à poursuivre toutes les personnes suspectes de ce crime; et les procès de sorcellerie se multiplient aux environs de Laon, où Bodin est procureur du roi. A quelque temps de là, en 1602, Henri Boguet, de Dôle, juge à Saint-Claude, en Franche-Comté, met au jour son *Discours des sorciers;* il engage tout juge à ne laisser échapper aucune sorcière, et les bûchers s'allument en ce coin du Jura plus nombreux qu'ailleurs[4]. En 1610, un conseiller du Parlement de Bordeaux, Pierre de Lancre, visite, à la recherche des sorciers, la terre du Labourd et il écrit son *Tableau de l'inconstance des mauvais anges, les démons*[5]; le livre paru, les procès de sorcellerie foisonnent. Entre le livre de Jean Bodin et ceux de Boguet et de Lancre se place la *Démonolatrie* de Nicolas Remy, procureur général de

---

1. Nous signalons plus loin les éditions nombreuses de ces livres. Les dates de ces éditions nous indiquent les périodes où la sorcellerie a sévi; les ouvrages cessèrent d'être réimprimés lorsque la contagion diminua.

2. Baudrillart, *Jean Bodin et son temps*, Paris, 1853; Georges Weill, *les Théories sur le pouvoir royal en France pendant les guerres de religion*, p. 159, Paris, 1891. Les *six livres de la République* de Bodin, tant vantés, ont été écrits en 1577, trois ans avant la *Démonomanie*.

3. Paris, Jac. Du Puys, in-4°. D'autres exemplaires portent les dates de 1582 ou 1587. Il y eut des éditions à Anvers, Arnault Conninx, 1586, in-8°, à Lyon, 1593, in-8°, à Paris et Lyon, Ant. de Harsy, 1598, in-8°, à Rouen, 1604, in-12. L'ouvrage a été traduit en latin par Lotarius Philoponus (Fr. Junius), Basileae, 1581, in-4°; Francofurti, 1590, in-4°; il y eut une traduction italienne, par Herc. Cato, Venezia, Aldo, 1587, in-4°; autres éditions, 1589 et 1592.

4. *Discours des sorciers, avec six advis en faict de sorcellerie, et une instruction pour un juge en semblable matière*, Lyon, Pillehote, 1602, in-8°; réimpressions : Paris, Binet, 1603; Rouen, Osmont, 1606, petit in-12; 2e édition, Lyon, Pierre Rigaud, 1608, in-8°; autre édition, Lyon, 1610.

5. Paris, Barjon, 1610, in-4°; 2e édition, 1613, Pierre de Lancre donne la figure du Sabbat. Il publia dans la suite d'autres ouvrages sur la sorcellerie, notamment : *Du sortilège, où il est traicté s'il est plus expédient de supprimer et tenir soubs silence les abominations et maléfices des sorciers que les publier et manifester*, 1627, in-4°.

Lorraine, qui fut écrite en 1592 et vit le jour en 1595. Nicolas Remy consignait dans son volume l'expérience qu'il avait acquise en instruisant de nombreux procès de sorcellerie et son livre eut pour effet de rendre ces procès encore plus nombreux; dans nul autre pays la sorcellerie n'a sévi davantage que dans le petit duché de Lorraine.

I.

Nicolas Remy naquit à Charmes vers l'année 1530[1]. Il se destina à l'étude du droit, et, comme, à cette époque, la Lorraine ne possédait pas encore d'université, il fit ses études en France, probablement à Orléans. Il prit le titre de licencié ès lois et pendant vingt et un ans il enseigna tour à tour la littérature et la jurisprudence[2]. Le 15 mars 1570, au moment où il atteignait la quarantaine, un de ses oncles maternels, François Mittat, se démit en sa faveur de sa charge de lieutenant général au bailliage des Vosges[3], l'un des trois grands bailliages entre lesquels se divisait la Lorraine; et, cinq années durant, il résida à Mirecourt, où il passa bientôt pour un excellent magistrat. Le 4 novembre 1575, le duc de Lorraine l'appela à Nancy et l'attacha à sa personne en qualité de secrétaire ordinaire[4]; l'année suivante, en 1576, tout en lui laissant sa charge de secrétaire, il le nomma membre du tribunal des échevins de Nancy[5].

Les échevins à Nancy ne formaient pas le conseil de la commune; c'était un tribunal ducal dont les membres, gradués en droit, étaient nommés par le duc de Lorraine; ils étaient au nombre de quatre ou six[6], ayant à leur tête le maître échevin,

1. Nous ne possédons qu'une biographie de Nicolas Remy sous forme d'un discours de réception à l'Académie de Stanislas. Elle est due au président L. Leclerc, et elle est en tous points excellente. M. Henri Lepage avait fourni à M. Leclerc toutes les mentions qui se trouvent sur Remy aux archives de la Meurthe. Cf. *Mémoires de l'Académie de Stanislas*, 1868, p. xxxix et suiv.

2. Dans les lettres patentes citées ci-après, il est qualifié de « licencié ès lois des Universités de France, où il auroit versé l'espace de vingt ung ans, faisant profession, la plupart d'iceulx, d'enseigner tant les lettres humaines que les droictz ».

3. Arch. dép., B. 39, fol. 205.

4. *Ibidem*, B. 45, fol. 115.

5. Il porte pour la première fois le titre d'échevin dans le compte du trésorier général de 1576 (B. 1172, fol. 166).

6. A l'origine, il n'y avait peut-être que deux membres : voilà pourquoi Nicolas Remy désigne ce tribunal sous le nom de *duumviri*.

choisi de même par l'État. Ils jugeaient les causes criminelles
dans l'étendue de la prévôté de Nancy ; cette prévôté comprenait,
outre Nancy, soixante-douze villages qui s'étendaient depuis
Frouard au nord jusqu'à l'extrémité sud du département actuel
de Meurthe-et-Moselle, à Affracourt, Xirocourt et Vaudéville.
Or, on remarque que, dans ces villages et dans la ville, furent
instruits, à cette époque, un grand nombre de procès de sorcellerie[1]. Nicolas Remy fut un juge très affairé.

Mais ce n'est pas tout. En Lorraine, il existait un très grand
nombre de tribunaux criminels : tribunaux ducaux (les autres
prévôtés), tribunaux seigneuriaux et tribunaux des communes.
Le tribunal d'un petit village, comme Amance[2], Arches[3],
Insming[4], Hessen[5], avait le droit de prononcer sans appel la
peine capitale. Ce tribunal communal était composé tantôt du
maire et de quelques échevins, tantôt de l'ensemble des habitants
d'une commune, de la *féauté ;* aucun de ces juges ne savait le

---

1. Nous n'avons trouvé aucune trace de sorcellerie à Nancy et dans les environs au moyen âge. Dans les extraits de la chronique attribuée à Florentin Le
Thierriat, on trouve bien le récit d'une scène curieuse qui se serait passée sous
René II, soit à la fin du xv° siècle. Une femme, Guillemette Lançon, vint s'établir au village de Saint-Dizier (aujourd'hui faubourg des Trois-Maisons de
Nancy). Elle passa toutes ses journées à l'église et on la regarda comme une
sainte. Mais elle fut prise d'une maladie « qu'aurait fin en neuf mois ». Un
prêtre, Louis Mousson, fut accusé par les commères du voisinage d'être le père
de l'enfant ; il se défendit avec énergie, soutint que Guillemette avait été ensor-
celée par un prêtre du nom de Michel Adam et qu'elle donnerait le jour à un
diablotin tout noir. On se saisit de Guillemette et de Michel Adam ; l'évêque
de Toul évoqua l'affaire ; on incarcéra la prétendue sorcière ; mais, sur ces
entrefaites, Louis Mousson prit la fuite et prouva ainsi sa culpabilité (*Recueil
de documents sur l'histoire de Lorraine*, 1868, 2° partie, p. 79-81). Mais on sait
qu'on ne peut attacher aucune confiance à ces prétendus Mémoires.

2. Cant. de Nancy, dans les Vosges. Amance avait jadis obtenu la loi de
Beaumont.

3. Les jugeants du ban d'Arches, cant. d'Épinal, jugeaient les sorciers des
villages d'Arches, Hadol, Le Roulier, Donnoux, Pouxeux et des hameaux dépen-
dant de ces localités. Ce sont ces jugeants qui ont prononcé la peine de mort
contre Antoine Grevillon, dont M. Charles Sadoul nous a raconté l'histoire.
Cf. *infra.*

4. Cant. d'Albestroff, aujourd'hui réuni à l'Allemagne. Le tribunal d'Insming
jugeait les procès de sorcellerie dans les villages environnants : Hunskirch, Réi-
ning, Wittersbourg, Petit-Tenquin (Klein-Tänchen), Gréning, Nelling. Cf. *Das
Elsass Lothringen*, art. *Insmingen* (*Meierei*). Ces diverses localités autrefois
dans la Meurthe, canton cité, ou dans la Moselle, cant. de Gros-Tenquin ou de
Sarralbe.

5. Cant. de Sarrebourg. Cf. *Ibidem.*

droit; beaucoup même ne savaient pas lire! Et combien de sorciers ou sorcières ont été condamnés par de telles juridictions à la peine de mort! L'on comprit qu'il était nécessaire d'exercer sur elles un contrôle, et il fut admis d'assez bonne heure qu'avant d'ordonner la question ou de prononcer une sentence capitale ces tribunaux demanderaient l'avis des échevins de Nancy. Ce qui était un usage devint bientôt une règle, une obligation[1]. On pensait, par cette consultation, éviter de fâcheuses erreurs judiciaires; on y voyait un autre avantage. On introduisait l'unité de législation dans l'enchevêtrement des juridictions. On superposait aux tribunaux seigneuriaux et communaux le tribunal du duc. L'échevinage de Nancy a contribué pour sa part à créer l'unité de la Lorraine.

En vertu de ces principes, tous les procès criminels du duché de Lorraine, — nous laissons de côté le Barrois, qui avait son organisation spéciale, — ceux de Lunéville comme ceux d'Épinal, ceux des terres ecclésiastiques de Saint-Dié et de Remiremont comme ceux du comté de Vaudémont ou de la seigneurie de Haroué, aboutissaient à Nancy et étaient examinés par les échevins. Beaucoup de ces procès étaient des procès de sorcellerie; et de la place des Dames où siégeait le tribunal dans la maison au change[2] partaient approuvées les sentences qui ont envoyé au bûcher d'innombrables victimes[3].

De 1576 à 1591, pendant quinze années successives, Nicolas Remy fut membre de ce tribunal[4]. Toutes les causes de sorcelle-

---

1. Cf. Charles Sadoul, *Organisation judiciaire de la Lorraine*, Nancy, 1898. Seules certaines enclaves lorraines en Alsace, Sainte-Marie-aux-Mines, Saint-Hippolyte, jugeaient sans en référer au tribunal des échevins.

2. La maison porte aujourd'hui le n° 19 de la place des Dames.

3. Sur ce tribunal, on consultera le mémoire de Guimet dans l'*Histoire de Lorraine* de dom Calmet, III, col. CCXXXIII; L. Leclerc, *art. cité*, notes 12 à 17; Henri Lepage, *les Offices des duchés de Lorraine et de Bar*, dans les *Mémoires de la Société d'archéologie*, 1869, p. 180; Krug-Basse, *Histoire du Parlement de Lorraine*, p. 21. Nous n'avons parlé ici que des attributions criminelles du tribunal des échevins. Au civil, le tribunal connaissait des affaires *personnelles* des gentilshommes de l'ancienne chevalerie, des nobles, anoblis et autres privilégiés; il s'efforçait d'attirer à lui les affaires *réelles*, empiétant sur la juridiction du tribunal des assises; mais, dans ces divers cas, des gentilshommes venaient siéger à côté des échevins. Les affaires civiles des roturiers étaient jugées en première instance par le prévôt; elles venaient en appel, — pour le cas où l'appel était autorisé, — devant le tribunal des échevins, et cela dans toutes les prévôtés du bailliage de Nancy.

4. Les maîtres échevins furent à ce moment Nicolas Olry (1572-1592) et

rie qui se sont produites dans le duché de Lorraine, durant ces années, lui ont passé sous les yeux, soit qu'il les ait jugées directement, soit qu'il ait examiné les sentences des tribunaux inférieurs. C'est son expérience de praticien qu'il a consignée dans sa *Démonolatrie* composée en 1592, alors qu'il sortait à peine de charge. Combien de sentences capitales avait-il prononcées comme échevin de Nancy? Il nous donne lui-même un chiffre dans le titre de son ouvrage : *Ex judiciis capitalibus non-gentorum plus minus hominum, qui sortilegii crimen intra annos quindecim in Lotharingia capite luerunt.* En ces quinze années, il avait envoyé au supplice 900 victimes, — un peu plus un peu moins; — c'est une moyenne de soixante condamnations capitales par an; et le duché de Lorraine était un pays fort petit; dans ce chiffre de 900 ne sont pas compris les sorciers qui ont été exécutés dans le Barrois[1] ni dans les terres des Trois-Evêchés de Metz qui appartenaient à la France et déchiquetaient

Nicolas Bourgeois (1592-1603). Parmi les collègues de Nicolas Remy, nous citerons Habellon et Mitard.

1. La sorcellerie dans le Barrois n'a pas encore été étudiée spécialement. Pourtant, il semble bien certain que l'épidémie a sévi avec beaucoup moins d'intensité que dans le duché de Lorraine. Il y a eu quelques exécutions sommaires dans le duché de Bar à la fin du xv⁰ siècle. Dans l'année 1473-1474, on fait à Bar le procès d'Alix, femme de Didier Hollier, de Hargéville, et de la femme Jacquot, du Plessis. Alix est condamnée à mort et ses biens sont vendus à l'encan (Arch. de la Meuse, Compte du receveur général, B. 507). En 1480, on exécuta à Bar Jeanne, veuve de Jeannesson, de Saulx (*Ibid.*, B. 508). Ces deux sorcières ont été jugées par le tribunal de l'Inquisition. Au xvi⁰ siècle, au temps où Nicolas Remy était échevin de Nancy et procureur de Lorraine, Jean-Baptiste Bournon, Jean Bourgeois, puis le fils de celui-ci, nommé aussi Jean, furent procureurs généraux du Barrois; ils ne paraissent pas avoir partagé les idées de Remy, et ils se montrèrent certainement plus doux que lui. Dans le Barrois non mouvant, il y eut bien quelques procès de sorcellerie et quelques condamnations devant les grands jours de Saint-Mihiel (cf. Bonnabelle, *Notice sur Saint-Mihiel*, Bar-le-Duc, 1889, p. 79). Trois femmes furent brûlées à Étain en 1616, une autre en 1619, deux autres en 1624 (Arch. de la Meuse, B. 1214, 1216, 1219; Bonnabelle, *Notice sur Étain*, dans les *Mémoires de la Société d'archéologie de Meurthe-et-Moselle*, 1878); d'autres exécutions eurent lieu à Souilly en 1583, 1599 et 1625 (Arch. de la Meuse, B. 1281, 1286 et 1290). A Saucy, il y eut des exécutions en 1581, 1586, 1594, 1595, 1615 (*Ibid.*, B. 1816, 1820, 1828, 1829, 1832). Mais ces exemples sont en somme assez rares; et il y eut encore moins d'exécutions dans le Barrois mouvant, qui relevait, au point de vue judiciaire, du Parlement de Paris. Nous n'avons trouvé mention que de quelques exécutions à Bar en 1573 (*Ibid.*, B. 568); une exécution à Pierrefitte en 1623 (*Ibid.*, B. 2873). Une autre femme y fut accusée de sortilège en 1599 (*Ibid.*, B. 2867; Bonnabelle, *Pierrefitte et les seigneurs de la maison du Châtelet*, p. 8). Cette observation nous prouve combien est grande la res-

le duché de façon si bizarre[1]. Il est naturellement difficile aujourd'hui de donner des statistiques exactes[2]; mais parfois à Nancy, où l'on exécutait les sorcières de la ville et *quelques* sorcières de la prévôté, — souvent ces sorcières étaient brûlées dans leur village, — on trouve trace de six ou même de huit condamnations capitales dans une année.

La manière dont Nicolas Remy remplissait ses fonctions de

ponsabilité de théoriciens comme Nicolas Remy. Dans les pays où ils détenaient l'autorité judiciaire, ils stimulaient le zèle de leurs subordonnés, et les procès se multipliaient.

1. Sur la sorcellerie à Toul, on consultera Albert Denis, *la Sorcellerie à Toul aux XVI*ᵉ *et XVII*ᵉ *siècles,* Toul, Lemaire, 1888, in-8ᵉ. Pour Metz, voir l'article d'E. Boutillier, *les Sorcières de Plappeville,* dans l'*Austrasie,* 1856, p. 149; Nerée Quépal, *Histoire du village de Woippy,* Metz, 1878, p. 104; Louis Gilbert, *la Sorcellerie au pays messin,* dans *le Pays lorrain,* 1907, p. 33. Les procès de sorcellerie étaient très nombreux en Alsace, et on lira avec intérêt l'excellent travail de Rod. Reuss, *la Sorcellerie en Alsace au XVI*ᵉ *et au XVII*ᵉ *siècle,* Strasbourg, 1872.

2. Dumont, *la Justice criminelle des duchés de Lorraine et de Bar,* 2 vol., Nancy, 1848, a relevé les noms d'un certain nombre de sorcières exécutées; mais cette liste est bien incomplète. Lepage, dans ses *Communes de la Meurthe,* a, à propos de divers villages, signalé les sorcières qui ont été exécutées. La plupart des actes de procès de sorcellerie ont disparu; nous en avons pourtant tenu quelques-uns entre les mains. Cf. Manuscrits de la Société d'archéologie lorraine, n° 135 (procès de 1602, 1619, 1625, 1633); Bibliothèque nationale, Collection de Lorraine, n° 466, fol. 7-81. On trouve aussi quelques actes dans les manuscrits de la Cour d'appel. Peut-être, en consultant les archives de la Cour des comptes, si admirablement conservées, arriverait-on à établir des statistiques précises. Chaque procès causait un certain nombre de frais pour l'information et pour l'exécution; ces frais sont consignés sur les registres des receveurs, et, souvent, dans les pièces justificatives, on trouve copie de la sentence capitale. Il faudrait dépouiller systématiquement ces registres et ces liasses; M. Charles Sadoul a commencé ce travail. Il a déjà trouvé l'indication de 1,800 sorciers ou sorcières brûlés à la fin du XVIᵉ et au début du XVIIᵉ siècle. Sur la sorcellerie en Lorraine, on consultera les monographies suivantes : Gab. Thomas, *les Procès de sorcellerie et la suggestion hypnotique* (discours prononcé à la rentrée de la Cour d'appel de Nancy, 1885). — Alb. Fournier, *Une épidémie de sorcellerie en Lorraine aux XVI*ᵉ *et XVII*ᵉ *siècles,* dans les *Annales de l'Est,* t. V (1891), p. 228. — De Chanteau, *Notes pour servir à l'histoire du chapitre de Saint-Dié* (contient une étude : *les Sorciers à Saint-Dié et dans le val de Galilée*), Nancy, Berger-Levrault, 1879. — Gust. Save, *la Sorcellerie à Saint-Dié,* dans le *Bulletin de la Société philomatique,* 1887-1888, p. 135 (M. Save estime à 600 le nombre des victimes pour l'arrondissement de Saint-Dié). — Charles Sadoul, *Antoine Grevillon, sorcier et devin au val de Ramonchamp, brûlé à Arches en 1625,* dans le *Pays lorrain,* t. I (1904), p. 145 et suiv. — Les deux livres suivants sont de purs livres d'imagination : Pierre Sternon, *les Moines et les sorcières d'Ancy au XVI*ᵉ *siècle,* Nancy, 1886; E. Badel, *D'une sorcière qu'aultrefois on brusla dans Sainct-Nicolas,* Nancy, 1891.

juge lui attirait la considération générale, et le duc récompensa,
à diverses reprises, son zèle. Le 9 avril 1583, Charles III l'ano-
blit; il voulait reconnaître ses loyaux services dans l'exercice de
son office, et aussi la manière dont il [avait rempli certaines
commissions qu'il lui avait confiées. « En chacune de ces charges,
disent les lettres patentes, il se serait comporté avec tel acquit et
satisfaction de son devoir que nous en aurions toujours reçu bon
contentement[1]. » Quelques années plus tard, le 1er août 1589, le
duc lui donna le titre de conseiller en son conseil privé[2], et Remy,
à cause de ses connaissances juridiques, s'y distingua, puisque
le conseil était une sorte de tribunal des requêtes et jugeait les
causes évoquées par le prince[3]. Enfin, le 24 août 1591, il le mit
à la tête de la justice en Lorraine, en le nommant procureur
général, en remplacement de Georges Maimbourg[4]. Le procureur
général avait juridiction sur toute l'étendue du duché, c'est-à-dire
sur les trois bailliages de Nancy, des Vosges et d'Allemagne; il
n'était pas attaché à un seul siège; il était ministère public non
seulement au tribunal des échevins, mais à la Chambre des
comptes, aux assises de Nancy, des Vosges et d'Allemagne, dans
les sièges inférieurs, s'il le jugeait bon. A lui de poursuivre les
criminels, d'ordonner les premières informations, de les faire
lui-même s'il l'estime à propos[5]. Dès lors, Nicolas Remy a livré
comme ministère public une guerre redoutable aux sorciers.
Il compte soixante ans. Mais l'âge n'a point refroidi son ardeur;
au contraire, pensant faire œuvre pieuse, il redouble de zèle. Il

1. Dom Pelletier, *Armorial de la Lorraine*, au mot Remy; on lui donnait
comme armes : « D'or, écartelé en sautoir d'azur, à deux serpents volants,
affrontés d'argent, mouchetés, allumés et armés de gueules, et pour cimier
un serpent de l'écu. »
2. Arch. de la Meurthe, B. 58, fol. 222.
3. Nicolas Remy fut chargé, comme conseiller, de diverses commissions.
A la fin d'août 1589, — nous sommes dans la période des troubles de la Ligue,
— le maréchal d'Aumont, gouverneur de la Champagne, avait envahi le Barrois
et tenté, le 6 septembre, sur Bar-le-Duc, un coup de mains qui échoua. Il
avait pratiqué des intelligences dans la place. Le duc Charles III, par commission du 26 septembre, chargea Nicolas Remy et un autre conseiller d'État,
Cuny Boucher, de faire une enquête sur ces faits et de juger les coupables
jusqu'à la sentence définitive inclusivement. D'après le jugement des commis-
saires, Jean Merle fut pendu, Castel écartelé. Jean Maucervel, avocat, et Nicolas Leschicault, orfèvre, durent payer de fortes amendes. Cf. *Lettres et instructions de Charles III relatives aux affaires de la Ligue*, dans la *Collection
de documents sur l'histoire de Lorraine*, 1864, p. 210-212.
4. Arch. de la Meurthe, B. 61, fol. 197.
5. Sur les attributions du procureur général, voir Krug-Basse, *op. cit.*, p. 28.

stimule les procureurs des bailliages d'Allemagne et des Vosges, les substituts et les officiers inférieurs, les exhortant à remplir leurs devoirs sans fausse pitié[1]; lui-même fait, dans le duché, de

1. Naturellement, le procureur général donnait aussi son avis sur les procès de sorcellerie qui étaient jugés dans les seigneuries particulières. En 1594, on signala de nombreuses sorcières au village de Wallerchen (Vaudreching), un canton de Bouzonville, dont l'abbé de Bouzonville était seigneur. L'abbé fit faire une information secrète, et, bien que les juges locaux inclinassent vers la douceur, les échevins de Nancy, consultés, déclarèrent que les inculpées devaient être appréhendées. Nicolas Remy, procureur, adressa à ce sujet à l'abbé Jean Sellier la lettre suivante autographe que nous avons trouvée dans la Collection de Lorraine, à la Bibliothèque nationale, n° 466, fol. 20, avec d'autres pièces de ce procès :

« Monsieur, Monsieur de Bouzonville.

« Monsieur, J'ay veu l'information que vous m'avez envoyée et trouve la chambrière du curé de Wallerichen fort chargée par icelle du crime de sortilège, tellement que je tiens qu'il y a matière de la constituer prisonnière en prison ferme et renvoyer sa partie formelle[a], pour avoir faict preuve suffisante de ce dont elle l'a defférée. Que sy le sieur woué en use aultrement[b], comme me l'écrivez, il abuse de sa vouerie, et sera bon d'en advertir le sieur procureur général du bailliage d'Allemagne, affin d'y intervenir et faire le dheu de sa charge. Quant à ce que vous m'écrivez aussy de ladite délinquante qu'elle s'est mise en la protection du sieur prévost de Château-Salins, cela ne l'exemptera d'être derechef appréhendée, veues les charges portées contre elle par la dite information; mais aussy conviendra-t-il, quant on luy dressera son procès et que on y donnera sentence deffinitive, y appeller le dit sieur prévost, pour s'estre la dite délinquante faicte bourgeoise de Marchis[c] sous luy, pourveu touteffois que ç'ayt esté à main saine. Touchant les autres impunités dont m'escrivez semblablement, ce sera bien faict d'en envoyer une déclaration particulière audit sieur procureur général du bailliage d'Allemagne, affin qu'il en face informer et y apporter pour l'advenir l'ordre qui en sera besoing[d]. Je vous baise les mains très humblement et prie Dieu, Monsieur, vous donner en santé continuelle très longue et heureuse vie. A Nancy, le VII° septembre 1594.

« Votre très humble et affectionné serviteur.

« N. REMY.

« P.-S. — J'ay reçeu quatre francs et demy de vostre homme, mais je vous remercie. »

a. La partie formelle est la partie qui accuse; on avait soupçonné les accusateurs de faux et on les avait arrêtés.

b. Les seigneurs de Burgesch, commune de Schwerdorf, étaient voués de Bouzonville.

c. On sait que les ducs de Lorraine avaient le titre de Marchis entre Rhin et Meuse. Le prévôt de Château-Salins fut en même temps « prévôt de la Marchise ». Les sujets des seigneuries qui voulaient acquérir la nationalité lorraine se déclaraient bourgeois de la Marchise et devenaient justiciables du prévôt de Château-Salins. Voir à ce sujet un mémoire d'un de ces prévôts, Austien Mélin, dans dom Calmet, *Histoire de Lorraine*, 2° édit., t. V, Préliminaires.

d. On voit que Nicolas Remy était d'accord avec l'abbé de Bouzonville : il faut que le procureur au bailliage d'Allemagne, — c'était Nicolas Weiss, — stimule le zèle des employés judiciaires sur les terres de l'abbaye.

fréquentes tournées pour découvrir les coupables ; il siège non seulement au tribunal des échevins, mais aux tribunaux inférieurs, pour requérir la peine de mort ; et comment de simples prévôts auraient-ils osé juger contre les conclusions de M. le procureur? Juge au tribunal des échevins, Nicolas Remy a fait 900 victimes : combien en a-t-il fait comme procureur? Il est difficile de répondre ; il faudrait sûrement doubler, peut-être tripler le chiffre. S'il avait donné à la fin de sa vie une nouvelle édition de la *Démonolatrie,* il aurait pu y ajouter de nombreux compléments. Ses tournées sont marquées par les bûchers. *Incedo per ignes* eût pu être sa devise[1]. En 1596, il parcourt tous les villages du bailliage de Nancy, et ces villages sont décimés[2] ; à la même époque, il visite Bertrimoutier dans le bailliage des Vosges et il y répand la terreur[3]. Remy exerça sa charge de procureur pendant quinze années, de 1591 à 1606, et ces temps, marqués en Lorraine par une grande prospérité, furent les sombres années de la sorcellerie.

Dans les loisirs que lui laissait l'exercice de ses charges, Nicolas Remy se livrait à sa passion pour les lettres. La robe du juge ou du procureur déposée, il s'adonnait, dans sa maison de campagne de Saint-Mard, près de Bayon, aux études plus douces, *amœniora studia.* Il taquinait la Muse en français et en latin ; il faisait de sérieuses études historiques ; il préparait ses harangues d'apparat. Plusieurs de ses ouvrages sont arrivés jusqu'à nous. Le plus ancien en date est la *Démonolatrie,* dont il nous raconte lui-même l'origine. Il repassait souvent en son esprit, pendant les vacances, les aveux que les sorciers avaient faits ; et il s'amusait, pour sa distraction, à les écrire en vers latins[4] :

Admirable matière à mettre en vers latins !

Il écrivait aussi en prose quelques réflexions sur la sorcellerie en général. Peu à peu, l'idée lui vint de réunir ces morceaux détachés pour en faire un livre, de même qu'on coud ensemble des bouts d'étoffe pour en faire un vêtement. Aussi redoubla-t-il désormais d'attention dans les procès et fixa-t-il avec soin en sa

1. Cette devise a été mise par le président Leclerc comme épigraphe à son discours.
2. Arch. de la Meurthe, B. 7314.
3. Lepage et Charton, *le Département des Vosges,* art. Bertrimoutier.
4. Un résumé en vers latins précède son livre de la *Démonolatrie.*

mémoire les détails de chaque affaire. Enfin, une année, la peste lui fit des loisirs plus longs; les tribunaux vaquaient en Lorraine; et pour charmer sa solitude, — *cum ruris solitudinem eblandiri aliqua ratione cuperem*, — il mit ses notes en ordre et écrivit son traité. Thierry Alix, qui, après avoir mis en ordre le trésor des chartes, était devenu premier président de la Chambre des comptes, parla du livre à Charles III[1]. Le duc exprima le désir qu'il fût livré à la presse, et, après toutes sortes de difficultés, il parut à Lyon en 1595[2]. Deux autres éditions furent données en 1596 à Cologne[3] et à Francfort[4]; l'ouvrage fut traduit en allemand[5]. Il obtint partout le succès le plus vif. Le jurisconsulte Charondas en fait un éloge enthousiaste : « C'est un livre rempli d'exemples notables et d'excellents discours mêlés de diverses sciences, pour montrer que de si abominables crimes doivent être sévèrement punis, sans y user de connivence ni dissimulation[6]. » L'œuvre est dédiée au fils du duc, au cardinal Charles, évêque de Metz et de Strasbourg, celui-là même qui deviendra plus tard le premier primat de Lorraine. Ce prince souffrait de violentes douleurs rhumatismales qu'il attribuait aux sorciers; il avait fait venir d'Italie pour l'exorciser des frères barnabites. Certes, il dut trouver plaisir à la lecture de ce volume, où l'anathème et la mort étaient prononcés contre ses prétendus bourreaux.

Ce livre est certainement un livre de bonne foi, comme disait Montaigne, et c'est ce qui en rend la lecture effrayante. A peu près

1. Tous ces détails sont empruntés à la préface de la *Demonolatrie*.
2. « Nicolaii REMIGII Sereniss. Ducis Lotharingiae a consiliis interioribus, et in ejus ditione Lotharingica cognitoris publici *Demonolatriae libri tres*. Lugduni, in officina Vincentii. M.D.XCV. » In-4°, Prélimin., 14 fol., y compris le titre, non numérotés, 394 p.
3. « Coloniae Agrippinae, apud Henricum Falckenburg. M.D.XCVI. » Petit in-8°, 16 fol. non numérotés et 414 p.
4. « Francofurti, in officina Palthenii. M.D.XCVI. » Petit in-12. L'éditeur a ajouté ce surprenant sous-titre : *Miris ac jucundis narrationibus, variarum naturalium quaestionum ac mysteriorum Doemonicorum discussionibus, valde suaves et grati adque sales movendos imprimis apti.*
5. « *Dœmonolatria d. i. von Unholden und Zauber Geistern, des Edlen, Ehrnverten und Hochgelarten Herrn Nicolai Remigii, des durchl. Hertzogen in Lothringen Geheimen Raths und Peinlicher Sachen Cognitoris publici.* Aus dem Latein in hoch Deutsch übersetzt durch Teucridem Aenaeum Privatum. Franckfurt bei Cratandro Palthenio, 1598. » Je n'ai pas vu cette traduction, elle est citée par Soldan, *Geschichte der Hexenprocesse*, t. II, p. 25, n. 2.
6. *Responses de droit françois*, éd. de 1637, p. 446, dans le chapitre : *Si les sorciers et sorcières sont dignes du dernier supplice.*

jamais le moindre doute n'a envahi l'âme du procureur; jamais aucun scrupule ne l'a effleuré. L'épigraphe de son livre est un verset de la Bible qui est déjà une sentence de mort : « Quand un homme ou une femme aura un esprit de Python ou sera devin, on le fera mourir[1]. » Et voici la conclusion : « Pour ceux qui ont souillé leur vie de tels crimes, je ne doute pas qu'il soit de droit de les tourmenter par toutes sortes de tortures et de les faire périr par le feu; il faut qu'ils soient un exemple aux autres et que la sévérité même de leur supplice soit un avertissement. » Et dans l'intervalle des 394 pages revient sans cesse le même mot : la mort! Et toutes les déductions de Nicolas Remy sont faites à grands renforts de citations d'auteurs grecs et latins et avec de véritables grâces littéraires, en une langue châtiée à laquelle on ne peut reprocher qu'un peu d'obscurité. Le procureur était nourri de la moëlle de l'antiquité, et il s'appliquait à bien écrire. Il comptait sur ce livre pour faire vivre son nom dans la postérité, pour rappeler aux arrière-neveux la grandeur de la tâche qu'il avait accomplie, les services qu'il avait rendus au christianisme et à l'humanité!

D'autres œuvres de Nicolas Remy nous sont parvenues. Il contribua à la rédaction de la coutume de Lorraine qui parut en 1596[2]. Le « nouveau style » exigeait des avocats la prestation d'un serment à la séance solennelle de la rentrée des tribunaux ou, comme on disait alors, « à l'ouverture des plaidoiries du duché de Lorraine ». La première fois que cette cérémonie eut lieu en 1597, le procureur général prononça un intéressant discours; dans un langage très élevé, il rappelle aux avocats leur devoir, non sans lancer à leur adresse quelques traits malicieux sur le choix des bonnes causes et des bons moyens, la modération des honoraires, la bienveillance dans les relations quotidiennes[3]. C'est peut-être le premier en date des discours de rentrée; la bibliothèque de Nancy en possède un exemplaire jadis donné par Remy

1. *Vir sive mulier, in quibus pythonicus vel divinationis fuerit spiritus, morte moriatur.* Lév. XX, 27.
2. *Les Coustumes générales du duché de Lorraine, ès bailliages de Nancy, Vosges et Allemagne,* Nancy, J. Janson, 1596.
3. *Recueil des principaux points de la remontrance faite à l'ouverture des plaidoiries du duché de Lorraine, après les Rois, en l'an 1597,* Metz, A. Faber, 1597, 30 p. in-4°. Florentin Le Thierriat a célébré ce discours en une pièce de vers qu'Augustin Digot a publié dans les *Mémoires de l'Académie de Stanislas,* 1849, p. 239.

lui-même à l'un de ses amis[1]. Puis il préparait une grande œuvre historique. Il amassait des matériaux pour une histoire de René II (1473-1508), et, en 1605, parut à Pont-à-Mousson le *Discours des choses advenues en Lorraine depuis le décès du duc Nicolas jusques à celui du duc René*[2]. C'est une œuvre remarquable qui dépasse singulièrement les chroniques du moyen âge; c'est la première en date des histoires parues en Lorraine. Remy fait un usage judicieux de la *Chronique de Lorraine* et du *Dialogue* de Jean Lud; il connaît aussi quelques-unes de ces chartes qu'avait si bien classées son ami Thierry Alix; le style est en général net et clair; pourtant on peut lui reprocher d'avoir accueilli quelques légendes que répétait la tradition orale. Nous savons aussi que Remy réunit en une collection les anciens édits et ordonnances de la province de Lorraine; le volume demeura malheureusement manuscrit; Nicolas Remy obtint en récompense 100 résaux de blé à prendre, trois années durant, sur la recette ducale de Châtel et de Charmes[3].

Ces travaux, aussi bien que la dignité de sa vie, assurèrent à Nicolas Remy la considération publique; on se tromperait gravement si l'on se figurait que ses contemporains se détournaient de lui avec horreur. Non, ses crimes étaient ceux de son époque, et le zèle qu'il déployait augmentait encore l'estime générale. Il vivait paisiblement à Nancy, pendant l'année judiciaire, en une petite maison de la rue du Haut-Bourgeois[4],

1. Fonds lorrain, n° 6481.
2. *Au Pont-à-Mousson*, par Melchior Bernard, in-4°, 196 p. L'ouvrage aura deux autres éditeurs, à Épinal, chez Pierre Houion, 1617, petit in-4°, 158 p., puis chez le même, M.DC.XXVI, 171 p. Cf. Beaupré, *Recherches sur les commencements et les progrès de l'imprimerie en Lorraine jusqu'à la fin du XVII° siècle*, p. 234; Pfister, *Histoire de Nancy*, t. I, p. 469. Nicolas Remy reçut pour ce travail du duc Henri II en 1609 la somme de 1,000 francs (Arch. dép., B. 1317, fol. 242). Henri II était reconnaissant à l'auteur de ce qu'il soutenait le droit des filles de succéder au duché de Lorraine. Le livre, au contraire, sera très mal vu du duc Charles IV, qui usurpa la couronne de Lorraine, en se fondant sur le principe de la masculinité.
3. Il fit ce travail après sa retraite; voir le compte général du trésorier de Lorraine pour 1611 (B.1332, fol. 236). Remy voulait publier ce recueil, Henri II s'y opposait « pour bonnes raisons ». Remy aurait-il retrouvé le testament de René II, consacrant la masculinité du duché de Lorraine, et craignait-il que son neveu Charles, — le futur Charles IV, — ne se fît une arme de ce document? Ce recueil est aujourd'hui perdu.
4. Voir les rôles des bourgeois de Nancy de 1589 pour la levée des sous de paroisse (B.7296).

entouré de sa nombreuse famille[1]. La ville de Nancy lui fit présent d'un beau tableau pour lui témoigner sa reconnaissance[2]. Le duc l'employa dans ses négociations diplomatiques. En 1594, le procureur général prit possession de la ville de Marsal, que Henri IV rendait à la Lorraine en vertu du traité de Saint-Germain[3]; les années suivantes, il assista à diverses conférences avec les agents du duc de Deux-Ponts, du comte de Nassau, de la communauté de Metz pour aplanir diverses difficultés de frontière inévitables en un pays où les enclaves étaient multipliées; partout il arriva à se rendre utile[4]. Aussi, en reconnaissance de ses services, le duc accorda, le 26 août 1599, sur la prière de sa belle-fille Catherine de Bourbon[5], au fils aîné de Nicolas, Claude, la survivance de la charge de procureur[6]; mais Nicolas Remy continua de l'exercer, tandis que Claude achevait ses études à Paris; ce n'est qu'en 1606, à soixante-douze ans, que le procureur prit enfin sa retraite et fut définitivement remplacé par son fils[7].

Nicolas se retira à Charmes, dont il avait fait une description enthousiaste dans son *Discours des choses advenues;* mais il se rendit encore, à plus d'une reprise, utile à ses compatriotes. Toutes les fois qu'une cérémonie importante se célébrait à la cour de Lorraine, on s'adressait à lui et on lui demandait une pièce de circonstance. Quand Marguerite de Gonzague, seconde femme du duc de Bar Henri, fit son entrée à Nancy, le 15 juin 1606, Nicolas Remy fut chargé de faire de cette cérémonie une description officielle en latin[8]. Quand, en 1608, le duc Charles III mourut,

1. Le 3 juin 1598, Nicolas Remy, âgé de soixante-huit ans, eut encore un fils qui fut baptisé sur la paroisse Notre-Dame (Lepage, *les Archives de Nancy*, t. III, p. 342).

2. Compte de la ville de 1605. Somme payée à Claude Henriet, dit Chalon, peintre à S. A., pour avoir repeint le tableau donné de la part de la Ville au procureur général (Lepage, *Ibid.*, t. II, p. 196).

3. Arch. dép., B. 1248, fol. 298. Somme payée à Nicolas Remy pour ce voyage.

4. Ces négociations nous sont connues par les dépenses faites par le procureur et qui ont été relevées sur les registres de la Chambre des comptes par M. Leclerc, *loc. cit.*, p. 27.

5. C'est la sœur de Henri IV. Sa requête en faveur de Claude est mentionnée expressément dans les lettres patentes.

6. Arch. dép., B. 70, fol. 109.

7. C'est à partir de cette année que Claude Remy touche son traitement.

8. *Quae sunt ad XVII Cal. Jul. An. M. DC. VI. honoris ergo exhilibitaque* (sic) *adventante primum ad Nanceium Sereniss. Margarita.* Clariloci ad Nanceium, excudebat Joannes Sauine typographus. Pour la description détaillée de

l'ancien procureur célébra, en un langage enthousiaste, les glorieux faits de ce prince[1]. Lorsque le fils de Charles III, Henri II, forma le dessein de faire son entrée dans sa capitale, le 13 septembre 1609, le peintre Florent Drouin fut délégué à Rémy, dans sa retraite de Charmes, pour conférer avec lui sur les vers et les devises à inscrire sur les arcs de triomphe[2]; l'entrée fut remise; elle n'eut lieu que le 20 avril 1610, et, sur le désir du duc, on évita tous frais trop considérables; mais on imprima les vers de Remy[3], et il figura, avec son fils, le procureur, au banquet qui fut donné à l'Hôtel-de-Ville[4]. Ainsi, jusqu'à la fin de sa carrière, il connut les honneurs. Il s'éteignit doucement à Charmes en avril 1612[5], entouré du respect de tous. C'était un fort honnête homme que ce Nicolas Remy, qui avait envoyé au bûcher 2,000 à 3,000 sorciers, dont les neuf dixièmes étaient sans nul doute des innocents[6].

Ch. PFISTER.

(*Sera continué.*)

---

la plaquette, voir Beaupré, *Recherches*, p. 239. Cf. Louis Davillé, *le Mariage de Marguerite de Gonzague*, dans *le Pays lorrain*, 1905, p. 75.

1. Voir le titre exact dans Beaupré, *Ibid.*, p. 244. Même endroit que précédemment.

2. Lepage, *les Archives de Nancy*, t. II, p. 204.

3. *Quae primum solennius in urbem Nanceium ingredienti Henrico II, duci Lotharingiae... Cives adornabant, nisi, ut sumptibus parceretur, vetuisset ejus Celsitudo*, Nanceii, 1610. En réalité, même les deux précédentes brochures, datées de Clairlieu, ont été imprimées à Nancy (*Histoire de Nancy*, t. I, p. 111).

4. Lepage, *Ibid.*, t. II, p. 205.

5. Nicolas Remy avait obtenu, le 7 mars 1609, de la libéralité de Henri II, une rente viagère de 300 francs. Or, sur les comptes du trésorier général pour l'année 1612, on lit : *Obiit au mois d'apvril*. Ajoutons que Nicolas Remy avait réuni une très belle bibliothèque. Le Musée lorrain et divers amateurs, entre autres M. Lucien Wiener, possèdent des livres qui lui ont appartenu.

6. Il nous reste de Nicolas Remy un portrait qui a été probablement gravé par Woëriot. Le procureur est représenté dans un médaillon ovale, autour duquel on lit : *N. Remigius a consiliis interiorib. illust. ducis Lothar. et in ejus duc. proc. gen.* C'est une physionomie intelligente, sévère ; les cheveux sont courts et le cou est entouré d'un collier de barbe. Jadis existait au Musée lorrain un portrait qu'on donnait pour celui de Nicolas Remy et qui a été reproduit par M. Leclerc en tête de sa *Notice*. Le portrait ne ressemble guère au précédent. Il a été identifié surtout par les armoiries qui y sont ajoutées. Il représente sûrement un membre de la famille Remy, mais nous inclinons à y reconnaître le procureur général Claude, fils de Nicolas. Voir sur ce portrait le *Journal de la Société d'archéologie lorraine*, 1857, p. 240-241.

NICOLAS REMY

SORCELLERIE EN LORRAINE A LA FIN DU XVI° SIÈCLE

(Suite et fin[1].)

II.

Après avoir esquissé l'histoire de la vie de Nicolas Remy, nous devons examiner de près sa *Démonolatrie*, sur laquelle il comptait pour faire passer son nom à la postérité et pour le rendre célèbre dans les temps les plus reculés; il ne se trompait que sur la nature de la célébrité que lui devait valoir son ouvrage.

En quoi consistait, d'après Nicolas Remy, le crime de sorcellerie? Nous avons déjà dit qu'au cours du xvi° siècle la croyance au Diable est générale. En Lorraine, le Diable porte les noms les plus divers. On l'appelle maître Persin, parce qu'il apparaît sous une couleur vert foncé; il se nomme encore maître Léonard, Napnel, Jolibois, Sautebuisson, etc. Parfois l'on fait une distinction entre ces sortes de démons : ce sont des personnages différents subordonnés l'un à l'autre. Le Démon apparaît sous des formes diverses aux personnes qu'il veut conquérir; il pince ses victimes au front, pour enlever le baptême, et les invite à assister au sabbat, qui a lieu sur une lande déserte, en un endroit écarté des habitations. Les sorcières se frottent d'un onguent et sont transportées à ce sabbat en général sur un balai ou bien sur un bouc. Ce sabbat a lieu en Lorraine le samedi et le mercredi, les démons étant occupés les autres nuits ailleurs[2].

---

1. Voir *Rev. hist.*, t. XCIII, p. 225.
2. Nous résumons ici ce que dit Nicolas Remy dans la *Démonolatrie*, p. 121 et suiv.

Les sorcières s'y donnent au Diable; elles dansent une ronde échevelée, mais masquées et retournées, la tête en dehors de la ronde. Puis elles prennent un repas en commun; mais toute nourriture est insipide; car le sel y fait défaut; suivant un calembour souvent répété, les plats y viennent de *Salamanque*. Il n'y a pas non plus de pain, puisque le pain rappelle l'Eucharistie. Pendant toutes ces orgies, les diablotins font une musique infernale, en frappant des tibias contre des crânes[1]. Nicolas Remy et les juges croyaient à la réalité de ces descriptions. Une fois pourtant le procureur a un léger doute. Une sorcière a affirmé qu'à telle heure de la nuit elle avait été au sabbat; et pourtant son mari a juré qu'à la même heure elle se trouvait tranquillement couchée à côté de lui. Remy ne peut pas ne pas accorder confiance à ce témoignage; il conclut qu'un sabbat imaginaire est aussi pernicieux qu'un sabbat réel; ce sabbat donne les mêmes émotions, provoque les mêmes lassitudes; une telle femme est bien la proie du Diable. A mort donc la malheureuse !

Mais, si hommes et femmes se rendent au sabbat, ce n'est pas seulement pour se procurer des plaisirs fatigants; ils veulent surtout obtenir du Diable le pouvoir de nuire à ceux qu'ils détestent. Maître Persin leur donne un onguent mystérieux, ou bien il leur apprend des paroles magiques; à l'aide de l'un ou des autres, ils vont provoquer le malheur de leurs ennemis. Ceux-ci languissent et dépérissent peu à peu. Ou bien il leur arrive un grave accident. Ils tombent et se cassent une jambe; ils n'entendent plus; ils voient double; des boutons leur poussent sur la figure; les maris deviennent impuissants. D'autres fois, les sorciers s'en prennent au bétail. Ils font trébucher la vache ou la chèvre de leur ennemi, les blessant grièvement. Ils tarissent, par leur pouvoir magique, le lait de ces animaux. Les sorcières plantent dans le mur de l'étable, au dehors, un couteau; et elles font sur lui le signe de traire la vache; elles prononcent le mot sacramental : « Je te trais au nom du Diable », et le lait coule réellement le long du couteau. Elles enlèvent la force nutritive qui est dans l'herbe broutée par les bestiaux; chevaux, taureaux, vaches mangent et dépérissent. Au contraire, cette nourriture profite à leurs propres bêtes qui restent grasses et bien portantes.

1. *Démonolatrie*, p. 141.

Ce qui frappe surtout dans ces stupides accusations, c'est la relation que les accusateurs établissent entre une rencontre fortuite avec un sorcier et un malheur arrivé souvent des semaines, des mois, des années plus tard. Dans un procès instruit à Amance, près de Nancy, en 1591, le herdier de la commune, — c'est-à-dire celui qui garde la *herde*, le troupeau, — est accusé de sorcellerie et les bergers qui vivent isolés dans les champs fournissent un nombreux contingent de victimes. Une femme dépose qu'elle a eu un jour avec l'accusé, nommé Bulme, une querelle à cause d'une vache qu'il lui avait perdue, et, dit-elle, environ un mois après, son mari tomba malade et mourut en cinq jours. Une autre femme certifie que son mari est mort six semaines après une querelle avec le sorcier. D'autres encore viennent dire qu'après une dispute de ce genre leur cheval ou leur verrat a péri au bout de quinze jours ou d'un mois. Et c'est sur des accusations de ce genre que Bulme et sa femme furent exécutés à Amance[1]!

Les sorcières ne s'attaquent pas seulement aux hommes et aux animaux ; dans leurs réunions nocturnes, elles rassemblent les nuages, qui bientôt se condensent en grêle et qui détruisent les moissons. Voilà pourquoi, dit Nicolas Remy, quand le tonnerre gronde, quand menace la foudre, il faut sonner les cloches ; car ces mêmes cloches qui appellent les fidèles à la prière chassent le Démon. Les sorcières sont encore accusées d'avoir suscité d'autres fléaux. En décembre 1586, la femme Odile Boncourt de Haraucourt, en novembre 1586, la femme Rose Gérardin d'Étival, en février 1587, la femme Housselot de Saint-Èvre ont avoué avoir suscité un très grand nombre de souris qui ont rongé toutes les racines et causé la disette[2].

Voici, avec quelques détails, les accusations lancées contre une pauvre femme de Nancy, nommée Lasnier (*Asinaria*) : elle avait l'habitude de mendier de porte en porte, et les aumônes qu'elle recevait suffisaient à son existence. Un jour elle frappa à la maison du bailli de Nancy[3]; mais le fils aîné de celui-ci

---

1. Amance, qui avait reçu la coutume de Beaumont, avait droit de haute justice. Toutes les pièces de ce procès ont été publiées par Henri Lepage dans l'*Annuaire de la Lorraine*, 1854 ; l'article a été tiré à part sous le titre : *Une procédure de sorciers au XVI° siècle*, Nancy, Grimblot et veuve Raybois.
2. *Démonolatrie*, p. 146.
3. Le bailli de Nancy de 1577 à 1607 fut Renault de Gournay, seigneur de

sortit à l'improviste et lui ordonna de revenir à une autre heure, car pour le moment les domestiques étaient occupés; la femme répondit par des injures et aussitôt notre jeune homme tomba face à terre comme s'il s'était heurté contre un caillou. Et il affirma aux domestiques accourus que l'accident n'était pas arrivé par sa faute, qu'il était poussé par derrière par une force supérieure et qu'il se serait certainement cassé un membre, s'il n'avait eu la précaution en tombant de faire le signe de la croix. Le Démon fit alors, dit Remy, de vifs reproches à la femme Lasnier d'avoir manqué son maléfice et lui donna l'ordre de surprendre le jeune homme avant qu'il eût fait sa prière du matin et se fût garanti par le signe de la croix. Or, un matin, le jeune homme ouvrit la fenêtre de sa chambre au premier étage et voulut saisir un nid qui se trouvait sur la muraille; il tomba la tête la première et on le rapporta évanoui à la maison. Il revint bientôt à lui et dit à son père : « Père, ne me faites pas de reproche; j'ai été poussé par derrière et on a lancé un objet contre moi. » Et en effet un gros morceau de bois fut ramassé à l'endroit où il était tombé. L'enfant mourut quelque temps après; la femme Lasnier fut aussitôt arrêtée. Interrogée par Nicolas Remy, elle fait des aveux; elle est condamnée à mort et exécutée le 14 juillet 1582. Remy nous raconte qu'aussitôt après la chute de l'enfant, le Diable était venu en personne féliciter la sorcière et il accumule, pour le prouver, une série de citations de la Bible[1].

Telles étaient les accusations portées contre les sorcières et qui devaient conduire presque toujours ces malheureuses à la mort. Dans l'ancienne procédure, il fallait qu'un accusateur se présentât et soutînt la vérité de son dire par serment, témoignages ou autrement. Dans les procès de sorcellerie, il n'y a plus d'accusateurs; il n'y a, comme pour les procès de l'Inquisition, que des dénonciateurs. Un individu a à se plaindre d'une femme qui l'a injurié, il ne veut pas payer son créancier; il dénonce la femme et le créancier comme soupçonnés de sorcellerie. Le dénonciateur ne risque jamais rien. Son nom n'est pas communiqué à l'inculpé. Même dans certains pays, — ce ne fut point le cas en Lorraine, — l'on plaçait aux églises ou aux maisons communes des troncs destinés à recevoir les dénonciations anonymes; les dénonciations

Villers. Cf. Henri Lepage, *les Offices des duchés de Lorraine et de Bar*, dans les *Mémoires de la Société d'archéologie lorraine*, 1869, p. 103.

1. *Démonolatrie*, p. 272.

lâches et méprisables! Sur ces dénonciations, l'officier public se
mettait en mouvement, souvent même il ne les attendait pas. Le
procureur général faisait des tournées en Lorraine et, par le
procédé de l'enquête, — qu'il est devenu odieux le mot *inqui-
sitio!* — il recherchait les coupables.

Sur toute dénonciation, sur tout soupçon du ministère public,
une *information* est ouverte[1]. On entend toutes les personnes
qui peuvent fournir des renseignements sur les inculpés et on
consigne avec soin tous leurs dires. Tous les actes de la malheureuse femme soupçonnée, — car la proportion des femmes sorcières par rapport aux hommes était de 9/10, — sont scrutés avec
soin et tout va devenir indice qu'elle est réellement sorcière. On
l'a appelée dans une querelle sorcière, et elle n'a rien répliqué;
elle n'a pas traîné son calomniateur devant les tribunaux; indice
sûr. Au contraire, elle s'est hâtée de poursuivre celui qui l'avait
injuriée; elle a voulu détourner les soupçons; indice sûr. On ne
voit jamais une femme à l'église; c'est, dit Nicolas Remy, qu'elle
s'est donnée au Diable. Elle court sans cesse à la messe, autre
indice; car une force irrésistible pousse les sorcières vers l'église;
constatation curieuse qui montre chez ces femmes une sorte de
folie religieuse. L'information est ainsi presque toujours défavo-
rable. La malheureuse est arrêtée et jetée en prison; à Nancy,
on la mène dans les tours de la porte de la Craffe.

Nous connaissons déjà les tribunaux qui vont la juger. Elle
n'est point renvoyée devant des inquisiteurs ou devant le tribunal ecclésiastique, l'officialité. Elle comparaît, comme les autres
criminels, devant la justice ordinaire, échevins, prévôts, justice
municipale. Les juges font venir l'inculpée devant eux et pro-
cèdent à son interrogatoire; c'est l'*audition de bouche*. L'un des
échevins, — nous supposons que le procès se déroule à Nancy,
— lui demande son nom, son âge, si elle sait de quoi elle est
accusée. A cette dernière question, en général, l'inculpée ne

---

1. Souvent le procureur général de Lorraine ou le procureur des Vosges ou
d'Allemagne requièrent les officiers judiciaires inférieurs, substituts ou prévôts
d'informer secrètement des cas de sortilège et vénéfice. Une réquisition de ce
genre a été publiée par L. Quintard, *Procès de deux sorciers en 1605*, dans les
Bulletins mensuels de la Société d'archéologie lorraine, 1906, p. 16. Il s'agit de
Catherine, veuve de Claude Bailliot, et de Claude, son fils, demeurant à Matain-
court (Vosges). On reprochait à Catherine de tenir et nourrir des crapauds dans
sa maison. Les deux accusés, qui n'avouèrent pas, furent condamnés au ban-
nissement.

répond rien. Finalement, le juge lui dit son crime et expose les charges qui ont été recueillies dans l'information ; il lui demande de se défendre. D'ordinaire, l'accusée se récrie ; elle se déclare innocente des méfaits qu'on lui impute. Le juge essaie toujours de l'effrayer par la violence de ses gestes, la véhémence de son langage. Il a recours à toutes sortes de ruses pour obtenir l'aveu attendu, l'aveu qui sera considéré par lui comme une véritable victoire. S'il y a deux inculpés, il ne manque d'affirmer au second que le premier a tout avoué, alors qu'il n'en est rien ; il se complaît dans les équivoques, les sous-entendus. Jamais, dans ces interrogatoires, l'accusée n'est assistée d'un avocat ; l'avocat est même toujours absent de ces tristes procès : une sorcière ne doit point être défendue. Du reste, l'avocat ne courrait-il pas de trop grands risques? La sorcière ne pourrait-elle pas lui jeter un sort? Mais qu'on admire la logique des croyances ! Il est admis que ces méchantes femmes ne peuvent rien ni sur les juges ni sur les bourreaux, qui, par une sorte de grâce d'état, sont à l'abri de leurs coups. Nicolas Remy nous raconte que le terrible onguent que maître Persin donnait aux sorcières perdait toute vertu dès qu'il était saisi par les juges. Lui-même, qui a été sans cesse en contact avec les sorcières, est resté toujours sain de corps et d'esprit, chrétien parfait. La femme Lasnier, de Nancy, interrogée par lui, lui lança cette apostrophe : « Comme vous avez de la chance que nous ne puissions rien sur vous, ô juges! Il n'y a point d'hommes que nous désirerions plus tourmenter que vous, qui poursuivez toute notre race par de tels supplices[1]. » Nicolas Remy pouvait procéder sans risque ni péril.

On trouvait des accusés, surtout parmi les femmes, qui avouaient dès le début. Il se présente ici un cas d'auto-suggestion fort curieux. La femme croit réellement qu'elle a conclu un pacte avec le Diable; elle le crie à son juge; et, en général, avec cet aveu, elle tient des propos incohérents et orduriers; elle se complaît dans la crapule. Ces femmes ont été désignées comme sorcières parce qu'elles sont des hystériques ; elles réalisent en quelque sorte les scènes qu'elles ont entendu raconter autour d'elles; oui, elles se sont données au Diable, elles ont assisté au sabbat qu'elles décrivent avec un luxe incroyable de détails.

1. *Démonolatrie*, p. 38.

REV. HISTOR. XCIV. 1ᵉʳ FASC.   3

L'hystérie est héréditaire; et voilà pourquoi souvent les filles ont été brûlées après les mères, parce qu'elles présentaient les mêmes symptômes morbides. La maladie chez des personnes faibles d'esprit est contagieuse; voilà pourquoi beaucoup de villages sont décimés[1]. Si la femme ne se suggère pas à elle-même toutes ces visions, le juge qui l'interroge les fait naître en son esprit. Ses questions sont si nettes, si précises qu'elle arrive à douter d'elle-même. Elle avoue. L'aveu est une condamnation à mort; le procès finit après l'information et l'interrogatoire.

Mais, après tout, ces aveux étaient rares; le plus souvent, l'accusée nie. Elle déclare qu'elle n'a point eu commerce avec Satan, qu'elle n'est point sorcière. Dès lors, on procède aux *recolements* et aux *confrontations*. Le juge convoque à jour et heure déterminés tous les témoins entendus dans l'information; il les interroge d'abord en l'absence de l'accusée; il leur demande s'ils persistent en leur première déposition; il les invite à y ajouter ou à en retrancher à leur gré; c'est le *recolement*. Puis, pour la première fois, l'accusée est mise en présence de ses accusateurs; et ici la Lorraine était en avance sur d'autres pays, où jamais la victime ne connaissait les témoins, où l'on continuait d'employer l'ancien système de l'Inquisition. Témoins et accusée sont interrogés contradictoirement sur les faits de la cause : c'est la *confrontation*. Celle-ci terminée, le procureur ou le substitut présent prend ses conclusions. Si elles tendent à l'absolution de l'inculpée, elles sont définitives; mais, avec des procureurs imbus de l'esprit de Nicolas Remy, de telles conclusions devaient être rares, — l'on en trouve pourtant des exemples. — Mais, en général, les conclusions sont *interlocutoires*. Le procureur peut requérir que l'accusée nomme des témoins à décharge; mais la malheureuse n'en trouvait presque jamais. Il peut requérir aussi que l'accusée soit soumise à la question; c'était le cas ordinaire. Quand le procès avait lieu loin de Nancy, l'on demandait sur ces conclusions l'avis des échevins de Nancy; mais presque toujours dans les procès de sorcellerie les échevins opinent pour la torture. A Nancy même, point n'était besoin de consulter personne,

1. Dans le petit village d'Azelot, au canton de Saint-Nicolas-de-Port, qui compte aujourd'hui 200 habitants, et qui en comptait à peine 100 autrefois, il y eut à la fin du xvie et au début du xviie siècle jusqu'à trente procès de sorcellerie. Cf. Lepage, *les Communes de la Meurthe*, art. Azelot.

et la sentence interlocutoire ordonnant la question était immédiatement rendue.

Avant de procéder à la question, l'on soumettait l'inculpé à un chirurgien ou à un médecin. L'inculpé, homme ou femme, était rasé des pieds à la tête « partout où poil se trouve », disent les procès-verbaux, par la *personne vile*, c'est-à-dire par l'homme qui tond les chiens et récure les égouts ; puis le chirurgien cherchait s'il retrouvait sur son corps la *marque du Diable*. De même que Dieu mettait son sceau sur certains élus en reproduisant sur leurs mains, sur leur flanc et leurs pieds les blessures du Christ, de même, dans les croyances de l'époque, le Diable marquait d'un signe ineffaçable la créature qui s'était donnée à lui. Nicolas Remy consacre tout un chapitre de sa *Démonolatrie* à cette marque diabolique. C'était au médecin à trouver ce signe, qu'on reconnaissait de la façon suivante : si à l'endroit du corps marqué par Satan l'on enfonce une longue épingle, l'inculpé ne sentira aucune douleur et pas une goutte de sang ne coulera de la blessure. Cette partie du corps est devenue tout à fait insensible :

Sanguis hebet, frigentque effetae in corpore vires

(la citation est de Nicolas Remy). Ainsi, en octobre 1590, on arrête à Briey la femme Claude Bogart. Après lui avoir rasé la tête, on découvre au sommet une cicatrice que les cheveux cachaient ; Claude affirme que cette cicatrice a été causée par une pierre qui lui a été lancée. Mais le chirurgien enfonce son épingle et déclare qu'en cet endroit le Diable a mis sa griffe sur sa créature. On découvre de même une verrue sur la jambe droite de la femme Muguet, arrêtée à Essey-lès-Nancy en juin 1591. Elle ne sent aucune douleur lorsqu'on y enfonce l'épingle ; mais, dès qu'elle est piquée à côté, elle pousse des hurlements effroyables. Signe diabolique, conclut Nicolas Remy, et il écrit : « Ceux-là errent cent et cent fois, ceux-là sont des fous qui prétendent expliquer de tels phénomènes par des causes naturelles. » N'en déplaise à Nicolas Remy, n'en déplaise à l'excellent abbé Lionnois, qui composait au XVIIIᵉ siècle une histoire de Nancy et qui faisait preuve d'un bien grand scepticisme en disant : « Les épingles de ces chirurgiens n'étaient-elles pas semblables à celles de nos joueurs de gobelets qui, en se perçant le front, ne se font

de mal que dans l'esprit des sots? », — de tels phénomènes existent
et la médecine actuelle les explique par des causes naturelles ;
cette insensibilité partielle est l'un des signes de l'hystérie ; elle
peut même être provoquée par simple suggestion du médecin.

Dans tous ces procès de sorcellerie, le médecin ou le chirurgien
doit partager la responsabilité du juge. Il procédait à l'examen
du corps, trouvait la marque et donnait son certificat, qui était
une condamnation à mort. Dans ce certificat, il ne constatait pas
seulement, il interprétait. Il affirmait que cette insensibilité était
causée par l'empreinte du Démon. Dans un livre de chirurgie,
paru en 1585, on lit : « Nul ne peut nier, il n'en faut douter,
qu'il y ait des sorciers ; car cela se prouve par authorité de plusieurs docteurs et expositeurs, tant vieux que modernes, lesquels
tiennent pour chose résoluë qu'il y a des sorciers et enchanteurs
qui, par moyens subtils, diaboliques et inconnus, corrompent le
corps, l'entendement, la vie et la santé des hommes et autres
créatures, comme animaux, herbes, l'air, la terre et les eaux.
D'avantage l'expérience et la raison nous contraignent le confesser, parce que les lois ont établi des peines contre telles
manières de gens[1]. » Singulier raisonnement : il y a des sorciers,
puisqu'il y a des lois contre les sorciers. L'auteur de ce livre est
Ambroise Paré, et peut-être le grand chirurgien, qui passait en
son temps pour un novateur hardi, a-t-il causé sorcellerie avec
Nicolas Remy, lorsqu'en 1575 il arriva en Lorraine pour guérir
la duchesse Claude de France, femme de Charles III.

Le médecin a donné son certificat ; mais il faut obtenir de l'inculpé lui-même l'aveu qu'il a eu commerce avec le Diable ; et
cet aveu lui sera arraché par la torture. Nous connaissons par
un livre de praticien écrit par Claude Bourgeois, maître-échevin
de Nancy après Nicolas Remy, quels modes de torture étaient
usités en Lorraine[2]. Il y avait quatre épreuves qui étaient gra-
duées.

C'étaient d'abord les *grésillons*. L'instrument était formé de
trois lames de fer qu'on rapprochait à l'aide d'une vis. On met-

1. Ambroise Paré, *Œuvres complètes*, éd. Malgaigne, t. III, p. 53. Ce passage,
tiré du *Livre sur les monstres et les prodiges*, ne se trouve que dans l'édition
de 1585.

2. *Pratique civile et criminelle pour les justices inférieures du duché de
Lorraine, conformément à celle des sièges ordinaires de Nancy*, Nancy,
J. Garnich, 1614, iv-53 feuillets in-4°.

tait entre ces lames le bout des doigts de la main ou du pied jusqu'à l'ongle et on serrait. La souffrance était atroce; la victime sortait de l'épreuve les doigts entièrement écrasés. Venait ensuite l'*échelle*. C'était une échelle ordinaire dont une extrémité touchait terre, tandis que l'autre reposait sur un tréteau à trois pieds du sol. L'accusé était étendu nu ou en chemise sur l'échelle, les pieds attachés au barreau inférieur, les mains liées, à l'autre extrémité, à une corde qui s'enroulait autour d'un tourniquet; on mettait en mouvement le tourniquet, et les bras, le corps entier s'allongeait. « L'accusé, dit Claude Bourgeois, souffre ainsi de grandes douleurs, tant à cause de l'extension violente de tout le corps qui s'allonge contre nature que pour les diverses parties affligées en cette extension, comme veines, artères, muscles, mais principalement les nerfs et tendons, qui sont toutes parties douées d'un sentiment fort exquis et conséquemment susceptibles de grandes douleurs. » Pour augmenter les souffrances de l'accusé, on lui faisait passer sous le dos un morceau de bois pendant qu'on l'étirait. On lui jetait aussi souvent de l'eau froide à la figure; on lui introduisait par un entonnoir une certaine quantité d'eau dans la bouche, ou encore l'on imprimait à cette échelle mobile des secousses savamment calculées.

Tandis que la victime reste couchée sur l'échelle, on lui infligera la troisième épreuve, les *tortillons*. Les bras et les jambes nus sont attachés par de grosses cordes aux montants, et la corde est serrée autant qu'il est possible. Puis entre les membres et la corde on passe des bâtons ronds qu'on emploie comme un tourniquet. La corde est serrée davantage encore; elle pénètre dans les chairs, qui sont de plus en plus comprimées en certains endroits et ressortent plus loin en bourrelets meurtris.

Enfin, si l'accusé n'a pas avoué, on a recours à l'*estrapade*. Au plafond de la chambre de torture est attachée une poulie, dans laquelle on passe une corde, semblable aux poulies dont se servent les maçons pour monter leurs pierres. L'accusé, en chemise, les mains liées derrière le dos, est attaché par la ceinture à ce crochet et tiré violemment en l'air. On lui fait exécuter ainsi un certain nombre de tours; parfois, pour augmenter sa souffrance, on étire le corps en attachant au pied de grosses pierres; Claude Bourgeois assure que quelques-unes de ces pierres pesaient de soixante à quatre-vingts livres.

C'étaient là les seules tortures autorisées en Lorraine par les échevins de Nancy. Et ils se croyaient des esprits libéraux. Ils prohibaient les modes plus atroces encore. Ils défendaient de faire asseoir l'inculpé sur une selle hérissée de pointes, de le pendre dans une cheminée pour l'enfumer, de le priver de sommeil pendant une longue période, en le tenant éveillé par des moyens artificiels. Ceux qui ont visité certains musées de torture d'Allemagne seront obligés de reconnaître que les échevins de Nancy ont été moins cruels que certaines justices d'outre-Rhin[1].

La torture est toujours administrée en présence d'un chirurgien. Celui-ci doit arrêter le bourreau quand il lui semble que le patient est à bout de forces; on ne doit pas détacher de l'échelle un cadavre; le fait s'est produit parfois. On commence en général par montrer à l'inculpé les instruments de torture; on lui explique la manière dont on s'en sert, les souffrances qu'ils produisent, et, devant cette menace, on l'interroge de nouveau; on le conjure d'avouer son crime. S'il persiste dans ses dénégations, le bourreau fait son office. Rarement une femme résiste jusqu'au bout. Tout à coup elle s'écrie que c'est trop souffrir; elle raconte tout ce qu'on veut; oui, elle a été au sabbat; elle a eu accointance avec le Diable. Le juge lui demande le nom de ses complices; elle nomme tous les noms qui lui traversent la tête, noms illustres ou noms ignorés, grands personnages de l'état ou pauvres mendiants. C'étaient de nouvelles victimes qu'elle désignait, et chaque procès en engendrait une série d'autres. Parfois le juge, pour obtenir plus vite l'aveu, usait de stratagème. Il promettait à la pauvre torturée sa grâce et une chaumière; mais il sous-entendait par restriction mentale la grâce d'être étranglée avant d'être brûlée, et la chaumière, c'étaient les bottes de paille du bûcher. Le juge aussi, dans la recherche des complices, désignait parfois un homme ou une femme par son nom : « N'étiez-vous pas au sabbat avec un tel ou avec une telle? » Ces pratiques, il est juste de le reconnaître, étaient condamnées par les échevins de Nancy. Claude Bourgeois écrit : « Il n'est loisible d'user d'artifices, de

---

1. Des procureurs lorrains demandaient des supplices plus terribles. Un procureur, Didier Colin, écrit sur un exemplaire de la *Pratique civile et criminelle*, de Claude Bourgeois : « Aucuns disent qu'il n'y a douleur si grande que celle qui vient de la distillation d'eau froide sur le nombril. Aucuns que les millepèdes, cloportes ou pourcelets Saint-Antoine, appliqués et retenus sur le nombril, font plus grand rage et tourment. » Cité par R. de Souhesmes, *la Torture et les anesthésiques*, dans les *Mémoires de la Société d'archéologie lorraine*, 1901, p. 10.

paroles mensongères ou captieuses comme de faire entendre au criminel qu'il confesse librement ce qu'on luy demande soubs espérance et promesse de pardon et autres, cela étant très pernicieux, et dont les juges practiquant tels abus et injustices en répondront devant Dieu, et, cela estant descouvert, debvront estre châtiés exemplairement par les juges supérieurs qu'il appartiendra » ; — et, en effet, certains juges ont été destitués pour n'avoir pas suivi ces préceptes. — Claude Bourgeois écrit encore : « Il ne faudra particulariser ou nommer personne, suggérer, — *le mot est dans le texte*, — ou désigner par habits ou autrement, ains faudra interroger généralement qui sont les complices. »

Le lendemain des aveux, l'accusée était interrogée à nouveau hors du lieu de torture. Il arrivait souvent qu'elle rétractait ses aveux antérieurs, qu'elle déclarait n'avoir su ce qu'elle disait, n'avoir parlé que sous l'empire de la douleur. Le juge aurait dû réfléchir à ses rétractations ; il aurait dû se rappeler le proverbe latin : *torquere est extorquere ;* il aurait dû se dire, comme plus tard l'auteur tragique[1] :

La torture interroge et la douleur répond ;

mais, dans ces rétractations, il voit une nouvelle manœuvre de Satan ; et l'accusée est remise aussitôt à la question[2]. Après les grésillons, l'échelle ; après l'échelle, les tortillons et puis l'estrapade. Quelques-unes résistent jusqu'au bout et sont renvoyées des fins de la plainte[3], mais le cas est tout à fait extraordinaire.

L'aveu une fois fait est aussitôt consigné par écrit : c'est la sentence de mort. Les juges n'ont qu'à en prendre acte et à prononcer en conséquence. Dans les juridictions inférieures, la sentence

---

1. Raynouard, *les Templiers.*

2. Claude Bourgeois se rend bien compte des objections qu'on peut faire à la torture : « La question est dangereuse, écrit-il ; le plus souvent l'innocent y confesse ; autrefois, le coupable malfaicteur l'endure et à ce moyen est absous. » Mais de ces prémisses il n'ose pas tirer la conclusion.

3. Quelques accusées très exaltées arrivaient à devenir insensibles à la douleur. Le juge le savait et voyait dans ce fait une manœuvre de Satan. Le Diable aidait ses suppôts : il se logeait sous les ongles et dans les poils. C'était un autre motif pour raser les victimes. Le diable leur avait appris des formules magiques qui supprimaient la douleur ; aussi on les exorcisait. Cf. R. de Souhesmes, *loc. cit.*, p. 5 et suiv. Les accusées qui ne manifestaient pas de douleur n'étaient pas relâchées ; on renvoyait seulement celles qui n'avouaient pas, malgré leurs évidentes souffrances.

est provisoire, les pièces du procès sont renvoyées aux échevins de Nancy; ceux-ci déclarent en général que le procès a été bien jugé, et, aussitôt leur réponse arrivée, les juges rendent la sentence définitive. A Nancy, il n'y a qu'une sentence définitive.

Nous donnons ici la formule de ces sentences de mort, prononcées par les tribunaux locaux, telle que nous la rapporte Claude Bourgeois; cette formule a été répétée des milliers de fois en Lorraine :

« Veu le procès extraordinairement instruit par Nous les prevôt *ou* Maire et gens de justice de N. (*ici le nom de la localité*), à la requeste du procureur d'office, contre N., prevenu et accusé de sortilège et vénéfice, sçavoir l'information, l'audition de bouche dudit accusé, recolements et confrontations, les conclusions dudit procureur en date du ..., notre sentence du ..., par laquelle aurions condamné ledit accusé à la question ordinaire et extraordinaire, l'acte et procès-verbal de ladite question, les conclusions définitives dudit sieur procureur et l'avis de Messieurs les maître eschevin et eschevins de Nancy (*c'est l'énumération exacte de tous les actes de la procédure; voici maintenant la sentence*), disons que, par ladicte procedure et par la confession dudict accusé, iceluy est suffisamment atteint et convaincu dudict crime de sortilege et vénéfice; de quoi l'avons condamné et condamnons à estre delivré entre les mains de l'exécuteur de haulte justice, pour par luy être exposé au carcan à la vue du peuple l'espace d'un demi-quart d'heure ou environ, puis mené et conduict au lieu où l'on a accoustumé supplicier les delinquants, et illec attaché à un poteau, y estre estranglé après qu'il aura aucunement senty l'ardeur du feu, son corps ars, bruslé et reduit en cendres, tous et chascuns de ses biens declarez acquis et confisqués à qui il appartiendra, les frais de justice pris sur iceux au préalable. »

Beaucoup d'accusés, pour ne pas affronter cette série d'horreurs, se donnaient la mort en prison. Que de fois ne trouve-t-on pas dans les archives des mentions comme la suivante : « 1593. Marguerite, veuve de Thiébaut le vigneron, demeurant à Belleau[1], accusée de vénéfice et de sortilège, étant détenue en prison de ce lieu, se serait par mains violentes précipitée à la mort. » Nicolas Remy reconnaît que les suicides en prison sont

1. Cant. de Pont-à-Mousson.

nombreux; il avoue par exemple qu'en juillet 1581 Didier
Finance, de Mandray[1], a échappé au supplice en s'enfonçant dans
la gorge un couteau qu'on avait oublié près de sa main, et il
ajoute : « Il me souvient qu'en cette année et l'année précédente
il s'est trouvé en Lorraine environ quinze personnages qui se
sont fait justice à eux-mêmes, pour ne pas être un exemple à
tous[2]. » Remy a horreur de ces morts : « J'ai hâte, écrit-il, d'en
venir à des procès qui eurent de meilleures issues, — *ad ea quae
exitus meliores habuerunt* », — et il raconte les supplices de
Jeanne, sorcière à Ban-sur-Meurthe, d'Anne Drigie, de Haraucourt, et de Didier Gérard, de Vennezey[3]. Le bourreau ne perdait pas tout droit si la victime se donnait la mort. Le cadavre
était exposé aux fourches patibulaires et ensuite brûlé.

La sentence définitive, une fois rendue, était aussitôt mise à
exécution. Un confesseur devait préparer la sorcière à la mort;
et nous pourrions répéter des confesseurs ce que nous avons dit
des médecins; jamais l'un de ceux qui avait reçu les dernières
confidences des victimes n'a protesté de leur innocence; si l'accusé niait encore au tribunal de la pénitence, le confesseur attribuait ces dénégations à une méchanceté endurcie et aux ruses du
Démon[4]. La condamnée, avant le supplice, était exposée quelques
minutes au carcan. A Nancy, cette exposition avait lieu sur la
place Saint-Èvre, tant que les prisons furent à la porte de la
Craffe. Plus tard, elle eut lieu dans la Ville-Neuve, sur la place
du Marché, devant l'hôtel de ville. Au-dessus de la malheureuse,
on plaçait un écriteau indiquant son crime : guenoche et sorcière.
On la livrait à la risée d'une multitude sans pitié et qui lan-
çait d'ignobles injures. Après l'exposition, la sorcière était
menée au supplice. ·Au début, devant le portail de l'église Saint-

1. Cant. et arr. de Saint-Dié, Vosges.
2. *Démonolatrie*, p. 347.
3. Haraucourt, cant. de Saint-Nicolas; Ban-sur-Meurthe, Vennezey, cant. de
Gerbéviller.
4. Nous devons pourtant citer un jésuite allemand qui osa protester. Frédéric Spee avait accompagné dans les environs de Bamberg et de Würzbourg de
nombreuses sorcières au bûcher, et, comme l'évêque de Würzbourg, Jean Phi-
lippe de Schönborn, s'étonnait que ses cheveux fussent blancs avant l'âge, il
répondit : « C'est à cause de la douleur éprouvée en conduisant des innocentes
au supplice. » Spee fit paraître en 1631 un livre où il s'élevait contre la sorcellerie : *Cautio criminalis seu de processibus contra sagas liber ad magistratus
Germaniae hoc tempore necessarius*. Sur ce livre, cf. Soldan, *Geschichte der
Hexenprocesse*, t. II, p. 187.

Èvre, elle faisait amende honorable, une torche noire à la main. Le cortège sortait par la porte de la Craffe et se rendait sur les bords de la Meurthe, à quelque distance de la route de Nancy à Champigneulles, en un endroit appelé le Paquis, où aujourd'hui se dresse l'usine du Pont-Fleuri[1]. Là le bûcher était dressé. Il se composait d'un cent de fagots et d'une corde de bois[2]. Au-dessus se dressait un poteau où la victime était attachée. La sorcière n'était pourtant pas brûlée, à proprement parler. A peine avait-elle senti la flamme que le bourreau l'étranglait. Le corps était ensuite brûlé et les cendres dispersées. On ne jetait vivantes dans le feu que les sorcières endurcies, celles qui avaient refusé de faire pénitence. A ces exécutions assistait une foule gouailleuse, — la même foule ignoble qui se presse aujourd'hui autour des échafauds.

Suggérées par le juge, des mères avaient avoué qu'elles avaient emmené au sabbat leurs enfants, jeunes garçons et jeunes filles de sept à dix ans. Ces enfants eux-mêmes avaient parfois avoué leurs forfaits; ils avaient décrit le sabbat, répété les chansons licencieuses qu'on y chantait; ils soutenaient avoir tourné la broche de Satan! Les échevins de Nancy n'osaient condamner ces malheureux; on se bornait à leur mettre les épaules nues et à les frapper trois fois de verges devant le bûcher où brûlait leur mère; et cette condamnation devint en Lorraine d'un usage courant. Mais Nicolas Remy s'élève contre ce qu'il regarde comme une faiblesse : « Je n'ai jamais pensé que de cette manière il était satisfait aux lois[3]. » Avec une férocité inouïe, dans un passage qui nous paraît le plus abominable de la *Démonolatrie*, il réclame contre les pauvres êtres la peine capitale. Il rappelle l'histoire des quarante-deux enfants de Béthel qu'Élisée avait fait manger par les ours, uniquement parce qu'ils l'avaient nommé vieux chauve. Et il veut que toute graine de sorciers soit anéantie.

Les enfants des sorciers pâtissaient encore d'une autre façon, même s'ils n'étaient pas impliqués dans les crimes de leurs parents. Tous les biens étaient confisqués au profit de l'État, et les malheureux, repoussés partout, restaient sans ressources. La

1. Au début du xvii⁰ siècle, il y eut quelques exécutions sur la place du Marché.
2. Voir les comptes des receveurs.
3. « Sed ne hac quidem ratione numquam putavi plene legibus esse satisfactum » (*Démonolatrie*, p. 200-201).

plupart des condamnés étaient pauvres, sans doute; mais il y en eut aussi de riches. On put soupçonner que le duc Charles IV envoya au bûcher Melchior de La Vallée, chantre de la collégiale Saint-Georges, non seulement pour compromettre sa femme Nicole, baptisée par le prétendu sorcier, mais encore pour acquérir son grand domaine de Sainte-Anne, sur la route de Laxou[1]. On a pu dire que les procès de sorcellerie étaient si nombreux en Lorraine uniquement parce que les biens des condamnés étaient acquis aux seigneurs[2].

Nous avons ainsi suivi la sorcière depuis son arrestation jusqu'à son supplice. Le jour où arrivait à la justice la dénonciation anonyme, elle était presque sûrement perdue. Comme ceux qui entrent dans les enfers, elle devait laisser toute espérance. Le drame que nous venons de raconter eut, au temps où Nicolas Remy fut échevin de Nancy, puis procureur général, de 1576 à 1606, soixante à quatre-vingts représentations par an[3]; et, après sa retraite et sa mort, l'impulsion donnée par lui dura. De 1606 à 1633, les bûchers s'allumèrent encore à mainte reprise; pourtant, peu à peu, le mouvement se ralentit et les rôles des échevins de Nancy furent moins encombrés. Le total des sorciers et sorcières brûlés ne laisse pas que d'être considérable; et cette épidémie de sorcellerie qui sévit sur le duché a fait plus de victimes que la peste; la sottise de l'homme est plus nuisible que les plus terribles fléaux de la nature. En l'année 1633, les Français occupèrent la Lorraine; le tribunal des échevins de Nancy fut supprimé; les magistrats français qui remplacèrent les magistrats lorrains étaient plus éclairés; puis, au milieu des guerres et de l'occupation étrangère, d'autres préoccupations absorbèrent les esprits; on laissa les sorcières en repos. Quand le duc Charles IV rentra dans ses états, en 1661, il y eut encore de-ci

1. On consultera, sur Melchior de La Vallée, Henri Lepage, *les Chartreuses de Sainte-Anne et de Bosserville* (Nancy, 1851), et un autre article du même, *Melchior de La Vallée et une gravure de Jacques Bellange*, dans les *Mémoires de la Société d'archéologie*, 1882, p. 257. Un autre procès célèbre fut celui d'André des Bordes, maître d'armes du duc Henri II. Cf. Henri Lepage, *André des Bordes, épisode de l'histoire des sorciers en Lorraine*, dans les *Mémoires de la Société d'archéologie*, 1857, p. 5-55. Nous comptons raconter prochainement l'histoire de ces deux procès.

2. En Allemagne, la confiscation n'était pas de règle. Voir Soldan, t. I, p. 453.

3. Il avoue avoir condamné à mort, de 1576 à 1592, comme échevin, 900 victimes : ce qui nous donne une moyenne annuelle de soixante, et les exécutions furent plus nombreuses après sa nomination de procureur.

de-là quelques exécutions. En 1661, Jeannon Maronde, femme de Jean La Ronze; en 1670, Jeannon, femme de Georges Grandidier, furent brûlées à Saint-Dié[1], en terre ecclésiastique, où les vieilles superstitions avaient poussé des racines plus profondes. Mais en 1682 fut rendu, sous l'inspiration de Colbert, l'édit qui défendait aux cours et aux tribunaux d'admettre dorénavant l'accusation de sorcellerie sabbatique; et cet édit fut appliqué à la Lorraine, que la France avait occupée une seconde fois en 1670.

Dans sa *Démonolatrie*, Nicolas Remy écrit ces mots : « Malheur à ceux qui ont conclu un pacte avec l'enfer... Mais malheur aussi à ceux qui cherchent à diminuer l'odieux d'un crime aussi horrible et exécrable, qui admettent les circonstances atténuantes de la crainte, de l'âge, du sexe, de l'imprudence ou d'autres excuses analogues. » En conséquence, dans l'exercice de son ministère, il a toujours refusé les circonstances atténuantes. Certes, Nicolas Remy eût été bien étonné si on lui avait dit qu'un jour il serait l'accusé. Soyons plus indulgent que lui; rappelons tout ce qui peut être dit en sa faveur : ses opinions étaient celles de son temps, et c'est à elles plus qu'à sa personne qu'il faut nous en prendre; il croyait faire œuvre agréable à Dieu, sauver la religion et la société; il pensait paraître au tribunal suprême la conscience pure et tranquille; il s'y serait même fait un argument des bûchers qu'il avait allumés. Mais pourtant il nous faut le condamner, parce qu'il lui manquait l'une des qualités que nous croyons indispensable au magistrat, la bonté. Peut-être avec plus de bonté aurait-il eu parfois des doutes et aurait-il été moins sûr de ses raisonnements. Avec plus de bonté, il eût été plus intelligent. Armé par la loi d'un pouvoir terrible, le magistrat doit se défier de lui-même et de sa raison, rechercher toujours les circonstances atténuantes et ouvrir son cœur à la pitié. Nicolas Remy ne fut pas un bon juge.

Ch. PFISTER.

---

1. Gaston Save, *la Sorcellerie à Saint-Dié*, dans le *Bulletin de la Société philomathique de Saint-Dié*, 1887-1888.

Melancholia and Witchcraft :
the debate between Wier, Bodin, and Scot

Sydney ANGLO

Professeur à l'Université de Swansea

> An other [man] there was which thought his Buttocks were made of glasse, inso
> much that he durst not do any thing but standing, for feare least if he should sitte,
> he should breake his rumpe, and the Glasse flye into peeces [1].

This amusing, and seemingly trivial, story concerning the delusions of a sixteenth-century victim of melancholia serves to introduce my subject which is, in
reality, not amusing at all, concerning as it does one of the more horrific aspects
of intellectual history : that is the persecution of witches. Nor is the subject trivial
for — as I hope to show — it implies matters concerning sixteenth-century habits
of thought, the use of evidence, and the status of authority, which are crucial to
any student of Renaissance ideas, and more particularly to those who are interested
in *folie et déraison*.

The man who thought that his buttocks were made of glass is one of several
examples given by the Dutch physician Levinus Lemnius in his treatise, *De habitu
et constitutione corporis*, to illustrate various types of melancholic persons and
their delusions. Elsewhere Lemnius had argued that disease is caused by the
humours, and not by evil spirits ; and that " Melancholicos, Maniacos, Phreneticos,
quique ex alia causa furore perciti sunt, nonnunque linguam alienam personare,
quam non didicerint, nec tamen esse Daemoniacos " [2]. And the idea, that those
afflicted with mental diseases are prone to visions and delusions, was not at all
unusual in the sixteenth century. Pomponazzi had suggested that melancholia
inspired its victims with extraordinary visions [3]. Cardanus had written at length
about the delusions of melancholia, and had observed the probable relationship
between ill-health and malnutrition on the one hand, and visions and witchcraft
belief on the other [4]. And many physicians, such as Durastantes and Leonhard
Fuchs, had described the evident connections between melancholia and the deception of the senses — especially of sight and of hearing [5].

---

[1] Levinus LEMNIUS, *The Touchstone of Complexions*, tr. Thomas Newton, London, 1576,
fol. 151r-v. Cfr the original version, *De habitu et constitutione corporis*, Antwerp, 1561,
fol. 141v.

[2] Levinus LEMNIUS, *Occulta naturae miracula*, Antwerp, 1559, Lib. II, caps. 1 & 2.

[3] Pietro POMPONAZZI, *On the Immortality of the Soul*, tr. W.H. Hay, in *The Renaissance
Philosophy of Man*, ed. E. Cassirer, P.O. Kristeller & J.H. Randall, Chicago, 1948, p. 373. The
Tractatus de immortalitate animae was first published in 1516 at Bologna.

[4] Hieronymus CARDANUS, *De rerum varietate libri xvii*, Basle, 1557, Lib. XV, Cap. 80.

[5] On Durastantes, see Lynn THORNDIKE, *History of Magic and Experimental Science*,
Columbia U.P., 1923-1958, VI, pp. 517-19. See also Leonhard FUCHS, *De curandi ratione
libri octo*, Lyons, 1548, Lib. I, caps. 29-34.

14

Now the relevance of all this to the witchcraft debate of the late sixteenth century is, I believe, obvious. Consider for a moment the intellectual bases of the whole complex of magical, demonic, and witchcraft belief. First, there was the authority of the Scriptures from which texts such as " Thou shalt not suffer a witch to live " (*Exodus* XXII.18), and stories such as that of the Witch of Endor (II *Samuel* 28), were cited *ad nauseam* by defenders of the witch persecution. Second, there was the authority of the Christian Fathers — and especially of Saint Augustine — which gave substantial support for belief in the interference of demons in the affairs of men. Third, there was the authority of classical literature where poets such as Homer, Vergil, and Ovid, were regularly cited as having historical validity. Fourth, there was the authority of the tradition of Neoplatonic magic, extending from the *Prisci Theologi* — Orpheus, Hermes Trismegistus, and Zoroaster — through Plotinus, Porphyry, and Iamblichus, to the widely-disseminated views of a writer such as Marsilio Ficino. Fifth, there was an enormous body of mediaeval scientific writing which served to confirm magical correspondences, astral influences, the operation of aerial spirits, the efficacy of talismanic magic in particular, and the possibility of working transitive magical effects in general. Sixth, there was the Christian faith itself, founded upon, and authenticated by, miraculous occurrences. Seventh, there was a mass of popular and folk belief which, in turn, gained an especial authority from an eighth basis : that is the accumulated evidence of innumerable legal processes where witches and magicians had been accused of diabolical practices, had confessed, had been found guilty, and had been duly punished.

All this added up to a towering edifice of authority which, in the sixteenth century, made belief in the reality of demonic magic much more likely, and intellectually much more respectable, than scepticism. How would it have been possible to undermine this edifice ? It was clearly necessary to shake the comprehensive authority of the Scriptures themselves. It was necessary to discredit much of the classical and patristic literature on the subject. And it was necessary, somehow, to destroy the seemingly conclusive evidence of the trials themselves — with their confessions, and their examples of demonic possessions, metamorphoses, and the like.

It was principally with this last class of evidence that the medical argument became relevant : that is in arguing from clinical observation of cases traditionally subject to demonic interpretations, but susceptible to a natural explanation. It might have been possible to attribute to disease a good deal of the material drawn from the testimony of witches — particularly those troublesome confessions which had been made, apparently, without the constraint of torture. Thus the relationship between melancholia, mental disease, and witchcraft, was a fundamentally important one ; and I propose, in this paper, to examine this problem as it was discussed in the writings of three very dissimilar late sixteenth-century thinkers : Johan Wier ; Jean Bodin ; and Reginald Scot.

The best-known, and most praised, sixteenth-century author who sought to utilise clinical observation to undermine witchcraft beliefs, was Johan Wier, a Lutheran physician who served Duke William III of Berg, Jülich, and Cleves, from 1550 till his death in 1588. His *De praestigiis daemonum* first appeared in 1563 at Basle ; and modern estimates of Wier's work have, in general, been very high. It has, indeed, become a commonplace to regard Wier as the first, and most important, anti-witchcraft writer ; to praise his common sense, his humanity, and his skilful deployment of medical evidence ; to enthuse over his allegedly liberal-minded scepticism [6] ; and even to see him as "the founder of modern psychiatry"[7]. However, very recently, Wier's role as a humane and intelligent critic of magic has been called into question : and, I think, rightly [8]. Of course it is not possible, within the confines of the present paper, to examine in detail the content of his vast and rambling work. But I believe that, even when we consider his own speciality — that is his opinions as a physician and as a diagnostician of mental disease — Wier is very much less impressive than his popular image.

Let us first consider the chapters which Wier devotes to disease as a source for witchcraft belief. He has little new to say about this problem. His views on which people are subject to delusions, and the kind of delusions to which they are subject, are precisely those of his predecessors in this field. Lemnius, for example, had pointed out that, though diseases are caused by humours and not by evil spirits, " spiritus tamen aëreos se iis, ut tempestatibus immiscere ac faces subdere " [9]. While Jason Pratz, in his important *De cerebri morbis*, had already made the connection which was so crucial in later discussions of the theme, and which was so destructive of many attempts to offer a wholly naturalistic explanation of the confessions of witches : " Accidit profecto daemones, ut sunt tenues, et incompraehensibiles spiritus sese insinuare corporibus hominum, qui occulte in visceribus operti valetudinem vitiant, morbos citant, somniis animos exterrent, mentes furoribus quatiunt, ut omnino alienum non fuerit de mania correptis ambigere, huiusmodo ne spiritu pulsentur [10]. "

Wier takes us no further. " Les gens plus sujets à estre assaillis de ces folies, sont ceux qui ont un temperament et complexion qui aisément obéit à une persuasion devenue telle, ou par les causes de dehors, ou estant touchee par les illusions du diable, ou essayee & tentee par le faux donner à entendre d'iceluy : ou comme estant instrument assez propre à sa volonté. Tels sont les melancholiques...[11]. " Thus Wier admits that certain folk are subject to delusions. Indeed, this is a major plank of his argument. But when he comes to explain how delusions come about, all that he can offer is the assertion that illness renders such people an easy prey to the wiles of demons ! And who are the easiest prey of all ? Wier can provide the answer to that question. " Le diable ennemi fin, ruzé & cauteleux, induit volontiers le sexe feminin, lequel est inconstant à raison de sa complexion,

---

[6] See, for example, E.T. WITHINGTON, " Dr. John Weyer and the Witch Mania ", *Studies in the History and Method of Science*, ed. C. Singer, Oxford, 1917, pp. 189-224 ; G. ZILBOORG & G.W. HENRY, *A History of Medical Psychology*, New York, 1941, pp. 207-35 ; H.R. TREVOR-ROPER, *The European Witch-Craze of the 16th and 17th Centuries*, London, 1969, pp. 73-75.

[7] Gregory ZILBOORG, *The Medical Man and the Witch during the Renaissance*, Baltimore, 1935, p. 205.

[8] See D.P. WALKER, *Spiritual and Demonic Magic from Ficino to Campanella*, London, 1958, pp. 152-156 ; E. William MONTER, " Inflation and Witchcraft : the Case of Jean Bodin ", in *Action and Conviction in Early Modern Europe*, ed. T.K. Rabb & J.E. Seigel, Princeton U.P., 1969, pp. 379-84 ; C.R. BAXTER, introduction to a facsimile ed. of the augmented French version (1579) of Wier's work. This last essay was written for the series *Bibliotheca Diabolica* : but the volume has not yet appeared.

[9] Levinus LEMNIUS, *Occulta naturae miracula*, fol. 97.

[10] Jason PRATZ, *De cerebri morbis*, Basle, 1549, pp. 213-14. At p. 262 Pratz makes a similar point concerning the way in which demons insinuate themselves into melancholiacs.

[11] Johan WIER, *Histoires Disputes et Discours des Illusions et Impostures des Diables, des Magiciens Infames, Sorcieres et Empoisonneurs etc.*, ed. Bourneville & Axenfeld, Paris, 1885, I, p. 298. I have used this reprint of the 1579 ed. throughout this paper.

de legere croyance, malicieux, impatient, melancholique pour ne pouvoir commander à ses affections : & principalement les vieilles debiles, stupides, & d'esprit
chancelant [12]. " And how does the enlightened Wier arrive at this point of view ?
Because this is attested in the Scriptures, Valerius Maximus, Fulgentius, Aristotle,
Lactantius, Saint Augustine, Gratian, and a veritable blizzard of legal glosses.

Wier now considers melancholy in general ; and, like his predecessors, he
presents us with a series of extraordinary cases of mental delusion ; explaining,
very significantly, how the Devil and his demons are able to exploit the corrupted
fantasy of the sick. " Et tout ainsi comme par les humeurs & fumees l'usage de la
raison est interessé es yvrongnes, es frenetiques & aussi es mélancholiques passions ; ainsi le diable, qui est un esprit, peut aisément, par la permission de Dieu,
les esmouvoir, les acommoder à ses illusions, & corrompre la raison [13]. " On this
basis, Wier is able to move on to specific instances ; arguing, for example, that
physical transformations — such as are alleged to take place in lycanthropy — are,
in fact, merely the deranged fantasies of the sick. However — and this is absolutely
typical of Wier — he immediately vitiates his own argument by adding : " Ou
bien il faut penser que ces loups sont les diables mesmes, qui ont pris ceste figure,
à celle fin de mieux enlasser en leurs deceptions ceste maniere de gens credules,
pour charger davantage les innocens, et rendre le Magistrat coulpable du sang
innocent [14]. "

In a subsequent chapter, Wier suggests that confessions in witch trials are the
result of the Devil driving the accused out of their senses. But, again typical of
Wier, this crucial attempt to discredit the accumulated evidence of numberless
trials is merely offered as an assertion, based upon earlier authority, which in any
case leaves the Devil — as it were — in full command [15]. And the same is true of
Wier's attempts to discredit belief in transvection, and in incubus and carnal
copulation between women and devils. The first he attributes to delusions caused
by drugs ; the second to delusions caused by disordered imagination.

Here, I think, we can clearly see Wier's inability to integrate his observations
within an ordered argument. He offers what is, ostensibly, a medical explanation
of women's delusions with regard to demonic sexual intercourse. With an accumulation of authorities Wier establishes that virgins always have an imperforate
hymen. Therefore, were the Devil to have real intercourse with them, the hymen
would be ruptured [16]. But Wier does not seem to see that, while he is perhaps
offering us a means of establishing whether or not intercourse has taken place in
any one specific case, he is in no way proving that such intercourse has not taken
place hitherto.

I could easily go on discussing Wier's *non sequiturs* in this way ; but I hope
that enough has been said to raise doubts even about his medical arguments. It is,
however, when one comes to set these within the larger context of his work, that

[12] *Ibid.*, p. 300.
[13] *Ibid.*, p. 313. Wier asserts that he could collect together " une infinité d'exemples, là où
vous pourriez voir les sens interessez en diverses sortes, par ce seul humeur, ou par les vapeurs
fumeuses de la melancholie, qui infecte le siege de l'esprit, dont procedent tous ces monstres
fantastiques " (p. 308).
[14] *Ibid.*, p. 321.
[15] *Ibid.*, pp. 323-7. Wier's case here rests on the argument advanced by Gianfrancesco
PONZINIBIO in his *Tractatus de Lamiis*. Wier cites the ed. which appeared in *Primum (-deci-
mum septimum) volumen tractatum ex variis iuris interpretibus collectorum*, Lyons, 1549, X.
[16] *Ibid.*, pp. 392-8.

the whole edifice comes crashing down. As already seen, Wier's medical position is precisely that of a Levinus Lemnius, or a Jason Pratz : there are mental illnesses which cause delusions ; but these mental illnesses, in fact, render their victims especially liable to demonic interference. An apologist such as Zilboorg has attempted to argue that when Wier talks about devils and demons, he is being merely figurative, not literal [17]. Now this is certainly true of Reginald Scot. But it is just as certainly *not* true of Wier. Wier's devils and demons are real devils and demons. They really do insinuate themselves into defective minds. They really do pose as wolves, or as other creatures to entrap men into sin. And they really do traffic with human beings. One example must suffice here to indicate hundreds of instances throughout Wier's work. The miracles whereby Pharoah's magicians transformed rods into serpents (always a crucial test-case in magical debates) may, says Wier, be explained in many ways : but the most likely explanation, in his view, is for us to remember " que les diables, par leur grande vitesse & alegresse peuvent oster & faire evanouir quelques choses au lieu desquelles ils peuvent supposer les dragons, des serpens, ou autres telles matieres " [18].

Wier's position is an impossible one. If the Devil and his host of demons can wreak physical effects ; can work corporeally ; and can traffic with men — as Wier constantly admits — then there remains scant logical objection to the belief that men might equally traffic with demons. Moreover — and this is the last nail in the coffin of Wier's reputation as an enlightened humanitarian — we must note that, while his *De praestigiis daemonum* is full of sympathy for falsely-accused old women, it is bitter against the male witch and magician who are to be punished with the full rigour of those very laws which Wier, conventionally, is supposed to have condemned [19]. Bodin recognised these weaknesses and used them as a stick with which to thrash Wier ; while Scot, also recognising these weaknesses, concentrated upon destroying belief in demons and in the Devil himself, as offering the only solution to the whole witchcraft problem.

Wier's work was immediately popular, and went through several editions, culminating in the huge augmented text issued by Jacques Chovet in 1579 [20]. In the following year there appeared the *Démonomanie des Sorciers* of Jean Bodin, in which the views of those who wished to destroy witches and magicians were systematically sustained, and which Bodin concluded with an impassioned *Refutation des Opinions de Jean Wier* [21]. Bodin's is, of course, one of the most famous names in the history of sixteenth-century thought : but his *Démonomanie* has presented a problem to its modern readers. Scholars have, generally, either avoided comment by concentrating their attention upon his *Methodus ad facilem historiarum cognitionem* and *Les six livres de la republique* ; or they have confessed that the *Démonomanie* poses an insoluble paradox : the learned jurist and political thinker who was also a rabid witch-hater and credulous malevolent : the great lawyer and intellect who nonetheless produced, in his *Démonomanie*, a " formless

---

[17] ZILBOORG, *Medical Man and Witch*, pp. 138-9.

[18] WIER, *Histoires*, I, p. 209.

[19] *Ibid.*, II, p. 323. Wier struggles with the problem of the punishment of witches and magicians throughout Lib. VI ; and he is, as ever, thoroughly inconsistent.

[20] Chovet's edition was a translation of the last and fullest Latin version. It includes Erastus's refutation and Wier's rejoinder.

[21] Jean BODIN, *De la demonomanie des sorciers*, Paris, 1580 ; second French ed., Paris, 1581 ; first German ed., Strassburg, 1581. All my references are to the first edition.

screed and dribbling mess " [22]. More recently, however, scholars have attempted to establish a closer relationship between Bodin's various works ; to see compatibilities and consistency both of opinion and of method ; and, more to the point, to regard the *Démonomanie* (and especially the *Refutation de Wier*) as a work of " devastating skill " ; where historical arguments are used with " devastating effect " ; and which, as a demolition of Wier, is " thorough and pulverizing " [23].

The question of the over-all consistency — or otherwise — of Bodin's thought does not concern us here. But the matter, the manner, and the coherence, of his attack on Wier certainly does. And I must state, from the outset, that I do not share the enthusiasm for Bodin's demonology shown by some of my colleagues. The *Démonomanie* seems to me to be the work of a man who is intellectually arrogant to the point of mental derangement.

In one respect, however, Bodin is consistent. Almost alone, amongst sixteenth-century defenders of the witch persecution, he does not do deals with his enemies. He does not concede that, perhaps, some visions are merely delusions caused by disease ; that witches are innocent victims of the Devil ; or that miraculous effects, such as transformations, are only illusory. For Bodin, witches and demons operate together ; they are real ; and they work transitive effects. Even metamorphosis is real ! And how does Bodin know all this ? Simply because, in order to deny it, " il faut donc condemner toute l'antiquité d'erreur et d'ignorance, il faut rayer toutes les histoires et bifer les loix divines et humaines comme faulces et illusoires, et fondees sur faux principes " [24]. With such an arsenal of evidence — and, one might add, even without it — Bodin was to find Wier an easy prey.

Bodin begins his refutation by expressing astonishment, and pointing out that his adversary was either " un homme tres-ignorant, ou tres-meschant " [25]. Since Wier's books demonstrate that he is not ignorant, then he must certainly be evil in setting out demonic incantations and magical figures. Bodin condemns Wier as a disciple of the notorious Agrippa : but, more significant, is an attack on Wier's use of the Scriptures which he has bent, twisted, and falsified to suit his own purposes. This is an attempt, by Bodin, to substantiate the traditional interpretation of the Bible in relation to witchcraft [26]. Also fundamental in Bodin's criticism is his attempt to discredit assertions that witches' confessions are untrue. Wier, says Bodin :

> dict tantost qu'il ny a point de paction, et tantost qu'on ne sçauroit le prouver, tantost qu'il ne faut pas croire la confession des Sorcieres et que c'est la maladie melancholique qui les tient. Voila la couverture que les ignorans, ou les Sorciers ont prise pour faire evader leurs semblables et accroistre le regne de Sathan. Par cy devant ceux qui ont dict que c'estoit la melancholie, ne pensoyent pas qu'il y eust des Demons, ny peut estre qu'il y eust des anges, ny Dieu quelconque [27].

Nevertheless, Wier confesses that there is a God ; and he admits that there are

[22] The *Démonomanie* was thus described by Lynn THORNDIKE, *op. cit.*, VI, p. 526.
[23] C.R. BAXTER, " Jean Bodin's Daemon and his Conversion to Judaism ", *Verhandlungen des internationalen Bodin Tagung*, ed. H. Denzer, Munich, 1973, p. 8 ; E.W. MONTER, *op. cit.*, pp. 377, 380. The latter article opens with a brief account of the difficulties facing Bodin's modern interpreters.
[24] Jean BODIN, *Démonomanie*, fol. 240v.
[25] *Ibid.*, fol. 218r-v.
[26] *Ibid.*, fols. 220 ff.
[27] *Ibid.*, fol. 225v. Bodin here points out that Wier's opinions, as set out in his *De lamiis*, contradict those set out in the *De praestigiis*.

good and evil spirits " qui ont intelligence et paction avec les hommes ". It is therefore impossible, argues Bodin, to attribute the transportations, maleficia, and other strange acts of sorcerers to melancholy. And far less :

> faire les femmes melancholiques, veu que l'antiquité a remarqué pour chose etrange, que jamais femme ne mourut de melancholie, ny l'homme de joye, ains au contraire plusieurs femmes meurent de joye extreme et puisque Wier est medecin il ne peut ignorer, que l'humeur de la femme ne soit directement contraire à la melancholie aduste, dont la fureur procede, soit qu'elle vienne *à bile flava adusta aut à succo melancholico*, comme les medecins demeurent d'accord. Car l'un, et l'autre procede d'une chaleur, et secheresse excessive comme dict Galen au livre *de atrabile*. Or les femmes naturellement sont froides et humides comme dict le mesme autheur, et tous les Grecs, Latins, et Arabes s'accordant en ce point icy [28].

Not only are women *not* melancholic, they are also healthier than men, says Bodin, confidently citing both Hippocrates and Galen.

> Jamais, dict Hippocrates, les femmes n'ont la goute ny ulceration des poulmons, dict Galen, ny d'epilesies, ny dapoplexies, ny de frenesies, ny de lethargies, ny de convulsions, ny de tremblement tant qu'elles ont leurs flueurs, ou leurs menstruës, et fleurs. Et combien que Hippocrate dict que le mal-caduc, et de ceux qui estoyent assiegés des Demons, qu'on appelloit maladie sacree, est naturelle : neantmoins il soustient, que cela n'advient sinon aux pituiteux, et non point aux bilieuz : ce que Jean Wier estant medecin, ne pouvoit ignorer [29].

Moreover, adds Bodin, there is a gross inconsistency in attributing to women " les maladies melancholiques ", while the praiseworthy effects of the melancholic humour — which makes men " sage, posé, contemplatif " — are scarcely compatible with the female sex. And Bodin cites Solomon to the effect that there is only one wise man in a thousand ; but no wise women at all. Thus Wier — seeing his veil of melancholy torn aside — had, perforce, to argue that " le Diable seduict les Sorcieres, et leur faict croire qu'elles font que luy mesme faict " [30]. And so, as far as Bodin is concerned, Wier's arguments based on melancholy have been utterly destroyed.

This rejection of the medical explanation for witchcraft beliefs is noteworthy for several reasons. For example, Bodin has nothing whatever to say about whether or not melancholia could ever be related to witchcraft ; or whether the delusions of melancholiacs — and other victims of mental illness — might ever have relevance to supposed magical occurrences. He rests his argument upon a simple assertion : women are not subject to melancholy. And he will accept no amount of clinical evidence to the contrary. He does not accept clinical evidence partly because he is quite unable to think in such terms ; and partly because he *knows* that he is right. And he knows that he is right because he can cite the authority of Hippocrates and Galen. However, when we look into his argument, we find that, even on its own terms, it is much less rigorous and much less learned than Bodin's modern admirers would have us believe.

In the first place, though he cites authorities to prove that women are healthier than men, and are free from melancholy, because of their menstruation, he omits to tell us what happens when women no longer menstruate. Yet a substantial number of which prosecutions concerned old women ; and Wier had carefully described the mental deterioration of the elderly female : though it was left to Scot

[28] *Ibid.*, fol. 226.
[29] *Ibid.*, fol. 226v.
[30] *Ibid.*, fol. 227v.

to make explicit the implication that this deterioration was due to the cessation of menses [31].

Secondly, Bodin cites the *De morbo sacro* as stating that " la maladie sacrée " (epilepsy) afflicts the " pituiteux " and not the " bilieuz " ; and he thinks that he is being terribly clever here. Wier, he says, had claimed that women are subject to black bile ; whereas Hippocrates demonstrated that epilepsy afflicts the phlegmatic. Hence women cannot be epileptic ! However, since Bodin himself has just denied that women are subject to black bile, it *could* follow that they are subject to epilepsy. Furthermore, Wier does not make an issue out of epilepsy as Bodin seems to suggest. And, in any case, the *De morbo sacro* specifically mentions bile, and not atrabile (*kolos,* not *melankolos*). Thus, on this point, Bodin's argument is quite futile.

Thirdly, while the *De morbo sacro* does say something approximately similar to Bodin's citation, Bodin omits to point out that elsewhere in the same work its author writes as follows :

> The corruption of the brain is caused not only by phlegm but by bile. You may distinguish them thus. Those who are mad through phlegm are quiet, and neither shout nor make a disturbance ; those maddened through bile are noisy, evil-doers and restless, always doing something inopportune. These are the causes of continued madness [32].

This passage, together with much else in the *De morbo sacro*, is prejudicial to Bodin's position. He does not, therefore, cite it.

Fourthly, Bodin writes thus : " Et combien que Hippocrate dit que le malcaduc, et de ceux qui estoient assiegez des Demons, qu'on appelloit maladie sacree est naturelle ", and so on [33]. However, the text of the *De morbo sacro* makes no mention of the sick being besieged by demons. This is simply a dishonest, and characteristic, gloss by Bodin himself.

Fifthly, while Bodin is accusing Wier of delving into matters beyond his competence — Wier's job, he says, " est de juger de la couleur, et hypostase des urines, et autres choses semblables, et non pas toucher aux choses sacrees " [34] — it is very apparent that the great jurist was himself ignorant of contemporary medical opinion. It was no longer sufficient to cite Hippocrates and Galen in such a slapdash manner in order to say all that was needed about any malady. Certainly, the flat assertions that women cannot be bilious, together with the parallel assertion that " les peuples de Septentrion tiennent aussi peu de la melancholie ", were gross and crude, even by the low standards of the most ill-informed Galenic medicine [35].

Bodin made two further forays into the field of medicine. First, when he attacked Giovanni Battista della Porta who had been cited with approval by Wier as an authority for establishing that witches might be using hallucinatory drugs [36]. Bodin's reference to Porta is suggestive : " On voit que l'Italien Baptiste en son

---

[31] See below, p. 202.
[32] See *The Sacred Disease,* tr. W.H.S. Jones, in *Hippocrates,* Loeb Classical Library : London, 1923-1931, II, pp. 175-7.
[33] BODIN, *Démonomanie,* fol. 226ᵛ.
[34] *Ibid.,* fol. 236.
[35] See Owsei TEMKIN, *Galenism : Rise and Decline of a Medical Philosophy,* Cornell U.P., 1973, pp. 95-151.
[36] Giovanni Battista PORTA, *Magiae naturalis sive de miraculis rerum naturalium,* first ed., Naples, 1558. For WIER's citation from Porta, see *Histoires,* I, pp. 377-9.

livre de Magie, c'est à dire Sorcellerie, et Wier s'efforcent de faire entendre que cest un unguent a force naturelle, et soporative, à fin qu'on en face experience [37]. " But, it will be recalled, Porta's work *Magiae naturalis* was certainly not principally concerned with witchcraft or diabolic maleficia. Yet it was all the same to Bodin. Experimental science is magic ; and magic — " c'est à dire sorcellerie ". In any case, says Bodin, Porta is doubly absurd : because no doctor, Greek, Arab, or Latin, used unguents on the back, arms, or thighs, to induce sleep ; and no ointments could possibly make people insensitive to fire and pain. No, says Bodin ; witches do fly ; they do attend sabbats ; and he can cite a vast number of *authorities* to prove it.

Bodin's other medical battle concerns incubus and succubus. Wier had explained such things as illusory. However, Bodin has *authorities* to establish the actuality of these demonic visitations : though confidence in his " devastating " intellect is severely shaken when we see that, against Wier's clinical observations, Bodin marshals the unimpeachable evidence of Horace, Lucan, and Homer [38].

Elsewhere, however, Bodin is on much stronger ground when confronting Wier with his own inconsistencies. Wier's powerful belief in the Devil, demons, and in all their evil doings, is the principal flaw in the physician's case. How, asks Bodin, can Wier say that it is the Devil who does things and not the witch, since the effects cease on the death of the witch ? After all, Satan is still there ! He does not die with the witch [39]. This is an interesting argument which was subsequently turned upside down by Reginald Scot who — with yet more relentless logic — pointed out that the effects (such as bad weather, illness, and so on) patently did *not* cease at the death of a witch [40]. But Bodin's case is that, as the soul and body operate together, so do the Devil and the witch — a partnership which he illustrates by the story of the theft of fruit by a blind man and a man with no legs. On being accused by the gardener :

> L'aveugle disoit, je ne voys goutte, ny jardin, ny arbres : L'estropiat disoit, je n'ay point de jambes pour y aller : Mais le jardinier leur dit, que l'aveugle avoit porté l'estropiat, et cestuy-cy avoit guidé l'aveugle, et tous deux ensemble avoient faict ce qu'ils ne pouvoient faire separement [41].

The Devil, says Bodin, must have willing partners. And, as he frequently points out, Wier accepts that the Devil is constantly attacking men with his almost infinite repertory of deceits and illusions ; and Bodin particularly hammers Wier's absurdly inconsistent argument that those who practise magic should be executed — but not " les Sorcieres " [42]. Wier had himself confessed that he had seen transvections ; while " tout son livre est plein des choses advenues contre le cours et puissance de nature qu'il confesse estre faites par le moyen des malings esprits " [43]. In any case, leaving aside questions of marvels, the real problem was the need to punish those who renounce God and give themselves up to Satan : " que Wier ne peut dire estre une action impossible ". Wier's arguments are built upon a ruinous foundation,

[37] BODIN, *Démonomanie*, fol. 233.
[38] *Ibid.*, fol. 232r-v.
[39] *Ibid.*, fol. 236v.
[40] See below, p. 201.
[41] BODIN, *Démonomanie*, fols. 237v-238.
[42] *Ibid.*, fol. 241.
[43] *Ibid.*, fol. 242v.

and Bodin neatly sums up his adversary's weakness : Wier " qui veut traicter en physicien les actions des esprits, dit en mil endroicts de ses livres que les Diables vont de lieu en autre, et dit vray " [44].

The unwillingness of physicians themselves to offer a totally naturalistic explanation for psychic phenomena, and, above all, the inconsistencies of Wier's demon-ridden universe, made witchcraft not merely feasible, but often decidedly the most likely explanation for the extraordinary situations they describe. This position can be seen in many writers who absorbed and adapted this ambiguous medical argument. We find it, for example, in the writings of Ludwig Lavater, Noël Taillepied, and, most strikingly, in Pierre Le Loyer whose summary of this position may serve to stand for many others.

> Et comme ainsi soit que le cerveau humain soit le siege de l'imagination, de la fantaisie, et de l'intellect, et que par iceluy, et par les organs et instrumens propres, les conceptions de l'ame soient mises en evidence, et poussées au dehors, si Diable voit que le cerveau soit offensé des maladies qui luy sont particulieres, comme l'Epilepsie, ou mal caduc, la manie, la Melancholie, les fureurs lunatiques, et autres passions semblables, il prend occasion de le tourmenter d'avantage, et s'emparant du cerveau par la permission de Dieu, brouille les humeurs, dissipe les sens, captive l'intellect, occupe la fantaisie, offusque l'ame [45].

The only answer to a Bodin, and to his massive weight of authorities, was to devise a system which renders witchcraft impossible. And this was the achievement of the last writer I wish to discuss : the English sceptic, Reginald Scot [46]. Scot wrote his *Discoverie of witchcraft* in response both to the increasing pace of witchcraft persecutions in England during the 1570's, and to the increasing campaign against witches, and the debate concerning spiritual and demonic magic, on the Continent. Several factors seem to have inspired Scot's work : genuine horror at the prejudice and stupidity of the judges in witch trials ; the fatuity of the charges brought against helpless and often senile women ; the way in which, to his mind, the evidence adduced in trials was totally inadequate and unsubstantiated ; the violation of accepted legal practice ; and the fact that his own religious convictions — reinforced, paradoxically, by an extremely sceptical temperament — seemed to invalidate even the possibility of magical activity. Furthermore, Scot appreciated, as few contemporaries did, the inconsistency and gross credulity of

[44] *Ibid.*, fol. 246v.
[45] Ludwig LAVATER, *Von Gespänsten vagieren, fälen und anderen wunderbaren Dingen,* Zurich, 1569 ; English tr. by Robert HARRISON, *Of ghostes and spirites walking by nyght,* London, 1572. Noël TAILLEPIED, *Psichologie ou traité de l'apparition des Esprits,* Paris, 1588 ; English tr. by Montague SUMMERS, *A Treatise of Ghosts,* London, n.d. Pierre LE LOYER, *IIII livres des spectres,* Angers, 1586. The last work is noteworthy in that it devotes its first 250 pages to an examination of the reality, or otherwise, of spectres ; attributing many phenomena to natural causes such as defective sight or hearing, or to mental disturbance. Yet, despite all this ; despite his belief that the visits of witches to sabbats are hallucinatory ; and despite his refusal to accept the reality of Nebuchadnezzar's metamorphosis ; Le Loyer concludes that there remain real instances of spiritual manifestations. My quotation is taken from the Paris (1605) ed. of Le Loyer, p. 146.
[46] There is no adequate study of Scot who is consistently misrepresented in modern works on witchcraft. The scanty information relating to his life — brought together in Brinsley NICHOLSON's excellent edition of the *Discoverie of witchcraft,* London, 1886 : repr. 1973 — is summarised and slightly augmented in the *Dictionary of National Biography.* Nicholson reprints the first ed., London, 1584, collated with the eds. of 1651 and 1665. There have been two twentieth-century eds. of SCOT's *Discoverie* : but both lack the crucial concluding *Discourse upon divels and spirits,* and are thus worthless to the serious student of Scot's thought. All my references are to the first ed. of 1584.

the apologists for witch-hunting, and the distance between their intellectual structures and the sordid trivialities of the persecution itself.

In the preparation of his *Discoverie* Scot followed the empirical and experimental bent he had demonstrated ten years earlier in an original horticultural study, *A Perfite platforme of a Hoppe Garden* [47]. Thus, not only did he study all the major demonological and magical writings of his time ; but he also interviewed people who had been involved in witchcraft cases, and discovered that even voluntary confessions to diabolic practices should be regarded with extreme scepticism. He experimented with feats which had baffled ignorant onlookers ; and he even attempted demonic conjurations to see whether or not they really worked [48].

Scot was appalled at a situation in which every adversity was attributed to witches ; and where, though there was a retributive God in heaven, yet " certeine old women here on earth, called witches must needs be the contrivers of all mens calamities " [49]. As soon as anything goes amiss, people cry out against witches and conjurors, though it is obvious that terrible things happen just as frequently when alleged witches are absent as when they are present, " yea and continue when witches are hanged and burnt : whie then should we attribute such effect to that cause, which being taken awaie, happeneth neverthelesse ? " [50] Moreover, Scot demands, if witches can indeed accomplish such feats, why should Christ's miracles have seemed at all remarkable ? Extraordinary powers are attributed to witches by " witchmongers, papists, and poets " : yet, when we examine the matter more closely, we find that such as are said to be witches are commonly " old, lame, bleare-eied, pale, fowle, and full of wrinkles ; poore, sullen, superstitious, and papists ; or such as knowe no religion " ; and, despite the bargain they are thought to have made with the Devil, they never receive " beautie, monie, promotion, welth, worship, pleasure, honor, knowledge, learning, or anie other benefit whatsoever " [51].

It is easy, in Scot's view, to see how an old women might earn herself a reputation for maleficence. She is usually poor and reduced to beggary ; she is refused charity ; she curses first one neighbour, and then another ; till, at length, everybody has at some time incurred her displeasure and imprecations. Eventually somebody falls sick, or dies ; whereupon the ignorant suspect witchcraft, and are confirmed in this opinion by unskilful physicians who use superstition as a convenient cloak for their own ineptitude. Other misfortunes are similarly laid at the poor old woman's door ; while she, in turn, seeing her curses taking effect, believes that she has indeed wrought magic. Thus, for Scot, this kind of witch is simply the innocent victim of a chain of circumstances and superstition [52].

In addition, Scot accepts that such poor old women are frequently subject to melancholic delusions and are thus easy victims for the kind of one-sided judicial system endorsed by Bodin. The evidence of their confessions — so important for

[47] *A Perfite platforme of a Hoppe Garden, and necessarie instructions for the making and mayntenaunce thereof,* London, 1574. There were further editions in 1576, 1578, 1640, and 1654.
[48] *Discoverie,* pp. 309, 352, 443, 478.
[49] *Ibid.,* p. 1.
[50] *Ibid.,* p. 14.
[51] *Ibid.,* p. 7.
[52] *Ibid.,* p. 8.

the witch-hunters — is worthless. Either it has been extorted by torture ; or, if apparently voluntary, it results from the mental illness of the accused persons.

> But these old women being daunted with authoritie, circumvented with guile, constrained by force, compelled by feare, induced by error, and deceived by ignorance, doo fall into such rash credulitie, and are so brought unto these absurde confessions. Whose error of mind and blindnes of will dependeth upon the disease and infirmitie of nature : and therefore their actions in that case are the more to be borne withall ; bicause they, being destitute of reason, can have no consent. For ... there can be no sinne without consent, nor injurie without a mind to doo wrong. Yet the lawe saith further, that A purpose reteined in the mind, dooth nothing to the privat or publike hurt of anie man ; and much more that an impossible purpose is unpunishable. ... A sound mind willeth nothing but that which is possible [53].

Like his predecessors in this field, Scot cites various instances of the extraordinary delusions suffered by melancholiacs ; but, unlike his predecessors, he does not vitiate his case by suggesting that such mental debility renders its victims easy prey to the Devil. For Scot, the natural explanation excludes the supernatural. If, he asks, melancholiacs can be so deluded :

> why should an old witch be thought free from such fantasies, who (as the learned philosophers and physicians saie) upon the stopping of their monethlie melancholike flux or issue of bloud, in their age must increase therein, as (through their weaknesse both of bodie and braine) the aptest persons to meete with such melancholike imaginations : with whome their imaginations remaine, even when their senses are gone. Which *Bodin* laboureth to disprove, therein shewing himselfe as good a physician, as else-where a divine [54].

Given this kind of mental sickness, continues Scot, we may well encounter confession offered voluntarily, " though it tend to the destruction of the confessor " ; and he provides an example, from his own experience in Kent, of a woman who had admitted to bargaining her soul with the Devil. Scot had interviewed the husband to check the details of the story ; and he writes that the confession was so freely given, and was so circumstantial, that " if *Bodin* were foreman of hir inquest, he would crie ; Guiltie : & would hasten execution upon hir ". Yet, in the event, the woman had been proven innocent. Just as in all other " strange, impossible, and incredible confessions ", the sequence of events in this case was a combination of external factors operating upon, and exciting, " this melancholike humor " [55].

Scot's answer to the entire problem of magical activity is the most radical advanced in the sixteenth century. Thus, while he appreciates the scope of *natural magic,* he denies completely the possibility either of spiritual or demonic magic. He denies, categorically, the operation of spirits or demons in human affairs. Indeed he virtually defines extra-terrestrial beings out of existence : either they are purely metaphorical expressions of mysteries beyond human comprehension ; or, more commonly, of psychological disorders and physical diseases perfectly susceptible to skilled medical treatment. For Scot, the Scriptures are simply an historic document chronicling the events leading up to the coming of Christ, and the events of Christ's life. The age of miracles ceased in apostolic times, and to seek further evidence for the Faith is to imply that Christ's own deeds had been inadequate. It follows from this that any other seemingly miraculous deeds

[53] *Ibid.,* p. 52.
[54] *Ibid.,* p. 42.
[55] *Ibid.,* pp. 43-45.

described in the Scriptures (when not performed by God's prophets or by Christ himself) could not possibly have been miraculous at all ; and it becomes necessary to seek non-magical explanations for stories such as the necromancy of the Witch of Endor, or the performances of Pharoah's magicians. What then was witchcraft ? Scot defines it as nothing but a cousening art :

> wherin the name of God is abused, prophaned and blasphemed, and his power attributed to a vile creature. In estimation of the vulgar people, it is a supernaturall worke, contrived betweene a corporall old woman, and a spirituall divell. The maner thereof is so secret, mysticall, and strange, that to this daie there hath never beene any credible witnes therof. It is incomprehensible to the wise, learned or faithful ; a probable matter to children, fooles, melancholike persons and papists [56].

*
* *

I would like to offer a few observations by way of conclusion. The three writers I have just discussed seem to me especially interesting in that they offer us three fundamentally different approaches to the same problem. Wier was a physician and an experimental psychologist, groping towards a new view of mental disturbances — and especially towards an understanding of the psychopathology of old age — by the accumulation of carefully observed case histories. And here, I think, we may accept the judgement of medical historians (at least with regard to this one important aspect of Wier's work) that his clinical observations were often brilliant, and that his methods, at many points, anticipate the work of later alienists [57]. However, having said this, it must still be emphasised that Wier's clinical observations concerning melancholia and other mental disorders were very imperfectly fitted into his refutation of the witch persecution. Indeed they were not, properly speaking, integrated at all : because Wier has no system. His arguments are riddled with major inconsistencies, and thus — despite his impressive work as a clinical psychologist — his attack on witchcraft beliefs can only be described as a totally unsuccessful attempt to reconcile two sets of irreconcilable ideas.

Bodin, on the other hand, in his *Démonomanie,* seems to me to stand as the archetypal sixteenth-century thinker whose methodology is largely confined to authoritative statements drawn from the past ; and who cannot even conceive of the value of empirical observation in the field of human behaviour. Despite their appearance of intellectual rigour, his arguments are full of inconsistencies scarcely concealed by a ruthless refusal to recognise the practical consequences of an intellectual position. This is particularly evident in Bodin's advocacy of torture and of the validity of any kind of evidence in witch trials [58]. Defenders of Bodin have argued that torture was by no means unusual in sixteenth-century legal processes : and I am aware that so eminent a critic as Pierre Mesnard has suggested that Bodin was, in this respect, unusually lenient for the period [59]. But I am sorry to say that I regard such arguments as sophistries which are sufficiently refuted by a glance at the text of the *Démonomanie* itself which advocates judicial

---

[56] *Ibid.,* p. 472.

[57] For some brief, confused, but useful observations on mental illness and old age, see Sona Rosa BURSTEIN, " Aspects of the Psychopathology of Old Age Revealed in Witchcraft Cases of the Sixteenth and Seventeenth Centuries ", *The British Medical Bulletin,* VI (1949), pp. 63-72.

[58] BODIN, *Démonomanie,* Lib. IV, *passim.*

[59] P. MESNARD, " La *Démonomanie* de Jean Bodin " in *L'opera e il pensiero di G.P. della Mirandola,* Florence, 1965, pp. 333-56.

149

procedures so one-sided that it would have been impossible ever to find any person accused of witchcraft not-guilty. One has only to consider Bodin's acceptance of the testimony of a condemned person — " Il se peut faire qu'elle sera veritable... que les Sorciers souvent mourir font les Sorciers : et que Dieu ruine ses ennemis par ses ennemies " — to see that with arguments such as these one can justify just about anything [60]. Thus the delusions of the elderly, the infirm, the insane, and the melancholic, present no problem for a thinker such as Bodin. He simply denies their relevance ; cites his Greek physicians, inaccurately ; and moves on.

Finally, Scot offers us a third approach to our problem : and it was a very unusual one. Unlike the majority of writers on magic, Scot was neither theologian, philosopher, lawyer, medical man, nor magus. He was a learned, independent-minded country gentleman, used to making decisions on his own initiative, and in evaluating what he read against what he observed. He waxed impatient with the manifest absurdities promulgated by erudite professionals who — it seemed from his position as a studious but pragmatic layman — advanced theories unwarranted by any evidence they had ever been able to adduce. Indeed, in his opinion, the matters upon which they discoursed could never, by their very nature, be productive of evidence. Scot banished magic of every sort from his conception of human affairs ; and were it not for his leap of faith in proclaiming his acceptance of the Word of God on the very basis of the miracles contained therein, his philosophical position might aptly, if anachronistically, be described as thoroughly positivist. From such a position, there was no difficulty with Wier's diagnosis concerning melancholy. For Scot this medical explanation of why old women confessed to impossibilities was but one naturalistic argument amongst many. They were sick, and in need of medical attention and social aid. Nor were they rendered susceptible to the wiles of the Devil and his minions on account of their debilities : for there were no devils or demons ; no planetary influences ; and no supernatural properties [61].

Scot's position was, in fact, more coherent and considerably more consistent than that of his hated enemy, Bodin. But in the century following the first publication of the *Discoverie of witchcraft*, there were no writers, either in England or on the Continent, who were able totally to reconcile themselves to Scot's extreme version of the double-truth ; and few were willing to subscribe to his thorough-going rejection of all magic. Unfortunately, it was only within the context of such a rejection of magic that the diagnosis of mental disease could be an effective weapon against the witchcraft persecution.

---

[60] BODIN, *Démonomanie*, fol. 193ᵛ.

[61] It is extraordinary that critics persist in treating Scot as a mere repetition of Wier. It is certainly true that Scot uses Wier both as a medical authority and as a source to undermine traditional interpretations of the Scriptures. But to write that " he accepted the arguments " of Wier ; and that, like Wier, he accepted the reality of witchcraft (TREVOR-ROPER, *op. cit.*, pp. 74-75), suggests no first-hand acquaintance whatever either with the text of the *De praestigiis* or with that of the *Discoverie*.

Discussion

Marc'hadour. — I would like to ask what was the date of Scott's *Discovery of witchcraft* ? its date of publication ?

Anglo. — 1584.

Marc'hadour. — How is it, since it seems that some form of censorship was applied by the Anglican authorities, that something which to me amounts to a denial of the devil, a positivistic view, went through the hurdles of censorship.

Anglo. — There are two things, I think. First, it is rather easy to overestimate the power of censorship, and its effectiveness. It was not as in modern times. There was censorship certainly, but it was very haphazardly applied. Secondly, as you probably gathered from my very brief resumé of a very big book, it is strongly anti-catholic. There are two main features. In the first place, of course, there is the medical argument which he uses, as I have tried to indicate. That is one way of demolishing evidence for witchcraft. The other is to show that a good deal of what passes for witchcraft-effects, or for magic in general, is in fact *tromperie* : tricks, or counterfeit. There exist jugglers and criminals. Now catholic priests are both criminals and jugglers ; and there is a good deal about this in Scot. This material is partly drawn from Wier ; but, whereas in Wier it is rather unsystematic, in Scot it is part of his general naturalistic argument. This is so strong and so effective, and Scot's is such a very racily written book, that I imagine that the thing which struck the contemporary reader was very much more its criticism of, and polemic against, Catholicism than its destructive arguments concerning Christianity in particular and religion in general. Scot seemed, superficially, sound enough, because he said a great deal to suggest that he was himself a believer. He offers a kind of double truth. He accepts the Word of God, absolutely, and he is a biblical fundamentalist. Unfortunately, he accepts the Word of God on the basis of the very miracles contained in the Word of God. It is a completely circular argument ; and he makes a great leap of faith. Ostensibly he is a Protestant — a good sound Protestant — and the greater part of his destructive argument, concerning the Devil and demons, is contained in a separate book placed at the end of his *Discoverie* : that is the *Discourse upon devils and spirits* which is presented as a kind of appendix. Now I suspect that a good many of his contemporaries never got as far as that appendix. Almost no modern readers do ! The *Discoverie* is a very big book — a very interesting and arresting book — but all the seeming juice of it, all the more obviously exciting material, is in the main body of the work. The *Discourse upon devils and spirits* is much more difficult, much less accessible, and it is an appendix ; and I honestly believe that a lot of people really did not understand what Scot was saying. On the other hand there were those who *did* come to understand ; and he was condemned, for example, by both James I and by John Rainolds, as a Sadducee. But his immediate contemporaries were, I feel, a little bit baffled. There is, by the way, a story that James I ordered that Scot's work should be burnt. This has not been substantiated : but though there is no contemporary evidence, it is very likely to be true.

Chaput. — I would like to have some more information on one aspect that you mentioned and that seems to me especially interesting in this conference. You suggested, at the beginning of your paper, that Bodin himself could have been mentally deranged. I would like just a comment on that. To me, it is for the first time that this thing has been said. On the one hand, those who say that witches suffer from melancholy you don't question their sanity ; on the other hand, Bodin says that they are not insane, but you mentioned that he could have been mentally deranged himself.

Anglo. — Let us go back to what I actually said. It seems to me that there has been a lot of controversy about Bodin's demonology. Many critics of Bodin actually find his *Démonomanie* frankly embarrassing. What I was really trying to suggest is that the kind of arguments that he advanced in the *Démonomanie* seem to me to be intellectually arrogant *to the point* of mental derangement. I do not say that he was mad, or that he was a lunatic, or even an idiot of some kind. But I think that there is a point where one can be so blind to an opponent's case, and so convinced that one is right — that one *must* be right — that it becomes almost a derangement. And that is actually what I meant. I find, in the *Démonomanie,* this kind of intellectual arrogance. Coming back to your point concerning a writer such as Wier. Well Wier is simply inconsistent. He is clearly not mad. Nor is he intellectually arrogant. We have before us three very different approaches. Bodin, on the whole, is consistent in his general attitude : I mean in his belief that there is magic. Wier simply doesn't know. Wier sometimes appears to think that there is ; and then he thinks that there is not. Some things are magically explained, and some things are not ; but, in the main, Wier's characteristic mode of argument is very laborious. He seeks explanations for things — which are often very obvious — in a very long-winded way. Now as for Scot : many condemned him, once his ideas began to be understood. When people started to realise the actual intent of his arguments, they didn't, in fact, say that he was mad ; they merely said that he was an atheist, and as such a person to be abhorred. But, from the point of view of your question, I don't think that Scot approaches the derangement of extreme intellectual arrogance. His arguments are really not expressed in that tone of self-righteous extremism. But I really did not intend to set up a model of a rational man as against a maniac : though there is a tendency to do this, of course. This is certainly what has happened with Wier. People see what appear to be rationalistic arguments in Wier, and therefore make him modern, in a way that he is not. In the same way, many critics of Bodin have accused him of writing a " dribbling mess ". These were Thorndike's words. The *Démonomanie* is sometimes regarded as a work beneath contempt. Yet, of course, to his contemporaries the weight of authorities would have appeared to have been with Bodin.

Céard. — Je voudrais poser un certain nombre de questions à M. Anglo, sans être toujours sûr qu'il n'y ait pas déjà répondu parce que je n'ai malheureusement pas la maladie de polyglottie et que je ne comprends pas tout. Par exemple, le problème de la preuve sur lequel vous avez apporté beaucoup d'éléments intéressants. Wier fait une interprétation fort curieuse du texte de l'Exode : « Tu ne laisseras pas vivre la sorcière », en indiquant que l'hébreu dit l'empoisonneuse et non pas la sorcière. J'aimerais savoir si cette interprétation est nouvelle ou si elle a une tradition.

Anglo. — As far as I know, Wier was the first person to appreciate the possibilities of this argument in anything like a serious way. He was, I believe, the first person who tried to establish that all the occasions in the Bible where something was normally translated as " sorcière " or " zauberer " were really misinterpretations.

He sought the advice of Andreas Masius, the great Hebrew scholar, to verify all his translations, and he advanced a whole series of new interpretations to establish that, in the Scriptures, there were no witches : that there were, in fact, poisoners, jugglers, ventriloquists — everything except witches. I think that Wier *was* the first to try to use this argument in order to undermine the authority of the Scriptures which provided one of the great bases of witchcraft belief. Naturally, every defender of the witchcraft persecution would argue from the Bible that " Thou shall not suffer a witch to live " ; and so on. Wier tries to give what seem to be more naturalistic explanations of these key passages in the Scriptures. Scot follows him in this ; but he is much more systematic and he makes much more orderly a case. Whereas Wier advances an argument, and then immediately cuts the ground from under it by saying that — though there may be naturalistic explanations, and though the Scriptures have been misinterpreted — nevertheless, in a case such as that of Pharao's magicians, it was probably the Devil who rushed around and got the serpents for them. This, of course, vitiates his naturalistic explanation. Whereas Wier did this kind of thing consistently — that is advances an interpretation and then promptly undermines it — Scot says that there is *only* a naturalistic interpretation. Witches were often merely jugglers who deceived people. The Witch of Endor, for example, is another *locus classicus* usually explained by demonic activity. For Wier it was probably a demon in the guise of the dead prophet. But for Scot it was a ventriloquist. There was no demon, no dead body : merely somebody speaking without moving her lips.

Céard. — Je vous poserai mes questions en vrac et vous y répondrez dans la mesure où vous avez le temps. Une remarque d'abord : Wier traite du problème en médecin, mais va bien au-delà, dit Bodin qui le renvoie à l'examen des urines. On se demande dans quelle mesure Bodin ne met pas un pied très avant dans le terrain des médecins, — de manière intéressante, parce que ses interprétations médicales me paraissent assez largement anachroniques à l'époque où il écrit. Elles sont encore, en ce qui concerne la femme, particulièrement influencées par de vieilles étymologies : *mulier*, c'est *mollis aer* ; la *femina* est de foi... moindre, *fide minima,* etc. Par exemple, pour un problème comme celui de l'épilepsie, bien des médecins de cette époque expliquent qu'au contraire c'est une maladie qui atteint plus fréquemment les femmes que les hommes à cause de la semence qui pourrit ; les hommes, eux, ont la chance d'y échapper largement. Taxil en donne une raison que je vous livre en vous demandant pardon pour les propos peu chastes que je vais prononcer : parce que les hommes, dit-il, « ont tousjours moyen d'ejaculer à la desrobee ».

Un autre problème que j'aurais voulu poser : celui de l'illusion. Il y a dans ce débat un personnage dont vous n'avez pas eu le temps de parler, mais qui est très intéressant : c'est Thomas Erastus (Johann Lieber), dont nous disions d'ailleurs un mot hier. Erastus, qui est un personnage très important — Mersenne en a fait grand cas et le père Lenoble le définit avec raison comme un Mersenne qui a eu la malchance de ne pas connaître Galilée — maintient qu'il faut poursuivre les sorcières. Il a gardé beaucoup de l'interprétation de Wier et il estime, certes, qu'il faut être un peu fou pour se donner au diable. Mais si on interprète absolument ce propos, il faudrait dire que la folie excuse, selon toute une tradition juridique dont on nous a bien parlé. Il se livre à toute une distinction entre l'imagination et la raison en disant que ces sorcières ont certainement l'imagination corrompue : autrement, elles ne renonceraient pas Dieu — et d'ailleurs elles prétendent faire des choses qu'elles ne peuvent pas faire. Mais leur raison n'est pas atteinte, car si elle l'était, elles ne cacheraient pas leurs méfaits. Il y a là toute une distinction d'origine médicale qui est fort intéressante et qui repose sur toute une interprétation des différentes facultés de la raison principale, qui place, en gros, la raison, faculté principale, au centre, dans le « palais royal », — *in regia,* comme on appelle souvent cette partie du cerveau — l'imagination constituant le vestibule et la mémoire le cabinet. Ainsi, très nettement, la raison des sorcières, elle, demeure entière. Voilà la distinction à laquelle il est obligé de se livrer. Mais cette analyse modifie complètement le sens de l'imagination qui n'est plus seulement la faculté de former des images et de les transporter au cerveau par le jeu des espèces et des esprits...

Dernière question que j'aurais voulu vous poser : c'est sur la notion du démon telle qu'elle s'exprime à travers ce très curieux débat. Car il semble bien qu'il y ait deux traditions qui s'opposent sans cesse et qui se rencontrent en même temps : celle d'un diable qui a sa place dans le plan de Dieu, qui est un serviteur de Dieu, qui n'agit que par son congé ; puis une autre interprétation, très marquée de manichéisme, qui fait du diable un contre-Dieu.

Anglo. — These are less like questions and more like supplementary information ! And I am very interested in what you have just said. I left Erastus out partly because of the time factor, and partly because I thought that somebody else might have discussed him. With regard to your first question : I agree, and indeed tried briefly to suggest, that Bodin's medical views were out-of-date ; and Scot actually accuses Bodin of being thoroughly incompetent to advance medical opinions. Your comment on Erastus was very interesting ; though I am myself unable to say whether the particular modification he made with regard to the relationship between the reason and the imagination — in order to establish the possibility of a witch's guilt — was peculiar to him. Of course, like so many writers on witchcraft, Erastus was very confused and scarcely consistent. I am thinking, especially, of the arguments he advances, in his *Dialogues contre les sorcières,* to refute even the idea that witches always have corrupt imaginations ; for they do not dream, he says, about their ordinary affairs ; and they reply precisely enough to questions. He accepts that melancholiacs might imagine virtually anything, yet denies that there is any similarity between men who believe that their genital organs have disappeared, and women who believe that they have had intercourse with demons. He says that witches confess to such practices as taking place not merely when they are asleep but also when they are awake — as though this effectively refutes all possibility that their convictions are due to mental disease. But he does try to cover his argument by saying that, while accepting that perhaps more female witches than men are deprived of their senses — and thus believe that impossibilities occur — nonetheless, this does not prove that, when they confess to such seeming impossibilities, they are *always* so deprived of their senses. And he refutes the argument that all such beliefs in demonic intercourse are simply melancholic dreams, by pointing out that, whereas no two melancholiacs ever imagine the same thing, witches at all times and in all places confess to similar activities. He does not see, as did Scot, that this argument is susceptible to a diametrically opposed interpretation. Your last question, about the two traditions of diabolic interference in human affairs raises vast problems : and I would only like to comment here that — like so much else in the field of magic — the two traditions seem completely irreconcilable. They pose fundamental difficulties for those who, like

Bodin, and like so many other advocates of the witch persecution, seem to accept simultaneously both the culpability of the witch and magician, and the notion that, in the last resort, everything is contrived and countenanced by God. " Avec la permission de Dieu " sounds so often like an inane parrot cry ; or as an after-thought added to remind the reader — who must have forgotten in the welter of case histories and authoritative statements on diabolic activity — that there was an omnipotent God in the heavens. And again I feel that there was no satisfactory way of reconciling a Devil who could do nothing without God's express permission, and a Devil who actively works against God. The only logical solution, but one scarcely acceptable in the sixteenth century, was Scot's position that there was no Devil at all.

De Grève. — Je commencerai par vous confesser que, jusqu'à présent, je n'ai pas pratiqué la démonologie de Jean Bodin. Mais après tout le mal que vous en avez dit, je suis très intéressé, surtout après vous avoir entendu rapprocher « Narr » et « narratio ». Il ne m'est pas apparu dans les réponses que vous avez fournies, si cette espèce de « comportement démentiel » de Bodin appartient au domaine de sa réflexion personnelle, c'est-à-dire au domaine de ses idées et de son raisonne-ment, ou bien au niveau de l'*expression* de ses idées. Certes, le fait que vous avez utilisé le terme d'arrogance me fait incliner vers la deuxième explication. S'il en est ainsi, je me précipite dans la démonologie de Jean Bodin.

Anglo. — It was in the second sense that I intented this. This, of course, is a rather personal reaction. But I think that one could demonstrate its validity, simply by analysing Bodin's arguments at length.

*

Gerlo. — Mesdames et Messieurs, sans vouloir surestimer l'importance de ce que nous avons fait, je crois pouvoir dire que le 5e colloque international organisé par l'Institut Interuniversitaire pour l'étude de la Renaissance et de l'Humanisme de Bruxelles a été un réel succès. Je voudrais souligner son caractère éminemment international. Les communications ont été présentées par des professeurs et cher-cheurs venant des Etats-Unis d'Amérique, d'Italie, de France, de Grande-Bretagne et de Belgique. Parmi les participants, d'autres pays étaient représentés, et notam-ment les Pays-Bas, la Pologne, la Suisse et le Canada. Les Actes prouveront, je crois, que nos travaux constituent un ensemble valable, pourtant très vivant, très varié.

Je terminerai par des remerciements. Je voudrais remercier tous ceux qui ont bien voulu s'embarquer dans notre nef : tout d'abord, les conférenciers, ensuite, tous les participants, pour leur patience et leur active collaboration. Je voudrais également exprimer ma gratitude à mon cher collègue Claude Backvis, qui a bien voulu présider deux longues séances de travail, et enfin à nos collaboratrices de l'Institut, qui ont pris sur elles l'organisation matérielle de ce colloque.

Mesdames, Messieurs, nous avons commémoré cette année le 500e anniversaire de la parution du livre imprimé, aussi bien aux Pays-Bas qu'en Belgique. Vous aurez constaté avec moi que l'imprimerie à ses débuts a été présente dans presque toutes les communications, de même que le livre imprimé illustré. Nous essaierons de tirer profit de cette circonstance lorsque nous publierons notre recueil.

Il y a eu un absent, et cela nous l'avons voulu ; c'est l'homme que nous avons commémoré il y a peu en Belgique, en France, un peu partout dans le monde, l'homme qui a écrit le livre le plus célèbre consacré à la folie. Je vais donc me permettre de faire appel à lui pour clôturer notre colloque, en citant les paroles au moyen desquelles la Folie prend congé de ses auditeurs :

> Je vois que vous attendez une péroraison ; mais vous êtes bien fous si vous croyez que je me rappelle un seul mot de tout le fatras que je vous ai débité. Un vieil adage dit : « Je hais le convive qui a de la mémoire. » En voici un nouveau : « Je hais l'auditeur qui se souvient. » Par conséquent, portez-vous bien, applaudissez, vivez, buvez, illustres adeptes de la Folie.

Charpentier. — Monsieur le Recteur, mes chers collègues, je me fais le porte-parole des participants de ce colloque (qui m'en ont priée), pour remercier les organisateurs, en tout premier lieu M. le Recteur Gerlo qui a eu la lourde tâche de lui donner corps, les conférenciers dont certains sont venus de fort loin pour nous apporter leur savoir et leurs réflexions, sans oublier celles qui ont assumé les ingrates tâches matérielles de secrétaire, et parfois les étudiants qui ont prêté la main à la manipulation des appareils. Je peux apporter ici le témoignage du « Huron », puisque c'est la première fois que j'assiste à ce colloque : j'ai été frappée par le très haut niveau des communications et des débats. Je dois aussi dire ma satisfaction de voir se dessiner des contradictions, des tensions grâce à quoi cet Institut n'est pas le lieu d'encensement dévôt d'une chose morte qui s'appellerait la Renaissance, mais celui d'une recherche dynamique et féconde.

Journal of Ecclesiastical History, Vol. 27, No. 1, January 1976

Religion and Magic in Elizabethan Wales: Robert Holland's Dialogue on Witchcraft

by STUART CLARK and P. T. J. MORGAN

Lecturers in History, University College of Swansea

Not much is known about Robert Holland, the only Renaissance demonologist to venture into print in the Welsh language. He was born in 1557 at Conway, the third son of a gentleman, and went eventually to Cambridge and into the Church of England. He took his B.A. at Magdalene in 1577–8, was ordained at Ely two years later and spent the 1580s preaching and schoolmastering in East Anglia. In 1591 he became rector of a crown living at Prendergast, near Haverfordwest in Pembrokeshire, and he was subsequently presented to Walwyn's Castle and Robeston West in the same county. As a result of the patronage of John Philipps of Picton, he was also incumbent of the Carmarthenshire parish of Llanddowror from at least 1594 until 1608. He is presumed to have died before the end of James I's reign, probably in 1622.[1]

Like so many other Anglicans of Puritan persuasion Holland regretted a misspent adolescence and sought to compensate in adult writings of extreme respectability. In his *Holie historie* (1594) he confessed that the race of his youth had been 'unadvisedly run' but hoped that a paraphrase of the Gospels in over fifteen hundred verse stanzas would 'withdraw vaine wits from all unsaverie and wicked rimes and fables, to some love and liking of spirituall songs and holy Scriptures'.[2] Another religious composition was conceived 'with a view to the great exaltation of godliness'.[3] Amongst the works he translated into Welsh were William Perkins's

We are indebted to Mr Keith Thomas for comments and suggestions on an earlier draft of this article.

[1] *Dictionary of National Biography; Dictionary of Welsh Biography* (and see the revised entry in *Y Bywgraffiadur Cymreig*, 1941–50, London 1970, 104); J. and J. A. Venn, *Alumni Cantabrigienses*, Pt. 1 ii, Cambridge 1922, 394; Thomas Erskine Holland, *The Hollands of Conway*, London 1893–9, repr. with additions, 1915, 26–39.

[2] Title-page and Dedication.

[3] *Darmerth, neu Arlwy Gweddi*, Oxford 1600. No original copy exists and the work is known only in Moses Williams, *Cofrestr o'r holl Lyfrau Printjedig* ('A Register of All Printed Books'), London 1717, sig. A6ᵛ. For details see Rev. William Rowlands, *Cambrian Bibliography (Llyfryddiaeth y Cymry)*, ed. and enlarged Rev. D. Silvan Evans, Llanidloes 1869, 72–3, 314.

31

catechism *The foundation of the christian religion* (1590)[1] and his *An exposition of the Lords prayer* (1592).[2] Impeccable Calvinist theology was matched with orthodox political and historical thought. Holland commissioned George Owen Harry's *The genealogy of James, King of great Brittayne* as a companion piece to his own Welsh translation of the *Basilikon Doron*.[3] The two works appeared separately in 1604 but the idea of combining them in the same publication would have made sound intellectual sense at the time, especially to Welshmen. The genealogy traced the Stuart descent via Cadwaladr and Brutus to Noah (and so by implication to Adam), thus underlining the Britishness of the royal heredity and the divine and patriarchal nature of kingship, the theme of James's treatise. A dedication by Holland spoke of the Druids as 'the first Founders of Philosophy in Europe'. In his own preface to the Welsh *Basilikon Doron* Holland also used the prophecy of Cadwaladr together with the claim that the Welsh had learnt their Christianity from Joseph of Arimathea to endorse the historicity of the British genealogy and the anti-Roman purity of Welsh Protestantism. Together, the two writers deployed a wide range of the historical arguments commonly and successfully associated with the political philosophy of divine right.[4]

Historical and antiquarian research seems to have linked a number of Pembrokeshire gentry in a wider literary circle at this time. Holland and George Owen Harry helped George Owen of Henllys in the preparation of his *Description of Penbrokeshire* and Holland composed an epitaph on Owen's death in 1613. Holland acknowledged help and patronage from Owen and also from one of the most prominent political figures in the county, James Perrott, who projected a major work of moral philosophy and completed a *Chronicle of Ireland* and a life of Sir Philip Sidney. John Philipps, William Herbert earl of Pembroke, John Canon, M.P. for Haverfordwest, the printer Richard Tottel and Humphrey Toy of Carmarthen were on the receiving end of this cultural activity.[5]

---

[1] Known only in the reissue by Stephen Hughes, *Catechism Mr. Perkins*, London 1672. For details see W. Ll. Davies, 'Short-title list of Welsh books 1546–1700, Part II,' *Journal of the Welsh Bibliographical Society*, ii (1916–23), 223. There was another Welsh translation of this catechism by Evan Roberts, printed in 1649 as *Sail Crefydd Gristnogawl*.

[2] *Agoriad byrr ar Weddi'r Arglwydd*, entered in the Stationers' Registers on 25 June 1599 as 'A booke in Welshe being Parkins uppon the Lordes Praier' but known only in Stephen Hughes, *Cyfarwydd-deb i'r Anghyfarwydd*, London 1677. See W. Ll. Davies, 'Welsh books entered in the Stationers' Registers 1554–1708, Part I,' *Journal of the Welsh Bibliographical Society*, ii (1916–23), 170; Rowlands, *Cambrian Bibliography*, 209–12. For Holland's translations of Perkins see W. Ll. Davies, 'Robert Holland and William Perkins,' *Journal of the Welsh Bibliographical Society*, ii (1916–23), 273–4.

[3] Details of the literary connexions between George Owen Harry and Robert Holland are in a Bibliographical Note by John Ballinger to *Basilikon Doron by King James I: Fragment of a Welsh Translation by Robert Holland, 1604*, Cardiff, 1931. The translation extended to Book I and approximately one sixth of Book II of the *Basilikon Doron*.

[4] W. H. Greenleaf, *Order, Empiricism and Politics: Two Traditions of English Political Thought 1500–1700*, London 1964, 83–4, 115–17; T. D. Kendrick, *British Antiquity*, London 1950, passim.

[5] H. A. Lloyd, *The Gentry of South-West Wales, 1540–1640*, Cardiff 1968, 204; J. Conway Davies, 'Letters of admission to the Rectory of Whitechurch', *National Library of Wales Journal*, iv (1945–6), 85–6.

32

Exactly when Robert Holland became concerned about witchcraft it is impossible to say. What is remarkable is that two of his Cambridge contemporaries whose ideas he must have known both wrote on the subject. The first was his younger brother Henry, who graduated from Magdalene in 1579–80 and who also spent the 1580s preaching in a Cambridgeshire parish. He was a noted Puritan scholar, the translator of Piscator's abridgement of Calvin and Richard Greenham's editor and eulogist. His *Treatise against witchcraft* appeared at Cambridge in 1590. The other university demonologist of the period was of course William Perkins, who graduated in 1581 and became a fellow of Christs and lecturer at Great St. Andrews. Although it was first published posthumously in 1608, his *Discourse of the damned art of witchcraft* may have dated from sermons delivered in Cambridge in the early 1590s.[1] English academic interest in demonology clearly reached its climax at around this time. The arguments of Henry Holland and Perkins were themselves replies to denunciations of traditional witchcraft beliefs made by the sceptic Reginald Scot in his *A discoverie of witchcraft* (1584). George Gifford, the Puritan minister of Maldon in Essex, also contributed two discussions in *A discourse of the subtill practises of devilles by witches and sorcerers* (1587) and *A dialogue concerning witches and witchcraftes* (1593). Finally, the controversy was brought to Scotland when James VI published his *Daemonologie* in Edinburgh in 1597.

It was at the height of this debate that Robert Holland produced his own dialogue on witchcraft *Tudor and Gronow*, although no copies of the original edition remain. According to Charles Edwards's account of books printed in Welsh in the sixteenth century it was around 1595 that 'Mr. Robert Holland ... made a short tractate against conjurors and wizards in the manner of a dialogue between Tudyr and Gronw.'[2] The form of presentation was common enough since it enabled discussions to consist of question and answer routines of almost catechetic regularity. However, Holland's intentions were pastoral and didactic, not intellectual. His

[1] H. R. Trevor-Roper, *Religion, the Reformation and Social Change*, 2nd ed., London 1972, 142.

[2] Charles Edwards, *Hanes y Ffydd Ddiffuant* ('History of the Unfeigned Faith') (facsimile of 3rd ed. of 1677, ed. G. J. Williams, Cardiff 1936), 204–5. The dialogue was reprinted by the Welsh publisher and educationist Stephen Hughes of Swansea as an appendix to his 1681 edition of the Vicar Pritchard, *Cannwyll y Cymru* ('The Welshmen's Candle'), 457–68, and appeared again in the subsequent editions of 1725, c. 1730, c. 1735, c. 1745, c. 1750, c. 1755, and 1766. The quotations given in this article are all taken from the 1681 edition. Hughes's own title for the dialogue might be rendered as 'Two Welshmen Tarrying Far From Their Country' but the title *Tudor and Gronow* (*Tvdyr ag Ronw*) comes from a manuscript copy of the text which appears to be earlier than 1681 in National Library of Wales, Cwrtmawr MS.114B, fols. 243–65. The dialogue is subtitled 'An argument between Tudor and Gronow, Tudor asking Gronow what meant it to cast a cat unto the devil, and he answering in various ways, question for question, reason for reason'. There is a modern edition of the text in Welsh in a collection of prose texts, edited by Thomas Jones, *Rhyddiaith Gymraeg, 1547–1618*, Cardiff 1956, 161–73. For a fuller bibliographical treatment see Robert Geraint Gruffydd, 'Religious Prose in Welsh from the beginning of the reign of Elizabeth to the Restoration' (unpublished D.Phil. thesis, University of Oxford, 1952), 374 n. 96.

33

brother had made an academic study of modern authorities like Bodin, Lambert Daneau and Niels Hemmingsen. With Perkins he helped to import the continental notion of the demonic pact into England. Robert, on the contrary, wished to write a short popular homily in a language and style that ordinary Welshmen could understand. If he had a model it was probably the least formal of the dialogues of the 1590s, Gifford's *Dialogue* of 1593, in which the two main participants are the very obviously village figures of the peasant Samuel and the schoolmaster/ preacher Daniel. Their Welsh equivalents are depicted in an exactly parallel conversation, Tudor anxious for reassurance on the nature and legitimacy of magic while ignorant of its moral and theological implications and Gronow sternly pedagogic in his deployment of the scriptural condemnations.

Indeed, the non-academic character of Robert Holland's Welsh demonology is best demonstrated by comparing his use of Scripture with that of more ambitious and influential writers. Texts such as those from Leviticus xx and Exodus xxii and examples like the witch of Endor and the magicians of Pharaoh on which Gronow's case is made to rest were certainly commonplaces, but since the interpretation of so many of them was open to question by 1590 one might have expected something more than simple citation.[1] As long ago as 1563 Johann Wier had suggested that the meanings of the favourite Old Testament *loci* ought to be reexamined from a philological point of view and a discussion along these lines (affirming orthodox exegesis) had appeared in England in 1575 when Daneau's *Les sorciers* was published in translation.[2] Bodin too had countered Wier's proposal in a special appendix to his *De la démonomanie des sorciers* (1580)[3] but it was enthusiastically endorsed by Reginald Scot. Scot wished to reduce the 'confessions' of witches and the claims of magicians to either purely imaginary events believed in only by 'children, fools, melancholic persons (and) papists' or frauds perpetrated by 'juggling' or 'cousenage.' The bulk of his *A discoverie of witchcraft* is in fact an attempt, following Wier, to reinterpret the many different Old Testament Hebrew words uniformly translated as 'witch' or 'magician' as referring instead either to *veneficium* or to a variety of legerdemains including augury, alchemy, soothsaying, sortilege and vaticination. Thus Scot translated the hebrew 'chasaph' in the classic injunction in Exodus xxii as 'poisoner' and explained the trickery used by the witch of Endor in I Samuel xxviii as a form of ventriloquism. Finally, he insisted that all scriptural texts which appeared to read as though the Devil and his spirits were corporeal beings with tangible qualities ought to be under-

[1] The Biblical texts cited are as follows: Exod. vii, xxii, 18; Levit. xix. 31, xx. 6, 27; Deut. xviii. 10–12; I Sam. xxviii. 3–7; II Kings xxiii. 24; I Chron. x. 13–14; Acts v. 36, xiii. 6; Gal. v. 20–1; James iv. 7; Rev. xxi. 8. There is also a reference to the historian Eusebius.
[2] Johann Wier, *De praestigiis daemonum, et incantationibus ac veneficiis*, Basle, 1563, Book II, Chap. 1; Lambert Daneau, *A dialogue of witches*, trans. T. Twyne, London 1575, Part I.
[3] Jean Bodin, *De la démonomanie des sorciers*, Paris 1580, 'Refutation des opinions de Jean Wier,' 220–5'.

34

stood not literally but 'significativelie' or metaphorically.[1] Later sceptics like Thomas Ady and Robert Filmer drew freely on Scot's massive learning. Henry Holland evidently appreciated the importance of his challenge and devoted a lengthy chapter of his dialogue to the subject of 'the witches mentioned in Scripture'. But his brother either did not realise that even before he wrote the exegetical ground had been removed from beneath his feet, or, with his audience in mind, chose to ignore the fact that demonologists who relied entirely on the Old Testament now needed to be etymologists as well. Gronow says simply, 'God's Word does show well enough everything necessary for our salvation'.

However, the significance of *Tudor and Gronow* lies outside the world of intellectualised demonology. Holland's inspiration came not from book learning but from his experience of rural society in the parishes where he served. As a result his secular knowledge is a mixture of gnomic truths and folk-lore which coloured the belief in magic and witchcraft at the popular level. Above all, his concern is not with the detection of actual witches and the definition of specific acts of *maleficium* but with the prevalence in his congregations of the superstitious reliance on demonic remedies for misfortune. Thus the imaginary conversation opens with a section on animal magic in the pre-veterinary age prompted by Tudor's doubts as to the meaning of the saying 'To cast a cat unto the devil' ('Bwrw cath i Gythraul'). This seems to have been an indigenous Welsh proverb[2] but there are literal instances of the practice elsewhere. In 1591 a number of Scottish witches investigated by James VI were alleged to have raised storms and destroyed shipping in the Firth of Forth by christening cats, attaching pieces of human flesh to their paws and, under instructions from the Devil and a local wizard, casting them into the seas off Leith and Prestonpans with cries of 'Hola'.[3] The pre-industrial world was a world of children and animals and both must often have been baptised.[4] However, in reply, Gronow chooses to emphasise the sacrificial implications of the proverb. He had heard recently in a conversation in 'Albania' of the case of a young farmer in which 'a plague came upon the livestock, and his oxen, his cattle and many of his horses died, and he, either from his own madness or from the counsel of another, I know not

---

[1] *Discoverie of witchcraft*, London 1584, 111–13, 139–50, 508–9.

[2] It appears in William Salesbury, *Oll Synnwyr pen Kembero ygyd* (dated 1546–53 by J. Gwenogvryn Evans in his facsimile edition, London 1902), xv; John Davies, *Antiquae linguae Britannicae, et linguae Latinae, dictionarium duplex*, London 1632, unpaginated Appendix of Welsh Proverbs; and James Howell, *Lexicon tetraglotton*, London 1660, Appendix 'Diharebion Cymraeg wedi ei cyfieithu i'r Saesoneg,' ('Welsh proverbs translated into English'), 8 (trans. as 'The devil take the curs'd cat'). The exact significance of the saying is obscure and was so in the seventeenth century; in an anonymous MS. collection of Welsh proverbs of 1663 it is entered with the comment 'rationem proverbi non intelligo'; National Library of Wales, Peniarth MS. 255, fol. 7.

[3] R. Pitcairn, *Ancient Criminal Trials in Scotland*, Edinburgh, Maitland Club, 1829–33, i. 211–12, 236–7; *Newes from Scotland declaring the damnable life and death of Doctor Fian, a notable sorcerer* (London, 1591?), repr. *The Gentleman's Magazine*, xlix (1779), 449.

[4] See the examples given by Keith Thomas, *Religion and the Decline of Magic*, Penguin ed. 1973, 41.

35

which, bound a live horse to a post, surrounded it with tinder, and set fire to it until it burned to ashes'. If this is Scotland (the Welsh for which is 'Alban') and if Holland had visited there since 1590 he could have witnessed the most virulent witch-craze in Scottish history. But the maltreatment or destruction of animals, including cats, was a very popular component of folk-magic and folk-medicine. Burning livestock to check cattle disease was common in Tudor England and in 1605 Sir Roger Wilbraham recorded a case identical to that mentioned by Gronow.[1] In Wales itself the phrase 'casting a cat to the Devil' was still being used in the late eighteenth century to describe the propitiatory sacrifice of farm animals, and modern accounts of Welsh folk customs associate the practice particularly with Celtic May-Day magic.[2]

Gronow turns next to the peculiarly English notion of the witch 'familiar', a belief that also reflected both folk superstitions and the obvious real significance of the domestic animal, especially in the lives of the old and lonely. Could demons metamorphose into various shapes in order to perform errands of maleficence? 'I have heard', Gronow confirms, 'an old witch and her daughter too when there were many good men listening, confessing that they kept a devil for a long time in the shape of a cat or a mouse or a flea or sometimes a hog, just as ever they pleased, and that they fed him drops of their own blood sometimes, and the old woman showed us the spots and traces where she dropped blood to him from her breasts!' This grotesque version of lactation and the pet names given to familiars again suggests that animals may have been treated like children, or at least that women who were past child-bearing and outside any household were nevertheless projected by their accusers as parodying maternal and familial behaviour. That some of the accused must have acted out these fantasies in fact is shown by the anger of the Newmarket woman whose toad familiar was subjected to the ultimate test—dissection at the hands of Dr. William Harvey.[3] Relationships of this kind were specifically condemned in the witchcraft statute of 1604 and when, as Gronow says, a flea could qualify as a familiar it was not difficult to substantiate accusations with 'evidence'. His other examples— rats and toads—were typical and confessions of their employment were certainly prominent in a number of Elizabethan trials, especially in Essex. Holland may well have known of these and other East Anglian cases for

---

[1] G. L. Kittredge, *Witchcraft in Old and New England* (reissued New York 1958), 96 and see 93–7, 148 on animal magic generally; *The Journal of Sir Roger Wilbraham, 1593–1616*, ed. H. S. Scott, *Camden Miscellany*, x, London 1902, 69.

[2] William Owen (-Pughe), *The Heroic Elegies and other Pieces of Llywarç Hen*, London 1792, xxxi; Pughe misreads 'caeth' (captive) instead of 'cath' (cat) and thus mistranslates the proverb. For modern accounts see Sir John Rhys, *Celtic Folklore Welsh and Manx*, Oxford 1901, 304–9; T. M. Owen, *Welsh Folk Customs*, Cardiff 1959, 98; D. Edmondes Owen, 'Pre-Reformation survivals in Radnorshire', *Transactions of the Honourable Society of Cymmrodorion*, 1910–11, 103–4.

[3] W. Notestein, *A History of Witchcraft in England from 1558 to 1718*, New York 1911, repr. 1965, 160–2. For many English examples of the use of familiars see Kittredge, 174–84; Thomas, 530–1; C. L'Estrange Ewen, *Witchcraft and Demonianism*, London 1933, 70–6 and passim.

36

they were reported in popular pamphlets and occurred not far from his Cambridgeshire parish.[1]

Sooner or later most demonologists had to consider the legitimacy of beneficent magic and this is really the main topic of conversation in Robert Holland's dialogue and the problem most relevant to the Welsh situation. After all, implicit in the ritual sacrifice of one animal was the belief that there existed a 'good' spell which would save the rest, and Tudor is anxious to put this to Gronow. Should recourse be had to charms and sorcery during illness or in cases of loss? What was the status of an apparently efficacious magical cure? 'What harm can come', he asks, 'of going to those whom God allows to do good?' Was it permissible to patronise a cunning man or wise woman who claimed counter-witchcraft powers? These questions seem to have been very pressing at the time *Tudor and Gronow* was written, and Perkins, Henry Holland and Gifford went to some lengths to expose and denounce the concept of 'white' witchcraft. Perkins went so far as to suggest that the Devil only employed an evil witch to inflict bodily injury in order that the victim might lose his soul by resorting to a wise woman or man for a remedy. The latter achieved 'a thousandfold more harme then the former', was 'the more horrible & detestable Monster' and, next to Satan himself, 'the greatest enemie to Gods name, worship and glorie, that is in the world'. It was no good pleading ignorance of the means used or the necessity of the benefits secured. 'No man', he insisted, 'may doe evill, that good may come out of it'. Charmers were in fact in greater demand than physicians but far better to sicken and die than resort to their 'insensible' and, therefore, ungodly cures. Perkins's *Discourse* actually finishes not with a blast against *maleficium* but with a definition of 'witchcraft' as anything, including so-called good magic, 'which cannot be effected by nature or art'. The corollary was unmistakable; 'Death therefore is the just and deserved portion of the good Witch'.[2] Henry Holland was as emphatic. It was possible, he thought, to draw a class distinction between the 'great master witches' who served in high places and the common sorcerers who deluded the 'rude people', the 'doating multitude'. But whatever the social standing of those who consulted magicians, their spiritual condition was no better than those 'meere Gentiles, & Pagans' whose idolatrous customs God had expressly forbidden to the Israelites.[3]

The third great Elizabethan text in the Puritan battle against good magic was George Gifford's *A dialogue concerning witches and witchcraftes*, the English work closest in spirit to *Tudor and Gronow*. Gifford naturally attacked black witchcraft although in rather a back-handed way; he argued that the physical banalities with which so many witches were charged were Satanic illusions to divert attention from what was really a mental war of altogether grander proportions in which the Devil was

---

[1] For examples see *Witchcraft*, ed. Barbara Rosen London 1969, 115, 182–9.
[2] *Discourse of the damned art of witchcraft*, Cambridge 1610, 174–8, 153–6, 255–6.
[3] *A treatise against witchcraft*, Cambridge 1590, sig. Dl'–D2', F4'–G2'.

37

merely God's vehicle. Men should, therefore, look beyond the punishment of witches to the spiritual implications of misfortune as a statement of God's anger. But they should be even more deeply aware of the true significance of counter-witchcraft as a tactic in Satan's strategy. 'Wisdom' was procured for wise men and women by hosts of fact-collecting demons who, by definition, could be withstood only by non-material weapons. No charm or sacrifice could restore health to man or beast; the Devil merely relinquished his blight at the right moment, giving credibility to the sorcerer involved but 'bewitching' his clients in the true sense of the word. A successful piece of thief magic simply meant that all the parties were damned, not just the originally sinning thief. There was in fact no fundamental distinction between any of the categories of 'witch' mentioned in Deuteronomy and all ought to be treated with equal severity.[1]

Historians are now in a better position to understand the part played by beneficent magic in the lives of the Elizabethan populace and why clergymen like Perkins and Gifford were more worried by it than by its maleficent counterpart. Alan Macfarlane has listed the cunning folk of Essex in the period and plotted the movements of their clients. He concludes that the county was 'covered with a network of magical practitioners' offering guidance at low cost particularly on health matters and stolen or lost property, in direct competition with the medical profession and the clergy but with some success and great popularity.[2] In Keith Thomas's *Religion and the Decline of Magic* black witchcraft is seen as only one of a number of popular assumptions about the nature and source of misfortune and the possibilities of redress. Because Catholic ritual, particularly the mass, had provided many physical objects and forms of words which seemed in themselves capable of producing occult effects, it had assumed in the popular mind the character of a powerful beneficent magic of aid, protection and cure against ills believed to have supernatural causes. Protestantism was of course extremely hostile to this superstitious aspect of religious practice, but its own attribution of all earthly effects, including calamities, to an inscrutable and ineluctable Providence and its stress on petitionary prayer and self-help failed to satisfy the need of ordinary men and women for some sense of magical control over their environment. Into the gap stepped the cunning men, charmers, astrologers and other non-ecclesiastical agencies for healing, detection, divination and counter-witchcraft. In this last respect Protestant preachers were particularly poorly equipped. As we have seen, they insisted on the existence of maleficent witchcraft and denounced it

---

[1] *Dialogue concerning witches and witchcraftes*, London 1603, see esp. sig. D3ʳ–H2ʳ; Gifford expressed the same views in his *A discourse of the subtill practises of devilles by witches and sorcerers*, London 1587, see esp. sig. Glʳ, Hlʳ–H4ʳ. For Puritanism and witchcraft in England see J. L. Teall, 'Witchcraft and Calvinism in Elizabethan England: Divine power and human agency', *Journal of the History of Ideas*, xxiii (1962), 21–36.

[2] A. Macfarlane, *Witchcraft in Tudor and Stuart England*, London 1970, Chap. 8, 'Cunning folk and witchcraft prosecutions'. Gifford wrote of one wise woman who had forty customers a week; *Dialogue*, sig. Hlʳ; Henry Holland thought that clients travelled up to thirty or forty miles for a consultation; *A treatise*, sig. Blʳ.

38

vehemently but, compared with the Catholic priest and the village sorcerer, they had little to offer in the way of practical remedies. In the last resort, said Perkins, the patience of Job was the proper response of the Christian to God's mysterious ways. 'Stand fast in faith and patience, and waite upon God for thy deliverance', was Gifford's counsel. Henry Holland listed Job's six preservatives as faith, prayer, a righteous life, the word of God, repentance and providential protection. Protestant writers saw good magic as their greatest rival in the affections of the people but it is no wonder that they failed to obliterate the distinction between white and black witchcraft on which it rested.[1]

Tudor's conversation with Gronow is a classic instance in a Welsh context of this conflict between magic and religion. Tudor testifies to the high respect given to wizards, soothsayers, astrologers and fortune-tellers by all elements of Welsh society, including even 'intelligent folks who know their Holy Scripture'. Of particular significance is his report of the open patronage given to such agencies by the Welsh gentry, who as exemplars of social conduct thus gave vital respectability to the magical profession. Besides, magicians provide useful advice and information as well as successful cures for man and beast; 'I know of one to whom many go from faraway to get spells for livestock and for men'. What is there but good in this social service; what, moreover, would the community do in their absence? 'We nowadays have no objection to pulling children through two fires, or to turn them on the anvil of the smith, or to put them on the edge or mouth of the mill (i gosod ymmhin neu hoppran y felin), or any other trick of that sort. As for wizards and astrologers and soothsayers and fortune-tellers and that sort, they are highly respected and liked with the best sorts, gentry and yeomen, all over the country, all of which tended to blind me so that I never thought God's Word could be against them, but rather that they were good people because all these think highly of them. As for witches and wizards, we just cannot do without them, for they do great good, in most folks' opinion, for livestock and men. Please make sure that you aren't making a mistake about this'.

Gronow will not compromise. But in his Calvinist eyes it is the spiritual sense of 'casting a cat to the devil' which has now become more significant than the literal. Since magical wisdom is alien to Protestant church ordinances, it must be demonic in origin. 'It's just as bad', he agrees with Gifford's Daniel, 'to go to the Devil himself as to go to the people who serve him and who get information and knowledge from him'. Just like the Demon to seize a man's soul at the instant when he believes he is doing least harm! Misfortunes are sent by God, 'who wants all men in their trials and tribulations to call upon Him not to go to the Devil to ask for his servants' help'. In fact, men despair of God's assistance and resort

---

[1] Thomas, passim, but see esp. 27–57, 87–9, 131–2, 209–332, 761–6; Gifford, *Dialogue*, sig. H3ᵛ; Henry Holland, *A treatise*, sig. H2ᵛ–H4ʳ.

39

to the supposedly more efficacious remedies of magicians and witches. Even so, 'the Devil can neither help nor hinder anyone save as God allows'. It is his intention 'to prove the faith of his children, as He allowed the Devil to prove Job, or to punish the ungodliness of evil men'. Gronow preaches the doctrines of necessary affliction, patience in adversity and confidence in the certainty that God will eventually stand by his saints in a covenant of grace that became commonplaces of mainstream English Puritanism. As for the reprobate, the very sign of their blindness is their readiness to use the occult. Gronow is suitably emphatic about their future; 'the same end shall befall all who resort to witches and magicians as befell Saul . . . the gaping yawning Demon is always ready to receive the soul and take it to endless measureless pains'. In the meantime, the magistrate must implement the Hebraic laws and follow the example of Josiah by purging Wales of magic. The remedy for private individuals like Tudor is to 'listen to God's Word, read God's Word, pray faithfully and fruitfully'.

The crux of this argument, as of the whole Protestant case against popular magic, was the calibre of religious life provided by the Church of England at the local level. Tudor hits the nail on the head when he retorts, 'But our ministers take no trouble to read and to show the Word of God to us, and as for a sermon, I never heard one ever in our parish church. The Bible is too expensive for a poor man to buy and to keep at home. God only knows how pathetic is the situation of the poor commonalty'. This was not an exaggeration of the situation in many areas of Wales. The Elizabethan Settlement was vitiated there by a chronic lack of preachers; in 1561 ninety per cent of the Welsh clergy were returned as incapable of preaching or teaching.[1] In his famous *A treatise containing the aequity of an humble supplication* (1587) John Penry lamented the ignorance, absenteeism and immorality of the official clergy and wrote that for 'one parish where there is one ordinary quarter sermon, we have twenty that have none'. Next year he added that there was not a single locality in Wales that had experienced a 'godly & learned' ministry for even six of the years since Elizabeth's accession.[2] The usual computation, made admittedly by biased witnesses like Penry, Walter Cradock and Vavasor Powell, was that there were no more clergy capable of preaching in Wales than there were counties. The language problem and the availability of Bibles were, as Tudor insists, crucial. At the end of their conversation Gronow pushes a 'little booklet' into his hand, presumably some Welsh devotional manual, but Morgan's Welsh Bible of 1588 was prohibitively expensive, and even

---

[1] Glanmor Williams, *Welsh Reformation Essays*, Cardiff 1967, 148; W. P. M. Kennedy, *Parish Life Under Queen Elizabeth*, London 1914, 36.
[2] John Penry, *Three Treatises concerning Wales*, ed. David Williams, Cardiff 1960, 36, 62. George Owen did accuse Penry of exaggeration, however, in *Description of Penbrokeshire*, ed. Henry Owen, Cardiff 1906, iii. 98–9. Owen believed that 'free chapels' caused the hopelessly disordered state of the Church in Pembrokeshire c. 1603; see B. G. Charles, 'The second book of George Owen's *Description of Penbrokeshire*', *National Library of Wales Journal*, v (1947–8), 280–1.

40

after 1630 when a cheap issue had been achieved, Welsh Puritans were still estimating the number of families per copy as between 20 and 500.[1]

The situation in Holland's own diocese must have been dreadful to a Puritan conscience. All the manifold physical and spiritual problems of the Elizabethan Church combined to make miserable preferments of its livings, even of the bishopric itself. Its value since the Reformation reduced by over a third, its parish tithes heavily impropriated by the cathedral chapter and by the Crown, St. Davids could muster 10 preachers (including the bishop) in 1579 and 14 in 1583.[2] In 1566 Bishop Davies begged that incompetent men should not be sent to West Wales; in 1583 his successor Marmaduke Middleton complained of 'very few sufficient men' and a 'want of preachers'. Over fifty years later, Laud, who could hardly bring himself to visit the diocese in 1622, endorsed an episcopal report which repeated 'that there are few ministers in those poor and remote places, that are able to preach and instruct the people'. In the early eighteenth century St. Davids was noted again as a diocese of non-residency and superstition.[3]

Indeed, in these circumstances it is hardly surprising that popular religion continued to be endowed with magical qualities and magic with functions expected of a religion. On the one hand, the Catholic ritual which survived extensively in Wales still appealed to the popular mind as having magical efficacy. In 1583, in what has been described as 'one of the severest denunciations of papist survivals ever to come from an Elizabethan bishop', Middleton forbade the elevation of the host, the churching of women, pilgrimages to holy places, the unlawful keeping of holy days and ringing of bells and the worshipping of images and pictures.[4] John Penry spoke of Welsh people requesting blasphemous prayers against specific illnesses and argued that living in the old faith was tantamount to signing a demonic pact. In 1628, Sir Benjamin Rudyerd described Wales and North England as scarcely Christian in belief; 'the prayers of the common people are more like spells and charms than devotions'.[5] Since, conversely, many actual charms in daily use were conglomerations of Aves, Creeds and Paternosters it is not surprising that

---

[1] Christopher Hill, 'Puritans and "the dark corners of the land"', in *Transactions of the Royal Historical Society*, 5th ser., xiii (1963), 82–4; T. Richards, *History of the Puritan Movement in Wales, 1639–1653*, London 1920, 11.

[2] J. Strype, *Annals of the Reformation*, iii, 1, Oxford 1824, 175; Glanmor Williams, 155–90.

[3] Kennedy, 36; Strype, *Life of Grindal*, Oxford 1821, 401; H. R. Trevor-Roper, *Archbishop Laud*, London 1940, 62; Laud, *Works*, Library of Anglo-Catholic Theology, Oxford 1853–60, v. 335–6; E. Saunders, *A View of the State of Religion in the Diocese of St. Davids*, London 1721, passim but see esp. 24–5, 35–7, 37–63.

[4] Glanmor Williams, 172; W. P. M. Kennedy, *Elizabethan Episcopal Administration*, London 1925, iii. 139–52; cf. the remarks about popular trust in the occult powers of saints and shrines in bishop Davies's funeral sermon for Walter Devereux, first earl of Essex, David R. Thomas, *The Life and Work of Bishop Davies and William Salesbury*, Oswestry 1902, 48–9.

[5] Penry, *Three Treatises concerning Wales*, ed. D. Williams, 34, 14–15; Hill, 'Puritans and "the dark corners of the land"', *Trans. of Royal Historical Soc.*, 5th series, xiii (1963), 96.

41

critics of superstition talked as though Catholicism and witchcraft were the same thing.[1]

On the other hand, in the absence of an adequate pastoral presence from the newly created Anglican Church, Welshmen availed themselves of the non-ecclesiastical services of professional magicians. The 'Good Wife' in Gifford's dialogue boasted that she knew a wise woman who 'doth more good in one yeere then all these scripture men will doe so long as they live'[2] and there are indications that the same situation may have occurred in Wales. In the first place, several manuals of popular astrology have survived from the period. A MS. in English and Welsh belonging to one Richard Jones and dated 1582 contains a treatise on 'Fate and Fortune' and extracts from a 'Compendious Description of Artificial Astrology' by 'John Nidar' (Johann Nider?).[3] In 1596 Thomas Evans of Hendreforfudd was copying out in Welsh calendars of saints days and planetary movements, zodiacal signs and influences and a work by 'E.D.' entitled 'Astronomy or Rule of the Stars or Sky-Gazing which is an art to know the running or course and power of the heavenly bodies'.[4] This last source also found its way into a commonplace book of astrology, prophecies and medicines compiled around 1600[5] by Thomas Wiliems of Conway, and there is another comprehensive collection of his almanacs and prophecies in a copy of 1692.[6] Huw Llwyd of Cynfal had a collection of magical books and equipment and a reputation for wizardry, as well as a record of military service in France and the Low Countries, although only a later copy of some herbal recipes remains to indicate the range of his interests.[7] Some Welsh wizards like John Evans and Arise Evans found their way to London, but there seem to have

[1] Perkins talked of 'Catholic witchcraft', in *Discourse of the damned art of witchcraft*, 25–6, and Henry Holland accused users of charms with being 'Papistes and rebellious Athistes', *A treatise against witchcraft*, sig. G1ᵛ. Immorality was another associated phenomenon; when he introduced Penry's treatise to the House of Commons, Edward Dounlee, M.P. for Carmarthen, spoke of 'the great idolatry begun again in Wales to an idol; of the number of people that resort to it; of the solitary [character] and closeness of the place, amongst bushes, where they abuse other men's wives; of the service . . . said in neither Welsh nor English tongue; and of the superstition they use to a spring-well, in casting it over their shoulders and head; and what ignorance they live in for lack of learned and honest ministers': J. E. Neale, *Elizabeth I and her Parliaments, 1584–1601*, London 1957, 153.

[2] Sig. M3ᵛ.

[3] National Library of Wales, Peniarth MS.172; the *Dictionary of Welsh Biography* lists a Richard Jones, stationer and printer of Welsh books in London 1550–80.

[4] National Library of Wales, Peniarth MS.187; Evans did, however, caution that it was not 'godly for a Christian to be too brightly exact or too searchingly curious' in wizardry and astrology; see fol. 54.

[5] National Library of Wales, Mostyn MS. 110.

[6] National Library of Wales, Cwrtmawr MS. 6.

[7] *Dictionary of Welsh Biography*; Rev. Elias Owen, *Welsh Folk-Lore: a Collection of the Folk-Tales and Legends of North Wales*, Oswestry and Wrexham 1896, 252–3; Gwyn Thomas, 'Dau Lwyd o Gynfal,' ('The two Llwyds of Cynfal' i.e. Huw Llwyd and his son or grandson, the Puritan Morgan Llwyd) *Ysgrifau Beirniadol* ('Critical Essays'), v, ed. John Ellis Caerwyn Williams, Denbigh 1970, 71–98; National Library of Wales, Peniarth MS. 123. For other MSS. collections of astrological and medical lore of this period in Wales see National Library of Wales, Cwrtmawr MS. 38, Peniarth MS. 171, Peniarth MS. 204, Peniarth MS. 206, and British Museum, Additional MSS. 14,882, 14,913 and 31,055.

42

been many who stayed at home catering for the more humble local market.

In addition, there is the evidence of prosecutions. In 1570 Hugh Bryghan of Pentrefelin was charged at Denbigh Great Sessions with using a crystal stone inherited from an uncle to identify thieves and locate stolen goods. For twenty years he had been satisfying customers with a rubric based on calling on Father, Son and Holy Ghost and making the sign of the cross.[1] Nine years later, Gruffydd ap David ap John and his accomplices were accused before Montgomeryshire J.P.s of practising 'inchauntements and wyxcraft' to procure the love of a local virgin.[2] Harry Lloyd told the Quarter Sessions at Caernarvon in 1632 that in order to make his neighbours rich he communed with friendly fairies and spirits every Tuesday and Thursday night. What is significant here is that the secular authorities, like the Calvinist theologians, tried to ignore the distinction between beneficent and maleficent magic which obviously existed in the mind of the defendant, as it existed in the mind of Holland's Tudor. Lloyd was actually charged with counterfeiting physic in order to use 'wicked & unlawfull arts (that is to say) fortunetellinge, Palmestry comon hauntinge & familiarity wth wicked spirits in the night time & comon cheatings & cusnages of div'se of his mats leadge people ... whereby he is dangerous to the inferiour sorte of people'.[3] Needless to say, cases were also heard where defendants did not claim to be acting for the good of the community and where the element of overt *maleficium* was always uppermost in the presentments. These are recognisably instances of accusation of witchcraft by injured neighbours and involved mainly women, such as the case of Katherine Lewis of Gumfreston, a parish close to Holland's, who in 1607 was charged with causing loss of goods and chattels by performing diabolical arts 'by the instigation of the Devil'.[4] However, it is with those who claimed occult powers *against* such witchcraft that Robert Holland is principally concerned and ultimately the role of the 'wise man' may be more significant as evidence of village life in early modern Wales than that of the evil woman.

In the meantime we have the testimony of two other witnesses who, like Holland, took the challenge from the magical profession seriously. There is a remarkable passage in Penry's *Treatise* where the failure of the new religion in Wales is blamed for the persistence of the old magic and

[1] G. Dyfnallt Owen, *Elizabethan Wales: the Social Scene*, Cardiff 1964, 62–3.
[2] C. L'Estrange Ewen, *Witchcraft and Demonianism*, 422.
[3] J. Gwynfor Jones, '"Y Tylwyth Teg" yng Nghymru'r Unfed a'r Ail Ganrif ar Bymtheg', (The fairies in Wales in the sixteenth and seventeenth centuries') *Llên Cymru*, viii (1964–5), 96–9.
[4] Francis Green, 'Pembrokeshire in by-gone days', *West Wales Historical Records*, ix (1920–3), 126–7; Bodleian Library, MS. Ashmole 1815, fol. 1 records a similar case in a nearby Pembrokeshire parish from the 1690s (we owe this reference to Dr. Frank Emery of St. Peter's College, Oxford). For other cases of black witchcraft in seventeenth-century Wales, see National Library of Wales, Llanfair and Brynodol Deeds, Bundle 115 (we owe this reference to Dr. D. W. Howell of University College, Swansea); C. L'Estrange Ewen, op. cit., 330–4, 422–4; D. Leslie Davies, 'The black arts in Wrexham', *Denbighshire Historical Society Transactions*, xix (1970), 230–3.

43

where 'magic' is again equated with catholicism. Speaking of those 'obstinate idolaters that would fain be again in execrable Rome', Penry says: 'Hence flow our swarmes of southsaiers, and enchanters, such as will not stick openly, to profess that they walke, on Tuesdaies, and Thursdaies at nights, with the fairies, of whom they brag themselves to have their knowlege. These sonnes of Belial, who shuld die the death, Levit. 20. 6. have stroken such an astonishing reverence of the fairies, into the harts of our silly people, that they dare not name them, without honor . . . Hence proceed open defending of Purgatory & the Real presence, praying unto images &c, with other infinit monsters.'[1] Vicar Rhys Pritchard's doggerel verses were also close to popular culture and many of them were known by heart. His 'Warning to the sick to beware of seeking help from the Sorcerers and Wizards' repeats Gronow's warning that magical 'healing' is spurious because it kills the soul, and offers the customary Protestant alternative; spiritual faith in Christ is the only genuine relief from affliction. In a longer stanza 'Against Conjurors' he catalogues the whole range of superstitions to which he believes the Welsh have always been addicted and for which they were originally expelled from England by the Angles and Saxons. These include the two symbolic sacrifices of children pleaded by Tudor, passing them through flames on Halloween and placing them on the 'mouth' or 'pin' of the mill.[2] In Wales wizards, sorcerers, conjurors, enchanters and seers are the 'apostles' whom the people prefer to follow; their pronouncements are the 'scriptures' they consult. This contradicts the Mosaic Law and ignores the warnings in Leviticus and Revelation. No heed is paid to the punishment of Ahaziah and Saul, the efforts of Samuel and Josiah to rid Israel of wizards or the patient response to tribulation shown by Job, Hezekiah, Naaman, Tobit, David and Jonah.[3]

Pritchard like Holland insisted that Welshmen must understand that demonic magic was a divine test of their spiritual condition, a temptation which the elect must overcome. But his somewhat frenetic tone suggests that Welshmen of the early seventeenth century often regarded it simply as a cheap and convenient local social service. Certainly the professional wise man (*dyn hysbys*) crops up frequently in later Welsh history, from the Rev. Dafydd Llwyd, curate, physician and magician of Ysbyty Ystwyth, who practised in early eighteenth-century Cardiganshire after learning his magic at Oxford after the Restoration, to Dr. John Harries of Cwrt-y-cadno, Carmarthenshire. Harries was a famous medicine-man with profound education and learning but he refused to answer queries unless the postage was prepaid. His son Henry who died in 1862 issued a

---

[1] John Penry, op. cit., ed. David Williams, 32–3.
[2] On children and fire see Deut. xviii. 10; II Kings xvii. 17 and II Kings xxi. 6.
[3] Rhys Pritchard, *Cannwyll y Cymru* ('The Welshmen's Candle'), ed. Rice Rees, 3rd ed., Wrexham 1867, 197 (stanza cxviii), 288–90 (stanza cci). Compare the poem of complaint 'against some evil habits of people in Wales' in S. Hughes and Hary Evans, *Cynghorion Tad iw Fab* ('Advice of a Father to his Son'), London 1683, 57–8, complaining of the frequency of worship of the Devil and sorcery.

44

prospectus listing his qualifications in nativities, fortunes, guidance for careers, monetary speculations and marriage and cures for sickness and disease. Other eighteenth-century *dynion hysbys* include Thomas Niclas of Conway and Edward Savage and John Morgan of Llangurig. In short, every locality of pre-industrial Wales seems to have had its magician as well as its preacher.[1]

Beneficent or white magic has had a continuous history in all such communities compared with the crazes over maleficent witchcraft that were limited to the sixteenth and seventeenth centuries. Even then no concerted campaign against black witches in Wales has been recorded. The preoccupation was rather with the proper means for redress in misfortune, and here the cunning man posed a greater threat to the Established Church. The village magician not only flouted the first commandment, he also directly challenged the pastoral monopoly and economic interests of the local ministry and undermined the people's piety. Hence, whenever an attempt was made to improve the quality of popular religious life, an attack on magic was its inevitable corollary. In Wales, a further consideration was the availability and linguistic merit of didactic literature in the Welsh language. Thus, the remarkable spiritual and devotional revival which began in Wales at the turn of the eighteenth century was supported by a spate of attacks in Welsh on sorcery designed for mass consumption. Much of the groundwork for this revival was laid in the 1670s and 1680s by resourceful Dissenters like Stephen Hughes of Swansea. The re-appearance of *Tudor and Gronow* in Welsh in 1681 and in many subsequent reprintings was itself significant. Hughes published it with Rhys Pritchard's verses and a pamphlet on *The Devil of Mascon* in order 'to stop the ordinary folk of Wales from now to go (as they usually do up to this very day) to conjurors, magicians and witches, to have their fortune told, and to get information about what they lose, and to get help for their cattle and their men in sickness (or rather to get help from the Devil through these people) and also to stop them from various other damnable habits, which Mr Holant mentions in this book'.[2] These damnable habits were fully reviewed in a later attack by T.P., *Cas gan Gythraul* ('The Devil's Bane') (1711), an 'encouragement to everyone not to go to conjurors',[3] while divine judgments on those who did were inventoried by Hughes's friend James Owen in *Trugaredd a Barn* ('Mercy and Judgment') (1687). At a time when English religious opinion was no

---

[1] Edmund Jones, *A Relation of Apparitions of Spirits in the Principality of Wales*, Trevecka 1780, 68–72, and *A History of the Parish of Aberystruth*, Trevecka 1779, 68–87; J. H. Davies, *Rhai o Hen Ddewiniaid Cymru* ('Some Old Welsh Wizards'), London 1901, passim; J. C. Davies, *Folk-Lore of West and Mid-Wales*, Aberystwyth 1911, 230–64; T. Gwynn Jones, *Welsh Folk-Lore*, London 1930, 119–44; Rev. Elias Owen, op. cit., 216–62; Sir John Rhys, 349–50; E. Hamer and H. W. Lloyd, *The History of the Parish of Llangurig*, London 1875, 110–19. On Harries, see esp. *Dictionary of Welsh Biography* and E. Jones, 'A Welsh wizard', *The Carmarthen Antiquary* (1945–6), 47–8. For evidence from modern Wales see W. Ll. Davies, 'The conjuror in Montgomershire', *Montgomeryshire Collections*, xlv (1938), 158–70.
[2] The quotation is at p. 50 of *The Devil of Mascon* which is paginated separately.
[3] This work contains the fullest treatment of witchcraft in Welsh in this period.

45

longer taking the matter seriously, reformers like Simon Thomas, John Prichard Prys and Rees Prydderch continued to denounce fortune-tellers, astrologers and charmers as seducers of the Welsh people.[1] It was Charles Edwards who remarked that since the faith was repaired 'the fairy folk (that is the familiar demons) are not so bold as they were in the time of Papistry, when they appeared in visible hosts to deceive folk by making merry with them'. Clearly the view was that the strengths of religion and magic varied in inverse proportion. 'It was a sign of the dawn of evangelical day', he continued, 'when the insects of darkness went into hiding'.[2]

However, the first attempt to evangelise the Welsh had been made not in the early eighteenth century but in the reigns of Elizabeth and James I. And it is in the context of the campaign to bring first generation Puritan piety to Wales that Robert Holland's interest in witchcraft and magic must be viewed. Between 1597 and 1603 the printer with whom he was closely associated, Thomas Salisbury, produced or planned to produce a whole series of items designed to improve the Welsh language and Welsh knowledge of the basic tenets of Perkins, Henry Smith and other English Puritans.[3] Holland may very well have been the chief translator in this 'battle of books' against ignorance and superstition. His interest was not in original work but in transmitting the values of the Cambridge of the 1570s and 1580s to ordinary Welsh people in a way that was intelligible to them. Minuscule in comparison with other more famous treatises on the subject, *Tudor and Gronow* has no significance in the grand intellectual strategy of classic Renaissance demonology. There is, for instance, only a passing reference to the great debate on the pathology of witchcraft. Robert Holland was in fact the Welsh Gifford and his work ought to be read in conjunction with that of John Penry and Rhys Pritchard not Johann Wier and Jean Bodin. What it lacks in subtlety it makes up in direct contact with reality. It is as additional evidence of the struggle between forensic Calvinism, with its reliance on Deuteronomy and Leviticus, and the patterns of life and belief in primitive village communities in the pre-industrial world that *Tudor and Gronow* qualifies for our attention.

[1] Geraint H. Jenkins, *Welsh Books and Religion, 1660–1730*, Chap. 8 (unpublished Ph.D. Thesis, University of Wales, 1974). One of the last English works to defend the reality of the occult was Richard Baxter's *The certainty of the worlds of spirits* (1691). For the correspondence on this subject which Baxter had with two Welsh scholars in the 1650s see Geoffrey F. Nuttall, 'The correspondence of John Lewis, Glasgrug, with Richard Baxter and with Dr. John Ellis, Dolgelley', *Journal of the Merioneth Historical and Record Society*, ii (1953–6), 120–34.
[2] Charles Edwards, *Hanes y Ffydd Ddiffuant* ('History of the Unfeigned Faith'), facsimile of 3rd ed. of 1677, ed. G. J. Williams, Cardiff 1936, 238.
[3] Details in Robert Geraint Gruffydd, 'Religious Prose in Welsh from the Beginning of the Reign of Elizabeth to the Restoration', 86–128, 366–78 (unpublished D. Phil. thesis, University of Oxford, 1952).

46

Reginald Scot and his Discoverie of Witchcraft: *Religion and Science in the Opposition to the European Witch Craze*

Leland L. Estes

Recent discussions of the major literary works of the witch craze of the sixteenth and seventeenth centuries have advanced significantly our understanding of this important episode in European history.[1] Clearly, our efforts no longer are controlled by the anticlerical and even antireligious sentiments that corrupted so much late nineteenth-century scholarship on this subject. Yet a more subtle nineteenth-century prejudice still remains with us. We still wish to believe that those who opposed the craze did so because in some fundamental way they were more enlightened, or more rational, or more scientific than those who accepted and even supported witch hunting. Recent anthropological research, however, stressing both the ubiquity and the intellectual integrity of a belief in witches, suggests strongly that this modern viewpoint is probably not correct. Certainly, this prejudice has seriously distorted our understanding of one important contribution to the witch debate, Reginald Scot's *The Discoverie of Witchcraft*.[2] Modern commentators have invested this book with an aura of scientific rationality that it ill deserves. A closer inspection, I believe, reveals an entirely different source for Scot's ideas and, more importantly, sheds some new light on what it really was that brought witch hunting in Europe to an end.

Modern interpreters generally agree on Scot's motivation. Wallace Notestein attributes Scot's opinions on witchcraft to his "scientific spirit"; instead of relying on the views of others, he "thought the subject out for himself." Sidney Anglo, in a recent article, describes Scot's method as that of "an independent-minded country gentleman, used to making decisions on his own initiative, and in evaluating what he read against what he observed." Anglo

---

1. Sydney Anglo, ed., *The Damned Art: Essays in the Literature of Witchcraft* (London, 1977).
2. Reginald Scot, *The Discoverie of Witchcraft* (London, 1584). There were later London editions in 1651, 1654, and 1665; the 1665 edition had some extra material added to it. Modern editions include those of Brinsley Nicholson (1886; reprint ed., Totowa, N.J., 1973); Montague Summers (1930; reprint ed., New York, 1972); and Hugh Ross Williamson (London and Carbondale, Ill., 1964). Because of the plethora of editions, I will give book and chapter numbers along with page numbers to the widely distributed Summers edition of 1972. Since this edition did not include *A Discourse on Divels and Spirits,* I will give the chapter and page numbers for the original 1584 edition of this treatise.

Mr. Estes is a junior fellow in the Institute for the Advanced Study of Religion in the University of Chicago, Chicago, Illinois.

444

actually refers to Scot as a "positivist." Even Keith Thomas, whose assessment of the *Discoverie* otherwise is balanced, argues that Scot's work was "no more than an elaborate application of a type of rationalist criticism already in vogue."[3] These authors portray Scot as not merely a precursor of the scientific revolution but as a full-fledged participant. However, a close scrutiny of the *Discoverie* and of Scot's other works does not support this view.

Much of Scot's reputation as a scientific rationalist arises from his extended discussion of various sleight-of-hand performances, which, as Notestein observes, occupies a large portion of his book.[4] Scot discusses at length the tricks of jugglers, the instruments of their trade, and the cozening to which they are so often given.[5] Yet, although Scot's exposition of legerdemain is extraordinarily interesting, it is for the most part derivative, as he himself was quick to point out. A goodly portion of it is copied word for word from books to which Scot very gladly directs the reader's attention.[6] More fundamental and to the point, the scientific methodology that Scot applied to the problem of legerdemain was rudimentary and unconvincing at best. This is not to say that he did not possess an acute observational sense. His work on the cultivation of hops clearly shows us a man with a strong, although not altogether exceptional, grasp of empirical detail.[7] And it cannot be denied that occasionally he speaks of the "notable and wonderful experiments and conclusions that are found in nature . . . through wisdom, learning, and industry."[8] He even attempted an experiment himself once in a great while, as when he tried to get some suspected witches to enroll him in the devil's league or when he claimed, in a marginal note, to have partially reproduced a trick first performed by one Brandon the Juggler.[9] But, on the

---

3. Wallace Notestein, *A History of Witchcraft in England from 1558–1718* (1911; reprint ed., New York, 1968), pp. 61, 62; Sydney Anglo, "Reginald Scot's *Discoverie of Witchcraft*: Scepticism and Sadduceeism," in *The Damned Art*, p. 134, repeating a similar quotation in idem, "Melancholia and Witchcraft: The Debate between Wier, Bodin, and Scot," in *Folie et Déraison à la Renaissance* (Brussels, 1976), p. 222; Keith Thomas, *Religion and the Decline of Magic* (New York, 1971), p. 579. Anglo has been cited favorably by several authors: Brian Easlea, *Witch Hunting, Magic, and the New Philosophy: An Introduction to the Debates of the Scientific Revolution, 1450–1750* (Atlantic Highlands, N.J., 1980), pp. 24–25; Brian P. Copenhaver, review of *Witch Hunting, Magic, and the New Philosophy*, by Brian Easlea, *American Historical Review* 87 (1982): 145; and Stuart Clark, "Inversion, Misrule, and the Meaning of Witchcraft," *Past and Present* 87 (1980): 98 n. 1.

4. Notestein, p. 65.

5. Scot, *Discoverie*, 13. 21. 181; 13. 31. 193; 13. 34. 199.

6. Ibid., 13. 33. 195–196; 13. 34. 199.

7. Reginald Scot, *A Perfite Platforme of a Hoppe Garden, and Necessarie Instructions for the Making and Mayntenaunce Thereof* (London, 1574). There were further editions in 1576, 1578, 1640, and 1654. For the impact of this book and an assessment of its contents, see G. E. Fussell, *The Old English Farming Books from Fitzherbert to Tull: 1523–1753* (London, 1947), pp. 11–12; Lord Ernle, *English Farming: Past and Present* (London, 1927), p. 92; W. H. R. Curtler, *A Short History of English Agriculture* (Oxford, 1909), pp. 89–91; Alan Bignell, *Hopping Down in Kent* (London, 1977), pp. 23–25.

8. Scot, *Discoverie*, 13. 16. 176, 177.

9. Ibid., 3. 6. 27; 13. 13. 174–175.

whole, Scot proceeds not by referring to the fruits of his own experience and experiments, but, in typical medieval and even Renaissance fashion, by citing the opinions and stories of others.

While Scot's modern commentators have systematically overvalued his practicality and his adherence to the canons of scientific inquiry, they have seriously underestimated his continued allegiance to the Christian tradition. Interestingly enough, this underestimation does not seem to have resulted from a lack of interest in his purely theological excursions, which are discussed in some detail by both Anglo and Notestein. Practically no one seems to have missed Scot's truly profound knowledge of both the Bible and the church fathers and his more than passing acquaintance with the scholastics. Yet, in the end, both Anglo and Notestein tend to reduce his theology to philosophy and even to psychology. Anglo argues, for instance, that for Scot devils have only a metaphorical and psychological significance; that they are just another name for evil desires.[10] If Anglo is correct, then Scot was little more than a deist. But is he correct? Did Scot deploy a quite remarkable biblical and patristic scholarship merely to cover himself? I believe not. Behind the facade of scientific rationality that modern commentators have imposed on Scot there lies a deeply religious man. His opposition to the witch craze found its source not in a deeper and more sophisticated construal of the facts, but in a theology that rejected the very possibility of witchcraft because, more fundamentally, it rejected the corporeal activity of created spirit.

Although Scot, especially in *A Discourse upon Divels and Spirits,* which was appended to the *Discoverie,* does provide a subtle, sophisticated, and consistent theology buttressed by a wealth of citations to biblical, patristic, scholastic, and contemporary sources, the first thing that strikes the casual reader is his virulent and often repeated contempt for and opposition to Catholicism. He describes the pope as the antichrist, accuses monks and friars of maintaining "their religion, their lust, their liberties, their pomp, [and] their wealth" by cozening their flocks, and declares that "their doctrine, in books and sermons teach and publish conjurations" to the end that people will "cast away their money upon masses and suffrages for their souls." Scot calls the sacrament of the mass an "uncivil and cruel sacrifice of popish priests" and compares it unfavorably to the Crucifixion because the Jews and Gentiles killed Christ only once, while priests "daily and hourly torment him with new deaths." He ridicules purgatory by arguing that all of the souls that once cried out for trentals have, since the Reformation, "all gone into Italy, because masses are grown dear here in England." He also vehemently opposes the worship of saints, the use of holy water, crosses, fasting on Sunday and other specially designated holy days, medicinal prayers, and

10. Anglo, "Scot's *Discoverie,*" pp. 109, 127–129.

other related Catholic practices. Running through and tying together all of the various attacks on Catholic doctrine is Scot's unwavering anticlericalism. "In all ages," Scot claims, "monks and priests have abused and bewitched the world."[11] His appetite for attacks on the clergy never seems satiated. Yet he never allows his detestation for clerical authority to develop into a criticism of authority in general. On the contrary, he is a firm supporter of the political and social hierarchy.[12]

While not ill disposed towards the secular establishment in England, there is little reason to believe that Scot had a very high opinion of English religion as commonly practiced. He could be very lavish in dispensing praise, but nowhere in the whole of the *Discoverie* does he have a good thing to say about the form and order of religion in the English church. In fact, he really says very little about that church at all. Even where he might compare it favorably to Continental Catholicism, he forbears. This forbearance might be explicable if we had some reason to believe that Scot was a Puritan, but we do not.[13] He was uninterested, almost ostentatiously so, in predestination or the problem of discipline.[14] And we have no reason to believe that he participated in any way in the Puritan agitation that swirled around him from the 1570s until his death. His name appears on none of the extant Puritan petitions or other similar documents. What is more, critics of the *Discoverie*, most notably Henry Holland, William Perkins, and James VI of Scotland, were virtually all Calvinistic in their theology; and none of them detected in that work a sympathetic attitude towards peculiarly Puritan modes of worship or belief. They refused to view Scot as a merely misguided fellow traveler.[15]

Where then might we place Scot on the religious spectrum? This is a difficult question, for neither of the two works from which we must reconstruct his theology was intended to cover more than a small portion of this subject. But it seems to me that the religious spirit that inspired Scot was

11. Scot, *Discoverie*, 7. 2. 74; 15. 23. 255; 15. 26. 258; 11. 3. 109; 11. 2. 108; 15. 39. 269; 3. 12. 34; 12. 10. 135; 12. 14. 142; 13. 19. 179; 15. 39. 268; Scot, *Discourse*, 24. 378. The "anti-sacerdotal, anti-authoritarian, and on occasion anti-sacramental" tendencies of Scot's thought remind one of the Lollards that had once been so influential in his part of Kent; see John A. F. Thomson, *The Later Lollards, 1414–1520* (Oxford, 1965), pp. 172–191, 244, 249.
12. Scot, *Discoverie*, 1. 8. 10.
13. John T. Teall, "Witchcraft and Calvinism in Elizabethan England: Divine Power and Human Agency," *Journal of the History of Ideas* 23 (1962): 22–23, has argued that "there can be little doubt that theologically [Scot's] sympathies ran far in the direction of Geneva." He bases this opinion on Scot's derogatory remarks about the sacraments, a slighting reference to Luther, a condemnation of the Brownists, and an occasional citation of Calvin. These are weak reads on which to stand. See also Christina Ross, "Calvinism and the Witchcraft Prosecutions in England," *Journal of the Presbyterian History Society of England* 12 (1960): 21–28.
14. Scot, *Discoverie*, 11. 4. 109; Scot, *Discourse*, 34. 400.
15. William Perkins, *A Discourse of the Damed Art of Witchcraft* (Cambridge, 1608); Henry Holland, *A Treatise Against Witchcraft* (Cambridge, 1590); James VI and I, *Daemonologie*, ed. G. B. Harrison (New York, 1966).

very much the same spirit that we find in the works of Desiderius Erasmus, even though they might not agree on each and every particular. Both men were theologically antidogmatic; both sought from the Bible rules for good living rather than reasons for contentious disputation.[16] Both men had a great love for classical erudition, and neither would have believed that the classics in any serious way conflicted with scripture. The two men were also firm opponents of clerical abuse, although it often seems that Scot opposed the very idea of an organized clergy. Interestingly enough, both Erasmus and Scot showed a distinct flair in their use of irony, and both men used this flair in order to contrast what they believed to be the simple ethical message of the Bible with the pomp, pretense, hypocrisy, and cruelty of their own age.[17] Of course, the two men were separated by the great divide of the Reformation. Erasmus would not have cared much for Scot's religious parochialism, though he might have understood it, and Scot certainly would not have supported Erasmus's attempt to maintain the integrity of the universal church. But in many highly disputed areas they adopted very similar positions, and we find Scot on more than one occasion quoting the Catholic humanist against the foibles and follies of his fellow Protestants.[18]

The connection between the two men, however, runs much deeper than my brief discussion of their general similarities might suggest and brings us back to the central topic of this article. Erasmus, in his biblical exegesis, severely limited the corporeal activities of demons. In his famous essay on the witch craze, Hugh Trevor-Roper argues that it was the skeptical attitude of Erasmus and other Christian humanists towards the demonic in nature that was responsible for the brief diminution in witch hunting that earlier scholars had detected in the first third of the sixteenth century.[19] When the craze broke upon the European world, the Erasmian exegesis was mostly ignored; but it was not entirely forgotten, and a few members of the literate classes continued to argue that demons and devils in the Bible were meant by God to have only a metaphorical or, at most, spiritual existence.

Certainly Scot was one of those who continued to argue in this way. In his biblical exegesis he greatly reduced the role of all subsidiary and merely

16. Scot, *Discourse*, 34. 400; 27. 382.
17. See, for example, Scot's retelling of the legend of Bishop Sylvanus (ibid., 4. 5. 45).
18. Ibid., 14. 5. 208–213.
19. Hugh R. Trevor-Roper, "The European Witch-Craze of the Sixteenth and Seventeenth Centuries," in *The European Witch-Craze of the Sixteenth and Seventeenth Centuries and Other Essays* (New York, 1969), pp. 129–130. Trevor-Roper, pp. 146–149, argues that Weyer was a disciple of Erasmus and that Scot was doing little more than copying his arguments from Weyer. It seems to me that, in fact, Weyer departed rather dramatically from the beliefs of Erasmus. Weyer was a great believer in the reality of demons. It was Scot who was the real disciple of Christian humanism. On the survival of Christian humanism in Elizabethan England, see James McConica, "Humanism and Aristotle in Tudor Oxford," *English Historical Review* 94 (1979): 314–315. McConica notes particularly the close connection in England between this Christian humanism and Aristotelianism (see below).

created spirits. He believed that such spirits tended to obscure and even to demean the only truly important relationship, that of humanity to God. Particularly, he granted to spirits only a "spiritual" and not a corporeal existence. Where in the Bible they might be "corporeally expressed," Scot argues, it is "for the help of our capacities," which often can understand such beings only by "parable or by metaphor." Spirits can only commune with humans spiritually and not bodily. But spirits do have a place in creation; they do really exist. For Scot, they are not themselves merely parables and metaphors, as Anglo would argue; but in the strictest possible sense, they are nothing more than the instruments of God "whose ministrations and services God useth." More importantly, they are also strictly subordinate to "the illumination of the inlighting spirit, which as it bringeth light with it to discover all spirits, so it giveth such a fiery heat, as that no false spirit can abide by it for fear of burning."[20]

As with other spirits, Scot argues, "the assaults of Satan are spiritual and not temporal." This is not to say, however, that Scot believed the devil to be powerless. Quite to the contrary.

> For whenever we find in the scriptures, that the devil is called god, the prince of the world, a strong armed man, to whom is given the power of the air; a roaring lion, a serpent, &c. the Holy Ghost moved us thereby, to beware of the most subtle, strong and mighty enemy, and to make preparations and are our selves with faith against so terrible an adversary . . . that we seeing our weakness, and his force manifested in such terms, may beware of the devil, and may fly to God for spiritual aid and comfort.

The devil "lyeth daily in wait, not only to corrupt, but also to destroy mankind; being (I say) the very tormentor appointed by God to afflict the wicked in this world [and the next] with his wicked temptations." But because the devil is spiritual, he cannot torment the physical man. In fact, he can do nothing physical at all, as, for instance, enter into a pact with a witch. Yet he can place "himself as God in the minds of them that are . . . credulous" to the end that they should "attribute unto him, or unto witches, that which is only in the office, nature and power of God to accomplish."[21] For Scot, the real dupes of Satan were not the witches, but the witchmongers!

To argue that Scot believed in the existence of Satan is not, however, the same as claiming that he interpreted all references to devils in the Bible as being to some really existing being. Much confusion has arisen over this point. For while Scot did believe that devils really existed, he also believed that biblical writers often used the word devil, or some related term, in a purely metaphorical or psychological sense. Such interpretations of scripture were well within the Catholic and even the Protestant exegetical traditions, as

20. Scot, *Discourse*. 16. 369; 20. 373; 29. 384; 13. 366; 10. 362; 34. 401.
21. Ibid., 12. 365; 31. 386; Scot, *Discoverie*, 5. 5. 57; 8. 3. 93; 15. 30. 262; Scot, *Discourse*, 31. 387; 32. 388; Scot, *Discoverie*, 1. 7. 9; 15. 26. 258; 10. 5. 103.

Scot makes abundantly clear. Concerning possession, for instance, he argues "that it is indifferent, and all one, to say; He is possessed with a devil; or he is lunatic or frenetic." Similarly, Scot suggests that the seven devils cast out of Mary Magdalene by Jesus were, in reality, "an uncertain number of vices."[22] Certainly, Scot's use of this exegetical technique is somewhat, although not altogether idiosyncratic. He is peculiar in the consistency with which he applies it to the problem of the lesser created spirits, that is, all spirits save Satan and the angels. But Scot was no regular trifler with the express word of God and, in fact, severely chastises "the Family of Love, and other heretics, as would reduce the whole Bible into allegory."[23]

An important question arises at this point in my argument: Are we to interpret the *Discoverie* based on our knowledge of what followed, refusing credit to that which is not fully scientific, or are we to take Scot's specific pronouncements seriously? Anglo finds in Scot a nearly perfect exemplar of the Enlightenment spirit. He has cast off the devil, he has cast off hell, and he has almost succeeded even in casting off God. He does not believe in witches because he does not really, down deep, believe in spirits. Of course, he is compelled by the darkness of his age to make certain concessions to the prevailing Christian consensus, but these concessions do not really reflect his own thinking on these matters.[24] I would argue, on the contrary, that Scot was a deeply religious man who first and foremost looked to his religion when he was trying to understand the nature of witchcraft and the witch craze. He found in this religion strong reasons for believing that witches did not really exist and that the craze was nothing more than an unfortunate delusion. This does not mean that he rejected the existence of spirits. He only rejected a certain formulation of the doctrine of spirits. In fact, Scot attacks those whom he believes would try to impose a purely materialistic view of reality. He will not allow "the ungodly and profane sects and doctrines of the Sadducees and the Peripatetics, who deny that there are such as devils and spirits." But neither would he countenance "the fond and superstitious treatises of Plato, Proclus, Plotinus, [and] Porphyrie ... who with many others write so ridiculously in these matters."[25]

The diminution of the corporeal role of spirits had, for Scot, certain important implications for the natural world. First and foremost among these implications was the regularity with which God ordinarily worked the divine will. "Neither does God permit any more, than that which the natural order appointed by him does require. Which natural order is nothing else, but the ordinary power of God, poured into every creature, according to his state and

22. Scot, *Discourse*, 14. 368; 13. 366, 367.
23. Ibid., 31. 386.
24. Anglo, "Scot's *Discoverie*," p. 129. "The truth of the matter is that Scot no more accepted the reality of spirits and demons than he accepted the reality of witches."
25. Scot, *Discourse*, 2. 353.

condition." A corollary of this view was that the age of miracles had ceased. This was not to assert that there was not anything such as a miracle or that Jesus did not really perform them. Scot believed that "it pleased God to manifest the power of Christ Jesus by . . . miraculous and extraordinary means . . . that his son's glory, and his people's faith might the more plainly appear." But after a certain interval, God allowed the power to perform miracles to lapse, so that, as Scot explained, such powers would not grow "into contempt."[26] In banishing miracles altogether from the contemporary scene, Scot was attempting to provide a solution for a problem that had plagued theologians almost from the beginning: how to differentiate a true miracle from a devilish one, or even from a wonder of nature. He argued that miracles no longer existed and that devilish marvels never did. Everything that transpires in the corporeal order must, except ontologically, have a purely natural explanation. Thus, we must not yield to the temptation to ascribe that which is natural to the "divine, supernatural, and miraculous" just because it exceeds our immediate comprehension. If we do, "a witch, a papist, a conjurer, a cozener, and a juggler may make us believe they are gods; or else with more impiety we shall ascribe such power and omnipotence unto them, or unto the devil, as only and properly appertaineth to God."[27]

Although Scot certainly was interested in the natural order, its explication, at least in the *Discoverie,* was not his primary concern. The fundamental problem that he posed for himself in that work concerned the relationship between the spiritual and the material worlds. He tried to show that it was both unbiblical and thus unreasonable to suppose that a human being could make a pact with the devil. This very clearly has little to do with science as we understand it. But in pursuing his argument Scot often uses the various "sciences" of his day to make his point. What animates and directs his discussions of contemporary science is, as one might expect, a profound distrust of anything that smacks of a spiritual explanation of a natural event. Such openly magical "sciences" as cabala and theurgy, which depended explicitly on the invocation or propitiation of spirits, he condemns out of hand.

> Their false assertions, their presumptions to work miracles, their characters, their strange names, their diffuse phrases, their counterfit holiness, their popish ceremonies, their foolish words mingled with impiety, their barbarous and unlearned order of construction, their shameless practices, their paltry stuff, their secret dealing, their beggarly life, their bargaining with fools, their cozening of the simple, their scope and drift for money doth betray all [these] art[s] to be counterfit.[28]

26. Scot, *Discoverie,* 1. 7. 9; 13. 21. 181; Scot, *Discourse,* 13. 367; 14. 367; Scot, *Discoverie,* 13. 10. 172.
27. Scot, *Discoverie,* 3. 18. 39; 5. 9. 62; 13. 16. 176; 15. 21. 252.
28. Ibid., 15. 42. 271. It might be worthwhile at this point is my argument to discuss the relationship between Scot and Cornelius Agrippa, whose *De occulta philosophia* Scot utterly rejected. Instead, he regularly appeals in the *Discoverie* to Agrippa's *De vanitate scientarum,*

Scot was not able to dispose of astrology quite as easily. After all, most astrologers claimed to be working naturally and not through the use of or appeal to a spiritual world. Even Scot had to admit, as did almost every other thinker of his age, that while the stars did not constrain one to act in a certain way, they did establish an inclination. But Scot also argued that, theoretically, there were too many other "causes which work together with the heavens" to make accurate prediction possible and that, practically, astrologers never seem to agree with one another. He was particularly incensed at those astrologers who dared to claim that even the miracles of Christ were a gift of the stars, and he used this manifest impiety of a few to attack the discipline as a whole. However, most astrologers, he thought, were simple cheats who used their ability to cast figures to defraud the public.[29]

Of Renaissance alchemy Scot knew very little. He never mentions Paracelsus nor any of his disciples. He probably knew of them indirectly through the works of Johann Weyer, Jerome Cardan, and Thomas Erastus, but there is no direct indication of this in the *Discoverie*.[30] Scot does seem to have had some knowledge of the medieval alchemists; the whole of book 14 is devoted to their refutation. But this knowledge seems to have been based solely on an acquaintance with their critics. Stories making fun of the alchemists and, especially, of their dupes he lifts bodily from Chaucer, Erasmus, Petrarch, and other late medieval writers. The tone of Scot's attack is far less splenetic than it was with astrology, cabala, and theurgy. It almost seems that the alchemical sections were included more as a diversion than as a serious attempt to deal with a profoundly disquieting problem.[31]

What then does Scot consider a "good" science? To whom does he appeal as the final arbiter on scientific matters? It is almost always to one of the great classical natural philosophers, particularly to Aristotle.[32] He never seems to have doubted the fundamental propositions of Greek science or to have challenged the reality of such notions as those of the elements or the humors. Modern writers, with a few important exceptions, are given short shrift. Of

where Agrippa completely repudiates the doctrines to which his name is usually attached. It is this total rejection of the "spiritual" sciences that Scot finds useful, as also Agrippa's well-known defense of a woman accused of witchcraft. See Scot, *Discoverie*, 2. 11. 20–21; 3. 5. 27; 5. 6. 58; 11. 21. 120; 15. 32. 263.

29. Scot, *Discoverie*, 11. 21. 120–122. Without here mentioning the Paduan Aristotelian Pietro Pomponazzi, Scot severely attacks his extreme astrological determinism. Elsewhere in the *Discoverie*, however, Scot uses Pomponazzi's *De naturalium effectuum causis sive de incantationibus* to some good effect against the witchmongers (see 7. 10. 81; 13. 4. 165; 13. 9. 172). Anglo is wrong, however, in claiming that Scot and Pomponazzi had a great deal in common ("Scot's *Discoverie*," pp. 132–134). No one doubts that Pomponazzi's appeals to the Bible and to Christian tradition were disingenuous. He seems to have been a thoroughgoing atheist. I argue that Scot was nothing of the sort and that his attack on the existence of witches had an entirely different base than that of Pomponazzi.

30. Interestingly enough, all three of these figures, for the most part, were anti-Paracelsians.

31. Scot, *Discoverie*, 14. 1–8. 204–216.

32. See Scot, *Discoverie*, 1. 6. 8; 3. 9. 31; 3. 11. 33; 6. 7. 70; 12. 23. 162; 13. 5. 166; 13. 7. 170.

over two hundred authors cited, only four who wrote on scientific topics after 1500 were given serious consideration by Scot.[33] It was to the ancient world that he looked for allies in his attack on the witch craze. "The heathen philosophers," Scot was convinced, "shall at the last day confound the infidelity and barbarous foolishness of our christian or rather anti-christian and profane witchmongers."[34]

But while Scot was scientifically conservative, he was not profoundly so. He realized that many things lay "hid in nature" and were thus unknown to the ancients. He argued strenuously for the continued exploration of the natural realm and accused those who would attribute every strange thing to spirits of being "sluggards, niggards, & dizzards" for whom "the secrets of nature are never opened." Science should be pursued, Scot believed, both because it "set forth the glory of God" and because it could be in "many ways beneficial to the Commonwealth: the first is done by the manifestation of his works; the second by skillfully applying them to our use and service."[35] Clearly, in this aspect of his thought, Scot comes very close to that of his younger contemporary, Francis Bacon.[36]

A Baconian tinge to Scot's science can also be discovered in his attitude towards natural magic, which, like Bacon, Scot was not disposed to swallow whole. Part of it, he believed, consisted in the "deceit of words" or "in the sleight-of-hand." But in it there was also much of interest and even profit. "In this art of natural magic," he believed, "God almighty hath hidden many secret mysteries."[37] Scot was attracted to the thought of Cardan and especially to his Neapolitan contemporary Giambatista della Porta, whose well-known work, *Natural Magic,* recently had been translated into English.[38] Jean Bodin had charged della Porta with sorcery, but this charge was rejected by

33. The four are Agrippa (see n. 28), Pomponazzi (see n. 29), Cardan (see n. 38), and della Porta (see below). Of course, Scot had to deal with the scientific aspects of the various demonologies that he used. Some commentators on the craze have argued that the *Discoverie* was little more than a copy of Weyer's *De praestigiis daemonum,* which deals with demonic diseases in some depth; but I must agree here with Anglo, "Scot's *Discoverie,*" p. 110–111, that there is not much similarity between the two men's approaches. Scot never dealt in any serious way with the various problems that the craze raised for medical theory and practice.
34. Scot, *Discoverie,* 12. 23. 162; 15. 30. 261.
35. Ibid., 13. 3. 165; 13. 4. 165.
36. Scot and Bacon had much in common. Bacon's response to the witch craze, however, was decidely ambiguous. See George Lyman Kittredge, *Witchcraft in Old and New England* (1929; reprint ed., New York, 1956), p. 331.
37. Scot, *Discoverie,* 13. 11. 174; 13. 3. 164.
38. Scot cites Cardan's two rambling encyclopedias, *De subtilitate rerum* and *De rerum varietate,* more often than any other works save della Porta's *Natural Magic.* See Scot, *Discoverie,* 1. 8. 9; 3. 3. 25; 3. 9. 31; 3. 11. 33; 5. 3. 55; 7. 15. 86–87; 8. 1. 90; 12. 15. 143; 13. 3. 164; 13. 4. 165; 13. 7. 169; 15. 41. 270. Yet there can be little doubt that Scot and Cardan were fundamentally at odds on several important issues. Cardan held that miracles, immortality of the soul, and the reality and corporeality of demons stood together (*De rerum varietate,* in *Opera* [Lyon, 1563], 15. 80–81. And while he did not support the hunting of witches generally, he was unwilling to concede that witches did not really exist.

Scot. He applauded the Neapolitan's attempt to explain naturally many things that heretofore had been attributed to spirits. The evil eye, for instance, was explained by suggesting the emission of certain "gross vapors proceeding out of [the] eyes," which he claims to have captured on a "looking glass." Scot recorded this and many other "experiments" of della Porta. He was especially interested in della Porta's work on soporific ointments and their production in suspected witches of delusions of flying and of attending a witches' sabbath.[39] In fact, most of the material borrowed from della Porta and from Cardan was of this nature, directed towards that which heretofore had been explained by reference to spirits and devils. Scot seems to have been seeking in natural magic explanations for phenomena which Greek science failed to comprehend adequately. He was trying to find some way of reducing the "wonderful" and "miraculous" to the ordinary course of nature.[40]

In this regard, Scot's attitude towards sympathy and antipathy is illustrative. He believed that many "strange effects" could be explained in this way, but he did not make a regular habit of appealing to this mode of explanation. It was the unusual that he attributed to this power, as, for instance, the "fact" "that a cocks comb or his crowing should abash a puisant lion." Nowhere did he adumbrate a general theory of sympathy and antipathy, and in more ordinary cases he was well content with the scientific principles of Aristotle. He even considered della Porta's explanations more palatable if they were buttressed, as they often were, by reference to some sound classical source.[41]

How then are we to rate Scot's science? I believe that it cannot be shown, as many writers have tried to do, that there was much of the scientific spirit in Reginald Scot. He was a diligent scholar, a clever polemicist, and a reasonably keen observer; he had a fine sense of humor, and, clearly, he was a humane man. But by any moderately strict use of the word, he was no scientist. Where at all possible, he relied, utterly without reflection, on the Greek scientific heritage. Where this broke down, and he did have the good sense to realize, at least intuitively, that Greek science was no longer the seamless garment it had been in the Middle Ages, he was willing to look elsewhere for an explanation. He was no diehard reactionary. But then neither was he a particularly fastidious progressive. Along with clever experiments concerning witches' ointments and involving complex optical devices, he also credited tales concerning the power of eagle's feathers and the curative value of precious stones.[42] This is not to say that Scot was any more

---

39. Scot, *Discoverie*, 12. 3. 124; 16. 9. 281–282; 10. 7. 104; 10. 8. 105.
40. Ibid., 15. 41. 270.
41. Ibid., 13. 8. 170–171; 16. 9. 281–282. I believe that Scot purposely avoided developing a theory of sympathy and antipathy so that he could avoid the difficulties that Cardan and della Porta encountered. Both men ended up providing explanations of witchcraft that witch hunters could use to justify their activities. Both men believed that there existed mechanisms in nature that could explain how old women might be harming their neighbors. Scot certainly wished to avoid this sort of conclusion.
42. Ibid., 13. 6. 166–168.

credulous than the bulk of his contemporaries. But, and this is really the point, he was not a great deal less so. He was not blind to the power of controlled experiment, but he did almost no experimenting himself. Like most of his contempories, he was under the spell of the printed word. Despite his many assertions to the contrary, he shackled his book to "well established" facts and his arguments to well-established authorities.

If Scot's place in history depended on the quality of his scientific achievement, he would rank very low indeed. It does not. Scot's achievement was not a scientific but a religious one. In his and Paul's words, he put on the "whole armor of God" and made war in the kingdom of the spirit. He waged a dogged, even vicious campaign against those "bastard devines" who would argue that God had populated the corporeal world with demons.[43] If from time to time this argument carried him from the realm of the spirit into the realm of matter, this did not mean that he had ceased doing theology and had started doing science but that he believed, as almost all of his contemporaries did, that theology encompassed both the spiritual and the material aspects of reality. But though Scot himself was not doing science, he and others like him were doing something extremely important for the scientific enterprise. By banning spirits from the corporeal world they were reducing the attractiveness of a "psychical investment" in a spiritual explanation and, conversely, increasing the value of purely natural ones. They were creating for the European world a metaphysical environment in which natural rather than supernatural explanations might triumph.

But if Scot was increasing the chances that natural modes of explanation would triumph in the long run, he was decreasing the possibility that his own particular intellectual program, the halting of the witch craze, would succeed in the cultural and religious environment of the late sixteenth century. In this regard it is worth noting that the 1584 edition of the *Discoverie* is today a relatively rare book and that it was not reprinted in English for almost three-quarters of a century after its first publication.[44] Scot's theology just was not widely acceptable. At no time in the early modern period, in fact, were most people willing to concede the merely spiritual existence of the devil. Not only would such a concession have been considered tantamount to atheism, but, perhaps more importantly, it would have been repugnant to common sense. Everyone knew that demons existed corporeally because almost everyone thought that they had had some kind of physical contact with them. Even Weyer, the most widely influential writer against the craze, was

43. Scot, *Discourse,* 12. 365; 8. 360.
44. It generally has been supported that Scot's book had been burnt by the public hangman on the accession of James I. This supposition is based on a passage in Gisbert Voet, *Selectarum Disputationum Theologicarum* (Utrecht, 1659), p. 564. However, there is not any other contemporary evidence that this occurred, and it now seems unlikely that such a burning ever took place. Consequently, it could not have had any bearing on the present availabilty of the volume.

intimately and directly familiar with the power of devils. He did not deny the corporeal existence of such beings; he only argued that those who were normally burned as witches had not actually made a pact with the devil but were suffering from some sort of illness.[45] Weyer sought neither to dispute the possibility of witchcraft religiously nor to demonstrate its absurdity by an appeal to science. What he did do, consciously or not, was to provide a framework of practical excuses for those who, probably for other reasons, wished to bring the hunting to an end but did not wish their opposition to the craze to be taken as opposition to the church or disbelief in God. This was also the line taken by those in the "Wurttemberg preaching tradition," discussed by H. C. Erik Midelfort, and by Scot's younger English contemporary, George Gifford.[46] The "practical" Scot was unwilling to make such a concession to common knowledge. From the high ground of his theology he was able to deny that which others took as empirically demonstrated. It should come as no surprise to discover that while he was occasionally cited by later critics of the craze, it was not until the last quarter of the seventeenth century, after witch hunting already had gone into a steep decline, that his specific arguments were taken seriously.

45. Johann Weyer, *De praestigiis daemonum et incantationibus ac veneficiis* (Basil, 1563), bk. 2, ch. 4.
46. H. C. Erik Midelfort, *Witch Hunting in Southwestern Germany: The Social and Intellectual Foundations* (Stanford, Calif., 1972), pp. 25, 56, 66, 194. On Gifford, see James Hitchcock, "George Gifford and Puritan Witch Beliefs," *Archiv für Reformationsgeschichte* 58 (1967): 90–99; Dewey D. Wallace, "George Gifford, Puritan Propaganda, and Popular Religion in Elizabethan England," *Sixteenth Century Journal* 9 (1978): 27–49; Alan D. J. Macfarlane, *Witchcraft in Tudor and Stuart England: A Regional and Comparative Study* (New York, 1970).

7

KING JAMES'S
DAEMONOLOGIE:
WITCHCRAFT AND
KINGSHIP

Stuart Clark

It is the glory of God to conceal a thing: but the honour of kings is to search out a matter. (Proverbs XXV. 2)

And hereunto I might add the disposition of King James, who was ever apt to search into secrets, to try conclusions, as I did know some who saw him run to see one in a fit whom they said was bewitched. (Godfrey Goodman, *The Court of King James the First*, J. S. Brewer, ed., 2 vols (London, 1839), I, 3)

James VI and I published his *Daemonologie* in Edinburgh in 1597, a slim quarto of eighty pages which went through two London editions in 1603 and was later translated into Latin, French and Dutch. Since it is neither original nor profound, its significance, in anonymity, would lie only in being one of the first defences of Continental beliefs about witchcraft in English. But as the work of James I it possesses quite unusual additional meaning and interest in the literature of demonology. It was the only book of its kind written by a monarch, naturally someone with enormous potential influence over the incidence and severity of prosecution. In fact, there is a good deal of evidence of James's personal involvement; and the origins of the *Daemonologie* can be traced to his part in bringing the witches of North Berwick to trial in Edinburgh in 1590–1. In addition, although its ostensible purpose was simply to refute the two major sceptics, Reginald Scot and Johann Weyer, the treatise was also intended, together with other theological and political writings, to demonstrate James's intellectual and religious *bona fides* as a ruler. Both in genesis and in content the *Daemonologie* may be read as a statement about ideal monarchy. Finally, there is a sense in which demon-

156

ism was, logically speaking, one of the presuppositions of the metaphysic of order on which James's political ideas ultimately rested. There is a temptation to view his concern for witchcraft as an isolated, even aberrant interest. He, on the contrary, thought of the *Daemonologie* as one of his most important works. This essay will argue that it was integral, indeed necessary, to his political career and mental world, and that only in this wider context can its various layers of meaning be fully understood.

I

It now seems clear that James showed no interest in witchcraft until the summer and autumn of 1590.[1] The idea that his affectionless childhood and violent political apprenticeship made him sensitive to the macabre and so receptive to the subject from an early age has been canvassed without becoming convincing.[2] He was certainly neurotic and easily terrified, and the fact that until 1587 Scottish politics centred on possession of his person did not help. Fontenay wrote that he was 'nurtured in fear' and Robert Johnston that his troubles 'molested his inward quiet'.[3] But his experiences were by no means unique in rulers of the period, and there is no actual evidence to support the psychological speculation that they inclined him to study witchcraft. His early work on the Book of Revelation, used to illustrate his supposedly abnormal preoccupations, could not have been *more* normal, given his education in the Protestant tradition that the Pope was Antichrist. The whole theory rests on the assumption that an interest in witchcraft and demonology needs some sort of special explanation, a misconception arising from the failure to see it in its appropriate context. What *is* significant in the case of James is that his belief in witchcraft was based on the demonic pact and the sabbat, and that he was almost certainly responsible for introducing these specifically continental notions into Scotland. Drawing on all the available evidence, Christina Larner has recently argued that he acquired them in the winter of 1589 during a six months' nuptial stay at the Danish court which included a meeting with Niels Hemmingsen, an authority cited in the *Daemonologie*. Until his return domestic cases were based on the primitive doctrine of *maleficium* or they were essentially political in character. Despite an act of 1563 against witchcraft, sorcery and necromancy, there was no really significant indigenous concern for persecuting witches at all.[4] It was James's personal diligence in the affair of North Berwick that dramatically changed the situation. In October 1591, after a year of unprecedented revelations, a commission for the examining of witches was issued and

157

the first period of intensive persecution in Scotland was given official recognition.

Although the principal North Berwick defendants were charged with a number of individual crimes, running the whole gamut of traditional witch activities, the central feature of their trials was communal devil-worship. On Halloween 1590 over a hundred local witches had supposedly sailed into the town in an armada of sieves and danced into the kirk to the sound of a trumpet. The Devil, a small black monster in gown and hat, addressed the assembly; 'his faice was terrible, his noise lyk the bek of ane egle, gret bournyng eyn; his handis and legis wer herry, with clawes upon his handis and feit lyk the griffon, and spak with a how voice'. Presenting his buttocks for the customary greeting he told them, 'Spair nocht to do ewill, and to eit, drink and be blyth, taking rest and eise, ffor he sould raise thame up at the latter day gloriouslie.' The proceedings reached their finale with the dese-cration of graves; 'thay opnit up the graves, twa within and ane without the kirk, and tuik of the jountis of thair fingaris, tais and neise, and partit thame amangis thame; . . . The Devill commandit thame to keip the jountis upoun thame, quhill thay wer dry, and thane to mak ane powder of thame, to do ewill withall.'[5] There was worse to come. To his horror James soon 'dis-covered' that a good deal of this diabolical energy had been expended on his own behalf. The accused were alleged to have convened another meeting with the Devil at Newhaven, also near Edinburgh, and been given the recipe for a mixture of venom of roasted toad, stale urine and adder skin with which to infect the royal linen. They had also asked the Devil to activate a wax image of the king which would then be destroyed by fire. Most amazing of all were the supposed plans for drowning James and his bride on their voyages to and from Denmark. Adopting a traditional procedure for raising tempests, covens of witches in Leith and Prestonpans had each taken cats, 'christened' them, tied to them 'the chiefest parts of a dead man' and, on a signal, cast them simultaneously into the seas off Edinburgh. There was even a report that Danish witches were involved in trying to destroy James's flotilla, of which one vessel was in fact lost.[6] Even this was not the end of the business. What had begun as a matter solely of witchcraft, albeit treasonable, was transposed into a political and dynastic key by the allegation that the toad poison and wax image had been specially commissioned by Francis Stewart, Earl of Bothwell, James's volatile cousin and figurehead of the ultra-Protestant opposition party. Each of the witches at Newhaven had apparently 'blessed' the wax effigy with the words, 'This is King James the Sext, ordonit to be consumed at the instance of a noble man Francis Erle Bodowell.' Bothwell protested his innocence but was committed to custody

158

in May 1591. After his escape a proclamation spoke of his having 'gevin himself ower altogidder in the handis of Sathan' and consulted 'nygro-manceris, witcheis, and utheris wickit and ungodlie personis'. The charges were never substantiated, but they certainly served to compound James's fears.[7]

The complex tangle of interests involved makes it difficult to see what reality, if any, lay behind these alleged crimes or to apportion exact responsi-bility for the confessions extorted from defendants.[8] But it is clear that James himself, his conversations with Hemmingsen fresh in mind, had a good deal of influence, and the supposition must be that the presence for the first time of Continental beliefs in Scottish indictments ('dittays') was his own work. It is evident from the pamphlet *Newes from Scotland* (1591), which reads very much like an official version of the trials, that he took a prominent part in interrogating the principals, and he claimed publicly that 'whatsoever hath bene gotten from them hath bene done by me my selfe'. Agnes Samp-son, for instance, was said to have been persuaded to confess 'by his owne especiall travell', though this seems merely to have meant extreme torture and the search for *stigmata sagorum*. Typical of the pedantic curiosity that never left him was his desire to confront the trappings and sometimes the very fact of magic. On Christmas Eve 1590 a demoniac was summoned to the royal chamber where 'suddenly he gave a great screach, and fell into a madness ... to the great admiration of his Majesty and others then present'. Sampson spoke of the procession into North Berwick kirk and the music and singing of the witches' congregation: 'These confessions made the King in a wonder-ful admiration, and he sent for the said Geillis Duncane, who upon the like trump did play the said dance before the King's Majesty; who, in respect of the strangeness of these matters, took great delight to be present at their examinations.'[9]

Remarkable evidence of James's active and vicious personal campaign can also be found in a letter to Chancellor Maitland in April 1591:

> Trye by the medicinairis aithis gif Barbara Nepair be uith bairne or not. Tak na delaying ansour. Gif ye finde sho be not, to the fyre uith her presesentlie, and cause bouell her publicclie. Lett Effie Makkaillen see the stoup tua or three dayes, and upon the suddain staye her in hope of confession. Gif that servis, adverteis; gif not dispatche her the next oulke anis, bot not according to the rigoure of the dome. The rest of the inferioure uitchis, of at the naill uith thaim.[10]

When eventually brought to trial on 8 May Barbara Napier was found guilty of consulting with witches but unexpectedly acquitted of treason. On 10

159

May James wrote demanding the death penalty; but at the end of the month he had decided to reverse the verdict by an assize of error, making doubly sure of the outcome by a prior 'consultation' with the assizors and by himself taking the chair. Both the assize and the royal presence were unprecedented. But Robert Bowes, the English ambassador, wrote, 'the King is earnest about it; it may open the way to other matters, and he would be present at the hearing'.[11] The dittay against the original jurors in the king's name was the fullest account of the North Berwick and other sabbats yet offered in court. The accused chose to yield to the royal will, whereupon James lectured them:

> For witchcraft, which is a thing growen very common amongst us, I know it to be a most abhominable synne, and I have bene occupied these three quarters of this yeere for the siftyng out of them that are guylty heerein. We are taught by the lawes both of God and men that this synne is most odious, and by Godes law punishable by death: by man's lawe it is called *maleficium* or *venificium*, an ill deede or a poyson-able deede, and punishable likewise by death.[12]

He had clearly grasped some demonological commonplaces and learnt to make capital of the famous text in Exodus. Whether or not he had already read Weyer or Scot, he anticipated their position: 'As for them who thinke these witchcraftes to be but fantacyes, I remmyt them to be catechised and instructed in these most evident poyntes.' Finally, in some closing remarks he foreshadowed the argument of Book III of the *Daemonologie* that, as in cases of treason, so in witchcraft trials 'infamous persones' might be admitted as witnesses, since 'none honest man can know these matters'. There was no need to worry about false accusation; as in the *Daemonologie*, James assured the assizors that only evil-doers were ever charged with witchcraft.[13] The speech shows that the kernel of his later arguments, and some of their logic, had already formed in his mind; he was convinced 'that such a vice did reigne and ought to be repressed'. Confirmation of these twin beliefs was the end-product of his extraordinarily close contact with the North Berwick witches and the starting point for his academic research in demonology.

Scotland's first witch craze lasted until 1597, but of James's actual presence at further investigations we have only glimpses. At the trial of Christian Stewart in November 1596 it was revealed that the accused had testified 'in presence of his Majesty' at a hearing at Linlithgow. On 16 September 1597 James wrote to the authorities at Stirling to ask them to bring a witch to Linlithgow 'that scho may be reddy thair that nycht at evin attending our cuming for hir tryell in that depositioun scho hes maid'.[14] More important, he was also involved in a series of cases at St Andrews in 1597 which were

160

192

strikingly reminiscent of the North Berwick episode. On 13 July Bowes reported that James had already spent more than a week examining charges against the university 'and for the trial and punishment of witches'. A great many had been condemned and executed for covenanting with the Devil, receiving his mark and renouncing their baptism. As in 1591 'sundry fantastical feats' had been brought to light and were to be set down for publication. The affair dragged on. A month later Bowes wrote that the king had been 'pestered and many ways troubled in the examination of witches', of which there were now 'many thousands'. Again, his life was in danger; the accused were alleged to have 'practised to have drowned the King in his passage over the water at Dundee at the late General Assembly of the Church there, and the life of the prince has been likewise sought by the witches'. On 5 September it was still being said that James had his mind 'only bent upon the examination and trial of sorcerers',[15] but these were the last recorded personal contacts with witches in Scotland, and there is nothing comparable in his dealings with them in England. Why was this so? In order to appreciate why his active involvement with witch-hunting and demonology was, in the end, short-lived we have to look beyond 1603 to the style and ideals of his English monarchy.

II

The notion that King James descended as a persecutor from the north, enacted a savage new witchcraft statute, and was responsible for many hundreds of executions in England was comfortably disposed of some years ago. The actual rate of prosecutions after 1603, at least in the strongly affected counties of the Home Circuit, was shown to have dropped from the Elizabethan level, while analysis of the legislation of 1604 revealed that it was only marginally more severe than the previous English act of 1563 and a natural reflection of informed opinion at the time. It is now agreed that although the new law codified aspects of the English attitude, bringing it more into line with Continental doctrines on the diabolical compact, the actual practice of the courts did not change very rapidly or, indeed, very much. The point at issue after 1604, as it had been before, was simply the power of witches to do harm.[16] In fact, not only does it appear that James's impact was much less than expected; in the end, there is little to suggest that he had any interest in propagating witchcraft beliefs in England at all. In explanation of this, it has become usual to suppose that he grew sceptical about the very reality of witchcraft as a result of cases like those in Lancashire

161

in 1612 and in Staffordshire in 1620, where accusations of bewitching were found to be fraudulent. In 1616 he was himself responsible for exposing a trickster at Leicester who had secured the execution of nine women and the imprisonment of six more by simulating possession. Certainly these cases affected the bench. There is no direct evidence of their effect on the king, but Thomas Fuller's verdict has often been quoted: 'The frequency of such forged Possessions wrought such an alteration upon the judgment of King JAMES, that he receding from what he had written in his Demonologie, grew first diffident of, and then flatly to deny the workings of Witches and Devils, as but Falshoods and Delusions.'[17]

The difficulty with this view is that a sceptical disposition and a reputation for probing impostures did not come to James late in life. He had scarcely arrived in London when he interested himself in the case of Mary Glover, a teenage girl suspected of counterfeiting possession.[18] In 1605 Sir Roger Wilbraham noted that the king had already solved two mysteries involving 'a phisicion that made latyne & lerned sermons in the slepe' and a woman who vomited pins and needles. The doctor was Richard Haydock of New College, Oxford. James heard him 'preach' one night, instructed the Earl of Worcester to examine him, and then frightened him into dropping his pretence by running at him with a sword and threatening to cut off his head. The case of the woman was very similar to that of Ann Gunter, whom James treated with a kindness so far removed from his behaviour in 1591 that she readily confessed her deceit and even secured a royal dowry.[19] Early in 1605 he investigated a prophet who spoke of imminent calamities, and had two bewitched women sent to Cambridge where university doctors certified that they were suffering from natural disorders. His pronouncements on the subject of marvels were equally indicative of a constant frame of mind. To Prince Henry he wrote that 'most miracles nou-a-dayes proves but illusions' and to an unknown correspondent that 'pretended wonders' and miracles 'should be all ways and diligently tested'. He was quite as blunt about the efficacy of the royal touch itself.[20]

Not so often recognised, but surely of more significance, is the caution which James showed in witchcraft affairs even before he left Scotland. In 1597 it was revealed that a Fifeshire witch Margaret Aiken had falsely accused a number of innocent women who were burnt. James felt obliged to revoke all commissions for the apprehension and punishment of witches on the grounds that honest citizens were not properly safeguarded against malicious or faulty charges.[21] On three occasions in 1597–8 the Scottish Privy Council upheld complaints from individuals accused of witchcraft and dismissed proceedings against them. Twice James intervened, once to

162

194

mitigate punishment and, in the case of the trials at Aberdeen in 1596–7, to order the authorities to drop all charges against two defendants who had been wrongfully accused by their enemies.[22] Even during the North Berwick affair, he was supposed to have shown a persistent incredulity. The writer of *Newes from Scotland* claimed that on hearing the confessions of Agnes Sampson 'his Majesty said they were all extreme liars'. Only her ability to repeat verbatim his pleasantries to Queen Ann on their wedding night was said to have convinced him that there was substance in her extraordinary dittay.[23] His determination to attend so many examinations, to scrutinise the evidence and even test the charms was itself, in part, an aspect of that 'fortunate judgment in clearing and solving of obscure riddles and doubtful mysteries' of which he always boasted. It seems quite compatible then for James to have always accepted the principles of witchcraft and yet, in each individual attribution that came to his notice, to have felt the need to be convinced, if possible by personal investigation.[24] In 1590–1 the evidence seemed overwhelming; on other occasions the same sceptical frame of mind uncovered fraud and trickery. Nor must we forget the very important point that James's famous detections were mostly concerned with child possession, a matter not essential to witch belief as it is set down in the *Daemonologie*. There is no evidence or suggestion that he ever changed his mind about the central canons of demonological theory, notably the possibility of the demonic pact.

However, if the King was not significantly more shrewd in the 1610s than in the 1590s and did not experience what R. Trevor Davies called 'a radical change of his views', we still have to explain his comparative lack of concern for English witchcraft. Partly, the answer lies in the far less virulent temper which surrounded it. The full force of the Continental persecution was not felt in England, where the courts were more sensitive, the use of extreme torture quite rare, and the charges often restricted to simple *maleficium* involving animal familiars rather than attendance at sabbats and other sensational matters. The Church of England did not wage a holy war against witches but against exorcists; and an exposé of exorcism by one of its most redoubtable scourges Samuel Harsnett was reported to have been presented to James soon after his accession.[25] Some English demonologists were also noticeably open-minded. Quite apart from Reginald Scot's comprehensive scepticism, reservations about aspects of witchcraft and witchcraft trials were expressed by George Gifford, John Cotta and even William Perkins. In this atmosphere the obsessive fear of witchcraft and magic never assumed the proportions it did elsewhere. In Ben Jonson's *Masque of Queens*, presented before James in 1609, a coven of hags is vanquished easily by Virtue and led bound before Fame's chariot. In *The Devil Is an Ass* (1616) Jonson's

163

character Pug, a junior demon allowed a day's mischief on earth, is repeatedly outwitted and has to be rescued from Newgate by Satan.[26] When the king earnestly inquired the answer to the well-known demonological teaser about the preponderance in witchcraft of old women over young, Sir James Harrington replied with a 'scurvey jeste' to the effect that 'the devil walketh in dry places'. Even James himself became flippant about the powers of dark-ness. In 1605 he informed Cecil that he was busy 'with hunting of witches, prophets, puritans, dead cats, and hares', but that Lord Montgomery had 'conjured all the devils here with his Welsh tongue, for the devil himself I trow dare not speak Welsh'.[27] One circumstance which undoubtedly eased his fears was the simple fact that English witchcraft and magic were rarely directed against his person. In this respect, it was the Jesuits who became the principal objects of his lively apprehensions. In his controversy with Bellarmine he waged a war of words against deposition and regicide by papal command. Since English priests proclaimed treason and were convicted of it, it was natural that he should regard them with a horror previously reserved for witches and speak of them as emissaries of the Devil. On the other hand, only one case of attempted bewitching of the king came to light, involving a schoolmaster called Peacock. Significantly James forgot his scepticism on the subject and reverted to former practices. Peacock was promptly committed to the Tower and tortured.[28]

Once again, however, the effect of the less compelling nature of English witchcraft and demonological opinion cannot in itself have been decisive. Before 1590 Scotland too was uninfluenced by Continental notions regarding witch practices, yet within a few years James's personal concern for the subject had contributed largely to a craze of the Continental type. The phenomenon of witchcraft was no doubt related to social conditions in the pre-industrial world, but the pattern of persecution could be influenced dramatically from above. Thus, to speak of James being mollified by the tenor of English witchcraft may be to put the cart before the horse. And while fear for his own life must have been a powerful motive for participation in the trials of 1590-1 it will not explain the writing of the *Daemonologie*. How then are we to account for the apparent change which took place in his attitudes after 1603? The answer must surely be that James became a witch-hunter and demonologist in order to satisfy political and religious pretensions at a time when they could be expressed in few other ways. In fact, he found in the theory and practice of witch persecution a perfect vehicle for his nascent ideals of kingship. In England these ideals did not change; they simply found alternative fulfilment.

It is patently clear, for instance, both from *Newes from Scotland* and from

164

his speech to the jurors of Barbara Napier, that James wished to play the part of the people's teacher and patriarch. But this desire existed independently of the fact that witchcraft was the matter in hand. It was integral to his view of monarchy as expressed in the *Basilikon Doron* and the *Trew law of free monarchies* and it led to his famous self-identification with King Solomon as the paradigm ruler. According to orthodox literature on the subject, the perfect prince was a model of virtue to his people, devoted to their welfare and education, sensitive in the care of religion and unity, respectful of rights, laws and advice, and above all wise and just in all his proceedings. For James too the images of monarchy were those of divine lieutenancy, father-hood and headship of the body politic. Brought up on a diet of treatises *de regimine principum* but continually thwarted in his ambitions as a ruler, it was natural that he should seize this early opportunity to unravel publicly, in court and in print, the mysterious vice of witchcraft, especially by drawing on the 'latest' Continental theories. Now the occasions for indulging in the *ex cathedra* were vastly multiplied after 1603, and James's passion for public debates and speeches need scarcely be emphasised. The point, however, is that his behaviour at Hampton Court, his harangues to Parliament and interference with its proceedings, his attempts to influence judicial opinion, even his brand of foreign policy, were only more elevated examples of the same obsession with the image of the philosopher-king which had involved him in the North Berwick affair. Another parallel and quite transparent piece of pedagogy was his public claim that he 'did upon the instant interpret and apprehend some darke phrases . . . contrary to the ordinary Grammer construction of them' in the famous Monteagle letter during the Powder Plot, a feat which was later magnified in a published account of the treason in just the way that *Newes from Scotland* had capitalised on James's witch-hunting.[29] The disputations at the universities, the mealtime seminars, the judgments in private cases all helped to divert the royal attention from any further investigation into the diabolical while satisfying the same instincts. The expression of his opinions in print was another extension of the desire to settle controversies and instruct his subjects. The *Daemonologie* was in this sense only one of the earliest of a long line of royal textbooks. At the other end of the scale, his intellectual appetite was whetted in less respectable and more trivial matters. One wonders to what extent his fascination with the details of the North Berwick conventions and with the Devil's 'mark' in particular was transmuted into the prurient interest he later showed in the sexual habits of his relations and courtiers.

But the most important ingredient of James's monarchy was surely his highly developed public religiosity. Nor in this instance was North Berwick

165

merely an occasion for indulging a certain style of government; demonology
was in fact intrinsically related to the presuppositions of godly rule. The
recurring theme of both the dittays of 1590-1 and *Newes from Scotland* was
that the king's Christian rectitude made him the Devil's principal target,
and yet at the same time protected him from all his machinations. This was
an issue which naturally arose whenever the role of authority in the war
against witchcraft was discussed. Demonologists like Bodin and Nicolas
Rémy, for instance, argued that the actual efficacy of magic and witchcraft
waned to the point of non-existence in proportion to the determination of the
public official in rooting them out; quite simply, the witch was disarmed of
her occult powers if brought face to face with the godly magistrate. James
discovered this argument at precisely the time when he was elaborating his
belief that the ruler was a divine lieutenant on earth, and incorporated it into
the *Daemonologie*:

> If they be but apprehended and deteined by anie private person, upon
> other private respectes, their power no doubt either in escaping, or·in
> doing hurte, is no lesse nor ever it was before. But if on the other parte,
> their apprehending and detention be by the lawfull Magistrate, upon the
> iust respectes of their guiltinesse in that craft, their power is then no
> greater then before that ever they medled with their master. For where
> God beginnes iustlie to strike by his lawfull Lieutennentes, it is not in
> the Devilles power to defraude or bereave him of the office, or effect of
> his powerfull and revenging Scepter.[30]

This fundamental principle of the politics of demonism is of crucial
significance. It transformed the very impotence of the North Berwick witches
into an affirmation of the truly divine nature (or the more powerful magic)
of James's early, and hitherto very hesitant magistracy. According to Agnes
Sampson's confession, which he personally extorted, they had wondered
why 'all ther devellerie culd do na harm to the King, as it did till others
dyvers', to which the Devil had answered, 'Il est un home de Dieu'.[31]
James could not have provided himself with a better statement of legitimacy,
nor, in the circumstances, from a more impeccable authority. Secondly, it
meant that the *Daemonologie* was not tangential to, let alone aberrant from,
his other early political writings. Its arguments complemented the Biblical,
historico-legal and patriarchal defences of monarchy attempted in the *Trew
law of free monarchies* and it dealt with one aspect of a kingship idealised in the
Basilikon Doron. Finally, it helps us to explain why James took his religious
duties with a seriousness which has recently been described as millenarian in
nature and content. In 1616 his editor Bishop Montagu claimed that the

166

paraphrase on the Book of Revelation composed around 1588 was the key to all the other royal works. W. M. Lamont has recently re-emphasised this point and argued that much of James's behaviour was inspired by a confidence derived from the Apocalypse. Millenarian kingship in its turn justified the persecution of witches; they were agents of Satan and swarmed more thickly as the end of Antichrist approached. James wrote in the *Daemonologie,* 'the consummation of the Worlde, and our deliverance drawing neare, makes Sathan to rage the more in his instruments, knowing his Kingdome to be so neare an ende'.[32]

If witch-hunting and the exegesis of Revelation were all that a Christian Prince could achieve in Scotland, the opportunities in England were once again so much more important. The caution enforced by the international diplomacy of the 1580s and 1590s was no longer necessary. From the position of subordination to which the Kirk had sought to depress him, James was suddenly given charge of a church which, in origin and ideology, was inseparably linked with the concept of the godly ruler. He could now take full advantage of what Lamont calls the 'centripetal millenarianism' of Foxe and Jewel, and associate himself with the Christian Emperor who would secure the final victories. The new role immediately occupied his attention, as Hampton Court again demonstrates. In 1609, his defence of the oath of allegiance gave him the chance to return to Revelation in order to demonstrate that the Pope was Antichrist. More generally, his close association with eminent scholars and divines, his insatiable appetite for sermons, his attempts to enforce conformity and his harrying of recalcitrants like Vorstius all reflected a scrupulous concern for the public obligations of godly rule that it had been simply impossible to satisfy fully before. Here too, then, we can see how James's essentially uniform ideals responded to the change in his circumstances after 1603, and how demonology was superseded as their most effective expression.

III

But what of the *Daemonologie* itself? What contribution did James make to the international debate on witchcraft and how successfully did he dispose of the sceptics? The treatise is a conversation between the demonologist Epistemon and the doubter Philomathes. Though one could scarcely speak of him as devil's advocate in this context, Philomathes is made to put the principal contemporary objections to orthodox opinions on magic and witchcraft. His role is thus that of a surrogate Weyer or Scot and identical to

167

that of Mysodaemon in Henry Holland's *Treatise against Witchcraft* (1590). Are the Biblical references to witchcraft decisive? Is magic really either harmful or unlawful? Do witches only imagine what they confess? How is it that God permits such evil? Epistemon is prompt to reassure his friend of the reality and power of the enemy. Magic and witchcraft, he says, are practices consistent with Christian belief and everyday experience; they are mentioned unambiguously in Scripture and confirmed by daily confessions. By permitting them God tests the patience of the elect, strengthens the faith of waverers, and punishes the wicked and reprobate. The Devil is given limited powers to entice the curious, revengeful and grasping into his service. His subtle and airy quality, his ageless experience of things and his profound knowledge enable him to perpetrate magical phenomena and acts of *maleficium* by which men are deceived and finally damned.

In magic and necromancy (Book I), the Devil permits himself to appear to be commanded in the performance of trivial feats by teaching magicians and spell-makers how to conjure him with charms. These have no intrinsic power and only work because the Devil co-operates with the charmer. Similarly, the effects of magic are not true in substance, for only God's miracles are real; they are in fact counterfeit, appearing to be true 'onelie to mennes outward senses'. In witchcraft (Book II) the Devil himself is commander and the witches his instruments, contracted into allegiance by a formal pact and marked as a sign of service. Again, there are agreed ceremonies and formulae, in this case for injuring men and beasts, but the means employed (excepting actual poison) are only the external forms for inward effects wrought by the Devil; just as the sacraments are outward means for God's inner workings. A twofold delusion is involved in that witches, like magicians, think themselves responsible for what is effected and, more important, believe themselves capable of doing things which are in fact 'against all Theologie divine, and Philosophie humaine'. Thus, while there are witches who hold actual sabbats, Philomathes is right to doubt some of their confessions. The world of spirits (Book III) is also filled with fabulous as well as real phenomena. Epistemon explains that there are spirits which haunt places, pursue and possess men and women and act as incubi and succubi. On the other hand, wraiths and werewolves are delusions. Nor can monsters be generated naturally, these, together with fairies, being products of the Devil's trickery. Against both magic and witchcraft the magistrate must fight unceasingly, the punishment in each case being death; the private man must amend his life and pray against the assaults of Satan.

These arguments were the stock-in-trade of orthodox European demonology. The absence of citations and case histories reduces James's book to

168

a fraction of the customary bulk, but it has all the other features of the typical Renaissance witchcraft treatise. The idea that demonology was best conducted in the catechetic form had been pioneered in the scholastic *Malleus Maleficarum* (?1486) and adopted by most major writers. Two dialogues which could have been actual models for the *Dæmonologie* had recently appeared in England, Lambert Daneau's *Les sorciers* translated as *A dialogue of witches* (1575), and Holland's *Treatise against Witchcraft*. Discussions of magic as well as witchcraft, of spirits and possession and of examinations and punishments were usual. Most writers in the field would have agreed with Epistemon's views—his definitions of magic and witchcraft, his theological and philosophical explanations of demonic activity, his Biblical exegesis, his lists of possible acts of *maleficium*, his account of the Devil, his description of remedies and penalties. Even when he appears to be sceptical, Epistemon follows a well-worn path. A popular but wrongly ascribed early Canon Episcopi which questioned the reality of night flight and sabbats was often quoted and had to be explained away by the authors of the *Malleus*.[33] Several sixteenth-century demonologists argued that spiritual transportation to sabbats, generation of children and monsters by incubus devils and metamorphosis of humans into wolves and other shapes violated natural and theological laws, and it therefore became traditionally permissible to cast doubt on these particular witch activities. The explanations why these things nevertheless appeared in confessions are often quite baffling and fall oddly upon the modern ear. What, for instance, are we to make of Nicolas Rémy's point that, absurd as it was to believe that anyone could really be changed into a wolf, so well were the witches endowed with the natural qualities of the animal that they differed 'but little' from the actuality? Or the generally held view that the Devil could totally disrupt human perception with sensory delusions and *glamours*, 'that thinges are beleved to be sene, harde, and perceyved, which notwithstandinge are no such maner of thinges'.[34]

James's own mixture of religious and naturalistic arguments and his confusion of the real with the illusory seem no less astonishing but are in fact quite typical. While allowing that witches can be bodily transvected through the air, Epistemon insists that they cannot pass through keyholes in the shapes of small animals. The Devil might create this impression by 'his woorkeman-shippe upon the aire', but it is in fact a physical impossibility. Similarly, the idea that witches can, as they confess, attend meetings in spirit only is against all theology; but the Devil creates the necessary dream in their minds, simultaneously illudes third parties into believing they have met them, and even commits the murders and injuries claimed by the witches while in the spiritual state. Henri Boguet used these same arguments when he 'explained'

169

the phenomenon of lycanthropy, and they are in fact a perfect example of the tortuous dialectic employed by all demonologists.[35] Some, it is true, felt reluctant to admit any exceptions to the power of witchcraft and to the reality of what was confessed; Bodin and Rémy (the latter not consistently) both argued that supernatural phenomena could not be subjected to the ordinary criteria of nature and physical causation but should be accepted on trust. James felt otherwise. By showing scepticism in the officially approved areas he hoped to 'saill surelie, betwixt Charybdis and Scylla', between doubting all and believing all. Although he condemned Scot as a Sadducee and suggested that Weyer was a wizard posing as an intellectual, he also criticised Bodin's *De la Démonomanie des Sorciers* (1580) as a product more of diligence than judgment.

In fact, Weyer's denouncement of witchcraft was in part only the logical *reductio* of James's own position. In the *De Praestigiis Daemonum* (1563) he argued that 'witches' were either innocent victims of ignorant physicians and superstitious clergy, or deceived into accepting their own culpability by the Devil, who took advantage of the hallucinations accompanying natural conditions like melancholy and nightmare. Whichever the case, the supposed pact on which conventional witch-theory was ultimately based, together with all the various witchcraft ceremonies, were illusions of the impossible. 'Witches' were harmless old women needing medical and religious guidance, not accusation and execution. Witchcraft was in fact a demonic imposture with no warrant in Scripture, a hideous lie perpetrated by the Devil in order to disrupt society. Now although there are strongly empirical and human-itarian elements in Weyer's argument it differs from normal demonological theory in degree only. All writers in the tradition, including James, agreed that though the Devil had superhuman endowments which enabled him to produce true effects, there were areas where God had made him impotent and where he was forced to deceive men's perception by *glamours*. All writers, including James, also admitted that in witchcraft the real agent of *maleficium*, true or illusory, was the Devil. And, as we have seen, orthodox demon-ologists had to allow for some deception of the witches themselves, some even admitting the similarities between witch phenomena and hallucinatory illnesses. Weyer simply extended these arguments until the witch became totally redundant in the effecting of *maleficium*, and the area of illusion wide enough to cover all rather than part of her confession. Otherwise he remained quite traditional and his discussions of devils, magic, possession and other matters were in essence as commonplace as those of Epistemon. Weyer even allowed the magician precisely that actual collusion with the Devil which he denied the witch.

170

James cannot have seen that theories of sensory delusion and mental illness were double-edged, for he comes perilously close to conceding Weyer's position. Lycanthropy is, he admits, a disease resulting from 'a naturall super-abundance of Melancholie'. Nightmare leads to physical sensations of constriction by 'some unnaturall burden or spirite'. Tales of fairies are produced by the Devil illuding 'the senses of sundry simple creatures, in making them beleeve that they saw and harde such thinges as were nothing so indeed'. In fact, 'all our senses, as we are so weake, and even by ordinarie sicknesses will be often times deluded'. These admissions are hardly com-pensated for by his actual refutation of the *De Praestigiis Daemonum*. Epis-temon bluntly denies Philomathes's suggestion (following Weyer) that the scriptural *loci* refer only to magicians and poisoners, and claims that Weyer's medical diagnosis is in any case the wrong one since witches, contrary to the symptoms of the melancholic disposition, are 'rich and wordly-wise, some of them fatte or corpulent in their bodies, and most part of them altogether given over to the pleasures of the flesh, continual haunting of companie, and all kind of merrines'.[36] Quite apart from the fact that neither argument deals satisfactorily with the difficulties raised by Weyer, both had been deployed previously with much Biblical exegesis and etymological and quasi-medical reasoning by Bodin. In his anxiety to be rational about some aspects of witchcraft James clearly failed to grasp the full significance of Weyer's adaptation of the theory of illusion. Nor did he appreciate the fact, ably demonstrated by Bodin, that Weyer's dismissal of witchcraft was funda-mentally incompatible with his orthodox acceptance of magic.

Like Bodin, Reginald Scot also wished to avoid the inconsistencies involved in rejecting some aspects of demonism while accepting others. But while Bodin opted for total credulity, Scot's *Discoverie of Witchcraft* (1584) attempted to demolish its very foundations. In an important appendix, Scot developed the view that the Devil and his demons were not to be conceived of as having corporeal existence or tangible qualities but rather as spiritual powers of evil, and that scriptural texts which spoke of them carnally were to be interpreted not literally but metaphorically and 'significativelie'. This, as Gabriel Harvey remarked at the time, 'hitteth the nayle on the head with a witnesse', for it destroyed at one blow the very essence of witchcraft and magic as physical collusions with spirits. Scot removed the Devil altogether from the world of material concepts and actions and reduced the belief in the demonic agency of physical events to a species of idolatry practised by 'children, fools, melancholic persons [and] papists'. Since the age of real miracles had passed with Christ, the only explanation left for the confessions of witches and the claims of magicians was that they were either purely

171

imaginary or produced by 'prestigious juggling' and 'nimble conveiance of the hand'. Thus, Scot adopted the suggestion that witches were often either sane and innocent or deluded by illness and 'dotage', but added a further dimension to the theory of deception to account for all phenomena attributed by Weyer to devils. This extra ingredient was 'meere cousenage' or leger-demain and it covered not only modern instances but Biblical episodes like that of the witch of Endor. Indeed, the main purpose of the *Discoverie of Witchcraft* was, following a proposal of Weyer's, to reinterpret the many different Old Testament Hebrew words uniformly translated as 'witch' or 'magician' but in fact referring either to poisoners or to a variety of fraudulent practices ranging from augury and alchemy through to necromancy and ventriloquism. In short, witchcraft was an impossibility, 'a cousening art, wherin the name of God is abused, prophaned and blasphemed, and his power attributed to a vile creature'.[37]

To this wholesale scepticism James replies simply that it is Sadducism to doubt the existence of spirits and likely to lead to a questioning of God him-self. This is not strictly fair. Scot did not deny that the Devil had been created as a living being but only insisted that he was 'ordeined to a spirituall proportion', the exact essence of which was hidden from man's under-standing. James, on the contrary, makes specific provision for the physical appearance of devils and spirits but admits rather weakly that the visible proof of corporeality which Scot demanded is 'reserved to the secreete knowledge of God, whom he wil permit to see such thinges, and whome not'. And although he too questions some of the physical attributes of devils, his general insistence on the physical reality of the witches' pacts and sub-sequent *maleficium* makes it impossible for him to concede Scot's principal point. Since Christ the 'appearances of Angels or good spirits' *has* ceased, but not those of 'abusing spirites'. Epistemon explains that whereas it is more difficult for Satan himself to have visible dealings with men and move 'familiarlie amongst them' since the era of Gentildom and the overthrow of Catholicism in England, nevertheless he compensates by the more frequent use of the medium of witchcraft and the other unlawful arts. It was to this passage that James later referred Archbishop Abbott, who had expressed doubts about the grounds for nullity *propter maleficium versus hanc* in the Essex divorce case. And he added, 'that the Devil's power is not so universal against us, that I freely confess; but that it is utterly restrained *quoad nos*, how was then a minister of Geneva bewitched to death, and were the witches daily punished by our law?'[38] The simple fact that witchcraft existed and was punished was sufficient refutation of Scot's arguments. James could not see it the other way round.

172

necessary to the world-view of order on which James's political philosophy rested, just as demonology in general has been seen as the logical extension of a whole cosmology.[41] In the sixteenth and seventeenth centuries political order was defended in terms of 'arguments by correspondence' in which analogies were drawn between parallel features of the various planes of the hierarchy of being. James's own use of this language involved the classic 'similitudes' between monarchy, divine power, patriarchal authority and the role of the head of the human body.[42] However, the cogency of the arguments for order also depended on the elaboration of a world of disorder. Recourse might be had to the idea of the decay of nature or to historical cases of dislocation, but the language often used was that of 'contrariety' in which the antitheses of orderly relationships were described. Especially persuasive was the image of the upside-down world, in which the normal patterns of authority were inverted by, for instance, the rule of the body over the head or of sons over fathers and subjects over princes.[43] The primary polarity in this way of thinking was of course God-Satan, the very prototype of what might be called the 'argument by antithesis'. Contrariety was thus a presupposition of Christian philosophy of history and political thought; Augustine's antithetical two cities and the contrasts drawn between monarchy and tyranny in medieval writings on the prince are paradigm examples. The Reformation concepts of election and reprobation, and the increasingly literal interpretation of the millennium and the activities of Antichrist encouraged still further the tendency to polarise experience. But antithesis was not confined to religious language. Its formal role in traditional logic and rhetoric guaranteed its use in a wide range of contexts. 'Contraries laid together', it was typically said, 'doe much set forth each other in their lively colours.'[44] The *mundus inversus* too was invoked in a number of ways, as a literary and artistic device, as the basis of fooling, comic drama and other entertainments, and as both a part of the mentality of popular revolt and a way of condemning it.[45]

James himself acknowledged the usefulness of the argument by antithesis in distinguishing monarchy from tyranny, 'for *contraria iuxta se posita magis elucescunt*'.[46] He also used the language of inversion to describe the disorder that would follow disobedience to kings. In 1609 it was Antichrist in the shape of papal supremacy which seemed the major threat; 'the world it selfe must be turned upside downe, and the order of Nature inverted (making the left hand to have the place before the Right, and the last named to bee the first in honour) that this primacie may bee maintained'.[47] But the most elaborate attempt to characterise disorder by inversion was surely to be found in Renaissance treatises on witchcraft. In describing its antithesis, orthodox

174

There is, then, little that is original in the *Daemonologie*, perhaps only the curious theory that witches can be carried bodily through the air like Habakkuk but only for the duration of one intake of breath. Nor are the objections of the two sceptics against whom the treatise is directed effectively met and overcome. Thomas Ady was later to complain with some justice that, 'blinded by some Scotish Mist', James had only 'written again the same Tenents that Bodinus and others had before written, and were by Scot confuted'.[39] It is true that James only intended to reason, as he said, 'upon *genus* leaving *species*, and *differentia* to be comprehended therein'. But it is doubtful whether it was possible any longer to write successful primers in orthodox demonology. Now that the interpretation of so many scriptural *exempla* was disputed, demonologists needed to be equipped to counter the intricate etymology on which sceptics like Scot, and later Ady and Filmer, were increasingly coming to rely. In this respect, neither the *Daemonologie* nor the new translation of the Bible made any headway. After Weyer, believers in witchcraft also had to argue the pathology of the subject. Here James seems to have been in a dilemma. His recognition of the effects of melancholy and nightmare and his readiness to submit bewitched women and children to clinical examination suggests an empirical open-mindedness. Indeed, he may even have learned something from Weyer's chapters on feigned possession. On the other hand, the argument *a posteriori* that witches are fun-loving hedonists because they attend spectacular orgies shows that he could not see beyond the myth to the real character of the majority of those accused.[40] Most important of all, after Weyer and Scot it was essential to find more satisfactory criteria for distinguishing the actual from the illusory. Hitherto the canons of theology had served this purpose. But so much had had to be attributed to the imagination and the corruption of the senses that the definition of what was real became less and less meaningful. In a sense, the diametrically opposed approaches of Bodin and Scot were the only logical solutions to this problem. By attempting to be reasonable about witchcraft without giving up his belief in its fundamental features James tried to find a compromise between common sense and faith. Like Weyer's it involved too many inconsistencies to be really successful.

IV

As we have seen, the interest of the *Daemonologie* lies elsewhere, in the circumstances of its genesis and as an early expression of an ideal kingship. In addition, there is an important sense in which, original or not, it was

173

205

demonologists presupposed an orderly world and so sustained it.[48] James summarised perfectly the purpose and the method when he wrote in his own *Daemonologie*, 'since the Devill is the very contrarie opposite to God, there can be no better way to know God, than by the contrarie'.[49] Conventional accounts of the nature of Satan, the character of Hell and the activities of witches owed much of their inspiration and cogency to this basic premise. The particular version of the upside-down world they offered, on which both the North Berwick dittays and the *Daemonologie* were based, must have confirmed many of James's political values.

The Devil, of course, *was* disorder, the first rebellious subject who tried to bring chaos to Heaven and succeeded in bringing it to man. Yet Hell itself was not simply a confusion. Although he disliked giving devils titles of honour or military ranks, James conceded that they 'could not subsist with-out some order', and theological justification for distinguishing between them on grounds of natural inequality could be found in Aquinas.[50] Renaissance demonologists and pneumatologists therefore drew freely on the language of political and military organisation. The vital point was that the order they discerned in the Devil's government was a spurious version of the legitimate order of divine politics; Weyer's demography of Hell, for instance, was entitled *Pseudomonarchia daemonum*. Demons co-operated only out of a common hate for mankind, not from the mutual love and respect for magistracy that cemented all properly constituted human societies. Moreover, 'that the inferior are subject to the superior is not for the benefit of the superior, but rather to their detriment; because since to do evil belongs in a pre-eminent degree to unhappiness, it follows that to preside in evil is to be more unhappy'.[51] To complete these inversions, the Devil's style of government was universally acknowledged to be tyranny, the antithesis of true kingship: 'the prince is a kind of likeness of divinity; and the tyrant, on the contrary, a likeness of the boldness of the Adversary'.[52]

In describing witchcraft itself, demonologists again concentrated on the systematic reversal of traditional priorities, symbolised by the contrariness which made witches do things back-to-front or left-to-right, 'in a ridiculous and unseemly manner . . . opposite to that of other men'.[53] The point was often made, as it was in the Scottish dittays of 1590-1, in connection with the dance, a widely used image of political harmony and considered to have in itself the power to teach participants and spectators the principles of order. In contrast, the grotesque gyrations of the sabbat were 'festes de desordre' and the dancers were not humanised but dehumanised by the experience.[54] Similarly, the Devil's liturgy was portrayed, as in the *Daemonologie,* as deliberately *un*ceremonious. It was a hideous parody or 'aping' of true worship

175

and therefore offensive to the sacramentalism in which state churches expressed their commitment to the orderly world. The sexual exploits of witches
also negated order, dethroning reason from a sovereign position on which
not only individual well-being but social relations and political obligation
were thought to depend. The surrender to passion was disorderly in more
than the physical sense; kissing the Devil's arse, like the Quaker refusal to
meet authority bare-headed, was a highly-charged symbolic act of political
defiance. A further inversion of good government lay in the anti-familial
aspects of witchcraft. It was notorious that witches were able to prevent the
consummation of marriages by ligature. Pierre de Lancre thought that they
also disordered the family by subverting patriarchal authority and destroying
filial love, and the dramatists Broome and Heywood made the upside-down
family a theme of their comedy of 1634, *The Late Lancashire Witches*. If
familial and political duties were analogous, if the state was based ultimately
on the actions of heads of households, then *maleficium* of this sort was especially
damaging. Above all, the condition of a society dominated by women must
have been seen as one of fundamental contrariety. 'I demand,' wrote Bacon
of the Amazons, 'is not such a preposterous government (against the first
order of nature, for women to rule over men) in itself void, and to be sup-
pressed?'[55] Finally, there was the fact that witchcraft was defined technically
in terms of re-baptism and a formal compact. The full force of this voluntary
rejection of the conventional world only becomes apparent if we recall the
non-sacramental implications of infant-baptism, but the main point is clear.
The activity of witchcraft was founded in the sin of disobedience, the primary
cause of disorder. Witches, like rebels and social climbers, were motivated by
pride and ambition; rebels, like witches, abused the sabbath and tried to
turn society and the state upside-down. Theorists of order and demonologists alike demonstrated the essential identity of these 'unnatural' treasons
by glossing the text from 1 Samuel XV. 23, 'For rebellion is as the sin of
witchcraft.' William Perkins, for instance, wrote:

> It is a principle of the Law of nature, holden for a grounded truth in
> all Countries and Kingdoms, among all people in every age; that the
> traytor who is an enemie to the State, and rebelleth against his lawfull
> Prince, should be put to death; now the most notorious traytor and
> rebell that can be, is the Witch. For she renounceth God himselfe, the
> King of Kings, she leaves the societie of his Church and people, she
> bindeth herself in league with the devil.

The political implications of witchcraft could not have been stated more
bluntly.[56]

V

Locating classic demonology in this way within the wider linguistic context of Renaissance political thought surely helps us to discern its essential rationality and intellectual appeal. Norman Cohn has recently said that the study of the mental world of late sixteenth- and early seventeenth-century magistrates may enable us to understand 'why so many of the educated and privileged *needed* to believe' in witches. The answer lies partly in the transposition into a specifically political mode of the principle of inversion, to which Cohn himself attributes the rise of the traditional medieval stereotype of the Devil-worshipper.[57] The conceptual world of men like Bodin, Rémy and James I was dominated by the principle of order, but the meaning of order could only be grasped by exploring its antithesis or 'contrary'. The existence of one was a necessary condition for the understanding of the other, and a single vocabulary was sufficient for the description of both. Hence their portrayal, in what seems to us morbid or absurd detail, of the deliberately disorderly aspects of witchcraft, notably the horrendous sabbat. With his fondness for the analogies which could be drawn between the government of the body, the family and the state, James must have been particularly sensitive to the unruliness which allegedly characterised demonism. But, like the Book of Revelation, both the confessions forced from the witches of North Berwick and his studies in demonology were also a source of comfort. At a vital stage in his early career they helped him to establish a view of monarchy and his own fitness for implementing it; but at a deeper level they reinforced his entire political philosophy. For the *Daemonologie* was not, as it were, a fresh statement about the world, but a re-statement of the need for order and its goodness, seen from a different perspective. Our understanding of James VI and I would not be complete without some attempt to come to terms with it.

Notes

1 The earliest evidence of direct contact is in R. Pitcairn, *Ancient Criminal Trials in Scotland*, Maitland Club, 3 vols (Edinburgh, 1829–33), I, p. 203 (case of Hector Munro); and *Calendar of State Papers relating to Scotland* (*C.S.P.S.*), X, pp. 348, 365 (case of Dutch prophetess of Leith).
2 See for example D. H. Willson, *King James VI and I* (London, 1956), pp. 26, 64–5, 81–2.

177

3 R. Ashton, *James I by his Contemporaries* (London, 1969), p. 2; Robert Johnston, *The Historie of Scotland*, trans. T. Middleton (London, 1646), in R. Buchanan, ed., *Scotia Rediviva* (Edinburgh, 1826), pp. 370–1.

4 Christina Larner, 'James VI and I and Witchcraft', in A. G. R. Smith, ed., *The Reign of James VI and I* (London, 1973), pp. 74–90. I am grateful to Mrs Larner for her advice on an early draft of this essay, and for permission to consult her PhD thesis: Christina Larner, 'Scottish Demonology in the Sixteenth and Seventeenth Centuries and its Theological Background' (Edinburgh University, 1962). On Scottish witchcraft in the period, see C. K. Sharpe, *A Historical Account of the Belief in Witchcraft in Scotland* (London, 1884); F. Legge, 'Witchcraft in Scotland', *Scottish Review*, XVIII (1891), pp. 257–88; and the records of individual cases in Pitcairn and G. F. Black, *A Calendar of Cases of Witchcraft in Scotland 1510–1727* (New York, 1938).

5 Sir James Melville, *Memoirs 1549–93*, Bannatyne Club (Edinburgh, 1827), p. 395; Pitcairn, I, pp. 211, 239.

6 *Newes from Scotland* (1591), repr. *Gentleman's Magazine*, XLIX (1779), p. 449; Pitcairn, I, pp. 211, 236–7, 245, 254; C.S.P.S., X, p. 365.

7 C.S.P.S., X, 501–2, 504–5, 530–1; Melville, p. 395; *Register of the Privy Council of Scotland (R.P.C.S.)*, IV, pp. 643–4.

8 M. A. Murray, 'The "Devil" of North Berwick', *Scottish Review*, XV (1917–18), pp. 310–21, suggests that Bothwell was in fact the 'devil' who preached at North Berwick, a theory shared by Montague Summers, *The History of Witchcraft and Demonology* (London, 1926, repr. 1965), p. 8. Helen Stafford, 'Notes on Scottish Witchcraft Cases, 1590–91', in Norton Downs, ed., *Essays in Honour of Conyers Read* (Chicago, 1953), pp. 96–118, is much more sceptical. Her account and that of William Roughead, 'The Witches of North Berwick', in *The Riddle of the Ruthvens and other Essays* (Edinburgh, 1936), pp. 144–66, are the best of the North Berwick trials. The full indictments are in Pitcairn, but there is important additional material in *Newes from Scotland*.

9 C.S.P.S., X, pp. 524, 430; *Newes from Scotland*, pp. 450, 394–5.

10 C.S.P.S., X, p. 510.

11 C.S.P.S., X, pp. 514–15, 519–20; Pitcairn, I, pp. 242–4.

12 C.S.P.S., X, p. 524.

13 C.S.P.S., X, p. 525; *Daemonologie, in forme of a dialogue* (Edinburgh, 1597), pp. 79–80 (all references are to the original edition reprinted in facsimile in the series *The English Experience* by Theatrum Orbis Terrarum, Amsterdam, 1969).

14 Pitcairn, I, p. 400; Black, p. 29.

15 C.S.P.S., XIII, pp. 56, 73, 78.

16 C. L'Estrange Ewen, *Witch Hunting and Witch Trials* (London, 1929), pp. 98–113; Alan Macfarlane, *Witchcraft in Tudor and Stuart England* (London, 1970), pp. 28–9, 200; G. L. Kittredge, *Witchcraft in Old and New England* (Cambridge, Mass., 1929, repr. New York, 1958), pp. 276–328; Barbara Rosen, ed., *Witchcraft* (London, 1969), pp. 19–29, 331–2; K. V. Thomas,

178

Religion and the Decline of Magic (Penguin edn, Harmondsworth, 1973), pp. 517–51. Wallace Notestein, *History of Witchcraft in England, 1558–1718* (Washington, 1911; repr. 1965), pp. 93–109, gives the least extreme version of the old view.

17 Quoted by Kittredge, p. 326. Classic expositions of James's supposed change of heart can be found in R. Trevor Davies, *Four Centuries of Witch Beliefs* (London, 1947), pp. 58–63, 76–84, and H. N. Paul, *The Royal Play of Macbeth* (New York, 1950), pp. 75–130.

18 Paul, pp. 103–12.

19 H. S. Scott, ed., *The Journal of Sir Roger Wilbraham, 1593–1616*, Camden Miscellany, X (London, 1902), p. 70; Edmund Lodge, *Illustrations of British History*, 3 vols (London, 1791), III, pp. 283–5, 287–8; Willson, p. 310; Kittredge, pp. 321–2.

20 *Historical Manuscripts Commission Records*, IX, Salisbury XVII (London, 1938), pp. 19–20, 22, 33, 36–7, 65, 222–3; J. Nichols, *The Progresses of King James the First*, 4 vols (London, 1828), I, p. 304; Kittredge, pp. 316, 319.

21 Andrew Brown, *History of Glasgow and of Paisley, Greenock, and Port-Glasgow*, 2 vols (Glasgow, 1795), I, pp. 39–40; *R.P.C.S.*, V, pp. 409–10.

22 *R.P.C.S.*, V, pp. 405–6, 448, 495; Black, p. 29 (case of Bessie Aitken); *Spalding Club Miscellany*, I (Aberdeen, 1841), pp. 163–4.

23 *Newes from Scotland*, p. 449; the fact that James was personally responsible for Sampson's confession supports Mrs Larner's view (*op. cit.*, pp. 84–5) that this report of his scepticism was, however, inserted in hindsight to enhance his reputation with English readers of the pamphlet.

24 Possibly a common attitude; see Alan Macfarlane, *The Family Life of Ralph Josselin* (Cambridge, 1970), pp. 191–2.

25 Notestein, pp. 73–92; Rosen, p. 313; Paul, pp. 107–8.

26 G. L. Kittredge, 'King James I and "*The Devil Is an Ass*"', *Modern Philology*, IX (1911–12), pp. 195–209, argues that Jonson was being openly contemptuous towards beliefs in witchcraft, particularly the idea of demonic possession.

27 Nichols, I, p. 492; *Historical Manuscripts Commission Records*, IX, Salisbury XVII, p. 121.

28 *Calendar of State Papers Domestic 1619–1625*, CXII/104, p. 125; Notestein, p. 399.

29 *A Discourse of the maner of the discoverie of the powder-treason*, in *Workes* (London, 1616), pp. 227–8, and *A speache in the Parliament House, ibid.*, p. 502.

30 *Daemonologie*, pp. 50–1; cf. Jean Bodin, *De la Démonomanie des Sorciers* (Paris, 1580), pp. 139–44, and Nicolas Rémy, *Demonolatry*, Montague Summers, ed. (London, 1948), pp. 4–5.

31 Melville, p. 395.

32 'To the Reader', *Workes*, D3ᵛ; W. M. Lamont, *Godly Rule: Politics and Religion 1603–1660* (London, 1969), pp. 28–52; *Daemonologie*, p. 81.

33 H. C. Lea, *Materials Toward a History of Witchcraft*, 3 vols (Philadelphia,

179

1939, repr. New York, 1957), I, pp. 178–80; *Malleus Maleficarum*, Montague Summers, ed. (London, 1928), pp. 3ff.

34 Rémy, *Demonolatry*, p. 113; Andreas Hyperius, 'Whether that the Devils Have Bene the Shewers of Magicall artes' in *Two Common Places taken out of Andreas Hyperius*, trans. R. V. (London, 1581), p. 47. On 'glamours' see Johann Weyer, *De Praestigiis Daemonum*, trans. as *Les illusions et tromperies des diables*, 2 vols (Paris, 1885), I, pp. 51ff; and Francesco Guazzo, *Compendium maleficarum*, Montague Summers, ed. (London, 1929), pp. 7–9.

35 *Daemonologie*, pp. 38–42; cf. Henri Boguet, *Examen of Witches*, Montague Summers, ed. (London, 1929), chapter 47. On types of demonological argu-ment in the period, see J. L. Teall, 'Witchcraft and Calvinism in Elizabethan England: Divine power and human agency', *Journal of the History of Ideas*, XXIII (1962), pp. 21–36; Wayne Shumaker, *The Occult Sciences in the Renaissance: A Study in Intellectual Patterns* (Berkeley and Los Angeles, 1972), pp. 70–107, especially pp. 91–9; and H. C. Erik Midelfort, *Witch Hunting in Southwestern Germany 1562–1684: The Social and Intellectual Foundations* (Stanford, 1972), pp. 10–66, who stresses the flexible and varied character of witchcraft theory.

36 *Daemonologie*, pp. 61, 69, 74, 52, 28–30. James seems to have had specific individuals in mind; in a manuscript of the *Daemonologie* which contains corrections in his own hand, the initials EM, RG and BN appear in the margin opposite the phrases 'rich and wordly-wise', 'fatte or corpulent', and 'given over to the pleasures of the flesh' respectively. Rhodes Dunlap, 'King James and some witches; the date and text of the "Daemonologie" ', *Philological Quarterly*, LIV (1975–6), pp. 40–6, suggests that these refer to three of the North Berwick defendants: Ewfame Makcalzane, the heiress of Lord Liftoun-hall, a Senator of the College of Justice; Richard Graham, client of Bothwell's; and Barbara Napier, wife of Archibald Douglas, burgess of Edinburgh.

37 Reginald Scot, *Discoverie of Witchcraft* (London, 1584), p. 472.

38 *State Trials*, T. B. Howell, ed., II (London, 1816), p. 801.

39 Thomas Ady, *A Candle in the Dark* (London, 1656), pp. 140–1.

40 James's socio-psychological appraisal of witchcraft was, however, influenced by the fact that some of the principal North Berwick defendants were of considerable social status; *Daemonologie*, pp. 28–30 and note 36 above.

41 H. R. Trevor-Roper, *Religion, the Reformation and Social Change* (2nd ed., London, 1972), pp. 177–83, 185, 192.

42 W. H. Greenleaf, *Order, Empiricism and Politics: Two Traditions of English Political Thought 1500–1700* (London, 1964), pp. 21–6, 58–67.

43 For examples of other analogous inversions in the world of disorder, see John Christopherson, *An exhortation to all menne to take hede of rebellion* (London, 1554), sigs T1r–T2r, T6v–T7v.

44 William Gouge, *Of domesticall duties* (London, 1622), 'Epistle Dedicatory'.

45 E. R. Curtius, *European Literature and the Latin Middle Ages*, trans. from the German by W. R. Trask (London, 1953), pp. 94–8; Enid Welsford, *The Fool:*

180

His Social and Literary History (London, 1935), pp. 197–217; Ian Donaldson, *The World Upside-Down: Comedy from Jonson to Fielding* (Oxford, 1970), *passim*; E. Le Roy Ladurie, *Les paysans de Languedoc*, 2 vols (Paris, 1966), I, pp. 405–14; Christopher Hill, *The World Turned Upside Down: Radical Ideas of the English Revolution* (London, 1972), *passim*.

46 *Basilikon Doron, Workes*, p. 155.

47 *A premonition to all most mightie monarches, Workes*, p. 307.

48 The same way of thinking is said by some theorists to underlie the labelling of deviance in modern societies; see, for instance, J. D. Douglas, 'Deviance and Respectability in the Social Construction of Moral Meanings', in *Deviance and Respectability: The Social Construction of Moral Meanings* (New York, 1970), pp. 3–30.

49 *Daemonologie*, p. 55.

50 *A premonition to all most mightie monarches, Workes*, p. 305; Aquinas, *Summa Theologica*, Part I, Q. 109, 'The Ordering of the Bad Angels', in A. C. Pegis, ed., *Basic Writings of Saint Thomas Aquinas*, 2 vols (New York, 1945), I, pp. 1012–16.

51 Aquinas, *loc. cit.*, p. 1014.

52 John Dickinson, trans. and ed., *The Statesman's Book of John of Salisbury* (London, 1927, repr. New York, 1963), pp. 335–6, 339; cf. Erasmus, *The Education of a Christian Prince*, L. K. Born, ed. (New York, 1936, repr. 1965), pp. 157, 174.

53 Rémy, *Demonolatry*, p. 61.

54 Compare Pierre de Lancre, *Tableau de l'inconstance des mauvais anges et demons* (Paris, 1612), pp. 199–212, with Sir Thomas Elyot, *The boke named the governour* (London, 1531), sigs K1r–M4v.

55 *Works*, J. Spedding, R. L. Ellis and D. D. Heath, eds, 14 vols (London, 1857–74), VII, 33.

56 William Perkins, *Discourse of the Damned Art of Witchcraft*, in *Works*, 3 vols (London, 1616–18), III, pp. 651, 639; cf. Isaac Bargrave, *A sermon preached before king Charles* (London, 1627), based on 1 Samuel, XV. 23.

57 N. Cohn, 'Europe's inner demons', *Times Literary Supplement* (14 March 1975), p. 278, and *Europe's Inner Demons* (London, 1975), *passim*; cf. the plea that demonology be seen in a wider intellectual context made by Teall, *op. cit.*, p. 36. I hope to explore the points made in the last section of this essay more fully on another occasion.

181

George Gifford and Puritan Witch Beliefs

by James Hitchcock

Although the Elizabethan Age has come to be regarded as a golden period in English history, an era of high culture and remarkable progress in many areas of life, it was also marked by a notable increase in superstition, the rapid growth of the "witch mania" which reached its climax in the following century. A sparsity of records from earlier periods makes comparisons difficult, but the number of witch indictments and executions seem to have increased steadily during Elizabeth's reign.[1] In 1563 a new witch statute was enacted by Parliament, renewing the provisions of an older law repealed at the death of Henry VIII in 1547.

Trevor Davies suggested quite plausibly that the increased prosecutions may have been inspired by the Marian exiles returning to England after 1558, men whose rigid Calvinist theology caused them to take a hard view of evil and to propose stern measures for its extirpation and who were acquainted with the vigorous witch prosecutions already in force on the Continent.[2] Certainly the Puritan mind did manifest interest in such proceedings, and the concurrence of rising Puritanism and renewed witch prosecutions seems more than coincidental.

However, those prosecutions also inspired able criticisms of witch beliefs by two men whose writings provoked some controversy in their own time and perhaps planted the seeds of doubt but do not appear to have had any immediate influence. The most important of the two was Reginald Scot, whose *Discovery of Witchcraft* (1584) went through a number of editions and was republished several times in later centuries.[3] The other, less well known in his own time and later, was the Essex vicar George Gifford.

Gifford approached the witch question systematically in two works – an exposition entitled *A Discourse of the Subtle Practices of Devils by Witches* (1587) and a fictional work called *A Dialogue Concerning Witches and Witchcraft* (1593, 1603). In the second especially, in the persona of the wise and humane Daniel, who dominates the debate, he formulated the objections to witch prosecutions that would be familiar in later times but were apparently not obvious to his contemporaries – that juries are too impulsive in convicting witches and ought to adhere to rigid standards of evidence, that the troubled

---

1. R. Trevor Davies: *Four Centuries of Witch Beliefs* (London, 1947), p. 17.
2. *Ibid.*, pp. 5–15.
3. The only reliable modern edition is Southern Illinois University Press (Carbondale), 1964. The 1930 edition by Montague Summers is abridged.

90

women accused of sorcery should be treated witch compassion rather than persecution, and that the Scripture forbids the spilling of innocent blood.[4] In the introduction Gifford himself expressed the belief that many prosecutions were hysterical and that a number of innocent people were killed.[5]

George Gifford's presence among the handful of Elizabethans who appear to have been concerned with the witch problem is surprising because his own background and character can in no way be interpreted to mark him as a sceptic or as a modern man. In fact he was a well established member of the very Puritan movement whose fanatic extremes are thought to have contributed to the witch fright, and his arguments against the prosecutions were drawn from the most orthodox and unimpeachable Calvinist traditions.

Only the bones of Gifford's biography are known, and they confirm his rigorous Puritanism. The circumstances of his early life are lost, but in 1568 he was a student at Hart Hall, Oxford, where Scot had also studied. Subsequently he transferred to the Puritan center of Christ's College, Cambridge, where he took an A. B. in 1569–1570 and an M. A. in 1573. He was probably the George Gifford, aged 30, who was ordained priest by Bishop John Aylmer of London in 1578. The following year he is known to have been a member of a Puritan synod in Essex, but this did not prevent his appointment in 1582 to the living of All Saints' with St. Peter's at Maldon, Essex.[6]

Little is known of Gifford's actual ministry, except that the mother of the Parliamentary diarist Sir Symonds D'Ewes was a member of his congregation and was edified by him.[7] However, Bishop Aylmer suspended him from office for nonconformity in 1584, apparently at the instigation of Archbishop John Whitgift of Canterbury, an ardent anti-Puritan. Gifford's offenses were probably liturgical. Despite the intervention of William Cecil and a petition of 52 parishoners urging his reinstatement,[8] he was tried before High Commission, although probably not imprisoned. He was never restored to his benefice.[9]

---

4. *Dialogue* (Percy Society Publications, 1843), pp. 72, 76, 81, 83, 99, 101.

5. *Ibid.*, p. 5.

6. *The Dictionary of National Biography*, ed. Leslie Stephen and Sidney Lee (London, 1921–1922), VII, 1179; Anthony a Wood, *Athenae Oxoniensis*, ed. Philip Bliss (London, 1815), II, 291–293.

7. D'Ewes: *Autobiography*, ed. James Orchard Halliwell (London, 1845), I, 114.

8. In 1586 a plot was hatched among some of his former parishioners to snatch Bishop Aylmer's offensive square cap as he entered the parish church in procession (T. W. Davids: *Annals of Evangelical Nonconformity in the County of Essex*, London, 1863, p. 68).

9. DNB, VII, 1180; Daniel Neal: *History of the Puritans* (London, 1837), I, 283; John Strype: *Historical Collections of ... John Aylmer* (London, 1701), pp. 109–112;

91

Instead he was given a privately endowed Puritan lectureship in the neighborhood of Maldon and continued his work. He remained an unchastened Puritan. In 1589 he attended the Cambridge synod and was among those subscribing to Walter Travers' *Book of Discipline*.[10] He was head of the Braintree classis until 1590, took part in meetings of the Dedham classis until at least 1589, and was a member of the Essex presbytery until at least 1597.[11]

Gifford's death was formerly given as 1620, but George Lyman Kittredge discovered that the will of a George Gifford of Maldon was probated in 1600,[12] indicating that he was dead by that year. The second edition of the *Dialogue* was apparently brought out posthumously.

His publications were prolific, and despite his own commitment to church reform he was a vigorous opponent of the Separatists and engaged in a pamphlet debate with Henry Barrow and John Greenwood, two of the London Separatist leaders, who were executed in 1593.[13]

Gifford took some pains to uphold the traditional view of the devil and of witchcraft. His Daniel remarked forcefully, "It is so evident by the Scriptures, and in all experience, that there be witches that work by the devil, or rather, I may say, the devil worketh by them, that such as go about to prove the contrary do show themselves mere cavillers."[14]

Gifford himself in the *Discourse* said that to deny the existence of witches is to deny God's word and is "gross" and "contumelious."[15] A good part of the earlier work is in fact taken up with a lengthy discussion of the various kinds of witchcraft described in the Old Testament, and Gifford denied that Pharoah's magicians could have worked their tricks by natural power, since this would imply that any of Christ's miracles could also have been worked by natural power.[16]

But the *Discourse* was essentially an argument against witch beliefs as they existed in Elisabethan England, and its arguments were complete in comparison

---

Live and Acts of ... John Whitgift (London, 1718), p. 152; Benjamin Brook: *Lives of the Puritans* (London, 1813), II, 273–278; Christobel F. Fiske: The Saneness of George Gifford, *Poet Lore*, XXI (1920), 210–223.

10. DNB, VII, 1180.

11. Roland G. Usher (ed.): *The Presbyterian Movement in the Reign of Queen Elizabeth* (Camden Society Publications, 1905), pp. xli, 9, 16, 19, 42, 94.

12. *Witchcraft in Old and New England* (Cambridge, Mass., 1929), p. 569.

13. For a summary of the controversy see Benjamin Hanbury (ed.): *Historical Memorials Relating to the Independents* (London, 1839), I, 49–62.

14. *Dialogue*, p. 18.

15. *Discourse* (1587), sig. A 2.

16. *Ibid.*, pp. 4–16, 28.

92

with the later work but sketched out much less forcefully and with little detail. In his introduction Gifford noted that the common people generally attribute too much power to the devil and to witches and that the clergy, who ought to reprove them, are generally silent.[17]

He perceives the witch mania, in a characteristically Puritan fashion, as a remnant of Catholicism. It is because the light of the Gospel was so long snuffed out in England that such things can be.[18] One of the worst aspects of Catholicism was its emphasis on magic – even its remedies against sorcery were based on the superstitions belief that mere words could be effective against the devil.[19] The true remedy is faith, but faith and repentance for sin are rendered impossible by the belief that the witches are the causes of evil in the world.[20].

In fact this belief is one of the devil's worst deceptions. He leads men to believe that he is under the control of the witches and thus obscures his real power.[21] Most important, he obscures the fact that he can operate in the world only because God allows him and his actions are a punishment for man's sinfulness.[22]

What appeared in the 1587 treatice as a reasoned theological position was repeated and elaborated by Gifford six years later with greater urgency. In the introduction to the Dialogue he remarked that witch prosecutions had grown more virulent in the meantime and that the innocent frequently suffered in the excitement.[23] He offered as a justification for the *Dialogue* the need of communicating with the common people, who were impervious to dry argument but who might respond to a lively, popular style of exposition.[24]

Probably Gifford was sincere in asserting this. Unlike Scot, who wrote with a certain scholarly detachment and seems to have lived as a country gentleman,[25] Gifford remained to the end of his life intensely involved in pastoral activity. As a true Puritan he felt personal distress at what he thought was the very low state of religious belief and practice in England. In 1581 he had published another dialogue, entitled *A Brief Discourse ... Termed the Country Divinity*, which portrayed the religious sloth and backwardness of the common people. Now, in 1593, he was writing "lest the ignorant sort be carried awry and seduced more and more by them [the devils]."[26] He felt concerned that innocent

---

17. Sig. A 2.   18. P. 43.
19. Pp. 30–31.   20. Pp. 54, 61.
21. P. 44.   22. P. 21.
23. Pp. iii, 5.   24. P. 5.

25. See the introduction by Hugh Ross Williamson in the 1964 edition of the *Discovery*.

26. *Dialogue*, p. iii.

93

blood should be spilled in fits of hysteria, but his concern was perhaps less for the innocent victims than for his own spiritual charges who incurred grave guilt in these proceedings and who continued blinded by superstition and ignorant of God's providence. Essex was one of the most active centers of witch prosecutions,[27] and in 1581, at St. Osyth, one of the most celebrated Elizabethan cases had taken place, involving thirteen women.[28]

Perhaps significantly, Gifford's hero Daniel had little to say about Catholic influences in the 1593 work. Gifford had apparently come to think that witch beliefs were more deeply rooted than any specific theological tenets and that the people, in attributing such great powers to the devil and the witches, espoused a kind of practical manicheeism which was thoroughly un-Christian.

The *Dialogue* is arranged as a dispute among three townsmen – Daniel, a learned, enlightened gentleman; M. B., a schoolmaster who shares most contemporary prejudices; and Old Samuel, the embodiment of popular superstition. Occasionally Samuel's wife interjects her opinions, which are even more extreme than her husband's.

Old Samuel begins by enumerating the most common witch superstitions of his contemporaries. He believes that every town has two or three witches, who spitefully or for hire kill and maim persons and cattle by the use of "familiars." The latter, which appear as small animals and are generally kept in bottles or baskets, are in reality diabolical imps and perhaps devils themselves. Possesion of them is crucial to the witch's powers.

There are also good witches – "white witches" or "cunning men" – who can also be found in most neighborhoods, although perhaps not in such abundance as their evil counterparts. They can discover the identity of secret malevolent witches and can prescribe remedial charms.[29]

Samuel concludes his exposition with a defense of the witch prosecutions. He admits that he has often served on juries which convicted old women on "common fame" or on the testimony of cunning men, but he asserts that this is necessary because the devil will not permit witches to confess.[30] The Schoolmaster echoes these sentiments and says it is better for the innocent to suffer than for true witches to escape unpunished.[31]

Probably these are arguments which Gifford encountered in his pastoral rounds, and Daniel responds to these superstitions very much like a learned Calvinist minister. Unintentionally he demonstrates the severe handicaps under

---

27. Trevor Davies: *Witch Beliefs*, p. 17; C. L'Estrange Ewen (ed.): *Witch Hunting and Witch Trials* (London, 1929).
28. Thomas Wright: *Narratives of Sorcery and Magic* (London, 1851), I, 205–219.
29. Pp. 8–10, 44–51, 102.   30. P. 102.   31. Pp. 4–16, 74.

which reformers labored. While his two opponents in the debate made constant reference to personal experiences and strong fears, Daniel could only respond with abstract arguments derived from logic and the authority of Scriptures. He led his hearers down tortuous metaphysical paths which they could only follow with difficulty.

Gifford's first concern was to show that common prejudices attribute too much power to the witches themselves and not enough to the devils. The ordinary witch tales described the devils, in the form of familiars, as being at the call of the witches, of committing themselves to more or less permanent service. Daniel challenges these ideas vigorously, asserting that the witches cannot command the devil, even though some of them believe they can, and that men are lulled into dangerous complacency by the belief that the devil is only operative when summoned by a conjuror.[32] The Schoolmaster is first perplexed by the question whether the witch is the master or the servant of the devil but finally yields to Daniel's arguments.[33]

This approach reveals the depth of Giffort's Calvinism and the direct relevance of his theology to his alarm over witchcraft. Just as one of Calvin's major concerns was to assert the absolute power of God in opposition to traditional theological limitations, so Gifford seeks to rescue the devil also from a kind of trivializing process which the theories of witchcraft have imposed on him. Evil as well as good must be seen in its full strength, and Daniel quotes the Epistle of Peter, in which the devil is described as "a roaring lion seeking whom he may devour," and then asks scornfully, "What then? Can you be so simple as to imagine that the devil lieth in a pot of wool, soft and warm, and stirreth not, but when he is hired and sent?"[34]

In the *Country Divinity* the Puritan character Zelot, who seems generally to express Gifford's beliefs, also stresses the devil's great power, and the theme is central to *Two Sermons Upon I Peter 5*, which Gifford published in 1597.

In Daniel's view men particularly fail to esteem the devil's power in not recognizing his great subtlety. The whole witchcraft mania demonstrates this, for by it the devil leads men to believe he is busy with trivial, when in reality he is concerned with great things.[35] The whole panoply of witch beliefs is filled with an obsessive concern for petty details and for minor quarrels, whereas the devil's real aim is to win men's souls.

By allowing cunning men to use Scripture to work minor wonders, the devil obscures the fact that they are his servants. Thus men who have recourse to

---

32. Pp. 33–34, 93–95.   33. Pp. 26, 31, 35.
34. P. 28.   35. P. 23.

them are really worshipping the devil, although they believe they are thwarting him. When the devil is apparently driven out of a man's body by exorcism he is actually driven deeper into the soul, because men have been led to put their faith in a superstitious practice.[36] As Daniel says, the devils' whole purpose is "to set up their kingdom, and to draw people after them, to seek help at their hands, and to worship them."[37]

These deceits abound in England as never before, because of the witchcraft scourge.[38]

Gifford's practicality, his intense pastoral concern, is never far from the surface of his writings, and it is perhaps this sense of urgency more than anything else which sets him off from the more speculative attitude of Reginald Scot.

The whole movement to seek out and to punish witches is seen to betray a profound lack of trust in God and a failure to appreciate His goodness. Gifford's Calvinism is fully apparent here, as he struggles to restore the concept of a completely sovereign God freed from the limitations placed on Him by misguided popular theology. "They think that the country might be rid of such spirits, if there were none to hoister them, or to set them a work. They imagine that they and their cattle should then go safe. Alas! poor creatures, how they be deluded! How little do they understand the high Providence of Almighty God, which is over all."[39] – "For the devils are chained up by God's most mighty power and providence, and in all things so far as letteth forth their chains, so far they proceed. Where men love darkness more than light, He hath given him leave to do many things."[40]

At the heart of this popular attitude Daniel finds an implicit denial of Christianity itself, a kind of pagan dualism which ascribes to evil a power equal to that of God. "Indeed, among the more ignorant sort he prevaileth much, when he toucheth those which embrace the lively word as sent from a witch. For many now do even quake and tremble, and their faith doth stagger. Hath he power (think they) over such as be cunning in the Scriptures, then what are they the better for their profession?"[41]

The devils, and the witches, seek for themselves the honor and respect which is due only to God.[42]

The full armory of Reformation theology is here turned against the witch mania, as Daniel insist that men's lack of faith is the chief condition for Satan's flourishing in the world and for God's permitting Satan and the witches to

---

36. Pp. 47–58.   37. P. 49.   38. P. iii.
39. P. 30.   40. P. 110.
41. P. 37.   42. P. iv.

96

exercise power over men. Few men have genuine faith, and the preachers do little to dispel the sins of ignorance which abound.[43]

Gifford remains an unrelenting moralist, a Puritanical preacher whose major intention is to lead his people to reform. In their personal sins he finds the real source of the devil's power and the flourishing of witchcraft. As Daniel says, "When a man professeth in words that he doth defy the devil and his works, and yet when it cometh to a trial of God's word, he is found to be seduced and wrapped in blind errors of the devil, in infidelity and evil works, in which he fulfilleth the will of Satan, and honoureth him in the place of God, shall we say that this is a good man because of his words and imaginations, and that he defieth the devil and his works?"[44] – "When as men have set so light by the hearing of God's voice to be instructed by Him, they are justly given over to be taught by devils, and to learn their ways."[45] – "... we must take heed of the common error which a multitude are carried so headlong withal, that they can by no means see, that God is provoked by their sins to give the devil such instruments to work withal, but rage against the witch as if she could do all."[46]

The final answer to the problem of evil, and the ultimate weapon against the witch and against Satan, is the standard Puritan program of personal regeneration and acceptance of the Bible. "The only way for men that will eschew the snares and subtleties of the devil and all harms by him, is this, even to hear the voice of God, to be taught by Him by His lively word which is full of pure light to discover and expel the dark mists of Satan."[47]

Gifford's answer to the problem of evil in the world, and more specifically the problem of witchcraft, was an original effort to solve these vexing questions in the light of the new Reformed theology. In this he was a genuine innovator.[48] Calvin himself had written nothing formal on the subject of witchcraft, although in a personal letter of 1545 he wrote approvingly of the prosecution of several

---

43. P. 87.   44. P. 16.   45. P. iii.

46. P. 36.   47. P. 114.

48. Reginald Scot had used arguments similar to Gifford's, and also compatible with Puritan theology, especially the idea that witches and devils plague man only with God's permission and that excessive credulity about magic is a failure to recognize that all wonders are from God (*Discovery*, pp. 25–36). John L. Teall, in: Witchcraft and Calvinism in Elizabethan England (*Journal of the History of Ideas*, 1962, pp. 21–36), argues that Scot was a Puritan, since he cited Calvin approvingly in his writings and slighted Luther. Very little is known of Scot's life. The tone of his work is generally more speculative than Gifford's, and whenever possible he offered naturalistic explanations of supposedly magic phenomena (*Discovery*, pp. 243–256). Gifford occasionally did this (*Dialogue*, pp. 34–41, 62–64, 67; *Discourse*, pp. 11, 55, 59), but his interests were overwhelmingly with theology and its practical implications.

97

alleged sorcerers in Geneva, who were thought to have caused a plague. He had apparently given the magistrates at least mild encouragement in their proceedings.[49]

William Perkins, roughly Gifford's contemporary and one of the greatest Puritan theologians, published a treatise on witchcraft in 1608, in which he emphasized the Scriptural proofs for its existence and strongly supported invoking the death penalty against witches.[50]

But in their theories of witchcraft both Calvin and Perkins appear chiefly as men of their times, who merely sought plausible theological justifications for common beliefs. Gifford's theories seem closer to the heart of Calvinist thought, in his strong denial that men can withstand evil by their own actions; his insistence that since witches are sent from God to plague men for their sins, men should accept these plagues until God chooses to remove them; and in his fierce rejection of all ritual magic. As John L. Teall pointed out, Gifford and Scot had such great conceptions of God that they could not conceive anything happening in the world which was not in some way due to His actions.[51]

In 1604 an even harsher witchcraft statute was enacted in England, whereby sorcery itself was made punishable by death and not, as previously, only those evil deeds worked through sorcery. Professor Kittredge suggested that Gifford was partly responsible for this law, since Daniel asserted in the *Dialogue* that, as Scripture says, witches should be liable to death for consorting with devils.[52] However, Gifford did not emphasize this point, and in context it seems more a concession to the letter of Scripture than a firmly held belief. Daniel actually used the remark to argue against witchcraft prosecutions, by asserting that contrary to common belief witches could not really harm people and that the existing law was therefore meaningless.[53] The new law of 1604 probably owed its major impetus to the credulities of James I.

But at the same time there is no evidence that Gifford tried to influence the authorities against the excesses. His concern remained always less with the objective effect of the mania on the accused than its subjective effect on would-

---

49. E. Doumergue: *Jean Calvin* (Neuilly-sur-Seine, 1926), VI, 46–37.
50. Teall, pp. 29–30.
51. *Ibid.*, p. 34.
52. *Witchcraft in Old and New England*, p. 297.
53. Professor Teall, in his brief treatment of Gifford, says that although he opposed blind fury he did favor prosecutions ("Witchcraft and Calvinism," p. 31). This is perhaps technically correct, but it overlooks the fact that the major force of Gifford's writings is to persuade his readers not to support the prosecutions. He leaves the inescapable impression that prosecutions are justified only rarely, and even this is a concession.

98

be Christians. His writings were also probably not influential. Wallace Notestein pointed out that unlike Scot, Gifford was not often attacked by staunch defenders of traditional beliefs.[54] At the end of the *Dialogue* Gifford himself, who showed in all his writings that he understood the popular mind better than most learned contemporaries, leaves the impression that Daniel's victory has been a very uncertain one. Old Samuel's wife is completely unconvinced, and Samuel himself and the Schoolmaster have bowed before Daniel's superior logic and personal force, but have not really been touched by the arguments.[55] Gifford's writings are important not for their contemporary influence, which may have been negligible, but as an example of the possibilities inherent in Calvinist theology and the Puritan temper.

ZUSAMMENFASSUNG

Obwohl der Puritanismus im allgemeinen wahrscheinlich zur Steigerung der Hexenverfolgungen im elisabethanischen England beitrug, so ist doch ein eifriger puritanischer Geistlicher in Essex, George Gifford, als einer der wenigen Kritiker des Hexenwahns hervorgetreten. In zwei Schriften (A Discourse ... of Witches; 1587 und A Dialogue concerning Witches; 1593) versuchte er, die Meinung der Laien gegen diese Hysterie zu beeinflussen. Calvin selbst scheint Hexenverfolgungen gebilligt zu haben; Gifford aber benutzte wirksam dessen Theologie, um dieses Unwesen zu entkräften. In Parallele zu Calvins Kritik an der Behandlung Gottes in der überlieferten Theologie argumentierte Gifford, der Hexenglaube lasse die Macht des Teufels als trivial und menschlicher Kontrolle unterworfen erscheinen. Der Teufel nähre absichtlich solche Vorstellungen, um seine wirklichen Absichten zu maskieren. Der Glaube an schwarze Magie und der Mangel an Bewußtsein für die persönlichen Sünden, die beide durch den Hexenglauben bestärkt würden, bedeuteten für den Teufel eine Hilfe bei seinem Bemühen, die Seelen der Menschen zu durchdringen.

Gifford scheint nicht einflußreich gewesen zu sein, aber seine Schriften sind wichtig, weil sie in der reformierten Theologie liegende Möglichkeiten, die kein anderer Theologe erfaßte, sichtbar werden lassen.

---

54. *History of Witchcraft in England* (Washington, 1911), pp. 72, 243.
55. P. 119.

ffolk=1Lore

TRANSACTIONS OF THE FOLK-LORE SOCIETY

Vol. LXIV]   DECEMBER 1953   [No. 4

SOME SEVENTEENTH-CENTURY BOOKS OF MAGIC
BY K. M. BRIGGS

A paper read before a meeting of the Society on January 21st, 1953

I HAVE chosen to speak about seventeenth-century manuscripts of magic, not beçause that was the only century in which they were rife but partly because that is the period I know best, partly because it is the last period in which they had real vogue, and partly because many of the manuscripts we possess were written at that time. They were almost certainly copies of much earlier ones, but some new elements may have been introduced, and with the spread of literacy the later manuscripts would tend to contain more popular notions and to be less exclusively learned than the earlier ones.

There would appear to be two opposite though parallel trends in folk tradition. In the first place the basic beliefs and assumptions of the people are taken by the most fully conscious minds of the community and formulated as science or shaped into arts, in the second these forms are broken down by oral transmission and become again the subject of folk study. These two trends are apparent in even the most literate civilization, though the first is more obvious in our culture and the second in a culture which contains few literate people. Both these trends are apparent in the magical writings with which we are dealing this evening. The books were produced by an educated, even a highly educated, class, with a long tradition of specialized learning behind it. The assumptions, however, upon which the most learned magicians worked were those of folk science. The doctrine of sympathies and of substitution appears again and again beneath their most elaborate charms, and the magic of names in all their spells. The spirits which they conjured up were angels, devils, fairies, and occasionally heathen gods. They used magical stones, amulets, plants and the blood and skins of animals, as the most

2 F

primitive witch-doctor might do. This is so obvious as hardly to need labouring, but, by the seventeenth century at least, the second trend is also apparent; and popular magic has broken into the elaborate, specialized technique of the learned magician. The greater part of the charms call for elaborate equipment, almost unlimited time, and a careful accuracy to which many of the operations of modern science are child's play; but scattered amongst these are spells and charms so simple that any old trot might use them. The day of the amateur magician had begun, or perhaps one should say had begun again.

From the early sixteenth century, and before it, the country seems to have been strewed with books of magic, and with friars and country parsons conjuring up their imps. The hill-diggers and over-turners of crosses against which an early Statute of Henry VIII was enacted must for the most part have begun their researches by conjuring the spirits who had been set to guard the treasure. We find the appropriate incantation in more than one of our manuscripts. The practice of setting a spirit to guard treasure was a very old one. Sometimes it was a Brownie or Dobie to whom it was entrusted, sometimes the spirit of the place, sometimes a man was killed to guard it. This last habit is said to have survived among pirates until the eighteenth century. There is an essay by Dawson Turner in *Norfolk Archaeology* (Vol. I) which gives an idea of how numerous the magical manuscripts and amateur magicians must have been just before the Reformation. A letter is appended to it from one William Stapleton, which appears to be addressed to Cardinal Wolsey. It is too long to be quoted complete, but an extract from it will show something of the way in which a magician went to work with his material; though, to judge from William Stapleton's own account, he was a singularly unsuccessful magician.

The two men with a " placard for treasure trove " were probably William Smith, and Amylion, a servant of Lord Curzon who had a permit from the King to dig for treasure. They seem to have made more from fining or blackmailing illicit treasure-diggers than from what they actually found. We cannot but sympathise with poor William Stapleton's difficulty in getting up in the morning, which was the original cause of all the trouble.

" To The Lord Legate's Noble Grace.
Whereas your noble Grace hath given me in commandment that I should inform your Grace of all such things as hath been done and committed by me, William Stapleton, Clerk, since the time of my coming from the Order of St. Bennett's in the County of Norfolk, that

is to say : First, I do ascertain your noble Grace that I, the said Sir William Stapleton, was a monk of St. Bennett's as aforesaid the XIXth year of the reign of King Henry the Eighth ; and being in the said Monastry, one Denys of Hofton did bring me a book called *Thesaurus Spirituum* and, after that, another called *Secreta Secretorum*, a little ring, a plate, a circle, and also a sword for the art of digging ; the which books and instruments I did keep for the space of half a year before I did come thence. And I and one John Kerver did give to the said Denys two nobles in pledge for the same ; and he said he had them of the Vicar of Watton, and left the said two nobles in gage for them. Then for because I had been often punished for not rising to mattins and doing my duty in the church, I prayed my lord to give me license that I might sue out my dispensation, and so he was contented. Howbeit for because I was poor, he gave me half a year's license for the purchasing thereof or else to return again to my religion ; which license had, I went that night to Denys of Hofton, and shewed him my license, and desired him to help me towards the purchasing of my said dispensation, who asked of me how I did like the said books ; and I said, well. And then he said, if you be minded to go about anything touching the same, I will bring you to two cunning men that have a placard for treasure-trove, by whose means, if I had any cunning, I might the better help myself. Whereupon he brought me to the said two persons with whom I agreed to go about the said business, in such wise that then they delivered me two or three books and other things concerning the said art of digging, and thereupon brought me to a place called Systern (Sidestrand) in the said County, intending to have gone about the said business. And as we went to make search of the ground where we thought the said treasure should lie, the Lady Tyrry, lady of the said ground, having knowledge thereof, sent for us, and so examined us of our purpose, and thereupon forbade us meddling in her said ground, and so we departed thence and meddled no further. And so I went to Norwich, and there remained by the space of a month ; and from thence I went to a town called Felmyngham, and one Godfrey and his boy with me, which Godfrey had a ' shower' called *Anthony Fular*, and the said boy did ' scry ' unto him (which said spirit I had after myself) ; but notwithstanding at such time as we had viewed the said ground and could find nothing there in no manner of wise, we departed to Norwich again, where we met with one unbeknown to me ; and he brought us to a man's house in Norwich where he supposed we should have found treasure, whereupon we called the spirit of the treasure to appear, but he did not, for I suppose of a truth there was none there ; and so from thence I came to one Richard Thony, and him required to help me to get my dispensation. And so he and other his friends, of their good kindness, gave me the sum of 46 shillings and 8 pence towards the suit of the same. And so I came to London, whereas I purchased a dispensation out of your Grace's Court for to be an hermit ; and so, after that was purchased, I went directly into Norfolk, and there shewed my license. And then they motioned

me that I should go about the said science again, and they would help
me to my habit ; to whom I made answer, that unless my books were
better, I would meddle no further. Whereupon they informed me that
one Leech had a book, to the which book, as they said, the parson of
Lesingham had bound a spirit called *Andrew Malchus*, whereupon I
went unto the said Leech, and his brother with me, whom they had
sent for before, and at my coming these had communication with the
said Leech, concerning the same. And upon our communication he let
me have all his instruments to the said book, and shewed me that, if
I could get the book that the said instruments were made by, he would
bring me to him that should speed my business shortly. And then
he shewed me that the parson of Lesingham and Sir John of Leiston
with others to me unknown had called up of late *Andrew Malchus*,
Oberion, and *Inchubus*. And when they were all raised, *Oberion* would
in no wise speak. And then the parson of Lesingham did demand of
Andrew Malchus, and so did Sir John Leiston also, why *Oberyon*
would not speak to them. And *Andrew Malchus* made answer, for
because he was bound unto the Lord Cardinal. And that also they did
entreat the said parson of Lesingham and the said Sir John of Leiston
that they might depart as at that time ; and wheresoever it would
please them to call them up again, they would gladly do them any
service they could ; and so they were licensed to depart for that time.
The plate which was made for the calling of Oberion by them hath
rested in the hands of Sir Thomas Moore, knight, since that I was
before him. And when I had all the said instruments, I went to Norwich, where I had remained but a season when there came to me a
glazier, which, as he said, came from the Lord Leonard Marquess, for
to search one that was expert in such business. And thereupon one
Richard Tynney came and instanced me to go to Walsingham with
him, where we met with the said Lord Leonard, the which Lord
Leonard did communicate with me concerning the said art of digging,
and thereupon promised me that if I would take pains in the exercising
the said art, that he would sue out a dispensation for me that I should
be a secular priest, and so would make me his chaplain. And, for a
trial to know what I could do in the said art, he caused his servant to
hide a certain money in the garden ; and I shewed for the same. And
one Jackson ' scryed ' unto me, but we could not accomplish our
purpose. Notwithstanding, incontinent after, one Sir John Shepe, Sir
Robert Porter and I departed to a place beside Creke Abbey, where
we supposed treasure should be. And the said Sir John Shepe called
the spirit of the treasure, and I showed to him ; but all came to no
purpose."

The method of scrying seems something similar to that of modern
spiritualists. The " scryer " would correspond to the medium and the
" shower " to the control. It is of interest to know that Cardinal Wolsey
was credited with a familiar spirit, as Thomas Cromwell was later, and it

is of even more interest to know that the spirit was called Oberion. Variants of this name occur in many books of magic, and though none of them is quite Oberon it seems likely that Shakespeare's spelling of the name was affected by hearing of this spirit. The instruments of magic, that is the sword, the pen, the jewel, the rods, the parchment, the wax, etc., for use with the book had to be made according to the directions in the book, and a spirit was generally bound to it by the ring or crystal which belonged to the book.

Now to examine some of the books of magic themselves. To begin with one mentioned by William Stapleton, there is a copy of *Secreta Secretorum* in the Bodleian Library. All books with this title may not be the same, but this particular copy is an example of theurgic magic. It deals almost entirely with the angels. To do it justice it is insistent that only good can be wrought by these means. For instance, there is a spell to make oneself irresistible to a woman, but a man may use it only on his wife. There are annotations to the manuscript in a later seventeenth century hand whose author is even more scrupulous. Beside the direction " to have thye owne good Angell who is of god Appoynted unto thee for a guyd all thy life " he has written " these are holy Angells of God and it is An Noble experiment and most Lawfull and whosoever can by a holy Life and prayer to God obtaine it may doe god's people much good, but this experiment requiereth A quiet religion and holy living to performe it ;" and he strongly advises against the experiment of Ascariell for enclosing spirits in a glass or crystal to give information about absent or dead friends, to find treasure, &c. There is a collection of strictly moral aphorisms in the book, but there are also recipes for many pleasant effects as to cause " A wood and greene Meadows and pleasant herbs and flowers " or " a table of delicate Dishes " to appear.

The most sinister recipe is under *Fumigations :* " Hermes saith there is nothing like unto spermaceti to Raise spirits suddenly, being compounded of spermaceti, lignum aloes and pepperwort and Muske saffron Red storage mixed with the bloud *of a Lapwing this being fumigated.* And if it be fumigated About Toombes or graves of the dead it causes spirits and ghosts of the dead to gather together as it is sayd."

One of the most widely diffused of the treatises on magic was *The Key of Solomon*, mentioned by Heywood in his *Hierarchy of the Blessed Angels.* This was a systematic treatise upon magic, not a collection of magical recipes like so many of the manuscripts. A copy is to be found in a well-known collection in the British Museum, Add. 36,674. A list of the contents will give some idea of the laboriousness of the magician's task, if he was to pursue his labours with any safety. The contents of Part I are :

1–3. Orisons to be sayde when you go conjure. &c
   4. Here followeth howe and after what sorte Pentacles must be made.
   5. Here followeth the way to work which is the cheyfest chapter of all.
   6. Here followeth how experyments for thinges that are stolne ought to be wroughte.
   7. Howe experyments to be invysible must bee prepared.
   8. Howe by what means experyments of Love ought to be wrought, as well in gettyng hyr whom thou desyrest as yn touching hir in her sleep, or talkynge with her.
   9. Here followeth an other waye whereby yt ys brought to passe that she shall dreame of thee.
  10. Of Experyments of favor and fryendshipp.
  11. Howe experyments for hatred ar prepared that any may be made deadly enemyes.
  12. An experyment to fayne a thinge to bee which indeade is false.
  13. Here followeth a way to bringe to passe any extraordynary experyment.

The second Booke of the Keye of Knowledge of Solomon

   1. What hour experiments ought to be wrought.
   2. Howe the conjurer must behave himself.
   3. Howe his fellowes must behave them.
   4. Of fastyng and watchyng.
   5. Of baths and howe they must be made.
   6. Of Apparell and all thereto belongyng.
   7. Of the knife belongynge to this Art.
   8. How the cyrcle must be made and how you must enter into it.
   9. Of water and ysope.
  10. Of fyre and lights.
  11. Of pen and inks.
  12. Of the blood of the bath.
  13. Of virgin parchment.
  14. Howe you must work with wax.
  15. Of the needle wherewith you must work.
  16. Of perfumes.
  17. Of cloth wherein you must lay your instruments.
  18. Of Images.
  19. Of hours to work in.
  20. Of the colours of the Planets.

The greater part of this book is concerned with ritual purity needed to safeguard the magician against the power of the spirits he raised. It does not contain much popular magic, but works by Names of Power, much as the ancient Egyptians must have worked. The ritual is founded on a long tradition, but rather a learned and literate than a popular one. But already the learning is in decay and popular elements are creeping in. Bound up with the Clavicula Solomonis are several other books of magic into which more popular elements enter undisguisedly. On the title page of the collection is written : "This Book was Tho. Brittan's the smal Cole man's and sold to Mr Bateman the Bookseller for the sum of Ten Pound five shillings, as appeared by his marked catalogue 40 1694. After it had the Lord Somers etc., for owners. Bot at St. Paul's Coffee Stall by J. Arnes." Cauius, Dee and Ashmole were among the authors. The contents of the book are :

The Book of King Solomon,
An Excellent Book of the Arte of Magick first begun mar. 1567, (This is by Dee.)
A notable Journall of an Experimental Magician,
An Old Book found among the Secret Writings of Dr. Caius,
Regulae utilissimae in artem Magicam cum multis aliis de arte Magica,
Certain strange Visions and Apparitions of Memorable Note. Anno. 1567.
A Catalogue of Mr. Bovey's Magical Books,
The Vision of Humphrey Smith concerning London,
Of Elizabeth Jennings being bewitched,
Compendium Heptarchiae Mysticae,
The Examination of several persons accused of witchcraft.

A mixed bag.

Amongst the elaborate recipes in these books are a few far simpler both in conception and execution. Here is, for instance, a straightforward example of sympathetic magic, employed in one of the main activities of the country magician, the discovery of theft :

The eye of Abraham. the noble experiment of Troy. To knowe who they be that have stolen anything out of your house, and to make them confesse the same.
Take argentum vivum and the white of an egge and mingle them together and make an eye upon a wall in this manner then call in all them that thou suspectest & tell them behold the eye, & his or her eye that stole the thing will water, if they will not confess take a copper key, & put it on the eye of the wall & strike upon it sayinge hare et jures vales, and the party that is guilty shall cry out myne eye myne eye. probat : est.

Presumably there is thought to be some connection here between quick-silver and Mercury, the god of thieves, which makes it particularly suitable. In the same manuscript we have something even nearer to folk tradition in a version of the night spell which was commonly spoken by the more superstitious of the yeomen around their properties at night. This one is something between the invocation of a saint and a piece of sympathetic magic. The mention of the two thieves in it makes it a protection against theft.

> *The Night Spell.* (From *Regulae Utilissimae.* Brit. Mus. MS. Addit. 36674, p. 89.)
>
> This charme should be said at night or against night about the place or field or about beasts without field, and whosoever cometh in he goeth not out for certaine.
>
> On 3 Crosses of a tree, 3 dead bodyes did hang, 2 were theeves, and 3rd was xst on whom our beleife is, Dismas and Gesmas, Xst amidst them was, Dismas to heaven went, Gesmas to hell was sent, Christ that died on that roode, for Maries love that by him stood, and through the virtue of his blood, Jesus save us and our good within and without and all this place about and through the virtue of his might let noe thief enter in this night : noe foot further in this place that I upon goe, but at my bidding there be bound, to do all things that I bid them do. Starke be their sineiues therewith & their lives mightles and their eyes sightles, dred and doubt them enclose about, as a wall wrought of stone so be thes crampt in the ton, crampe and crookeing and fault in thier footing, the might of the Trinity, save these goods for me. In the name of Jesus, holy benedicite all about our goods bee, within and without and all place about, then say 5 pr. nrs., 5 av. & i cred. etc.

A Latin version follows, but without the rather impressive curses of the English ones.

> Disparibus miseritis pendent tria corpora varius
> Dismas et Gesnas medio divina potestas.
> Alta petis Dismas infelix infima Gesmas,
> His versis discas ne furta tu tua perdas.

These spoken spells are less common in the manuscripts than the charms and incantations that were meant to accompany ritual action. A quantity of them were used both by the witches and the ordinary countrymen, but only a few have found their way into magical manuscripts. They have in common with the ordinary conjurations of the magicians a strong admixture of holy names, and also of the apochryphal incidents objected to by the authors of *Malleus Maleficarum*. An example not to be found in a manuscript but in popular tradition is probably well known to you. It is the toothache charm :

> Peter was sitting on a marble-stone,
>   And Jesus passed by ;
> Peter said, " My Lord, my God,
>   How my tooth doth ache! "

Jesus said, " Peter art whole!
And whoever keeps these words for my sake
Shall never have the toothache!"

Even more curious is that broken-down medley of spells recited by little
Jennet Device at the first Lancashire witch trial :

Upon Good-Friday I will fast while I may
Untill I heare them knell
Our Lords owne Bell,
Lord in his messe
With his twelve Apostles good,
What hath he in his hand
Ligh in leath wand :
What hath he in his other hand?
Heavens doore key,
Open, open Heaven doore keyes,
Steck, steck, hell doore.
Let Chrizum child
Goe to it Mother mild,
What is yonder that casts a light so farrandly,
Mine owne deare Sonne that's naild to the Tree.
He is nailed sore by the heart and hand,
And holy harne Panne,
Well is that man
That Fryday spell can
His Childe to learne ;
A Crosse of Blew, and another of Red,
As good Lord was to the Roode.
Gabriel laid him downe to sleepe
Upon the ground of holy weepe :
Good Lord came walking by,
Sleep'st thou, wak'st thou *Gabriel*,
No Lord I am sted with sticke and stake,
That I can neither sleepe nor wake :
Rise up *Gabriel* and goe with me,
The stick nor stake shall never deere thee,
Sweete Jesus our Lord, Amen.

The first quatrain of this is said to be the witches' password, which
enables them to attend Mass without compromising their dedication to
the devil, at the end is an immunity spell and in the middle is one form of
the White Paternoster, of which the most widely known version is the
folk prayer " Matthew, Mark, Luke and John—Bless the bed that I lie
on." The version nearest to the Devices' is to be found in White's *Way
to the Church*.

White Paternoster, Saint Peters brother,
What hast i'th t'one hand? white booke leaves.

What hast i'th t'other hand? heaven yate keyes.
Open heaven yates, and steike hell yates :
And let every crysom child creepe to it owne mother.
White Paternoster, Amen.

A verbal spell of the same kind to stop bleeding is to be found in *A Book of Experiments out of dyvers authors*, dated 1622. (MS. Bod. e Mus 243). It runs :

" God that was borne in the borough of bethlehem
& baptised in the water of flem Jordayne
The water was both wylde and wode,
the chylde was both meeke and goode.
He blessed the floude,
& still it stoode.
With same blessinge that he blessed the floude
I doe blesse the bloude
By virtue of the childe so goud. & say 5 pater nosters, 5 avies & 2 creedes."

Akin to the spoken spells are the written amulets to be carried about the person. The collector of the Book of Dyvers Experiments seems to have great faith in these, particularly in those taken from the psalms, as, for instance, " To take Birds, Wryte the 103 psalme on virgin parchment & hange it on a tree & you shall have byrds enough therein ", or " For a childe crying and cannot slepe write the 8 psalme Domine Deus Noster & laye it to the infants right arme & he shall sleepe quyetly ".

Another amulet is made by writing the names of the three archangels, Raphael, Michael and Gabriel on a laurel leaf, and while you carry it your enemies will in no wise be able to touch you.

Various country charms with plants and animals are to be found in these homelier books of magic. Thyme, rue and hyssop are among the herbs most commonly recommended ; thyme especially for fairy charms, which I shall deal with presently ; for they are some of the most interesting.

Vervain was considered one of the most potent herbs, and many versions of the charm for gathering it are to be found in the handbooks of magic. In the beginning of *Incantamenta Magica* (MS. Bod. Rawl. D. 252) is an addition, written apparently by a Northerner, which contains a rhyme very like that given by Reginald Scot :

Haill thou holy herb ; growing upon the ground.
In the mount of Calvarie thair was thou found.
Thou heallis manie greif, and stanches manie wound,
In the name of Sweit Jesus I tak thee from the ground.

Halliwell Phillipps gives a longer version from a manuscript in the Chatham Library at Manchester :

> All hele, thou holy herb vervin,
>   Growing on the ground ;
> In the mount of Calvery
>   There wast thou found ;
> Thou helpest many a greife,
>   And stenchest many a wound.
> In the name of sweet Jesus,
>   I take thee from the ground.
> Oh Lord, effect the same
>   That I do go about.
> In the neame of God, on Mount Olivet
>   First I thee found,
> In the name of Jesus,
>   I pull thee from the ground.[1]

These spells speak of vervain as a medical herb, but it had various other uses, chief among them being to procure love and favour. In our *Booke of Experiments taken out of dyvers authors*, we find various formulas for gathering vervain, and uses to which it can be put. For instance there is " *ffavor to have.* Gather verven on midsummer even fastinge & out of deadly sinne with 3 pater nosters. 3 avies & 2 creedes & beare it about thee." Or an even simpler one to obtain love is ; " Rubbe vervin in the bale of thy hande & rubbe thy mouth with it & immediately kisse her & it is done."

In the French nursery rhyme, *Anne of Brittany* vervain was used as a divinatory herb, but its most familiar use was as a *fuga daemonis*. " Vervain and dill ", as Aubrey reminds us, " Hinder witches from their will ". St. John's wort, another midsummer herb, was sometimes coupled with it instead of dill. Thomas Jackson, who tells us nearly as much about superstition as Aubrey, has a passage on this.

> I well remember a tradition, that was olde, when I was young, better beleeved by such as told it, then if it had beene Canonicall Scripture. It was of a maide that liked well of the devill making love to her in the habit of a gallant young man, but could not enjoy his company, nor he hers, so long as shee had *Vervine* and *S. Johnsgrasse* about her : for to this effect he brake his minde unto her at last in rime :

> *If thou hope to be Lemman mine ;*
> *Lay aside the St Johnsgrasse, and the Vervine.*[2]

[1] J. O. Halliwell-Phillipps. *Nursery Rhymes and Nursery Tales of England.* ed. cit. There is also a version of it in White's *Way to the True Church.* 1610. (To the Reader.)
[2] T. Jackson, *A Treatise Containing the Originall of Unbeliefe, Misbeliefe or Misperswasion.* 1625. p. 177.

Of all fruit trees apples were the most magic. To sleep under an apple tree rendered one liable to be carried off by the fairies, the witches often worked ill by the gift of an apple, apple skins were used in divination, and apples themselves were often used in experiments for love and favour. A somewhat hazardous way of assuaging enmity was to cut the word *yava* on an apple and throw it at one's enemy.; and amongst the love spells we find :

> Take an Apple in thy hande as it hangeth on the tree & wryte in yt these names followinge. *Anaell, Satnell, Asiell* & then saye *I conjure* thee Apple of Apples by the name of these devels, which deceptfully deceaved Eve in paradyce, that what woman soever it be that doth eate or tast of this Apple that she may burne in love of me. Saye this 4 tymes upon the Apple & then geve the Apple to what woman you will.

In the same book celendine gathered in the morning of St. Peter *ad vincula* is a useful preservative from prison.

Moles were considered uncanny things, and often used in country charms. Here is one *To have money always*. " Take a mole in March and make a purse of the dryed skynne, and with a hawk's fether and the bloude of a batt wryte thes names Rosquilla dunstallum, & looke what summe you have in your purse, & so much you shal fynde al ways."

Spells against witchcraft were a large part of the countryman's armory, and these are liberally represented in the magical books. Here is one with the patient's urine :

> " Put five spanish needles into an egge through the shell & seethe it in the uryne of one that is bewytched, & whyle it is seethinge the witch will come without doubt. prt est. prt est prt est."

Here we have the belief in the power of steel and of fire and the magic quality of eggs, as well as the sympathetic charm with the patient's urine, with which the witch had presumably been before in some kind of malign contact.

One of the most interesting manuscripts which I have come across, from our point of view, is the early seventeenth-century treatise in the Bodleian, e Mus 173. This has some general directions, but it is chiefly remarkable for the variety and scope of its recipes. It begins in an orderly way with directions for the consecration of the magician's instruments, his book and stone, and the making of the circles of Moses and Solomon for conjuration of angels ; and the licence for them to depart, then it slips suddenly into a recipe " to make a woman burn in love ". It returns to a more legitimate arrangement in the description of " the circle of defence for the master and his fellowes to stand in, ether in feelde or towne," and " how to excommunicate spirits that will not appeare in ther invocation ". After three more recipes it continues with the names of spirits to be called up in an earthy circle, and an experiment of Saymay for treasure in the seas, to bring the spirit Bilgal into a crystal ; and the most convenient experiment by which a master might call a spirit into a crystal without help from a scryer or assistant. Then we have *circulus aquaticus*, for spirits of the water to get treasure out of the sea. The spirits invocated are Azuriel, Azael and Elevotel, but the circle serves for all watery spirits, and was possibly that used by Owen Glendower. It is followed by another excommunication of spirits that will not appear, which would have been useful to Glendower if the spirits were as disobedient as Hotspur suggested. It then goes on to an experiment to get eight princes of darkness out of hell, unto whom all spirits are obedient, which is followed by an experiment to bring down angels. After that the book becomes frankly a collection of miscellaneous recipes, of which there are eight to find treasure, seven for love, six to raise spirits in the crystal, five against theft, five medical, five cures for the bewitched, three excommunication of spirits, two charms against witches, two for raising the fairies, as well as some odd recipes such as that " a sword or knife shall not hurt thee " and " to make soldiers courageous ". This is not a complete list of the contents of the book but it gives a fair idea of the proportion in which the recipes occur. They vary in source and type from bookish Latin invocations to a truly folk method of gaining a fairy familiar, which I believe to be unique in its traditional quality. Just before it we have directions to call Oberion into a crystal stone, which proceeds in the usual way with a conjuration by the name of God, by the angels, archangels, etc., followed by a dismissal ; it was always wise to have a good formula of dismissal. There are several simple spells as one for a horse that is bewitched, or any other beast : " Three biters have bitten thee, three betters have bettered thee. In the name of the Father and the Son and the Holy Ghoste, 3 persons in one trinitye, Stand up bayarde a God's name. Say this 3 times, and make crosses on him with your hand and he shall be cured." There is also a simple means of discovering whether a person or beast is bewitched. If you regard his eye and see no image of yourself in it, then he is bewitched. Walter de la Mare in his notes to *Come Hither* calls this the mark of a witch, but in the magical books I have only found it as a sign of being bewitched.

There are several other interesting recipes in the book, as one to see the spirits of the air, for which a lapwing's blood is needed ; but to me the cream of the book is *Experimentum Optimum Verissimum for the Fairies*.

Before it, by way of contrast, here are the well-known fairy spells from Elias Ashmole's manuscript in the Bodleian, Ashmole 1406.

Fairy Spells contained in MS. Bodleian. Ashmole 1406.

An excellent way to gett a Fayrie, but for my selfe I call margarett Barrance but this will obtaine any one that is not allready bound.

First gett a broad square christall or Venus glasse in length and breadth 3 inches, then lay that glasse or christall in the bloud of a white henne 3 Wednesdayes or 3 Fridayes : then take it out and wash it with holy aqua and fumigate it : then take 3 hazle sticks or wands of an yeare growth, pill them fayre and white, and make soe long as you write the spiritts name, or fayries name, which you call 3 times, on every sticke being made flatt one, one side, then bury them under some hill whereas you suppose fayries haunt, the Wednesday before you call her, and the friday followinge take them uppe and call hir at 8 or 3 or 10 of the clocke which be good plannetts and howres for that turn : but when you call, be in cleane Life and turne thy face towards the east and when you have her bind her to that stone or Glasse.

An Ungt. to annoynt under the Eyelids and upon the Eyelidds evninge and morninge, but especially when you call, or finde your sight not perfect. [That is, an ointment to give sight of the fairies.] pt. [precipitate?] sallet oyle and put it into a Viall glasse but first wash it with rose water, and marygold flower water, the flowers be gathered towards the east, wash it til the oyle come white, then put it into the glasse, ut supra. and thou put thereto the budds of holyhocke, the flowers of mary gold ; the flowers or toppes of wild time the budds of young hazle, and the time must be gathered neare the side of a hill where fayries use to go oft, and the grasse of a fayrie throne, there : all these putt into the oyle, into the glasse, and sett it to dissolve 3 dayes in the sonne, and thou keep it for thy use ; ut supra.

To Call a Fairy.

I, E. A. call the. Elaby ; Gathen : in the name of the. father. of. the. sonne. and of the holy. ghost. And. I adiure. the. Elaby. Gathen : Conjure. and. Straightly : charge. and Command. thee. by. Tetragrammaton : Emanuell. messias. sether. panton. cratons. Alpha et Omega. and by. all. other. high. and. reverent. names. of allmighty. god. both Effuable. and. in. Effuable. and by. all. the. vertues. of the holy. ghost. by the dystic grace. and. foreknowledge. of. the. holy. ghost. I. Adjure. and commande. thee. Elaby. by. all. the. powers. and. grace. and. vertues. of. all. the. holy. meritorious. Virginnes. and. patriarches. And. I. Conjure. thee. Elaby Gathon. by. these. holy. names. of God. Saday. Eloy. Iskyros. Adonay. Sabaoth. that thou appeare presently. meekely. and myldy. in. this. glasse. without. doeinge. hurt. or. daunger. unto. me. or any other. livinge. creature. and to this I binde. thee. by. the. whole. power. and. vertue. of. our. Lord. Jesus. Christ. I. commande. thee. by. the. vertue. of. his. uprisinge. and. by. the. vertue. of. his flesh. and. body. that. he. tooke. of. the. blessed.

Virginne. Mary. Empresse. of. heaven. and. hell. and. by. the. hole. power. of. god. and. his. holy. names. namely. Adonay. Adonatos. Aloy. Elohim. Suda. Ege. Zeth. and heban : that. is. to. say. Lord. of. vertue. and. king. of. Israell. dwellinge. uppon. the. whole. face. of. the. earth. whose. seate. is. in. heaven and. his. power. in. earth. and. by. him. &. by those glorious. and. powerfull. names. I binde. thee. to. give. and. doe. thy. true. humble. and. obedient. servise. unto. me. E.A., and never. to depart. without. my. consent. and Lawfull. Authoritie. in. the. name. of. the. Father. and. the. holy. trinitie. And. I Command. thee. Elaby. Gathen. by. all. Angells. and. Arkangells. and. all. the. holy. company. of. heaven. worshippinge. the omnipotent. god. that. thou. doest. come. and. appeare. presently. to. me. E.A. in. this. christall. or. glasse. meekely. and. myldely. to. my. true and. perfect. sight. and. truly. without. fraud. Dissymulation. or. deceite. resolve. and. satisfye me. in. and. of. all. manner. of. such. questions. and. commands. and. Demands. as. I. shall. either. Aske. Require. desire. or. demande. of. thee. and. that. thou. Ellaby. Gathen. be. true. and. obedient. unto me. both. now. and. ever. heareafter. at. all. time. and. times. howers. dayes. nightes. mynittes. and. in. and. at. all. places. wheresoever. either. in field. howse. or. in. any. other. place. whatsoever. &. wheresoever. I. shall. call. upon. thee. and. that. thou. Elaby : Gathen : doe. not. start. depart. or. desire. to. goe. or. departe. from. me. neyther. by. arte. or. call. of. any. other. Artist. of. any. degree. or. Learninge. whatsoever. but. that. thou. in. the. humblyest. manner. that. thou. mayest. be. commaunded. to. attend. and. give. thy. true. obedience. unto. me. E.A. : and that. even. as. thou. wilt. Answer. it. unto. and. before. the. Lord. of. hoste. at. the. dreadfull. day. of. Judgment. before. whose. glorious. presence. both. thou. and. I. and. all. other. Christian. Creatures. must. and. shall. appeare. to. receive. our. Joyes. in. heaven. or. by. his doome. to. be. Judged. into. everlastinge. Damnation. even. into. the. deepe. pitt. of. hell. there. to. receive. our. portion. amongst. the divell. and. his. Angells. to. be. ever. burninge. in. pitch. fier. and. brimstone. and. never. consumed. and. to. this. I. E.A. Sweare. thee. Elaby. Gathen. and. binde. thee. by. the. whole. power. of. god. the. Father. god. the. Sonne. & god. the. holy. ghost. 3. persons. and. one. god. in. trinitye. to. be. trew. and. faithfull. unto. me. in. all. Reverence. humillity. Let. it. be. done. in. Jesus. Jesus. Jesus. his name. quickly. quickly. quickly. come. come. come. fiat. fiat. fiat. Amen. Amen. Amen. etc.

The call ut supra is to call Elabigathan A. Fayrie.

You will notice that all the precautions of ordinary necromancy are taken here, and that there is very little to distinguish the fairy from a ghost. The fairy is raised into a crystal, and in the second spell Elaby Gathan is addressed not as an elemental, but as a spirit that has a stake in the great Day of Judgment. The recipe in e Mus 173 is very different :

In the night before the newe moone, or the same night, or the night after the newe moone, or els the night before the full moone, the night of the full, or the night after the full moone, goe to the house where the fairies mayds doe use and provyde you a fayre and cleane buckett or payle cleane washt with cleare water therein and sett yt by the chimney syde or where fyre is made, and having a fayre newe towell or one cleane washt by, and so departe till the morninge. then be thou the fyrst that shall come to the buckett of water before the sonne ryse, and take yt to the lyght, that you find upon the water a whyte ryme like rawe milk or grease. take yt by with a silver spoone, and put it into a cleane sawcer then the next night following come to the same house agayne before 11 of the clocke at night, making a good fyre with sweet woods and sett upon the table a newe towell or one cleane washt and upon yt 3 fyne loaves of newe mangett, 3 newe knyves with whyte haftes and a newe cuppe full of newe ale, then sett your selfe downe by the fyre in a chaire wyth your face towards the table, and anoynt your eyes with the same creame or oyle aforsayd. Then you shall see come by you thre fairy mayds, and as they passe by they will obey you wyth beckinge their heades to you, and like as they doe to you, so doe to them, but say nothinge. suffer the fyrst, whatsoever she bee, to passe, for she is malignant but to the second or third as you like best reatch forth your hand and pluck her to you, and wyth fewe words aske her when she will apoynt a place to meete you the next morninge for to assoyle such questions as you will demand of her ; then if she will graunt you suffer her to depart and goe to her companye till the houre appoynted, but misse not at the tyme or place, then will the other in the meane tyme whyle you are talkinge with her, goe to the table and eate of what is ther, and then will they depart from you, and as they obeye you doe you the like to them, saying nothinge, but letting them depart quyetlye. Then when your houre is come to meete, say to her your mynd, for then will she come alone. Then covenant with her for all matters convenient for your purpose and she will always be with you, of this assure yourself for it is proved.

Here we find ourselves in an entirely different world from the magician's study, and the elaborate precautions with which he hedged himself. There is no circle here, no invocations of the name of God, no crystal stone, no curses nor attempts at supernatural coertion. It might be the beginning of a fairy story, indeed it seems part of one. It is clear where the scum came from that was found on the water. Though the three fairy damsels seem to have come alone on the second night, on the first the fairy mothers must have come and washed their babies' eyes. This was the magic ointment which gives fairy sight in so many of our earliest fairy tales, from William of Newbury's *Fairy Midwife* down to the story of Cherry of Zennor.

The preparations made for the fairies are startlingly like those made in the thirteenth-century play, *Le Jeu de Feuillie*[3] by Adam de la Halle. A bower was prepared for these fairies, but there were the white-handled knives, bread and wine, and clean linen, and one fairy out of the three was malignant. Otherwise the preparations remind us of a Midsummer Eve custom vividly described by Bovet in his *Pandaemonium*, 1684. The household had been disturbed by the attempt of two young maid-servants to find out their future husbands. Bovet happened to visit the house the next day, and the maids were called up to give him an account of their experience. The elder of the two was the spokesman.

> We had been told divers times, that if we fasted on *Midsummer* Eve, and then at 12 a Clock at night laid a cloath on the Table ; with Bread, and Cheese, and a cup of the best Beer, setting ourselves down, as if we were going to eat, & leaving the door of the Room open ; we should see the Persons whom we should afterwards Marry, come into the Room, and drink to us : Accordingly we kept a true Fast all the day yesterday, unknown to any of the Family ; and at night having disposed of my Mistresses to Bed, we fastened the stair door of their Rooms, which came down into the Hall, and locked all the doors of the Yard, and whatever way besides led into the House, except the door of the Kitchen, which was left open into the Yard for the *Sweethearts* to enter ; it being then near twelve a Clock, we laid a clean cloath on the Kitchen Table, setting thereon a Loaf and Cheese, and a Stone Jug of beer, with a drinking glass, seating ourselves together in the inside of the Table, with our faces towards the door : We had been in this posture but a little while, before we heard a mighty ratling at the great Gate of the Yard, as if it would have shook the House down, there was a jingling of Chains, and something seemed to prance about the Yard like a Horse, which put us into great terrour and affrightment, so that we wisht we had never gone so far in it ; but now we knew not how to go back, and therefore kept the place where we were : my Master's Spaniell (for the young Captain was then alive) got against the door of the stair foot, and there made so great a noise with houling, and ratling the door, that we feared they might have taken notice of the dis-turbance ; but presently came a young man into the Kitchen, [*here one of the young Ladies interrupted her, saying, Housewife, it was the Devil* to which the Maid replied, *Madam I do not believe that, but perhaps it might be the Spirit of a Man*], and making a bow to me, he took up the Glass, which was full of Beer, on the Table, and drank to me, filling the Glass again, and setting it on the Table as before, then making another bow, went out of the Room. Immediately after which, another came in the same manner, and did the same to the other Maid (whom she named, but I have forgot) and then all was quiet, and after we had eaten some Bread and Cheese, we went to Bed.[4]

[3] Œuvres Complètes du Trouvères Adam la Halle. Paris, 1872.
[4] Bovet. *Pandaemonium, or the Devil's Cloyster.* London. 1684. p. 212.

2 G

On the more elaborate, magical side we have a spell in which three spirits appear, of which the last is the best disposed, and which has something of a fairy-tale quality, but it has the elaborate protection of the circle and the conjuration and the blood, moreover even the third spirit is too dangerous to be trusted.

A method of obtaining help from some unspecified spirit.
      (Brit. Mus. MS. Sloane 1727. p. 18.)
      If thou wolde have whatsoever thou desirest : first thou must gett a Lapwing and lett him blood in a glasse, and close it that noe ayre enter in, and when you would worke : goe ply. to a woode, and first hold a bright sword in thy hand and say these words (which must be written in an Abortive) with the same blood. and in the entring into the wood begin and say thus Betha suspensus in ethera superea enpion, emprogudum, pamelion angius Marius Egripus fons floriseme desede baldithe sapors ana velarca siras : but these are truer : beltha suspensus Mathea Superea Implex pamilion ananrius fons floris Trosdogod Baldachia. Sarius Mars. these are the words in negromancy : then arise one thy feett and make a circle four square with the said Sword ; and in every corner of the circle make Solomon's pentacle and between every pentacle a Crose ; and then stand against the east in the midst of thy circle with thy sword in thy hand saying the words aforesaid, 2, 3, 4 times or as often as occasion requireth : and when thou hast saide there shall appeare a knight on a horse with a Gos-hawke on his hand : the which will say what will you aske : why call you me, I am redy to fulfill all your will : but answer nothing att all keeping thyselfe short from him : but beholding still the circle till he be past and thou arise upon thy feet and say againe towards the North as a foresaide and Anon shall come one other knight more fayor than the firste & more semely then the other with a goshauke on his hand : but answer him not neither behold but as thou didst the other : and he shall vanish away : thou say as aforesaid Beltha etc. turning westward and anon the third knight shall appeare. more beautyfull and fayer than any of the rest riding on a horse with a goshawke one his hand Crowned with a diadem of Gould the which shall say behold I am here weary for Labor all the day : wherefore tell me what thou wouldst : and you may trustily say what you will unto him : and he shall presently Answere thee : asking the if thou wilt have his fellowshipp : but thou shalt denie him and leave him : and as soon as he shall here that word he shall pass from thee : and soe leave untill the next day : and the next day come againe and thou shalt find what thou desirest : *Approved*.

Here then are a few gleanings from some of the more accessible books of magic. I have selected the recipes that seemed to me nearest to the ordinary country practices, but of course these are only a few, and further research might discover many that are more significant.

WITCHCRAFT IN SPAIN: THE TESTIMONY OF MARTÍN DE CASTAÑEGA'S TREATISE ON SUPERSTITION AND WITCHCRAFT (1529)

DAVID H. DARST

Associate Professor, Spanish and Humanities, Florida State University

INTRODUCTION

In 1529 a little known Franciscan friar named Martín de Castañega published a brief treatise in Logroño entitled *Tratado muy sotil y bien fundado de las supersticiones y hechicerías y vanos conjuros y abusiones; y otros cosas al caso tocantes y de la posibilidad e remedio dellas.* It was the first independent book on witchcraft composed in a vernacular language to reach print, [1] and—most surprisingly—it wasn't republished until 1946. [2] In 1530 or 1531 a work with virtually the same title appeared by the famous professor and theologian Pedro Ciruelo; [3] and it was re-edited ten times in the next two decades, thereby totally eclipsing its predecessor. The editorial history of Castañega's *Treatise on Superstition and Witchcraft* is all the more lamentable because the book is not only saner and more rational than Ciruelo's on general issues but also truly sceptical in matters of bewitchments, possessions, and conjurations. To understand Castañega's place in the history of witchcraft, however, one first must comprehend the various guises that witchcraft took during the Middle Ages and the pre-modern periods.

Thanks to the recent investigations of such admirable scholars as Norman Cohn [4] and Richard Kieckhefer, [5] we are finally beginning to understand fully the nature of the hysteria that swept sixteenth and seventeenth-century Europe, plus the nature of public and learned opinion on witches before 1500. Cohn's

book traces from antiquity to the Renaissance the presence of the characteristic accusations made against witches of erotic debauches at sabbats, infanticide and cannibalism, group devil worship, and night-flights. All of these were of course pure fantasy. "There is in fact no serious evidence for the existence of such a sect of Devil-worshippers anywhere in medieval Europe," avers Cohn. "One can go further; there is serious evidence to the contrary" (p. 59). He shows that these traits—despite their total fabrication— were used universally against the established society's enemies, most notably by the Romans against the very Christians who would centuries later use the tags against their witches. Cohn also demonstrates that people were punished for these fantasized crimes only where the authorities deemed it expedient to eliminate a certain group from society. Before 1500, moreover, there appeared to be little desire to prosecute people for witchcraft. Although the typical witch beliefs were in the air, they were not used against anyone except in unusual circumstances. The prevalence of an accusatory form of criminal procedure rather than an inquisitorial one aided to hold down the number of witch trials, yet the chief reason was that in the Middle Ages the authorities were reluctant to believe the accusations made against those accused of witchcraft.

The classic example of an increasing willingness on the part of some authorities to act against people accused of witchcraft is the bull *Summis Desiderantes Affectibus* published by Innocent VIII in 1484. The motivation behind the bull was clearly political, having to do with jurisdictional problems in northern Germany between the local priests and civil authorities and the Roman Inquisition. Innocent states that "not a few clerics and lay folk of those countries . . . are not ashamed to contend with the most unblushing effrontery that these enormities are not practiced in those provinces, and consequently the aforesaid inquisitors have no legal right to exercise their powers of inquisition in the said provinces." [6] To prove them wrong, Innocent gives to the inquisitors Heinrich Kramer and James Sprenger complete authority and liberty to proceed against any and all heretics in those

---

[1] Earlier books in the vernacular were either translations from the Latin, never published, or touched only tangentially on witchcraft. For a complete account of books on the subject before Castañega's, see Rossell Hope Robbins, *The Encyclopedia of Witchcraft and Demonology* (New York: Crown, 1959), pp. 145–147. Robbins, ironically, does not even mention Castañega or his treatise.

[2] Agustín G. de Amezúa (ed.), *Tratado de las supersticiones y hechicerías* (Madrid: Sociedad de Bibliófilos Españoles, 1946).

[3] *Reprobación de las supersticiones y hechicerías* (Alcalá, n.d.). It has recently been translated into English by Eugene A. Maio and D'Orsay W. Pearson, *Pedro Ciruelo's A Treatise Reproving All Superstitions and Forms of Witchcraft* (Rutherford: Fairleigh Dickinson University Press, 1977).

[4] *Europe's Inner Demons: An Enquiry Inspired by the Great Witch-Hunt* (New York: Basic Books, 1975).

[5] *European Witch Trials: Their Foundations in Popular and Learned Culture, 1300–1500* (Berkeley: University of California Press, 1976).

---

[6] In *Malleus Maleficarum*, Trans. Montague Summers (New York: Dover, 1971) pp. xliii–xliv.

PROCEEDINGS OF THE AMERICAN PHILOSOPHICAL SOCIETY, VOL. 123, NO. 5, OCTOBER 1979

provinces, threatening those who would impede the inquisitors with excommunication.

In 1486 Kramer and Sprenger published their handbook for future witch hunters entitled *Malleus Maleficarum,* in which they defined the characteristics of witchcraft and the procedures to be used against witches. The authorities thus had their permission in the bull and their procedure in the treatise. Thenceforth the number of accusations and trials increased proportionately, mainly because, as Cohn points out (pp. 251–253), it was deemed expedient to believe the published notions on witchcraft. Cohn thus concludes: "The great witch-hunt can in fact be taken as a supreme example of a massive killing of innocent people by a bureaucracy acting in accordance with beliefs which, unknown or rejected in earlier centuries, had come to be taken for granted, as self-evident truths" (p. 155). Cohn gives no valid reason for the prevalence of the ensuing witch-craze, as Hugh Trevor-Roper calls it,[7] that swept Europe from 1560 to 1680; but Marvin Harris does. He notes that the question should not be why the authorities suddenly decided to stamp out witchcraft, but rather why they were so obsessed with creating it. He answers that it was to subvert the anxieties of the lower classes about their living conditions onto a scapegoat and away from the upper classes. "The practical significance of the witch mania," Harris explains,

was that it shifted responsibility for the crisis of late medieval society from both Church and state to imaginary demons in human form. Preoccupied with the fantastic activities of these demons, the distraught, alienated, pauperized masses blamed the rampant Devil instead of corrupt clergy and the rapacious nobility. Not only were the Church and state exonerated, but they were made indispensable. The clergy and nobility emerged as the great protectors of mankind against an enemy who was omnipresent but difficult to detect.[8]

Kieckhefer's close investigation of the witch trials supports Cohn's assertions and indirectly proves Harris's radical theory. Kieckhefer makes the essential distinction between "sorcery," which is maleficent magic usually involving mysterious rites and invocations, and "diabolism," which entails submission to the devil. The former was a perennial aspect of village peasant life; the latter was a purely learned notion imposed on the masses from above. After a thorough examination of reliable documents, Kieckhefer asserts: "The idea of diabolism, developed and elaborated on the Continent, was evidently the product of speculation by theologians and jurists, who could make no sense of sorcery except by postulating a diabolical link

between the witch and her victim" (p. 36; see also pp. 78–79). Therefore, "in those courts which were most likely to transmit learned notions, the charge of diabolism was most likely to occur" (p. 37).

Witchcraft, in sum, was for the most part a literary artifice.[9] It began slowly with the Church fathers incorporating folktales into their writings and treating them as gospel truth, after which everyone followed the established "authority" as proof for their assertions about witchcraft.[10] St. Thomas Aquinas's statements on the existence of demons, incubi and succubi, transmutation, and the devil's pact especially made self-evident truth out of what had earlier been supposition. Furthermore, the forbidden nature and sexual aspects of witch lore could not help but to shock and tantalize both prosecutors and offenders. R. E. L. Masters therefore correctly likens witchcraft to a "collective art work": "As such, it might be regarded as the ultimate esthetic expression of an era notable for its excesses: the combination of an impossible ideal of asexuality, accompanied by a hatred of the flesh, with a practical libertinism seldom rivaled in all of history. This gigantic phantasy was a delusion insofar as it was mistaken for objective reality, leading to the most savage attempts at suppression of the imaginary offenses accepted as authentic by both the offenders and those who judged and punished them".[11]

A vicious cycle thus emerges where the scholars, preachers, and inquisitors say that certain characteristics would prove a person to be a witch, and then the person accused is forced through torture to confess she has done those things, thereby proving with "experience" the truth of the authorities' statements. That witch is then compelled to implicate others—as proof that there were organized sects allied against Mother Church—and those others are in turn induced to declare they committed the same crimes. With all that ponderous evidence to substantiate the scholars' assertions it was virtually impossible for anyone to deny the existence of witches; and there are even cases where crazed women actually turned themselves over to the authorities claiming they were truly witches.

The keystone to the whole fabrication appears to be

---

[7] *The European Witch-Craze of the Sixteenth and Seventeenth Centuries and Other Essays* (New York: Harper Torchbooks, 1969), pp. 90–192.

[8] *Cows, Pigs, Wars and Witches: The Riddles of Culture* (New York: Random House, 1962).

[9] The literary origin of the witch-craze is now common knowledge. See, among others, Rossell Hope Robbins, p. 144: "Witchcraft was a notion evolved primarily by the Inquisition and opposed by the people (with a handful of lawyers and physicians); it was learned, not popular. Only later, after decades of pounding in the new doctrine, did public support for the delusion grow."

[10] The question of "authority" and "proof" is taken up at length by Wayne Shumaker, *The Occult Sciences in the Renaissance* (Berkeley: University of California Press, 1972), pp. 74–80.

[11] *Eros and Evil: The Sexual Psychopathology of Witchcraft* (Baltimore: Penguin Books, 1962), p. 146.

the existence of a bureaucratic system—the Inquisition—capable and willing to undertake the systematic prosecution of people called witches, plus credence in the legality and efficacy of judicial torture; for, as Hugh Trevor-Roper notes, it was torture that lay, directly or indirectly, behind most of the witch trials of Europe, creating witches where none were and multiplying both victims and evidence. Trevor-Roper thereby concludes: "All the evidence makes it clear that the new mythology owes its system entirely to the inquisitors themselves. . . . The Hammerers of Witches built up their systematic mythology of Satan's kingdom and Satan's accomplices out of the mental rubbish of peasant credulity and feminine hysteria; and the . . . mythology . . . once launched, acquired a momentum of its own. It became an established folklore, generating its own evidence, and applicable far outside its original home" (pp. 116–117).

Now, where does Martín de Castañega stand in this swirl of evidence? If he had lived in the fourteenth or fifteenth century, he would be most definitely in the camp of what Kieckhefer calls "Medieval Rationalism": "Instead of condemning and burning witches, the authors of these texts condemned the superstitious belief that such occurrences are real" (pp. 38–39). Yet by writing almost half a century after the publication of the *Malleus Maleficarum,* and after having been a spectator at the famous Pamplona witch trials in 1527, one must consider Castañega one of the few sceptical minds of the time. The inquisitor Avellaneda who was in charge of the Pamplona trials, for example, believed and followed all the current absurdities about witches. [12]

The *Treatise on Superstition and Witchcraft* has two separable parts. The first eleven chapters treat almost exclusively "diabolism," and the last thirteen chapters are concerned mainly with "sorcery." The first part thus speaks of the two inimical churches, diabolical rites that parody Christian ones, satanic pacts, witch-flights (but quite hesitatingly), apparent transmutations (for which he gives scientific reasons), infanticide, plus incubi and succubi, all of which come from literary sources cited by Castañega. He especially culls biblical references, proving, in effect, every one of the above topics except incubi and infanticide with references to similar instances in the Bible. If it's stated in the Bible, declares Castañega, then it must be true. He likewise depends on four other unsinkable authorities: St. Augustine, St. Thomas Aquinas, the *Canon Episcopi* that apeared in the *Decretum* of Burchard of Worms, and John Gerson's *De erroribus Circa Artem Magicam Reprobatis.* These sources never lie, so Castañega uses them liberally to sub-

stantiate what occurs in the Bible. They thereby form a bridge between the events in it and the plausibility for the same things to happen in sixteenth-century Spain. In sum, the literary quality of the chapters on diabolism is undeniable.

In Castañega's favor, nevertheless, is the total absence of remarks on the infamous devil's mark, explicit worship of the devil as lord and master (although witches are accredited with paying homage by kissing his nether parts), sabbat meetings, flying on anointed sticks, group sex, and all the other morbid paraphernalia that the *Malleus Maleficarum* [13] and other contemporary works associate with the trade. Furthermore, Castañega sees clearly the reasons for someone wishing to become a witch. All the cases he discusses stem from a desire to learn secret things, or to gain riches, or to satisfy carnal appetites. There is absolutely no credence given to the idea of a witch doing evil purely for the sake of doing evil. He also notes that most witches are old and poor women who have recourse to the devil solely because they foresee no other way to satisfy their carnal and material needs. And, quite contrary to what the *Malleus* says, Castañega claims the witches receive immense sexual delight from their nefarious lovers. The general impression from the first eleven chapters is that Castañega discounts as many of the popular and learned beliefs as he can without having to deny the validity of the Bible; almost everything concerning witchcraft is false, in other words, except for those doctrinally undeniable events in the Scriptures.

The second half of the treatise has a totally different tone. Castañega refutes diabolical activities for virtually every topic he discusses, instead offering medical reasons or citing as cause the imagination of the person afflicted. His arguments are thus to dissuade belief in witchcraft, to prove that diabolical intervention normally does *not* exist. He specifically attacks the belief in any supernatural or magical benefits from king's cures, the evil eye, amulets, exorcisms of animals, and weather making. He is especially distressed at demented, hysterical, or epileptic people being considered possessed by the devil and subsequently exorcised. Many, he asserts, fake the possession, others are medically ill, and some think they are possessed but aren't. One person he knew had nothing wrong with her until the priest tried to exorcise her, after which she actually showed the characteristics of a possessed person. As Alonso Salazar was to comment scores of years later when he investigated claims of witchcraft in the same region of Spain: "I deduce the importance of silence and reserve from the experience that there were neither

[12] See Julio Caro Baroja, *The World of the Witches,* trans, O. N. V. Glendinning (Chicago: University of Chicago Press, 1964), pp. 143–151.

[13] These physiological and psychological aspects of the *Malleus* have been studied by Gregory Zilboorg, *The Medical Man and the Witch* (New York: Cooper Square, 1935), pp. 1–64.

witches nor bewitched until they were talked and written about." [14]

Also in Castañega's favor is the total absence of any mention of torture or the Inquisition. In the long chapter on excommunication (Chapter XVIII), for example, only proper judicial procedures are described; and in the sections on weather makers he recommends scorn and disbelief rather than arrest and interrogation. He even goes so far as to imply that people accused of diabolical possession should be exorcised only as a last resort, and then without a crowd and through the quiet counsels of religious men and honorable matrons. In all of these postures he specifically denies the advice Kramer and Sprenger suggest in the *Malleus Maleficarum,* and he even belies much of what his equally cautious contemporary Pedro Ciruelo claims in the *Treatise Reproving all Superstitions and Forms of Witchcraft.* Ciruelo sees many of the "natural" events, such as the evil eye, amulets, curing with saliva, and tempests, as coming directly from witchcraft. Castañega attributes real natural curative or medicinal powers to them. Ciruelo, in other words, is more credulous about witches and their influence, while Castañega is more credulous about "natural" events and medicinal cures. Concomitantly, Ciruelo never attributes anything to the imagination, yet Castañega includes without exception the person's imagination as a potential source of delusion. Castañega even goes so far as to recommend that doctors should at times use vain and superstitious remedies, such as hanging an oak acorn around the person's neck to cure the fever, because the patient who believes in those remedies will have more faith in his doctor and will in his imagination think he is going to be cured faster (Chapter XV). In fact, medical information and terminology abound in Castañega's treatise, and they are sorely lacking in his contemporary's work. Castañega, for example, sees excommunication not as a punishment but rather as a medical problem. He calls it "a medicine to guard against spiritual sickness (as is *a jure* excommunication) or to cure sickness (as is *a judice* excommunication)," and recommends charity and works of mercy "because the medicine that is given to cure or preserve ought not to deny or impede the acts that favor a return to health" (Chapter XVIII). This is a far cry from the terrifying instructions for torture and punishment found in the third part of the *Malleus Maleficarum.*

The following translation of the *Tratado de las supersticiones y hechicerías* will let Castañega speak for himself to the numerous scholars of witchcraft who know no Spanish. It is a complete translation that adheres to the original Spanish as closely as facile comprehension allowed. All names have been anglicized and the few obscure references have been annotated in the text. Hopefully, when such collections of witchcraft documents as those of H. C. Erik Midelfort, [15] Alan C. Kors, [16] and E. William Monter [17] are compiled in the future, the sound and rational views of Martín de Castañega will not be absent. [18]

[14] Cited in Charles Williams, *Witchcraft* (Cleveland: Meridian Books, 1959), p. 253. See also Baroja, pp. 184–189.

[15] "Were There Really Witches?" in Robert M. Kingdon (ed.), *Transition and Revolution* (Minneapolis: Burgess, 1974), pp. 189–233.
[16] With Edward Peters, *Witchcraft in Europe 1100–1700* (Philadelphia: University of Pennsylvania Press, 1972).
[17] *European Witchcraft* (New York: John Wiley, 1969).
[18] The preparation of this study was made possible (in part) by a grant from the Program for Translations of the National Endowment for the Humanities, an independent federal agency.

A TREATISE ON SUPERSTITION AND WITCHCRAFT

I. THE DEVIL ALWAYS DESIRES TO BE HONORED AND ADORED AS GOD

The devil always has an overweening estimation of his own power and procures to be honored and adored as God, which is clearly seen in his fall and during the times of the Gentiles. He showed this self-estimation when he said to Christ: "All these things will I give thee, if thou wilt fall down and worship me" (Matthew 4:9). For this reason Christ called him Prince of this World (John 12:31). If the devil thus dared to confront Christ, knowing him to be a very perfect and complete man (although he might not have had sure knowledge of his divinity), why should anyone marvel if the devil does the same and tempts thereby earthlings he knows to be weak sinners? Those who are not attracted by such temptations should give thanks to God and have compassion on the others who are deceived by such allurements.

This is the way the devil nowadays procures simple Christians and curious folk not well versed in the faith, as well as those who are inordinately inclined to temporal riches, honors, and vanities, to licentious carnal delights, and to the vain investigations of occult matters: he deceives them as he did the first woman by promising them wisdom and knowledge of things that cannot be achieved through natural means, such as knowledge of secret events that occur in remote

parts. Since all naturally are inclined to know—and
especially about occult and other hidden matters—
thus it happens that many curious and less intelligent
persons are deceived either by a greed for abundant
knowledge or by a cupidity for achieving and having
those things they desire with an inordinate appetite.
Seeing that their own efforts are not enough, they
accept the aid of the devil, who as their lord, protector,
and master promises those things.

The devil tempts and often conquers anyone who is
inclined to worldly pomps and honors, as happened
with Pope Sylvester II (999–1003). He was a monk
named Gerbert who abjured Christ, made a pact
with the devil, and took up necromancy and the
magic arts so as to have everything he wished. With
the devil's help he was made Bishop, then Archbishop,
and finally Pope. At the end of his life, however, he
recognized his error and died a Catholic.

The devil also easily blinds and brings under his
tutelage those who do not bridle their carnal appetites.
One example is Salomon (I King 11) who by his blind
and licentious desire for women committed idolatry
and built temples to idols and demons. He also composed exorcisms and superstitious conjurations (in
a book known as *The Key of Salomon*) with which
in times past people conjured demons and cast them
out of human bodies. Another example is the story
of Saints Cyprian and Justina. A student named
Agladius, burning with desire for Justina, sought the
aid of the necromancer Cyprian to conquer the girl
with incantations; but the virgin Justina caused the
devils to flee by making the sign of the cross. When
Cyprian saw the power of the cross to be greater
than that of the devil, he converted to Catholicism.
Both eventually became martyrs (in 304). Temptations and superstitions in matters like these occur
every day among young students.

The devil also tempts and deceives those who desire
and procure to know secret, occult, and future things,
as happened with Saul (I Samuel 28), who consulted
that pythoness to learn who would win an upcoming
battle.

No one should consider it strange that the devil
tempts poor people who desire inordinately temporal
things, since he did not hesitate to tempt even Christ
by offering him worldly riches; yet he saw our Lord
despise them all. We see every day in our own experience how poor women and needy clerics take up
the office of conjurers, witches, necromancers, and
diviners in order to maintain themselves and have
enough to eat; and they always have their houses full
of people. We read the same about the prophet
Balaam (Numbers 22), a covetous and ambitious
necromancer. In this way the devil has his disciples
and following, and he attempts to create a congregation with them.

II. THERE ARE TWO CHURCHES AND CONGREGATIONS IN THIS WORLD

There are two churches on earth: the Catholic and
the diabolical. The Catholic church is the congregation of all faithful Catholics, united under one God
whom all adore, by one faith that all confess, with
one baptism that all receive. The diabolical church
is in general all the unfaithful who are outside of the
Catholic church; it is not properly speaking one
church, because they do not adore nor believe in the
one true God, nor confess the one true Catholic faith,
nor receive or have a holy sacrament that is effective.
Although many think that Jews and Moslems believe
and adore the one true God, this belief is false; and
if one persists in affirming it he can be considered a
heretic. Neither the Jews nor the Moslems adore the
three-in-one God; and, as Saint Augustine says, this
is God, and no other. Christ said that if you believe
in God you must also believe in him, and it is impossible for someone to reject him yet adore and honor
the God his father who sent him. Jews and Moslems
therefore do not believe in the true God, but in a
false God.

In the diabolical church there is no union, but only
many diabolical congregations distinct from each other
with no agreement or participation among them; nor
do they make up one body, as the particular Catholic
churches do who are all the same universal church,
which is a mystical body whose head is Jesus Christ.

III. AS THERE ARE SACRAMENTS IN THE CATHOLIC CHURCH, SO THERE ARE EXECRATIONS IN THE DIABOLICAL CHURCH

As in the Catholic church there are sacraments ordained and established by Christ who is true man
and God, so in the diabolical church there are execrations ordained and fixed by the devil and his ministers.
Although circumcision was a sacrament God gave a
long time ago to Abraham (Genesis 17), one can't
say now that the circumcision the Jews use is or was
ordained and established by God, since the way Abraham did it has ceased. What the Jews now have is
like the Moslem rite, which isn't ordained by God
but by the deceit of the devil and his ministers. Such
ceremonies are called execrations because the sacraments are vessels of grace by the virtue of which those
who take them receive grace; and those who take the
execrations receive neither virtue nor grace, but rather
incur the sin of heresy, which is the worst of all sins.

Besides the circumcision that the Jews now use and
that is similar only in appearance to the matter, manner, and ceremony of the true circumcision that God
gave to Abraham, the diabolical church has other ceremonies and execrations in imitation of the sacraments
of the Catholic church, and we popularly call them
superstitions and witchcrafts. To understand this it
is necessary to note that Christ ordained the Catholic

sacraments with very clear non-rhetorical words in common items that are found under ordinary circumstances, such as water, bread, wine, and oil. The diabolical execrations, on the contrary, are neither performed with clear words nor with things that are found under ordinary circumstances, but with unguents and potions made from rare animals and birds, and with obscure and rhymed words. Those rare things are not more appropriate for the effect that the devil and his ministers intend, but the devil wants his disciples to put great diligence in looking for them so that God's law will be despised and the devil himself will be honored as God with divine honors, and so they will put little or no hope in God, confiding in those vanities, and so that the deceits of the devil will be more hidden and less known, and so that the malice of those who occupy themselves with those things will be inflamed when they procure them with fervor and curiosity. The devil responds to those who do these ceremonies with ill will and malice, because the Catholic sacraments have value and work by way of grace and are signs instituted by God to give grace; but the diabolical execrations work by way of the diligence, antipathy, and malice that the devil creates.

As we said of the Old Testament ceremonies to which God responded with his grace according to the devotion with which they were undertaken, God responds likewise with his grace to those who take holy water and the consecrated host according to the devotion with which they are received and not because they are efficacious signs instituted by Christ. But because the more difficult a thing is the more man will endeavor to find it, the devil does not wish that his own execrations and enchantments be based on things easily found; nor does God consent it, because by that difficulty men avoid getting involved in superstitions and witchcrafts. Sometimes, however, the devil's ministers will use common things for signs; for a woman burned at the stake confessed that the devil gave her and two other companions some rocks to throw into the sea and then the sea became so rough that later in the afternoon twenty-two men were drowned trying to enter the harbor. Since by their own nature some objects have no more value than others, the devil uses and responds to common signs as well as to difficult ones according to his whim, noting if the signs deceive those to whom they are directed; and God permits this to happen to those already confirmed in their errors, for the Prophet says: "So I gave them up unto their own hearts' lust" (Psalms 81:12). Thus they go running after vain inventions.

These ceremonies and execrations are many times bodily ointments imitating the sacraments that are also celebrated with ointments because Christ means Anointed One, and the anointed Christians ought to be bodily and spiritually anointed when they receive their name because bodily anointment is a sign of the spiritual anointment of grace. Who besides someone who had faith in the sacraments of baptism, confirmation, ordination, and unction would say that they were anything but superstitions, with so many ceremonies and ointments? The sacrament of extreme unction looks like true witchcraft when they anoint the eyes, ears, nose, mouth, hands, back, and feet of the sick person. Isn't it what witches do to invoke the devil's aid? Well, since the devil always wishes to usurp the divine offices and have the mannerisms and dissimulations and colors that he needs to become an angel of light, he copies the sacraments; yet he mocks them by using dirty and abominable things that are difficult to find. This is contrary to the substances used for the Catholic sacraments, which are made of clean objects necessary to human use and easily found. The devil wishes that the form be with obscure, ugly, rhymed words for which diligence and study are needed; and this too is contrary to the form of the sacraments where simple, clear, and clean words without complications are used. The devil's intention is evil, and so isn't righteous or Catholic, and therefore it can't be good; all of which is contrary to the intention of the sacraments, which are good and holy so God can concur with his grace.

As for God's concurrence, it's worth noting here that if there isn't any fault in the sacrament, nor in he who receives it, the grace for which the sacrament is ordained follows immediately without fault. In the diabolical execrations and ceremonies, on the other hand, although all possible things are observed, the effect does not always follow as it does when God concurs in the sacraments. The sacraments are efficacious signs, that is, they have such efficacy by divine pact, and God can't help but to concur if there is no fault in the other part. The diabolical execrations are not efficacious signs, for neither by their nature nor by the institution of the devil can they have efficacy or power because only God can promise and give such infallible efficacy and no created being, because the creature does not always have God's permission for such effects except when it pleases God who, in his secret counsel and wise judgment which is hidden to us, does it for our good. Nor are there other reasons for the permission God gives except for those that are commonly stated about why God permits Jews, Moslems, Gentiles, and heretics to live in the world. The commonly held reasons are: first, to confirm the weak in their faith, because there are many who are Catholics in not having any error in their understanding but do not have some Catholic truths so well rooted as could be desired. Such people, seeing the confession of those who have been deceived by the devil's illusions, are confirmed in their faith and are made fervent instead of pusillanimous.

Second, to manifest the faith of those firm and well-founded in the faith, as one reads of Job, who was tempted and ill treated by the devil (Job 1). As Saint Paul said: "There must be also heresies among you, that they which are approved may be made manifest among you" (I Corinthians 11:19). Third, God permits these things as punishment for the obstinate. As the Apostle said: "God gave them over to a reprobate mind, to those things which are not convenient" (Romans 1:28). From these the fourth reason results and follows: to manifest the goodness and grandeur of God, who would not permit evil to be born in the world if from it great goods did not come.

Such execrations and diabolical bewitchments will be much more evil and superstitious and worthy of punishment if the rituals are composed or done with holy relics or objects dedicated to the divine religion, like holy water or the host or pieces of a consecrated altar or with words from the church rites. Although they may only mix similar terms and symbols for evil ends other than the church ordains, the more saintly objects they make use of, the more the ceremonies are odious to God and injurious to the church.

IV. WHO THE DIABOLICAL CHURCH'S MINISTERS ARE

The ministers of these diabolical execrations are, according to John Gerson (in *De Erroribus Circa Artem Magicam*), all those consecrated and dedicated to the devil by an express or occult pact. To understand this one must note the following explanations. An express pact with the devil is of two kinds. One is so clear and express that with formal words, denying the Faith, they profess anew to the devil in his presence, who appears to them in any form and figure he desires to take. They give him complete obedience and offer him their body and soul.

I met some of these witches and saw some burned and reconciled. One man said that the devil made him deny God and the Faith, but the devil could never make him deny Our Lady. He was a small, old man, and he recognized his sin and was reconciled. I could say the same about many others with whom I spoke and conversed, and I heard from their own mouths and depositions the ways that they first fell into error.

Others have an express and explicit pact with the devil, not because they have once spoken to him or seen him in some well-known aspect, but because they make the pact with his disciples, who are other enchanters, witches, or sorcerers. These people take the same vows as the others; for, although they never speak to the devil and have never seen him in any figure, they themselves renounce their faith and make a pact to serve the devil. They do the same ceremonies that other witches do or those that the devil teaches them and inspires them to do. Both of these

types of people are consecrated to the devil by express pact and are commonly called witches (*brujos*) or *jorguinos* or *megos*, which are corrupt words. *Sorguino* (commonly pronounced *jorguino*) comes from the word *sortilego* (L. *sortilegus*, conjurer), and the word *mego* comes from *mago* (L. *magus*, magician), whose meanings are common and clear in the writings of the Scholastics and appear in various chapters of the *Decretum* (of Burchard of Worms). The name *bruja* is from the Italian (I. *bruciare*) and means to burn or to sear, because the punishment for such conjurers and magicians is burning at the stake; and thus the name was given to them, but with the Spanish pronunciation rather than the Italian.

An implicit or occult pact is also of two kinds. Some make an occult pact with the devil without either denying or renouncing the formalities of the Catholic faith, yet at the same time they believe and take part in diabolical ceremonies and invocations. These people have an occult and tacit pact with the devil because hidden within such execrations and ceremonies and superstitions is apostasy of the Christian faith; for he who has confidence in something other than Christ or who asks for aid from someone other than Christ is against Christ and his law. These people are commonly called witches (*hechiceros*). There are others who don't believe in any of these things, but sometimes they consent and practice them, assuming that any remedy will do to achieve bodily health or some other thing they need; and these people commit mortal sin and also have an occult pact, although not as serious as the other kinds.

V. WHY THE DEVIL HAS MORE FEMALE DISCIPLES THAN MALE ONES

There are more women than men consecrated and dedicated to the devil. The first reason is because Christ forbade them to administer the sacraments, and therefore the devil gives them the authority to do it with his execrations. The second reason is because women are more easily deceived by the devil, as is shown by the deception of the first woman, to whom the devil had recourse before going to the man (Genesis 3). The third reason is because women are more curious to know and investigate occult lore, since their nature denies them access to such matters. The fourth reason is because women are more talkative than men and can't keep a secret; and thus they teach others, which the men don't do as frequently. The fifth reason is because women are more subject to anger and are more vindictive. Since they have less strength and means to avenge themselves on people with whom they are angry, they procure and seek vengeance and favor of the devil. The sixth reason is because the spells that men cast are attributed to some science or art, and the common people therefore call them necromancers and not warlocks. Such were the evil sorcerers of the Pharoah (Exodus 7), whom scholars call magicians. They made serpents to appear and disappear in the King's presence by means of the devil's ministry, counteracting thereby the true miracles that God did through Moses. Balaam (Numbers 22) was also a necromantic prophet. But women, since they don't have any art or science as an excuse, can't be called necromancers (although Juan de Mena called Medea a necromancer for poetic reasons in *El laberinto de la fortuna*), rather they are called *megas, brujas, hechiceras, jorguinas,* or *adevinas* (soothsayers), as was also that pythoness to whom Saul had recourse to learn if he would win or lose an upcoming battle against the Philistines (I Samuel 28). In truth, there are just as many warlocks consecrated to the devil who pass for necromancers as there are simple women, because the devil does not respond or aid the invocations and conjurations of the necromancer by reason of any power or efficacy that the magician's art has over the devil, for there is no such science or art unless the two have made a pact. Thus the real difference is not among the ministers of the devil but among the different manners the devil uses to deceive and contract familiarity with men; so he will be the best necromancer who best follows and complies with the devil's will, and not he who knows the most arts and formulas, as in a true science.

Most of the women are old and poor rather than rich and young, because after they become old the men don't pay any attention to them. They therefore have recourse to the devil, who satisfies their appetites. This is especially the case if the women were inclined and given to vices of the flesh when they were young. The devil deceives this kind of old woman by promising to satisfy her appetites, and he actually keeps his word in a way that will be described in Chapter XI. There are also more poor and needy women because, as with the other vices, poverty is often the occasion for many misdeeds in people that don't have a strong will or much patience. Since they think the devil will tend to their needs or respond to their desires and appetites, old and poor women are more easily deceived than young girls are, for the devil promises them nothing will be lacking if they follow him. No one should marvel that the hags don't receive anything they can use, however, because God doesn't consent that the devils have so much power to deceive people. If Satan had permission to give gold and silver to his disciples, I don't think anyone could be found to punish the wayward ones. The devil therefore only shows them great treasures, which he would indeed give if God would permit it. That will happen at the time of the Antichrist, but at present it is all deceit.

VI. HOW THOSE CONSECRATED TO THE DEVIL CAN FLY THROUGH THE AIR

Many doubt that witches can fly through the air and walk on water, as some say; and many church doctors have denied it. Therefore the following rule must be stated: knowing that flying through the air is possible, that it has been seen several times, that it and similar things are proven by scripture, and that the very persons deceived by the devil confess it to be so, there is no reason why it should not be believed. We read that the angel carried Habacuc from Judaea to Babylon with the food that he was taking to the reapers so that Daniel, who was in the lion's den in Babylon, could eat (Daniel 14, Vulgate Edition). Scripture also reports that the angel pulled Habacuc off his horse by the hair to show thereby the angel's ability to carry away a man. We likewise read that during the temptation of Christ the devil carried him from the desert to the pinnacle of the temple in Jerusalem; and afterwards he carried him from there to a high mountain where he showed him all the kingdoms of the world (Luke 4, Matthew 4). It is also said that the enchanter Simon Magus tried to ascend to heaven while Saint Peter was preaching about Jesus Christ. He was carried through the air in everyone's presence by demons who transported him to another spot to deceive and make people believe he had been carried to heaven. His ruse would have worked except for the prayers and petitions of Saint Peter, which were so effective that the devils deserted Simon Magus and he fell from aloft, burst open, and died (from the apocryphal *Acts of St. Peter*).

One must assume that if Simon Magus attempted such a novelty in public he had flown through the air many times before, crossing large expanses in little time with the aid of the devil. Are we therefore supposed to doubt it, since the devil has the power and man the obedience to him if God permits it and gives permission for it to happen? And one should also believe that God permits the devil to carry his disciples through the air, for God let himself be carried thusly to the above mentioned places. It appears, then, that since it is possible and since the witches themselves confess they go to strange and remote lands, it ought to be believed; although sometimes it is fairly obvious that the witches were deluded.

It is necessary to remark, however, that as we read and discover how the devil and any other good or bad angel by natural powers and virtues can carry someone through the air and over water, God permitting it, we also read how people can be driven out of their senses, which the doctors call ecstasy. During these ecstasies they have revelations of great secrets and of things that occur in remote areas, and these people think they are there. Thus we read of Saint Paul, who says he was caught up to the third heaven (II Corinthians 12:2), which is the Empyrean; and he says he does not know how it happened, bodily or spiritually. It therefore appears that being out of his senses and not using them, *in extasi mentis* caught up, he saw secrets that he didn't have permission to describe, and he wasn't sure in what way he was in heaven, bodily or spiritually. The devil can in his own way disturb the human senses, especially during a heavy sleep, to make a person think he is in the place that the devil represents to him.

There are apparently two ways the devil ministers to his disciples. Some really go to faraway lands and remote places by the devil's aid; others, carried away out of their senses as in a heavy sleep, have diabolical revelations of remote and occult—and often false— things, whereby they many times affirm what is not true. These latter are deceived by the devil, yet take pleasure and delight in those things as if their bodies were really there. All disciples, whether of the first or the second kind, have an explicit and express pact with the devil and he with them, and they are called *brujos*.

Not even the Council of Ancyra in the *Canon Episcopi* is against what I say; and because so many are deceived by its statements I will state clearly what the *Canon* reprobated and condemned, summing it up in four conclusions. First, Diana and Herodias, as the *Canon* says, were two normal women killed and not resuscitated. To say that live women converse with the dead, as those wicked women affirmed, is an error, a public deceit, and an illusion of the devil. Second, Diana and Herodias were wicked and faithless women when they lived. To affirm they were goddesses or that there was some divinity, power, or grace in them is a manifest error and blasphemy. Third, it is false to believe that the devil, because he can appear in various shapes, forms, and natures, can actually convert things to other substances and natures, like converting a man into a fox or a goat or some similar thing and afterwards returning the person to his original form, as many evil persons have said and affirmed. Fourth, it is possible that when wicked people think they walk through the air they are only imagining it by the devil's deceit, as declared above. These are the errors that the *Canon* wishes to eliminate and condemn, but it doesn't deny the possibility of what I have explained above.

VII. HOW THE DEVIL'S DISCIPLES CAN TAKE VARIOUS SHAPES

No one should doubt that the devil can feign various shapes as often as he likes to deceive or frighten people. Reason demonstrates this and experience is a good witness that it has often happened, for it is documented in the lives of the Egyptian church fathers. The devil can do the same thing for his disciples, whom also he can show and transport in the shape he desires without losing any of their substance and volume, so well can Satan make and feign a deceit for the eyes of those that would see it. Some ex-

amples can be found in the lives of the saints, for such was the case in Saint Augustine's discussion about Ulysses' companions, whom that famous sorceress *mega* Circe transfigured into beasts (*City of God,* XVIII, 8).

The devil can also make himself and his disciples invisible or partially so. The reason is this: eyesight tires from the visible rays that proceed from the visible thing, as is demonstrated in perspective. The devil can cause those visible rays to become tied up in such a way that they represent the figure he desires; or he can divert the rays so they don't go straight to the eyes looking at it. Thus the thing would be invisible, since it would not be seen by the eyes looking at it. Christ appeared thusly in the guise of a pilgrim and a gardener, and another time he made himself invisible when he hid in the temple. By the same process the devil transports his disciples invisibly or in any desired shape without taking or changing any of the true substance, quantity, and volume that the person has, as is read of Simon Magus. But these people can't leave their houses except through windows or open doors, and if they are closed the devil opens them. They can't leave through a window or door smaller than their body either, because the devil can't take away or diminish the volume of the body, nor the body's necessity to occupy space; so they need the same size door or window a person of normal size and measure needs. Although they could leave in the apparent form of a bird or a cat or a fox, or totally invisible, they still couldn't leave through a space smaller than a normal body occupies. The devil's disciples themselves confess to this, and if someone should claim otherwise it would be a blatant lie.

VIII. HOW THE DEVIL'S DISCIPLES REVERE AND ADORE HIM

In the Catholic church the subjects kiss the hand of their spiritual and temporal elders and leaders as a sign of spiritual and temporal obedience, and they kiss the foot of the Pope as a sign of absolute and total obedience and reverence, and God on the mouth, as the bride requests in The Song of Songs (1:2), for in the church it is a sign of peace. Well, for the devil, who is a tyrant that mocks his subjects, it is necessary that they kiss him in the most dishonest part of his body, and the reason is this. As the prize and reward of virtue is honor in this world and glory in the next, thus what vice merits is scorn and dishonor in this world and pain in the next. For as are the lord and his vassals, so are the signs of reverence shown him, and God desires that for greater confusion such reverence be made to him who is admired as a god and lord. As the Prophet said: "Confounded be all they that serve graven images, that boast themselves of idols" (Psalms 97:7). The very people deceived by the devil confess that they do these things.

IX. THE SACRIFICES THAT SATAN'S DISCIPLES MAKE TO HIM

Once God ordered Abraham to behead his very beloved son Isaac and to sacrifice the boy as a demonstration of obedience (Genesis 22). This was not because God wished such a sacrifice, shedding Isaac's blood, as appeared in the command; it was to declare and manifest Abraham's faith and obedience, who, in order to comply with God's command, was indeed going to behead and sacrifice his beloved son.

Concerning Jephthah's vow and sacrifice of his daughter (Judges 11: 30–40), that was not a proper deed nor did God desire Jephthah to complete the vow he made by sacrificing and beheading his only daughter. God does not wish such offerings nor sacrifices that involve the shedding of human blood, with the exception of martyrdom, where the good and pious unjustly receive death with wonderful patience from the hands of their persecutors. This kind of offering and sacrifice is very acceptable to God.

Many of the ancient and most solemn diabolical sacrifices were celebrated with human blood, offering, beheading, and sacrificing daughters and sons to the devil. For this reason the devil in the past caused his disciples to make sacrifices in which they offered up children and covered the temples in human blood as if they really took pleasure in it. Today his disciples do the same thing, as is recounted of the idolaters of the New World; and where sacrifices can't be done publicly the devil makes disciples kill children in the most subtle and secret ways possible. Many witches who serve as mid-wives do this, or they suck human blood in secret and hidden ways that the devil shows them. Although this seems like a crazy thing and many don't believe it, one nevertheless believe that the devil procures in every manner and way possible to offend men and to deceive his disciples and followers. Even those who did these things confess to them.

X. HOW ONE CAN INHERIT DISCIPLESHIP TO THE DEVIL

It is common opinion among the superstitious that a diabolical discipleship or ministry can be passed on from one person to another as an inheritance, but it is obvious that no one can be deceived by the devil except by his own express or occult consent, as is stated above in Chapter IV. Therefore, if a daughter or niece inherits diabolical discipleship from her mother, it's only by her true and proper own consent; yet this consent can entail no more than not turning away from what is suspected to be evil. Thus, if a Jew or a Moslem who does not believe in baptism should consent to it and should receive baptism as Christians receive it, he would nevertheless have

really received baptism and have become a Christian, so that if he should ever come to believe the Faith, he would not have to be baptized again. Likewise, if someone were to receive something from her mother or grandmother or any other witch as a sign that she was being left discipleship to the devil as an inheritance, even though she should not believe it, it is the same as giving license and authority to the devil in order that he do with her what he did with her predecessor.

XI. HOW DEVILS PARTICIPATE WITH THEIR DISCIPLES

Although evil people enjoy and find great sport in doing anything evil, there are certain evils that by nature given more delight than others, such as acts of venery and carnal deeds. For this reason the devil deceives his followers and disciples with the bait of carnal acts, holding them thereby in his power. He seduces women by taking the form of a man, and men by taking the form of a woman, as scholars have often determined; for devils can be incubi or succubi. They are called incubi when they take the form and position of the man to seduce women, and succubi when they take the body and position of the woman to seduce men.

The devil receives absolutely no physical pleasure from these acts because he doesn't have either the body or the nature necessary to feel any corporeal or carnal delight, since he is a pure spirit and is made of spiritual substance. The bodies that he takes for such a sordid act are not true bodies of some formed and living matter; therefore neither in them nor in their nature, which is spiritual, can he feel any alteration of carnal delight. The diabolical followers and disciples, on the other hand, receive immense pleasure by communicating and participating with devils; much more, in fact, than with ordinary men and women, because there is nothing to impede the carnal delight, and the devil provides all that is needed to increase it. But it's quite unnecessary to go further into this matter.

XII. WHY MEDICINE MEN ARE NOT WITCHES, AND THE CURATIVE POWERS THEY HAVE

Many doubt the gifts and curative powers of medicine men (saludadores), especially with rabid dogs and poisonings. It is therefore necessary to note than many natural curative powers are so hidden from human understanding in this life that many times we see marvelous cures and we don't know the reason for them, except that such is the property of natural things and that it is hidden from us. An example is the natural property of the magnet for attracting steel, for none can explain it. I knew a woman who deceived girls and simple women with a magnet. She told them that she could make their boyfriends and husbands love them so much that they would never look at other women and never leave them. To do this she took that stone, which attracted from one side and repelled from the other, and saying some words and phrases so it would look like a spell she put a sewing needle in the palm of her hand or on a table and then put the magnet near the needle. She showed the needle not to move toward the stone (because the repelling side was placed near), and said that the boyfriend or husband didn't love that particular person, but that she would cast a spell so the man would love her so much he would never part from her. She then neared the stone to the needle again, muttering certain phrases, but now with the attracting side close. The needle jumped to the stone and stuck to it, and thus the simple girl believed the the spell worked.

Amber and jet when dry, clean, and cold and shined against one's clothing have the same property, attracting dry straw. The same is also true for many herbs and rocks. One is used in rings to treat a bad heart, while the unicorn's horn is an antidote for poisons; and other similar things have natural properties and virtues that nature has impressed on them. There is no other reason for this except that all divinity and honor possible have been given to nature. If in the presence of some natural cause a certain effect follows, and in its absence the effect stops or goes away, then we must conclude that the effect followed and proceeded from some natural cause. When there is an eclipse of the sun, for example, certain effects on the elements and on human beings are caused which don't occur when the moon is in another aspect or part of the sky. We conclude that the moon in such an aspect with the sun was the cause of those effects.

In the same way one can argue for other effects that proceed from natural causes, as in the above examples. We shouldn't attribute such works to miracles, for learned churchmen state we should never conclude that something is a miracle that can be produced naturally (although by means hidden from us), because the miracle is a work that natural forces cannot accomplish. One must also reasonably presume that human bodies are as capable of receiving such natural powers as are animals. Thus, because of unique complexions or according to one's temperament, some person could have a natural property hidden to human understanding that would appear to be miraculous in comparison to the powers of normal men. Some men thereby have a saliva when fasting that can kill serpents, and every day we see saliva cure mange, scabs, and wounds without applying any other medicine. Some men have complexions that give this hidden natural power to their breath, their saliva, and even their touch, by reason of the temperament of the complexional qualities. Thus the four humors, which are choler, blood, phlegm, and

melancholy, are in some human bodies organized in such a temperament and harmony that a hidden natural power comes from it which is medicinal enough to counteract the effect of poisons, the diversity of which is tied to the temperament of the humors.

It is clear that those with such natural powers should not be condemned, because according to the rules of nature any power not repugnant to nature should be attributed to it whenever it is shown to be so; and thus it is clear that those who have and use these natural powers (and they are not found in abundance, but only very rarely) can be called medicine men because they give health and counteract some poisons. Some men are better at this than others, and some do it in one way and others in another, because not all have that hidden power equally nor in the same way, since they don't have the same humors which are needed for it in their temperament. It is thus patent that such a virtue can be found among the non-Christians as well as the Christians and among the evil as well as the good, because it is not a moral power but a natural power that comes from the body's unique complexion; and thus it is wrong to reprimand or condemn as suspect or superstitious those who have these virtues simply because we can't explain them. Although we know it to proceed from a natural and bodily hidden power which is not repugnant to the natural complexion of the human body any more than it is to rocks, herbs, and some animals, some people continue to be deceived into considering those who perform such acts to be holy men. They should be shown that since it is also normal for a Moslem or a non-Christian to have the same power, it can't be due to saintliness or goodness.

XIII. THE POWER THE KINGS OF FRANCE HAVE TO CURE SCROFULA

What I said in the last chapter leads me to question the power the kings of France had to cure scrofula, because that power had to be either natural or supernatural. It couldn't be natural because the natural celestial influences and the bodily complexions reign, influence, and do their operations in natural bodies, not in offices or in artificial things. If the king of France didn't have such a natural power before he was king, in other words, it's not possible for him to have acquired it afterwards simply by becoming king, because, as I said, a person can only have the ability to cure sicknesses with his saliva or his breath or touch because of unique bodily complexions influenced by the heavenly bodies and constellations. This power doesn't come suddenly either, but over a period of time, as medicines and natural remedies work although in more secret and subtle ways, as I explained about the medicine men.

This power of the French kings doesn't appear to be supernatural either, because, as the theologians state, God doesn't do miracles or give such grace to men because they are kings or have titles and offices, whether ecclesiastical or secular, but rather because of the person's merits as a testimony to his saintliness. Such were the miracles of Saint Martin and of Saint Nicholas, and of many other saints. God also gives the power to do miracles to those who preach the truth of the catholic faith where and when there is need, although the priest may be evil and a sinner. Of similar things Christ said: "Many will come to me in that day, Lord, Lord, have we not prophesied in thy name? and in thy name have cast out devils? and in thy name done many wonderful works? and then I will profess unto them, I never knew you: depart from me, ye that work iniquity" (Matthew 7: 22–23). This power was also given to show to the pagans the reverence and honor of the name of Jesus Christ, as is read in Acts 19; but such grace and power for doing miracles can never be inherited with the office and royal scepter.

This custom of curing by French kings had its origin with Saint Louis IX, King of France (1214–1270) and grandson of the king of Castile. He was a saintly man who merited from God as a testimony of his saintliness the power to cure those afflicted with leprosy and the plague, and from him the later kings have taken the custom of laying their hands on those suffering from scrofula. They select the afflicted who instill less horror and repulsion in the noble classes. The king places his hand in a certain way on their throats, saying some appropriate words. Many are easily healed, but not all; which makes it appear that it didn't come from any power that can be proven, since it can't be natural or supernatural, for no virtues are given to a person because of some temporal office. Yet I don't condemn those who go to a king to be cured, because they don't go to him believing him to be a sorcerer; nor am I saying that no power was passed on to later offspring by that virtuous king who worked those miracles so long ago, because it is certainly possible for God, whose limits are boundless, to have done it. Nevertheless, since such a proposition goes against reason, authority, and the true history that I know, I don't dare to affirm it because miracles are not easily proven among the faithful of today. One could say with more reason that the Pope has the power of curing the sick because he is the successor to Saint Peter, who did so many miracles that the sick were cured by only his shadow. Since we don't have any proof for this, there is much less reason to believe the king of France can do it; nor does experience convince us, since it is said (and it is true) that the devil can do similar things.

Because this case has been declared by so many learned men and is praised so highly in public, I wished to state some doubts about it with the hope of illuminating those who know and understand these matters. If they know some particular secrets about this matter that go beyond the general rules I have stated, let them tell me so I can also praise the Lord who gave such grace and left it as an inheritance for sinners. If they have no proof, let them acknowledge the truth of my arguments and, recognizing human weaknesses, keep quiet about the matter.

I declare the same about the English rings that they say the king blesses so they can be used to cure a nervous disorder known as cramps (*calambrio*). I doubt they work any better than an ordinary ring of the same metal. If it weren't for the overactive imagination of the person who trusts in it, who would favor the ring over natural remedies? Also, since no ring is capable of receiving supernatural power, including one blessed by a king (who in truth hasn't the power or merit to aid such a process), it appears to be a deceit of he who blesses it and even a bad joke on he who wears it to think that the blessed ring should have more power than any other metal without that benediction. Again, if there is indeed some foundation to the belief, I would like to know about it.

XIV. TO GIVE THE EVIL EYE IS A NATURAL ACT AND NOT WITCHCRAFT

The natural expulsive power, which is one of the powers of the nutritive faculty, expels and throws from the body all the impurities that can't be used for sustenance and maintenance of the body. What is thickest is expelled by the nether parts that nature provided for that purpose; and what is not so thick comes out of the natural windows, like the mouth, the nose, and the ears; and what is more subtle through the pores and spongy parts as sweat; and what is the most subtle is expelled by the glassy parts of the eyes. Thus the most subtle impurities of the body come out through the eyes like rays, and the more subtle they are the more they penetrate and are most infectious.

This is how a menstruating woman can stain a new and clean mirror with the rays that come from her eyes, because the body's natural powers at such a time throw off corporeal impurities, and the most subtle ones come from the eyes and thereby dirty the mirror. If at such a time the woman should stare closely at a tender and delicate child she would imprint on him those poisonous rays and distemper his body in such a way that he would be unable to open his eyes or to hold his head up. Even her breath could harm him, because it is harsh and smelly at that time, which is a sign of the corrupt and indigestible humors, as we say of the wolf, who corrupts and fouls the air with his breath and thus makes men hoarse with it (see Albertus Magnus, *De Animalia*). Some have this infection and poison more than others, especially old women who no longer menstruate, because they then purge more impurities through the eyes and have a bad complexion because of their age. The look of such women is therefore more dangerous, and they should never stare closely at the eyes of young babies nor kiss them on the mouth. Moreover, even more poison is administered when they do this with malice because of the activity of the imagination, and this would be a mortal sin against the fifth commandment.

Mothers should take care to guard their beloved children from similar looks and treatment, especially when the children are young and delicate, because they have less power to resist the poisons. Mothers who suspect such actions should tie pieces of mirror to the baby's locks over the eyes, because they will look at the mirror before the eyes of the child, and thus the infected rays strike the mirror on the forehead and not the eyes of the creature. When mothers suspect that their child is infected by the evil eye, they shouldn't go to old healers (*santiguaderas*) or witches but should use steam treatments of odorous herbs and incense and similar aromatic things, and as quickly as possible, continuing it for some days. This is the best natural remedy for it. Nor should mothers suppose that the sickness comes only from witches and is always a part of witchcraft, because it is a natural thing that can come from any indisposed person; although it is true, as I say, that it can be increased and made more intense by malice in the heart of she who looks at the child, and thus it may be done by some malicious person or witch or sorceress that wishes to do harm to innocent creatures to serve her lord the devil, as explained in Chapter IX.

XV. MEDICAL PREPARATIONS ARE NEITHER SUPERSTITIONS NOR SPELLS

The natural medicines and practices of doctors are not to be condemned, although to some they appear to be superstitions and vanities. An example is wearing certain roots around the neck to cure some sicknesses that medicine can't cure; for sometimes doctors order a patient to wear the peony root or the seeds of it around the neck for epilepsy, and for quartan fever they recommend live insects such as crickets or locusts and spiders. For other sicknesses they have similar ways that *prima facie* appear to be superstitions or idle fancies, for which reason they are not used. Yet if a doctor should use them without malice because he finds other doctors wrote about them, there is no reason to be suspicious, because many times the patient's imagination is fortified with them and they therefore aid in achieving a rapid cure. Furthermore, as I said in the chapter on medicine men, the virtues of natural things are so hidden that we can't explain them rationally, and for this reason many times men judge them to be vain and superstitious.

Other things that are done with a mixture of words and ceremonies without natural objects are not medicines but true superstitions, even though they are found written about in the medical books, especially since most of those doctors were pagans, such as Hippocrates, Galen, Avicenna, and many others. As we Catholics, when we lack natural remedies and recipes, seek aid from the saints so that God may supply what natural powers lack, so back then they resorted to diabolical superstitions and invocations, with which Apollo was accustomed to cure. The medicines of his son Asclepius, according to Isidore of Seville (*Etymologies,* IV), cured men with these superstitions and preparations for five hundred years until the time of Hippocrates, who was the first to use natural medicine. The devil aided and responded to what those ancients asked so they would remain in error and so they would be the authors of them for future generations.

For such superstitions one uses every kind of figures, characters, ceremonial observations, and secret words, none of which can have natural power, nor are capable of it, nor ever had any. While these things can naturally aid in a cure because the patient would have his imagination more set on being cured, they have no curative powers in themselves. Only natural remedies which are certain and not superstitious, although they may be unknown and remote from human understanding and appear impertinent and idle, as seen in the natural examples cited above, are efficacious cures. Nevertheless, if a Catholic doctor does every reasonable thing to cure a tertian fever and still finds the fever not breaking, he may order the patient to hang a green oak acorn around his neck, assuring him that as the acorn dries the fever will go down. This remedy won't be superstitious nor would a wise doctor condemn it as such, although he may call it idle and impertinent. He would see it aided the patient's imagination and his faith in the doctor; for the sick person would believe he would recover more quickly from the tertian fever.

When all these things fail, the imagination and strength of the patient should rest on a confidence in God, aided by the customary devout and Catholic means of the church, and not with things Catholic and wise doctors condemn as suspect and superstitious. A perfect example of the latter is consulting a witch who cures broken ribs by splitting or breaking a reed or cane and afterwards joining the parts while saying certain words in a secret way. This is superstitious, because that joining of the split parts is not natural since the parts would not be joined without those words; and the words themselves are unnatural, because no words can ever have natural powers for any effect. The whole remedy therefore has no natural power to cure and put together broken ribs, thereby arguing for an occult pact with the devil.

Thus, it is clear that washing away certain words and letters written in the bottom of a cup and drinking that water to cure some diseases or to undo curses between husband and wife are indications of an occult pact with the devil. All the other words and ceremonies that are done and said, as tying a ribbon or cord and reciting certain words to trap wolves and foxes and to catch snakes or other serpents, are suspect and superstitious, for there is no natural power in any of these things.

Nor is it enough to say that the effect follows from what they desire and ask because, as said above, the devil can respond with an effect to deceive those who are occupied with these superstitions, so they are more suspect the more they succeed. These people are not excused from sin by using saintly and good words either, because the more saintly the words used the more suspicious are the deeds. The vain superstition of some churchmen who dress up in stoles to gather the seeds of the fern plant that they say flowers and seeds on Saint John's Eve is also subject to condemnation. They circle the place where the ferns grow with crosses and read the bible and do ceremonies so the devil won't disturb the gathering of the seeds. All of this is public deceit by the devil, because there are no seeds, and even if there were the devil wouldn't need them nor would he care who should gather them. Yet there is no doubt that the effect for which those seeds are gathered, according to the fabulous opinion of the vain folk, are for service to the devil rather than for God. Therefore, those who indulge in that act should be punished as superstitious, for the very devil scatters those seeds they find in that circled space and over the blankets that are placed to catch them so that they should believe them to be from the fern and for the effects they imagine and so they won't cease to do those ceremonies and believe in those vanities on such a holy day of the year.

XVI. AMULETS AND RELICS ARE NOT SUPERSTITIOUS NOR SUSPECT

Many times the authorities order the amulets (nóminas) made by religious and devout people to be taken from the churches. The amulets usually are nothing more than some holy words from the scriptures or signs of the cross; but these amulets can indeed be used for devotional purposes. The objection is to the ceremonies surrounding them, such as the proper time of day, or whether written on a certain virgin parchment, or hung with certain threads, or similar superstitions. Especially objectional amulets are those where one reads that he who carries it won't die in water nor in fire nor in childbirth nor by arms, and similar words; as if there are figures on them besides the cross or words other than those used in the Church.

The amulets worn for devotional purposes are not prohibited, and one can assume that God will look piously on that devotion and will succor the person's

needs. This would not be done unless by the devil if one were to use the amulets with suspicious and superstitious words and figures.

It is also not evil to drink the water used to wash chalices or relics or to sprinkle it on sick livestock. Men likewise sometimes out of devotion and without any superstition ask for the oil from the lamp that burns before the image of a saint or the Holy Sacrament and the water from the wounds of the image of Saint Francis, not to use it evilly, but to receive it and use it with great devotion, desiring to remedy their sicknesses or those of their livestock. As John Gerson says in *Astrologia theologizata*, XXI, if the devil responds to invocations and superstitions, God and his angels respond much better to saintly invocations, because the correct faith, unfeigned devotion, and saintly intentions of the simple and devout merit much more.

XVII. IT IS NOT LICIT TO UNDO ONE CURSE WITH ANOTHER

Speaking now as a philosopher even more than a Catholic theologian about the nature of evil, no good can come from bad, although by accident it could be that some good would follow from an evil, as when a murderer enters into a religious order and lives saintly, which he would not do if he hadn't committed that murder. The envy of Jacob's children against their brother Joseph was a similar case. They sold him to the Ishmaelites, which was the cause that he should later be governor of the whole kingdom of Egypt and the savior of his brothers (Genesis 37). Yet by nature evil never is ordained for any good, nor can its end be such.

It is true that God would not permit evil unless good men were to reap good fruits from it, because for the good and chosen people all things happen well and are converted into profit; yet this does not naturally come from evil, but from the goodness of God and the good people who imitate him and help in this, who gather the odorous flowers from the thorns and squeeze sweet honey from bitter flowers. Evil people, on the contrary, gather bad fruit for their perdition from the goodness of the virtuous, as when the Jews became shameless and worsened from the good examples of Jesus Christ. So it is clear that no one ought to do evil thinking that some good will come of it because, besides the fact that Saint Paul prohibits it (Romans 3:8), common sense proves it to us.

It likewise follows that in order to remedy the bodily health of some person, no one ought to do anything that isn't licit and honest and that isn't a natural and honest medicine and remedy. Lacking this, they can use natural remedies with medical counsel, as declared in Chapter XV. When all natural remedies fail, they should have recourse to God and confide only in him without other superstitious invocations and vain observations of ceremonies. But they ought to note that the remedies to countervene the obvious bewitchment of someone who is clearly bewitched or cursed not only have to be licit, according to the common opinion, but even have to be freer, clearer, and more untainted of all suspicion than are other remedies prescribed for other natural sicknesses.

Since the devil had part in the curse, he would come and respond to the smallest sign of invocation or superstition, and he would take part in the cure and remedy; and then it would be true that by the power of Beelzebub, prince of demons, the sorcerer had cast out the devil and his curses. The devil himself will also aid in an exorcism by leaving the premises in order to contract a discipleship with that exorcist or sorcerer, who would be more daring to gain a foothold in similar businesses, seeing that his exorcisms and conjurations work so well. For this reason it is necessary that a curse's remedy not be another curse or anything that even appears to be one, but it should be free of all suspicion. Chapter XXI explains the forms of licit exorcisms to undo curses.

XVIII. THE DERISIVE AND IGNOMINIOUS EX-COMMUNICATIONS OFTEN FULMINATED WTHOUT FOUNDATION AGAINST ANIMALS

In the beginning God created man with so much perfection that not only did the inferior powers and senses of sensuality obey the superior ones of rationality but all the beasts and corporeal creatures were obedient to him also. He had superiority over them by his most excellent nature, as now, and also because of the total subjection and obedience that they had to him so much so that if he had persevered in that justice and perfection fire would not burn him, nor air fatigue him, nor water drown him, nor anything on earth would harm him or give him pain. Not even the fierce beasts would hurt him, for they would be at his command. But when he sinned the order of nature became perverse as a sign and punishment for the disobedience that he committed against God. Sensuality raised its head against reason, and all the beasts and corporeal creatures became man's enemies. From thence forward they do not obey him, as experience shows, for they offend his person and temporal goods in various ways. Although Christ established the sacrament of baptism, with which original sin (with the eternal torment related to it) was taken away, he did not wish to assuage the corporeal and temporal pains that we suffer for that sin, nor do irrational creatures obey baptized people more than infidels who never received any sacraments. The few exceptions are those who merit it from some singular reason, such as the saints of the primitive church, who demonstrated special powers and signs in order to found it; and one also reads of some saints who were not burned by fire, others who walked on water,

others who humbled fierce beasts at their feet, and did similar marvels.

Now that the first perfection and even the personal merits (for which God many times heard men and succored them in their need) are lacking, we take recourse to superstitions and diabolical invocations so that the devil will do (God permitting it as an angry judge of our sins) what God himself would have done as a pious father if we had not been so obstinate with him.

In some parts, for example, they are accustomed to proceed against the locust, that destroys their crops, in a legal way, naming lawyers for each side and alleging their rights before an ecclesiastical judge, proceeding and sentencing against the party that is found in error. A sentence of excommunication is drawn up against the locust and all sorts of censures are fulminated against it, and it has been proven that the locusts leave that district or that they all die. This ·kind of thing has been done in many parts, and all of it is superstitious and diabolical, in much offense of God, and an injury to the holy mother Catholic church.

For that reason I decided to declare here briefly the matter of excommunication in regard to its substance and its efficacy, as the theologians consider it, leaving the lengthy particulars to the lawyers; because this is the main door through which the devil has entrance to tempt and deceive those who through it actually hand over the church itself to the devil's power, as in the primitive church the apostle did when the devil visibly possessed them and tormented them (1 Timothy).

There are two methods of excommunication, one in relation to God and another in relation to the church. Speaking in relation to God, all mortal sins, but only they, are grounds for excommunication; for by committing a mortal sin one is parted from God and loses the grace by which he was united with him. Thus Saint John says: "He that dwelleth in love dwelleth in God, and God in him" (1 John 4:16); and in another place Christ said: "He that abideth in me, and I in him the same bringeth forth much fruit" (John 15:5). Moreover, the only way God can be in the just more than in sinners is by the grace that the just have and sinners lack; and by this absence of grace that comes from sin we say that God is not in them, nor with them, but parted from them. As Isaiah said: "Your iniquities have separated between you and your God, and your sins have hid his face from you" (Isaiah 59:2), and Christ said: "If a man not abide in me, he is cast forth as a branch, and is withered" (John 15:6).

Any mortal sin by which one normally loses grace is in this way an excommunication by God, and all other excommunications are founded on this doctrine. This type is called "minor," because although that

person is parted from God and the sacraments (which no one in mortal sin can take without committing another sin) he is still not parted or deprived of the temporal goods of the church nor is he made incompetent to hold offices, benefices, and church posts; nor is he parted from contact with the faithful, because the Church gathers to it the just and the sinners, symbolized by the evangelical net that catches good and bad fish.

Speaking of excommunication in regard to the church militant, it is a documented moral condemnation entailing an official ecclesiastical sentence and censure that deprives the man of his goods, of his public and general favors in the church, and of human contact with his fellow Catholics. When pronounced in the required form, this becomes a "major" excommunication. To understand this definition, one should note that the authority the church has to pronounce a public sentence of major excommunication is founded on the rule that Christ established when he said: "If thy brother shall trespass against thee, go and tell him his fault between thee and him alone; if he shall hear thee, thou hast gained thy brother. But if he will not hear thee, then take with thee one or two more, that in the mouth of two or three witnesses every word may be established. And if he shall neglect to hear them, tell it unto the church, but if he neglect to hear the church, let him be unto thee as a heathen man and a publican" (Matthew 18: 15–17). This means that you may not consider him a brother as before in regard to conversation and communication. The Pharisees, who held themselves as observers of the law, followed this rule and would not speak nor have contact with the publicans nor the gentiles.

The reasons for excommunication can now be given. First, contumacious disobedience of a true, express nature (or reasonably judged and interpreted as such) against the church and its commandments is required. Contrarily, it is also clear that when the person is prepared to do what the church orders him, he can't be subject to excommunication; nor can any other creature incapable of such disobedience, like irrational creatures, be excommunicated.

Second, Christ ordered the act of excommunication only against those men who are capable of glory, which appears in the above stated rule as well as in what he added, saying: "Verily I say unto you, Whatsoever ye shall bind on earth shall be bound in heaven; and whatsoever ye shall loose on earth shall be loosed in heaven" (Matthew 18: 18). This means that there is such a brotherhood between the church militant and the church triumphant that everything you bind and loose justly and without error to the church militant, which reigns on earth, will be bound and loosed to the church triumphant, which is glory. It doesn't refer to every living thing, how-

ever, but only to man and those things enclosed and subject to man's service. He also of all things on earth can be bound and loosed to the churches militant and triumphant; so one can't extend excommunication to anything except men who are capable of glory.

Third, excommunication presupposes union and communion, and thus he who was never united with the church by the faith that is received and promised in baptism nor was received in the communion of the faithful can't be excommunicated, that is, thrown out of the union and communion. It is therefore clear that ecclesiastical excommunication cannot be used on the infidel who was never baptized nor received into the flock of the church. The reason is this. Excommunication is imposed to identify and separate the disobedients and rebels of the church from the others who are obedient to it. Since the infidels are identified and parted from the church by definition, their excommunication would be superfluous and derisive. Contact with infidels is therefore not prohibited as it is with excommunicated people.

Fourth, excommunication is only promulgated for mortal sin committed through blatant disobedience of the church's precepts and commandments. In some cases before such disobedience is committed a censure is imposed to prevent the crime and impede the blame with the fear of punishment. This is the kind of sentence imposed on those who would try to lay hands on a cleric or religious person, who practice simony and usury, and other similar cases that are of such a nature that the church is concerned about impeding and hindering them.

The church has the authority to impose indiscriminately major excommunication on any who commit such sins so that *ipso facto* they incur the stated sentences and censures. These cases are called *a jure* because they are imposed by the councils and synods that have authority to order and establish laws; and they are promulgated against those that would commit such crimes so they won't commit them. In other cases the ecclesiastical judge can proceed in an ordinary way or by way of a commission to adjudicate cases of individuals who ignore express orders of obedience or who express declared disobedience against the church. For such cases he promulgates censures against the rebellious and disobedient part, and this kind of excommunication is called *a judice vel ab homine* because it comes from a man and particular judge. Whoever the judge may be, even if he were the Pope, a sentence in one particular case does not make a law, and for this reason it is called *ab homine vel a judice,* and not *a jure* as the first.

The efficacy that major excommunication has is its power to part, deprive, and make useless to the excommunicated person spiritual and temporal goods of the church and of human contact with the faithful who are its members, both in public and general acts and in hidden and particular ones. He is obliged to accept this segregation from divine offices and human contact with the faithful, and the latter are obliged to part from him when the person is denounced by an ecclesiastical judge with the proper authority. If someone should lay hands on a clergyman, moreover, and the deed were so well-known that future communication were certain, although the person were not yet denounced, the faithful ought to part from him and he from them.

It is notable that excommunication does not bar from human contact those who are obliged by divine or natural law to the service of the excommunicated person. The person's wife, children, servants, slaves, farm hands, and all other servants are therefore free from this positive law, because it is not presumed that the excommunicated person's arrogance against the church will be rewarded by communicating with them. Since excommunication is a medicine to guard against spiritual sickness (as is *a jure* excommunication), it follows that excommunication does not deprive one of doing works of mercy and charity, because the medicine that is given to cure or preserve ought not to deny or impede the acts that favor a return to health. Likewise, he who wishes to have contact with an excommunicated person can do so if it entails such things as giving him alms if in need or giving him charity, which are acts to attract him to the knowledge and obedience of the church, turning him from his error and obstinacy.

All others who may have contact with excommunicated persons after public denunciation and notification by name incur the sentence of minor excommunication. The gravity of the sin will be according to the amount of contact and the extent of the disobedience. If someone should have contact with an excommunicated person to spite the prelates of the church, he will in no way be excused from mortal sin. If, on the other hand, someone has contact because the opportunity arises unexpectedly or out of shame or human complaisance and affable social graces, making always some changes in the words normally used with people not excommunicated, it is no more than venial sin. The minor excommunication that is incurred by open contact with excommunicated persons, although it is most often a venial sin, nevertheless deprives the person of the church sacraments, because the efficacy of minor excommunication is that it deprives the sacraments in such a way that he who incurs the sentence of minor excommunication, even in a case where he only sinned venially, sins anew if he is not absolved before receiving the sacraments. Those who communicate with minor excommunicated people do not incur excommunication nor do they sin because of that contact, for a minor excommunication does not pass to a third person.

Some conclusions can hopefully resolve and sum up this matter. The first conclusion is that excommunication itself does not spiritually kill man nor part him from God; the mortal sin does. No major excommunication kills in itself nor brings on sin; it only marks and denounces spiritual death, as symbolized in the knife of Saint Peter that didn't kill but only cut the ear. In other words, it notifies and denounces to the ears of the excommunicated person and the other faithful members the death of him who is disobedient and rebellious against the church and its prelates. The knife is for cutting the rotten member from the same body; that is, to part the disobedient from those obedient to the church, which is the mystical body of Christ whose members are all the obedient. The knife is also like a lance to open the abscess of the stubbornness and pride of the disobedient person so he can cure himself by becoming humble and coming to the knowledge of his disobedience.

The second conclusion is that God alone absolves excommunication with his grace, which he fuses into the soul of the contrite person; and the priests his ministers aid in this with the sacrament of penitence.

The third conclusion is that sometimes one is absolved by God and goes to heaven from his great contrition on dying, and he is still excommunicated from the church because that contrition is not valid unless he received sacramental absolution. Since one is the law of God and of one's conscience, and the other the exterior law of the church, the person remains excommunicated and expelled from the church in body and human acts until he is actually absolved by an exterior law by him who excommunicated him and has authority to absolve him.

The fourth conclusion is that the pain of the excommunicated, as far as the church is concerned, is more corporeal than spiritual, because the church judges what it sees and what by human wisdom it can achieve; and thus it can't exercise its knife except on exterior things, by which it wishes to notify and give to understand interior things. The church thus deprives the excommunicated person of the bodily reception of the sacrament and of bodily contact in human acts and church offices, in public and in private, general and particular, and of the goods of the temporal church, like offices, benefices and honors. All those acts are corporeal and exterior pains, and by them are denoted the interior privation of spiritual goods.

The fifth conclusion is that many times it happens that someone is excommunicated from the church when he is united in charity with God, for the church at times makes mistakes in its legal procedures. The witness whom the judge receives are not always the four evangelists, nor men who never lie, and if they don't tell the truth the ecclesiastical judge may condemn an innocent man. Yet although the person could be in God's grace, innocent and blameless, that sentence must be upheld as if it were correct; for if the man was proceeded against juridically and there were no other flaw save the falsity of the witnesses, which no judge could know about, the judicial process is not at fault. Moreover, according to some church fathers and modern lawyers, although the judge should know about the falsity, he could still sentence *secundum allegata et probata,* and condemn the innocent person on the merits of the process. Otherwise all human justice would be disturbed and confounded, and justice would be lost, since none of us would be certain of its validity. The innocent person that is thus condemned ought to work and procure by the best and most honest means he can to seek remedy and absolution, without scorning the judge's sentence that proceeded thus and condemned him.

The sixth conclusion is that sometimes one is condemned to excommunication who is not bound either to God or to the church, as when a judge does not proceed juridically or is corrupted to give the wrong sentence, or the causes for promulgating the sentence are so unjust as to contain intolerable error in such a way that it would appear unjust to any knowledgeable man and he would judge it as such. In a case like that one should definitely not heed the sentence.

After considering the aspects of excommunication and its efficacy succinctly declared here, it is clear how scandalous and injurious to the church a feigned excommunication against the locust and other similiar reasonless creatures can be, applying the ultimate remedy the church has for humbling and punishing proud disobedient Christians to brute animals and irrational creatures. What makes it worse is that it is a diabolical invention inspired by Satan in the hearts of some evil Christians and heretics who mock the great and excellent authority that Christ left to the church by enacting such processes and promulgating and fulminating such censures and sentences (although it can be that afterwards by their example others have done it out of simpleness and stupid ignorance).

The ecclesiastic that acts as judge for such a process and orders such a sentence and fulminates such censures can't be excused from the grave crime he commits, because by reason of his office he is obliged to know that such a process is not Catholic and that it is a grave offense against God, an injury to the holy mother church, a scandal for the simple folk who from his example will do others, and a scorning of the keys that Christ left to the church. Such people, especially the ecclesiastics who get involved in these things, merit to be punished severely by their bishops and prelates. They deceive themselves with the profit they find in it, because if the locust goes away or disappears or dies, they argue by this experience that excommunication is not only

profitable and has a power against men but even against similar animals. To this I say that it is not so bad to have done it as to insist that it was done well and to affirm that excommunication has such power and efficacy. The first is to have little or misplaced faith, but the second is a formal heresy by reason of the affirmation with persistence and obstinance. Therefore, no one should insist that excommunication can be extended to anything or anyone other than those baptized and united at some time with the church, so the second error won't be worse than the first.

I have already shown in how many ways the devil can work marvelous feats which neither the power of men nor all the corporeal creatures can resist, and how the more the superstitions are suspect and dangerous, the more times the effect follows or what is asked for is granted. For clarification of this, I now wish to give some reasons for persuading why this is true. Let's begin with the perennial dilemma of Christian faith: why in our good and ordered Catholic petitions we are often not heard by God, and why so few times we receive what we ask from his just wisdom, hidden to us.

Among the answers that I give to you, the first is that God does not hear us or does not respond to our petitions as quickly as we desire in order to test and declare our virtue and patience. If he permits evils to prove and show the goodness and beatitude of a virtuous person, as was the case with Job, he will more easily deny us the good that we request. Thus, many times he does not grant goods that we ask of him when we ask so that we can be affirmed better in humility and our virtue and patience will be more manifest.

The second reason God does not respond to a just and Catholic petition is so that our desire may become more inflamed. God therefore defers giving us what we ask so that, according to Saint Augustine, we may learn to persevere in what we desire. As Saint Gregory noted, desires become inflamed and increase with delay.

The third reason that God doesn't respond immediately to what we ask is so that he may grant it to us at a more proper time, as Saint Augustine preached. Some things, for example, are not denied to us but are given at a more convenient time, as with the doctor who orders medicines for his patient.

The fourth reason that our Catholic petitions are not heard is that we don't keep the conditions required for the prayer to be heard, which are necessary circumstances for perfect prayer, as that done with much humility, because the prayer of the humble rises to heaven; or that done with much fervor, because Christ abhors the pusillanimous; or that done with perseverance without weakening, because those who persevere achieve what they ask, and they only ask for things that pertain to and favor salvation of the soul, because—if we have a complete and principal care for spiritual things—God will not forget to assure for us the corporeal and temporal things. And since very rarely do all these circumstances and conditions occur in prayers, it follows that few times are we heard and succored in our necessities.

The fifth reason that we are heard few times is because most often we pray for what is actually not to our benefit, and God knows better what our needs are. Christ spoke in this regard to brothers James and John: "Ye know not what ye ask" (Mark 10:38).

The sixth reason, decisive in these times, is because we don't have the virtues nor the merits to be heard and granted what we petition. Isaiah says: "When ye make many prayers, I will not hear: your hands are full of blood" (Isaiah 1:15), which means full of sins.

For these reasons and others—that I abstain from putting here to shorten the argument—God does not hear us, I mean does not respond to our Catholic petitions and invocations when and in the manner we ask. Yet as I have said and declared, the least times we think we are heard, and even when he hears us, as his gifts are more spiritual than temporal and corporeal, they come in silence and without fanfare. When they are corporeal, as with bodily health, and temporal, as in the accumulation of wealth, God does them so they appear to come about naturally. Thus one argues well and clearly that when with superstitions and suspect things and strange invocations in the church we easily achieve what we ask of things in the corporeal and temporal sphere, outside of all natural course, they don't come from the pious hand of God but from the devil (God permitting it for the sins of those that practice those superstitions), as declared above in Chapter III. For the devil doesn't consider the virtuous circumstances that are required to order that prayer and invocations be efficacious, nor does he function as a doctor who follows the rules that govern our sickness and weakness. He always responds with the work and effect of what they ask when they call on him, if he has licence to do it. And often God does not deny him it, at the request of the same who hand themselves over to the devil (even in an occult pact), for many times God concedes with ire what he denies with mercy. It is clear, then, that the more suspect and dangerous are people's superstitions and non-Catholic petitions, more often and more easily do they achieve what they desire and ask. Thus no one should blind himself with the profit that he sees before him, for the harm that comes unawares is always the worst. The devil makes the locusts flee or kills them and does the same with other irrational creatures (who perhaps are devils in the figure of those animals) because he can do it easily; and he does it to mock the authority that Christ left to the church and to deceive those that participate in such processes and censures, making them lose thereby the true faith in the church's authority by substituting a false and heretical belief, which is to believe that excommunication can be extended to and has an effect on non-rational creatures.

XIX. CONCERNING CONJURERS AND THEIR SUPERSTITIOUS SPELLS TO CREATE CLOUDS AND STORMS

The conjurers and their conjurations of clouds and tempests are so public in this kingdom that there is no town that doesn't have one on the public payroll and a sentry-box in the bell tower or some other high place so the conjurer can be closer to the clouds and the devils. This error is so shameless that they offer to ward off all hailstorms for that year, and they persist and bet on it with other neighboring conjurers (and these many times are the village priests). At the time of the spells they say and boast that they play with the clouds as with a ball, and predict which sorcerer they will throw the storm to. Some, who presume to be the wisest, make circles and stand in them and say that they go so quickly to where the devils are that they lose their shoes, and they come out of the circle exhausted and boast of their endurance. They set limits within which spells will work, and they procure to cast the clouds out of their district into their neighbor's or into another designated place.

Anyone with normal intelligence can recognize these acts are vain, evil, superstitious, and diabolical. The madnesses, simplicities and idiocies that they explain are to be laughed at, and even to be scorned. They affirm that when the cloud bursts from their spells they convert the hail into water. If they were natural philosophers they would know that the hail that they fear is water first and only afterwards is frozen into hail, as the philosopher Aristotle says, per antiparistasim, which means fortification by the nearness of one's contrary. By this mechanism the great heat of the nearby air contracts and fortifies the coldness of the water, which falls as if fleeing from its contrary in such a way that the drops of water are frozen and fall and become hard as rock very quickly. According to the Philosopher, as well as common opinion, this is normally done in the lowest region of the air, which is hot and close to the earth. The hail therefore usually falls on very hot days and in the afternoon when the sun is the hottest, from a very low black cloud that hails near the earth. When the hail falls mixed with heavy drops of water, it is a sign that there isn't enough heat to freeze all the drops of water. When it hails at night, that hail was frozen in the middle region of the air, not in the manner explained above but by the extreme coldness of that region, in the way that Albertus Magnus explains;

and that rock will be smaller and rounder, because it descends from so high. The hail that freezes here below is larger and not so round, because from where it freezes to the ground there is little time to take such a round form from its movement, losing something of its size. Wherever the water may freeze into hail, first the vapor was converted into water, and later that water was frozen and converted into hail; yet the conjurers think that by their spells the hail changes into water. It would be better if they should ask God that the water that falls not turn into hail, which is a lesser marvel, without working to turn the hail into water, which is difficult to do in so short a time and is a greater marvel, especially in the same air where it was frozen.

They have for these things some superstitious spells composed of a few ignorant repetitions (and they prize them if they are written on virgin parchment) in which are many parts of the Mass and sacramental words, for they think that since these words turn bread into the body of Christ and wine into his blood, they will also turn hail into water. They tie together without concert or order a multitude of words and, while making the sign of the cross, they threaten the cloud saying: *Per ipsum crucem, et cum ipso cruce, et in ipso cruce. Si ergo me queritis sinite hos abire, titulus triumphalis, miserere nobis.* They then add with babylonian confusion: *Eli, eli, la mazabathani, agla, aglata tetragrammaton, adonay, agios, o theos, ischiros, athanatos, eloim,* and as many Hebrew, Greek and unknown names as they can find. They act as if powerful secrets and great mysteries were enclosed in the words they don't understand, and as if God were of the condition of men, who are always more benevolent and liberal to foreigners who speak to them in their native language. They remind me of the convert who when a Jew called himself Jacob and when a Christian Diego; and although the name is the same in both languages, he was always happier that they call him Jacob rather than Diego. I knew a convert who blessed those who called her Rachel, and was displeased when they called her Isabel; and those who look for such names to call on God think the same about him.

XX. CONCERNING EXORCISTS AND EXORCISMS FOR POSSESSED PEOPLE

There are other singular exorcists who exorcise people possessed by the devil, and sometimes they are the very types discussed above, and have special diabolical ways to do it. They make some circles on the ground with certain signs and letters inside written in a special way, and they make the possessed person kneel inside that circle. As soon as the exorcist says certain words the person loses his senses and makes frightful gestures and shouts loudly and says unintelligible words and many times curses those present. The exorcist forces him to say who he is (I have seen this type of thing happen). The possessed person responds that such a devil as Satan or Beelzebub is the lord of that body; and sometimes he says the soul of certain dead people are there with him. He speaks in their name, representing their person; and if they died on the battlefield they ask for water as if dying of thirst, and if they were drowned at sea they make gestures as if they were coughing up water, and if they died of sickness they speak like a sick person, and other similar deceits happen. The people cruelly put incense pots around the possessed person, stick handfuls of rue under his nose, and beat him, during all of which the exorcists show themselves to be ministers and disciples of the devil and deceived by him.

The reason is this. Although Christ and his apostles cured many possessed people, casting out devils from their bodies, one doesn't find that the souls of dead men were in human bodies, nor do the theologians and philosophers confirm this. The exorcists therefore ought not to affirm nor hold true that there are souls wandering in torment, inhabiting live bodies and tormenting people, as these exorcists deceived by the devil presume and think. Second, the circle that they make with those figures and letters is a thing of superstition and express demonic invocation. It should come as no surprise that where first someone was not possessed, except for some emotional or cerebral disorder, the devil responds to the invocation and call. This is very clear, because while the person comes whom they say is bewitched in mind and composure and says he is only sick, they insist that he has spirits; and after putting him in the circle and beginning the exorcism the person changes and loses his senses, which indicates the diabolical effect of the circle and the spell. Third, the torments they inflict on the body don't offend or hurt the devil, but since he doesn't enter human bodies (God permitting it) except to torment them, the exorcists serve him in this, tormenting the body as he desires; and he complains that they hurt him so they will inflict more pain. Fourth, they ask him to explain if they could speak to some dead person, and in what state he is in, Hell or Purgatory, and if they can help with some benefices; and similar reasons and conversations occur, all of which is superstitious and diabolical and a manifest deceit of the devil. Fifth, they set a day for the casting out of the devils, and the devil takes the day for when he and all those with him will leave. Every time the exorcists cast them out the devils make a big show of coming out one by one and going away, but with license to return to the same body the next day. They take this license from the very exorcist, who gives it as a minister and disciple by way of agreement, and says that he does it to cure better and assure the patient from thence forward, because he would not be sure of his promise nor the cure if he did not make first an agreement with the devil. All this designates an express diabolical pact, and only the very people deceived or the most simple and ignorant would not recognize it all as superstitious and an express pact with the devil.

XXI. THE LICIT AND CATHOLIC EXORCISMS FOR WITCHES AND SORCERERS

As for the remedy of curses, one must first see if they are well-known and manifest or deceits and human fictions, as I will explain later about feigned possessions. When the curses are true, which can't be easily denied, because the doctors speak of them, pointing out matrimonial impediments, there are express decrees for exorcising them; and since it is wrong to remove one curse with another, as I said above, one must seek remedy and liberation from God. One should first seek confession with good and wise confessors, with much preparation and the strength of a clean conscience because God many times permits these things as a punishment for our sins or to test our faith and virtue. He should receive the Holy Sacrament many times devoutly with the mass of the chains of St. Peter, and after the mass he should read the Gospel of St. John, *In principio erat verbum*, with much faith. He should reverently kneel with much devotion at the phrase *Verbum caro factum*, kissing the earth with much humility in memory of the son of God, who to free us from the devil and his power descended from heaven to earth, taking our nature in the virginal womb of Our Lady the Virgin Mary. He should pray the Creed many times devoutly and with much faith, and note the symbolism of *Quicunque vult*. He should wear some true relics around his neck, with the Gospel of *In principio*, but without other suspect objects, as is declared in the chapter on amulets. He should take home some holy water every Sunday to sprinkle around the house, especially the bedroom and bed; and he should take holy bread every Sunday before breakfast, and always bring with him a cross, which is the thing that makes devils flee, and marking with it he should say the name of Jesus. He should drink the water used to wash the utensils for the Mass and the relics; and it is even a thing of much devotion to drink the water used to wash the wounds of the image of St. Francis.

By doing these things, which are devout and Catholic, he can trust in God that he will be heard. If God doesn't hear him, he should believe it is not because God is deaf, but because God knows better what aids us and what we merit, and serves us in that way. Thus we ought to leave all to his will, after having made our just and reasonable diligences, without looking for other curious and dangerous ways and with-

out tiring from persisting in these devout and Catholic methods.

XXII. THE DEVOUT AND CATHOLIC SPELLS FOR CLOUDS AND TEMPESTS

Since we have seen that the conjurer's way to cast a spell on clouds and tempests is vain, dangerous, superstitious and even scandalous, the Catholic way will now be given.

When one is afraid of some storm clouds that gather on the horizon, where there is the custom to ring the bells as an emergency signal, they should sound the alarm for all the people to gather in the church, or those who can, and the priest should light all the candles, open the relicary and take out the host with much awe and reverence, and put it in the chalice that is in the middle of the altar. With all devoutly kneeling, they should sing or say in plain song the *Salve Regina,* along with the prayers that are normally said in public prayer services, as long as they are from the missal. When the priest or some other ordained person finishes this, dressed in his surplice with his stole around his neck, he should read loudly the Gospel of *In principio erat verbum* in plain song from the altar. After the Gospel the congregation should take the most revered and holy cross they have in the church and go to the cemetery, stopping in the corner closest to the storm, singing or saying in plain song the antiphons of the lauds of the Exaltation of the Cross, which are these: *O magnum pietatis opus: mors mortua tunc est, quando in ligno mortua vita fuit. Salva nos, Christe Salvator; per virtuten crucis, qui salvasti Petrum in mari, miserere nobis. Ecce crucem Domini, fugite partes adverse, vicit leo de tribu Juda, radix David alleluya. Nos autem gloriari oportet in cruce domini nostri Jesuchristi. Per signum crucis de inimicis nostris, libera nos Deus noster.* And they should also say the *Benedictus Dominus Deus Israel* with this antiphon: *Super omnia ligna cedrorum tu sola excelsior, in qua vita mundi pependit, in qua Christus triumphavit, et mors morten superavit in eternum.* And they should finish with the prayer of the Cross. Next, if the time and place allow it, they should confront the storm with the cross and say the litany of the Saints in the same plain song until finishing it all, with everyone responding devoutly, and they should conclude with the Gospel *Missus est* in the same devout tone.

If all these devout and Catholic diligences are done as well as possible, God may still permit them to be punished, or test their faith and patience, as he did when he permitted that furious wind and storm to destroy the houses where the children of Job were, because the devil can't do any more harm than God permits him to do, as is clear in the same book of Job, Chapter 1. We therefore ought not to lose patience or leave our upright ways to please God with foolish inventions and vain superstitions, for anyone in his right mind will say that our way to seek God's aid conforms better to reason and the doctrines of the Saints than a way with suspect and non-Catholic words and ceremonies. God gives the devil license to inflict punishment for people's sins through superstitious invocations and dangerous conjurations, as he did with those people in Egypt. Sometimes also God permits people to be deceived by the same sin, for the devil makes them believe that by their invocations and spells they were freed from the storm, to have them thus blind in that error, although in truth the damage the devil does them will be worse, not only to their souls but even to their estates when and where they least suspect it.

You should therefore leave aside the diabolical superstitions and invocations and take up the sure, devout, and Catholic ones. Nor do I think you should use ancient Hebrew names, as I said before, except the sweet name of Jesus, which Saint Paul praises and names so much; for the angels in heaven respond to this name, and the men on earth, and the devils in Hell. There is no other name equal to it, and it is above all else a legitimate name to be invoked. It is vanity, lack of faith, superstition, and even a judaizing trick to use the name of the ancient Hebrew in Catholic and Christian invocations as if the old names were worth more than the new ones. They are especially dangerous for those with little knowledge, because they may say other unknown and diabolical words with those Hebrew and Greek ones. Nor should you think the word *tetragrammaton*, which is a Greek word, has more virtue than any other word, like *pentagrammaton*, for example. *Tetragrammaton* doesn't mean anything special; it is simply a greek word in the genitive plural that means all the words or sounds composed of four letters, as are the Latin words *mons, pons, vita, mors,* and the Spanish words *asno, mulo, gato, rato*. Every one of these words is a *tetragrammaton*, because it has four letters. The name *pentagrammaton* is also a Greek word of the same case that means all words composed of five letters, as are *demon, lepra, plato, berta,* and many others that it is not necessary to name. It is unwise to put in Catholic invocations and prayers confusing sounds and words that may mean good saints or bad ones, as are the above mentioned Greek words. If in ancient times under the old law this word *tetragrammaton* was held in much reverence, it was because by it they conceived a word that referred only to God, composed of four Hebraic characters, that could not be named or pronounced until the coming of Christ, meaning thereby that God in his infinite being could not be described by any name. After that infinite being became flesh, however, he is called Jesus, which means Savior; and therefore the apostles and

disciples of Christ only did miracles in the name of Jesus. You won't find in all the Epistles of Saint Paul, even though he was a Jew, any ancient Hebrew name for God, nor did the translator put it in his translation, and much less the word *tetragrammaton;* but you will find the name of Jesus five-hundred times. You won't find such ancient names in other parts of the New Testament either; but the name of Jesus, who brought us health and freed us from the power of the devil, appears many times. The saints, and even the unholy exorcists who pretended to be disciples of Jesus Christ, when they wished to do miracles and cast out devils, didn't cast them out with ancient Hebrew and Greek words but with the name of Jesus. Christ's disciples therefore said to him, "Lord, even the devils are subject unto us through thy name" (Luke 10:17). Of those who falsely usurped his name, Christ said: "Many will say to me in that day, Lord, Lord, have we not prophesied in thy name? And in thy name have cast out devils? And in thy name done many wonderful works?" (Matthew 7:22). Yet now Catholics are not content with only this name, but resuscitate the Greek and Hebrew names that the Latin Church on Good Friday names and buries as dead, to be no more bothered with. Say therefore many times these sweet names Jesus and Mary, and read the litany of the Saints, and believe me and don't try to cure yourselves with other ancient or unknown words.

XXIII. THE CATHOLIC DECLARATION AND REMEDY FOR THE BEWITCHED AND POSSESSED

There remains the problem of bewitched and possessed people, and it is worth noting that you can be possessed by the devil in one of three ways. First, as his subject and prisoner; second, as his disciple by an express or occult pact; and third, as the innocent object of his torment.

The chief exorcist of the first type of possession was Jesus Christ, who by his own authority (being God and man), threatening them with his finger, cast out devils and made them be quiet; and by his power and authority he gave the same ability in his name to his apostles and disciples. One also reads how Saint Bartholomew and other saints could hold devils prisoner and make them visible.

The magicians of the Pharoah in the times of Moses were of the second type, as was Simon Magnus in the times of the Apostles. In our times there was a famous necromancer (Joanes de Bargota) held in great respect by the populace in the kingdom of Navarre. They considered him a person who could discover and say marvelous and secret things and could cure unknown diseases because of an express pact and familiarity with the devil.

Of the third type were Saul, before whom young

David played his harp so he would forget the devil's torment (I Samuel 16), the daughter of the Cananean (Matthew 15), and that person who was dumb and blind from the devil's torment (Matthew 12:22), whom Jesus cured along with many others who were possessed by the devil.

The Pharisees, blinded by envy, denied Jesus could cast out devils and accused him of being a magician and necromancer who was obeyed by devils through his familiarity with Beelzebub. They said he exorcised and invoked minor devils of little power by the power of Beelzebub, prince of Devils. This is what they meant when they told him he had a devil, for they didn't accuse him of being tormented in the third way nor did they think such a thing, according to the common opinion the Pharisees had of him. First, because the person tormented by the devil is often blameless, and they claimed Jesus had a devil because they wanted to defame him and falsify his doctrine. Second, one can't presume that a devil who pretends to be a prisoner and subject to a necromancer would torment his master, nor as with Saul, possess him, because that would not be a good way to deceive. There is also no reason to say the Antichrist will be possessed by the devil, rather he will have him at his command by familiarity and by express pact with him. Third, he who is possessed, bewitched, and tormented by the devil never has a clear mind nor talks normally, nor is of tranquil character, and exactly the opposite is seen in Jesus Christ. So those blind people blurted out in anger the words of John 10:19–21, without thinking what they said and motivated by the dissension they had between them.

Those who are possessed by the devil in the second way, by pact and familiarity, speak and do marvelous things with too much precision. An example is Balaam, who was this kind of necromancer and prophesied and spoke and said marvels, both present and future. Many authentic and true sayings in the Holy Scriptures are proof of this, although some were spoken by diabolical disciples of devils, because the spirit of prophecy is a gift that can be in the good and the bad. The Pharisees judged Christ to have a devil out of envy, and defamed his doctrine and disdained his miracles. May Nicholas of Lyra (in *Postillae Perpetuae in Universan Scripturam*) pardon me, for he says the Pharisees held Christ for a possessed person like Saul, meaning that he prophesied by being bewitched and possessed. Lyra either didn't look well or didn't remember when he said this what he had read of Saul, who although he was possessed had other periods of true devotion that lasted a short time, and in that time of devotion (when the spirit of God was present) he prophesied and was elevated in spirit among the prophets, and not when the devil tormented him. Thus they didn't say Christ was possessed by the devil, but that he was a deceitful

necromancer who had an express pact with the devil. The tyrant emperors and their lieutenants likewise pursued the Christians for being necromancers and deceivers rather than for being possessed or bewitched.

To determine who are bewitched or possessed or tormented by the devil, one first must note and examine with much vigilance what spirits are those who supposedly possess the person. It has been found from experience that some people, especially women, by their own malice sometimes pretend they are bound, cursed, or bewitched, because of some problems they have with their husbands or for strong carnal passions they have for someone or for terrible temptations of the flesh that the devil ignites in them. Sometimes the exorcists themselves also participate in these deceits. This can be seen and recognized in the possessed person's gestures, if they are good and healthy, and in the lucid and happy intervals they have, when they drop their mask or when they speak to you of those things in their heart. I know by experience that there are these types of people. They give bad examples of themselves, and have perished through their evil ways. I knew a religious priest, who has now passed away, that with only one disciplining with the whip cast the spirits out of one of these kinds of women. She confessed her treachery and the cause of her malice, and the cause was one of the above mentioned. Don't believe them nor marvel at the gestures they make when you speak with them. Don't exorcise or bless them or show them good will, because the woman who is faking her possession makes more frightful gestures than the devil would grant her to make. The spectators also become more frightened watching her.

It could also be that similar people when favored by the devil would do more and say more than if they were left to their own devices, because the devil favors them and the others who associate with them by deceit and he gives them strength and aid to pursue and achieve their evil thoughts and desires; for this is his goal, and he desires disciples more than tormented bodies. After recognizing the sickness, the remedy will quickly follow; and it is that one should never cure them with a crowd watching, nor by giving them credit for what they do, but by good counsels of religious men and honorable matrons, or with the exorcism of the reverend father I mentioned earlier.

There are others that are sick with natural diseases unknown to the doctors of our land, and here also there are more women than men that are sick with some kind of mania or cerebral weakness or depression and failing of the nerves or similar hidden sicknesses. Often, because the doctors don't recognize the cause of the illness nor know how to remedy it naturally, they say that the women have spirits or demons. Sometimes the patients say marvelous things during these illnesses, recognizing people they never saw or speaking words and reasons they never heard or thought. They say they see the devil or someone who is absent or dead, and other similar things; and with ugly bodily shaking and gestures they convince those present they must be possessed. But a good natural philosopher (whom we assume the doctor to be) will recognize how all these things are natural sicknesses and diseases. The concurrence of celestial constellations and the aspects of celestial bodies with the humors and complexion of those sick with such symptoms are accidents that naturally follow and occur in the human bodies of those subject to such sicknesses. The remedy for these illnesses should be procured naturally with natural medicines, comforting the brain, purging the melancholic humor, strengthening the heart, controlling food and drink with a diet prescribed by a learned doctor who is well acquainted with the illness.

There are other possessed persons who really are possessed and tormented by the devil; and we cannot deny this because Jesus Christ and his disciples cured them many times, as is written in many parts of the Holy Scriptures. One should also note that often the bodily sickness of which we spoke is a way for the devil to have entrance to torment badly disposed and sick bodies. This seems clear from the phases of the moon. When its phases change with the sun or cross with Saturn or move away from it, the devil is found to torment the body more or less, as appears also in one that Christ cured, who was a lunatic (from *luna*, moon). This is because the natural dispositions of the human body are subject to the movements of the celestial bodies, and since the devil knows the brain (by such movements and aspects) to be more humid, or the heart weaker, or the melancholic humor more predominant, or similar alterations in the disposition of the human body, thus he torments more on one day than another, and at one hour than another, as one who uses nature to do evil. In the same way that his disciples persecute more the poor and underprivileged, so the devil torments more those whose natural power and bodily complexion are contrary or in disorder; and he does this to make the person lose patience and to curse the moon and the sun and all God's creation, including God himself as creator of all things. Women are more tormented during these times because they are subject to depression, have a weaker heart and a more humid brain, are more subject to the stars, more subject to the passions of anger and fury, weaker to resist temptations, and change course with the slightest wind. Where the devil finds these accidents and dispositions, he thinks he has an open door; but not having antecedents nor natural inclinations, he doesn't have as much license nor the same appetite for evil. The remedy for such things should begin with God, and jointly one

should try to cure the body (as stated above) of those who have interior natural sicknesses such as a weakness of the brain or the heart.

Beyond this, which is natural, Catholic spiritual forms to frighten the devil away exist, for which all aid should be asked of God; and to him alone ought one to have recourse to impede the devil's entrance to torment a person and to deny and revoke the license that the devil has to do it. One therefore ought not to use suspect remedies to undo curses or bewitchments, since one person alone is the cause; and if after those diligences the person is still tormented and persecuted, do what is written above about exorcisms. If a healthy person should find himself tormented and possessed by the devil, as was Saul, there is no better remedy than that I described to free oneself of curses and bewitchments. They can change the mass, reading the section of the Gospel where Christ cured the daughter of the Cananean, or the verses about the possessed mute. They should never do anything besides what I described above, because, spiritually speaking, that is the music of David that remedied Saul's possession, and with that the person is strengthened and made one with the will of God.

XXIV. A CATHOLIC EXHORTATION AGAINST SIMPLEMINDED AND SUPERSTITIOUS CHRISTIANS

Finally, I exhort and warn all Christians in the name of Jesus Christ to heed this doctrine, to note the difference between the two lords, the one true, who is Jesus Christ our Redeemer, Creator, and Glorifier, and the other a tyrant, the devil, condemned eternally, our first enemy and subtle deceiver. He who serves Satan most will be the least free, and will suffer the worst pains and torments. Contemplate the Catholic Sacrament of the Holy Mother Church, all saintly and clean, ordered and established by Christ for the remedy of our sins; and look with clear eyes at the filth, vanity, and foolishness that the diabolical execrations and bewitchments bring to deceive and condemn the devil's disciples and followers. Think about the mocking and ridicule that the devil heaps on those who follow him, and the honor that comes to those who follow and serve Jesus Christ, plus the glory and goods that await them in the other world. To free oneself from the ties and deceits of the devil, one should devoutly hear mass on all holy days, listening closely to the sermon, and as often as possible confess with good confessors when the church requires. For those who are most tempted by the devil, be obedient to all the Church's commandments, and fear incurring any excommunication, and don't go too many days without taking communion. Don't commit any frivolities that the Church forbids, nor say prayers or words the Church doesn't use; and when there is any doubt, speak to your priest or confessor. Simple women shouldn't cure children or other people, especially with words and things that they wouldn't want learned men to see and hear. Nor should you go to those inclined or dedicated to these cures. Procure to ignore things you don't need to know or that tax your brain; don't be curious about occult things, desiring to know what you can't naturally learn; and always live with fear of going against the faith of the Holy Mother Church and its commands, proposing never to part from the Catholic faith. Pray the Creed often where the articles of faith are stated when you get out of bed and at night before retiring. Make the sign of the cross, naming Jesus Christ often, and say the creed and the other prayers you know, especially the Lord's prayer and the Ave Maria. I beseech the preachers who visit these lands to teach and declare these things, for they are most necessary and profitable and more meritorious to those who preach than other vain and curious speculations. I also humbly suplicate all prelates and other religious men, by whose negligence their subjects fall into deceits and errors, that they watch over and order these remedies provided rather than attending to other things which are of civil and temporal interest, because the latter properly belong to civil investigators. The *Canon Episcopi* specifically orders this. Thereby freeing their sheep from the diabolical snares and guiding them along the true and sure road, they will merit double honor in this world and infinite glory in the next.

INVERSION, MISRULE AND THE MEANING
OF WITCHCRAFT

I

WE NO LONGER READILY UNDERSTAND THE LANGUAGE OF EARLY MODERN witchcraft beliefs. Demonological classics like *Malleus maleficarum* (1486-7) or Jean Bodin's *De la démonomanie des sorciers* (1580) seem to reveal only an arcane wisdom. It is not apparent what criteria of rationality are involved, nor how the exegesis of authorities or use of evidence support the required burden of proof. Since individual steps in the argument are difficult to construe, its overall configuration often remains impenetrable. And the accounts given by other authorities like Nicolas Rémy and Pierre De Lancre of the ritual practices of witches and demons, notably those associated with the sabbat, appear sensational and absurd. Faced with such refractory meanings, some past commentators have tried to put Renaissance demonology to the test of empirical verification by asking if it described, albeit in exaggerated or symbolic form, the actual activities of real agents. Agreed (largely) that it did not, that there were no witches in fact, they turned with relief to sceptics like Johan Wier who, even at the height of prosecutions, cast doubt on the reality of witchcraft phenomena by offering non-magical theories of causation. And with intimations of rationalism of this sort historians have continued to feel an intellectual affinity.[1] A second popular approach has been the explanation of learned witchcraft beliefs in terms of social and socio-psychological determinants, especially those thought to be at work in the designation of criminal actions or the persecution of demonized "out-groups". This too has had the advantage of bypassing the problem of their meaning by reducing them to epiphenomena; tracing them, for instance, to the periodic social need to relocate moral and cultural boundaries by means of accusations of deviance,[2] or, again, to the

---

[1] Two surveys of witchcraft studies are H. C. Erik Midelfort, "Recent Witch Hunting Research, or Where Do We Go from Here?", *Papers Bibliog. Soc. America*, lxii (1968), pp. 373-420; E. W. Monter, "The Historiography of European Witchcraft: Progress and Prospects", *Jl. Interdisciplinary Hist.*, ii (1971-2), pp. 435-51. For a recent trenchant estimation of the intellectual quality of demonological arguments, see S. Anglo, "Melancholia and Witchcraft: The Debate between Wier, Bodin and Scot", in A. Gerlo (ed.), *Folie et déraison à la Renaissance* (Brussels, 1976), pp. 209-22.

[2] Applications of labelling theory to early modern witchcraft include K. Erikson, *Wayward Puritans: A Study in the Sociology of Deviance* (New York, 1966); E. P. Currie, "The Control of Witchcraft in Renaissance Europe", in D. Black and M. Mileski (eds.), *The Social Organization of Law* (London, 1973), pp. 344-67.

neuroses which are said to accompany the repression of erotic or irreligious impulses in devout minds.[3]

Yet there is surely prima facie reluctance to dismiss Bodin as a victim of obscurantism or delusion, let alone regard a whole tradition of discursive argument, successfully sustained for nearly two hundred years, as essentially irrational.[4] What is at stake are the criteria for interpreting a past world of thought without recourse to anachronism or reductionism, an issue recently debated by historians of ideas in a number of analogous inquiries. In the case of the history of political theory Quentin Skinner has persuasively defended a model of explanation in which the claim (stemming from Collingwood) that meaningful action can be sufficiently accounted for in terms of agents' intentions is complemented by J. L. Austin's stress on the performative quality of utterances. Since its explanatory force depends on seeing the point of a specific textual speech act for the author, Skinner also emphasizes the Wittgensteinian principle that what it makes sense for anyone to say is relative to a linguistic context or "language game". In political theorizing the intention to persuade presupposes such a framework of shared meanings in which certain concepts and rules for applying them in argument have a conventional life. It is these changing conventions of discussion which pre-empt anachronistic readings by limiting the range of possible meanings which a textual utterance can be said to have. Likewise it is the criteria of sense and nonsense which they embody to which appeal must first be made before cases of apparently bizarre rationality are rejected on the grounds of incoherence.[5]

Such a methodology has already rescued Hobbes's *Leviathan* from a series of critical mythologies; others like it have established the internal cogency of styles of thought like those associated with divine right monarchy or millenarian politics where little sense could previously be discerned.[6] The implication is that if the rationale which originally in-

[3] N. Cohn, *Europe's Inner Demons: An Enquiry Inspired by the Great Witch-Hunt* (London, 1975).

[4] A point effectively emphasized by H. R. Trevor-Roper, "The European Witch-craze of the Sixteenth and Seventeenth Centuries", in his *Religion, the Reformation and Social Change*, 2nd edn. (London, 1972), pp. 121-2, 183-4.

[5] Q. Skinner, "Meaning and Understanding in the History of Ideas", *History and Theory*, viii (1969), pp. 3-53; Q. Skinner, "Motives, Intentions and the Interpretation of Texts", *New Literary Hist.*, iii (1971), pp. 393-408; Q. Skinner, "Some Problems in the Analysis of Political Thought and Action", *Polit. Theory*, ii (1974), pp. 277-303.

[6] Q. Skinner, "The Context of Hobbes's Theory of Political Obligation", in M. Cranston and R. Peters (eds.), *Hobbes and Rousseau* (London, 1972), pp. 109-42; Q. Skinner, "Conquest and Consent: Thomas Hobbes and the Engagement Controversy", in G. E. Aylmer (ed.), *The Interregnum: The Quest for Settlement, 1646-1660* (London, 1972), pp. 79-98. Cf. W. H. Greenleaf, *Order, Empiricism and Politics: Two Traditions of English Political Thought, 1500-1700* (London, 1964), pp. 1-13, 58-67; W. M. Lamont, *Godly Rule: Politics and Religion, 1603-1660* (London, 1969), pp. 13-15, and *passim*. A comparable case in the history of historical thought is the interpretation of Vico's *New Science*; see B. A. Haddock, "Vico: The Problem of Interpretation", *Social Research*, xliii (1976), pp. 535-52.

formed the literature of witchcraft is ever to be recovered, we must begin not by assuming some sort of mistake on the part of the authors but by locating individual texts in the linguistic framework, possibly extending far beyond demonology itself, in which they were expected to make sense as utterances of a certain kind. This would involve establishing what Skinner calls the "range of descriptions" available to writers in a demonological tradition. It might lead us into a world where the criteria for saying that something was possible or impossible or made sense or nonsense were highly idiosyncratic. But Wittgenstein's point is not that these rules may not vary between language games but that their existence is the minimum formal condition for any linguistic engagement.[7] Thus, if it could be shown that it did in fact make sense within such a world for scholars like Bodin and De Lancre both to accept the reality of witchcraft phenomena and attribute witches with certain ritual practices, then initial doubt about the felicity of demonological arguments would simply disappear. There would be no cause to look for an explanation of them other than that they followed recognized linguistic conventions, that they were part of what Peter Winch has called "a coherent universe of discourse".[8]

Doubtless the task of decoding the meaning of witchcraft texts in this way would be an enormous undertaking. In what follows I have chosen only one, albeit characteristic idiom, the stress on contrariness and inverse behaviour in demonism. Part at least of our puzzlement over this particular way of thinking and writing about witchcraft can be successfully removed by filling out the prevailing conventions of discourse, particularly political discourse, in the sixteenth and seventeenth centuries. Of central significance are those arguments considered appropriate for identifying and contrasting the key conditions of order and disorder. I want to argue that Renaissance descriptions of the nature of Satan, the character of hell and, above all, the ritual activities of witches shared a vocabulary of misrule, that they were in effect part of a language conventionally employed to establish and condemn the properties of a disorderly world.

II

That witches did everything backwards was as much a commonplace of scholarly demonology as it has been of romantic fiction since.

[7] P. Winch, *The Idea of a Social Science and Its Relation to Philosophy* (London, 1958), pp. 15, 21-33, 40-52, 108.

[8] P. Winch, "Understanding a Primitive Society", *Amer. Phil. Quart.*, i (1964), p. 309. Contrast Cohn, *Europe's Inner Demons*, where it is a reluctance to accept the "manifestly impossible" elements in evidence for the reality of witchcraft events that sustains a view of demonology as an intellectual fantasy and leads to a search for an alternative socio-psychological causation. This appears to raise the same difficulties over an independent reality that Winch finds in the work of E. E. Evans-Pritchard.

But in this respect they were not alone. Throughout the late medieval and Renaissance period ritual inversion was a characteristic element of village folk-rites, religious and educational *ludi*, urban carnivals and court entertainments. Such festive occasions shared a calendrical licence to disorderly behaviour or "misrule" based on the temporary but complete reversal of customary priorities of status and value. One typical recurring idea was the elevation of wise folly over foolish wisdom. Another was the exchange of sex roles involved in the image of the "woman on top" or in transvestism. Clerical parodies of divine service substituted the profane for the sacred, and low for high office. Most pervasive of all were mock political authorities, the *princes des sots* or "abbeys" or "lords of misrule" who presided over ephemeral commonwealths complete with the paraphernalia of serious kingship but dedicated to satire and clowning.[9] Often these various modes of topsy-turvydom were invoked simultaneously, as in the ecclesiastical Feast of Fools or the activities of the French urban confraternities, the *sociétés joyeuses*. Sometimes one relationship was explored; the street charivari in which partners in unequal or violent marriages were ridiculed by the symbolic ride backwards focused on the dangerous social and moral inversions implied when familial disorder threatened patriarchal rule.[10] Similarly "barring out" the master in English grammar schools has been shown to depend on assumptions about the limits of pedagogic government over pupils, especially with the onset of the vacation.[11] Whatever the case, however, seasonal misrule involved not simply riot or confusion but conventional styles of ritual and symbol associated with inversion — recognized forms of "uncivil rule".

It would be remarkable if no links could be established between these forms of inverted behaviour and descriptions of demonic practices, flourishing and declining as they did in the same period. Certainly there were borrowings from accounts of sabbat rituals where the world upside-down was an important theme of festival occasions at court.[12] Conversely the demonologist Pierre Crespet located the witches' dance in a tradition including the bacchanalian revel, early

[9] E. Welsford, *The Fool: His Social and Literary History* (London, 1935), pp. 197-217; N. Z. Davis, *Society and Culture in Early Modern France* (London, 1975), pp. 97-123, "The Reasons of Misrule", and pp. 124-51, "Women on Top"; P. Burke, *Popular Culture in Early Modern Europe* (London, 1978), pp. 182-91; R. Muchembled, *Culture populaire et culture des élites dans la France moderne* (Paris, 1978), pp. 173-7.

[10] Davis, *Society and Culture in Early Modern France*, pp. 105-7, 116-21, 139; E. P. Thompson, " 'Rough Music': le charivari anglais", *Annales. E.S.C.*, xxvii (1972), pp. 285-312; R. Mellinkoff, "Riding Backwards: Theme of Humiliation and Symbol of Evil", *Viator*, iv (1973), pp. 163-4; J.-C. Margolin, "Charivari et mariage ridicule au temps de la Renaissance", in J. Jacquot and E. Konigson (eds.), *Les fêtes de la Renaissance*, iii (Paris, 1975), pp. 579-601.

[11] K. V. Thomas, *Rule and Misrule in the Schools of Early Modern England* (Reading, 1976).

[12] See pp. 123-5 below.

Christian transvestism and the masquerades of the *Maschecroutte* of contemporary Lyon.[13] The inferior clergy of late medieval France celebrated Christmas and the New Year with burlesques which were readily attributable to God's ape — singing in dissonances, braying like asses, making indecent grimaces and contortions, repeating prayers in gibberish, censing with puddings or smelly shoes and, above all, mocking the sermon and the mass with fatuous imitations. As late as 1645 the lay brothers of Antibes marked Innocents' Day by wearing vestments inside out, holding liturgical books upside-down and using spectacles with orange-peel in them instead of glass.[14] According to the social reformer Philip Stubbes, English rural practitioners of misrule encouraged in their soliciting for bread and ale what was in effect a propitiatory sacrifice to Satan as well as a profanation of the sabbath.[15] In France attempts were made by Jean Savaron and Claude Noirot to link the history and etymology of popular entertainment with those of witchcraft; Savaron thought that masquerading was a form of demonic sabbat (*la feste de Satan*).[16] Moreover carnival devil-figures could be seen taking an important part in processions and even organizing festivities.[17]

But even if they shared no specific types of inversion, both festive behaviour and learned demonology were dependent on inversion itself as a formal principle. And this allows us to apply to witchcraft studies some of the questions currently being asked by historians and anthropologists about the meaning of misrule. To some extent attention has concentrated on the practical benefits accruing to a community from what is actually done at times of ritual licence. For instance it is argued that traditional institutions and values are reaffirmed by the mockery of offenders against social codes, the deflation of pretentious wisdom and overweening authority or simply the open expression of grudges borne against neighbours. In this fashion, misrule strengthens the community by symbolic or open criticism and its moderating in-

[13] Pierre Crespet, *Deux livres de la hayne de Sathan et malins esprits contre l'homme et de l'homme contre eux* (Paris, 1590), pp. 246-55.

[14] E. K. Chambers, *The Mediaeval Stage*, 2 vols. (Oxford, 1903), i, pp. 317-18, cf. pp. 294, 305, 321, 325-6; Welsford, *The Fool*, pp. 200-1.

[15] Philip Stubbes, *The Anatomie of Abuses* (London, 1583, S.T.C. 23376), Sigs. Mi^v-Mi^r.

[16] Jean Savaron, *Traitté contre les masques* (Paris, 1608), pp. 3-4, 15-16; Claude Noirot, *L'origine des masques, mommerie, bernez, et revennez es jours gras, de caresme prenant, menez sur l'asne a rebours et charivary* (1609), in *Collection des meilleurs dissertations, notices et traités particuliers relatifs à l'histoire de France*, ed. C. Leber, 20 vols. (Paris, 1826-38), ix, pp. 35-8; cf. Nicolas Barnaud, *Le miroir des francois* (n.p., 1581), pp. 488-93, where an attack on "mascarades" and "mommeries" develops into one on witchcraft; Guillaume Paradin, *Le blason des dances* (Beaujeu, 1556), pp. 81-8.

[17] Pierre Le Loyer, *IIII livres de spectres* (Paris, 1586), pp. 228-9, quoting Ludwig Lavater, *De spectris, lemuribus et magis* (Geneva, 1570); Burke, *Popular Culture in Early Modern Europe*, p. 195; M. Bakhtin, *Rabelais and His World*, trans. H. Iswolsky (Cambridge, Mass., 1968), pp. 263-8.

fluence.[18] Alternatively the same carnivalesque practices have been associated with innovation and protest because they offer freedom to explore relationships potentially corrosive of existing structures and therefore not normally tolerated.[19] Neither of these readings is particularly helpful when applied to demonology. For although the differing social functions are largely seen as latent in the behaviour, some attribution of intentions to agents is required in each case. In the first, we would therefore be committed to something like Margaret Murray's theory that Renaissance witchcraft consisted of rites of inversion actually performed by folk worshippers of a surviving Dianic fertility cult.[20] And the second would involve accepting the connections which Le Roy Ladurie has claimed existed between conceptions of revolt based on a "fantasy of inversion" shared by rural peasant insurrectionists, festival fools *and witches* in southern France at the end of the sixteenth century.[21] Yet the accredited historical evidence for maleficent witchcraft comes very largely from allegations or from stereotyped confessions; we therefore have few grounds for attributing witches with intentions of any kind, whether re-integrative or innovatory in character.

This forces us back on a second set of issues relating to misrule, concerning the conditions which must obtain if inverted behaviour is to be seen as having not only various social-functional uses but any meaning at all *as* an act of inversion. The starting-point here must be the fact, emphasized many years ago by Enid Welsford and recently reiterated by Natalie Davis and Keith Thomas, that misrule necessarily presupposes the rule that it parodies. Thus the fool could only flourish, in fact or in literary imaginations, in societies where the taboos surrounding divine kingship and sacramental worship were especially rigid. The street theatre and cacophonous, "rough" music of the charivari were effective precisely because all other ceremonial occasions were solemn; while turning social or sexual status upside-down, and the laughter it provoked, only began to make sense in a world of simply polarized hierarchies.[22] The degree of meaningfulness of carnival misrule there-

[18] Thomas, *Rule and Misrule in the Schools of Early Modern England*, pp. 33-4; V. Turner, *The Ritual Process: Structure and Anti-Structure* (London, 1969), pp. 166-203.

[19] Davis, *Society and Culture in Early Modern France*, pp. 103, 122-3, 130-51. For a survey of theoretical accounts of inversion, see B. Babcock, "Introduction", in B. Babcock (ed.), *The Reversible World: Symbolic Inversion in Art and Society* (London, 1978), pp. 13-36.

[20] M. A. Murray, *The Witch-Cult in Western Europe: A Study in Anthropology* (Oxford, 1921), *passim*, esp. pp. 124-85.

[21] E. Le Roy Ladurie, *Les paysans du Languedoc*, 2 vols. (Paris, 1966), i, pp. 407-14.

[22] Welsford, *The Fool*, p. 193; Davis, *Society and Culture in Early Modern France*, p. 100; Thompson, " 'Rough Music': le charivari anglais", p. 289; Thomas, *Rule and Misrule in the Schools of Early Modern England*, p. 34; K. V. Thomas, "The Place of Laughter in Tudor and Stuart England", *T.L.S.*, 21 Jan. 1977, pp. 77-81.

fore depended on the extent of familiarity with such orthodoxies. And the performance of ritual inversion was only successful if accompanied by possibly complex acts of recognition. An example from modern anthropology is McKim Marriott's failure to comprehend the Indian village festival of Holī as an actor but his subsequent understanding that its apparent disorder was "an order precisely inverse to the social and ritual principles of routine life".[23] Reverting to the language of use, there is the further suggestion that, simply in obliging the spectator to see the conventional world in the guise of its opposite, misrule embodies a cognitive function that, in part at least, must be essentially conservative — a restatement of the normal from a "ritual viewpoint". Stronger still is the claim that only by exploring this contrary perspective can men make themselves conceptually at home in a world of unchanging polarities.[24]

With these considerations in mind we can sketch the sort of linguistic context in which Renaissance accounts of the contrariness of witchcraft rituals were intended to make sense. For it is certain that what was required of both the spectator of festive misrule and the reader of demonological textbooks was formally, and perhaps even substantively, the same. The full force of an account of the sabbat such as De Lancre's, and indeed the cogency of demonological argument as a whole, depended on what might be called the sufficient conditions of the intelligibility of inverse behaviour being met. What was demanded was an act of recognition with three distinguishable elements: first, a general awareness of the logical relation of opposition, without which inversion could not even be entertained;[25] secondly, a familiarity with the relevant linguistic and symbolic conventions under which a specific action might be seen as one of inversion, the most important of these being the "world upside-down"; and thirdly, the grasping of just what positive rule or order was implied by any individual act of ritual witchcraft. By re-invoking these criteria we would in effect determine the range of descriptions governing the meaning of learned witchcraft beliefs.

III

Misrule involved the exchanging of roles or qualities which were themselves opposites or could be reduced to opposites; in the first instance, therefore, its impact was relative to an understanding of what it was for (say) wisdom to be opposite to folly, male to female, or authority to subjection. To some degree, of course, such dual classifications have no *history*. Discussions of the formal oppositions holding between terms or propositions have not changed since Aristotle's *De*

---

[23] Cited by Turner, *The Ritual Process*, pp. 185-6.
[24] *Ibid.*, pp. 176, 200-1.
[25] Babcock (ed.), *The Reversible World*, p. 27.

interpretatione, and there is an obvious sense in which all thinking and acting depend on the analytical relationship between judgements of opposition. Nevertheless some intellectual movements have positively encouraged this sort of cognition and the utterances and actions appropriate to it. In the sixteenth and seventeenth centuries a predisposition to see things in terms of binary opposition was a distinctive aspect of a prevailing mentality. What is remarkable, however, is the extraordinary pervasiveness of the language of "contrariety", the most extreme of the relations of opposition. To a great extent this reflected the dominance of an inherited metaphysic. But it was also associated with two features peculiar to that period: a linguistic preference for standardized forms of argument and expression based on antithesis, and a preoccupation with the extreme poles of the religious and moral universe. Thus it becomes possible to attribute the era of witchcraft beliefs with an especial sensitivity to the idea of opposition and a consequently heightened appreciation of what was involved when the orthodox world was reversed or inverted.[26]

In the system of ideas which informed early Greek religion and natural philosophy, material flux and moral variety were traced to the interplay of contrary entities in the world.[27] Of particular importance was the Pythagorean view that such primal disorder could be transcended by obedience to laws of proportion; hence the existence of analogous processes of *concordia discors* in mathematical reasoning, musical harmony, physical health, moral improvement and ultimately the universal structure of things. Both Plato and Aristotle endorsed a theory of the generation of opposites from opposites, the former in the course of the argument for immortality in the *Phaedo*, and the latter as essential for the explanation of all process. Aristotle argued that the categories in respect of which things were capable of changing were always one of two contraries and that change was therefore matter moving between the contrary poles represented by the possession or privation of some form or forms.[28] In the case of Christian metaphysics the need was to give a dualistic account of the imperfections which marred the Creation without extending this to first principles; to stress, that is, both the contrasting and correlative aspects of good and

[26] For parallel instances in non-European cultures, see R. Needham (ed.), *Right and Left: Essays on Dual Symbolic Classification* (London, 1973), esp. pp. 76-7, 294-8, 307, 327, 351, 358-62 (inversions associated with death), and pp. 369-90 (disorder, inversion and witchcraft among the Lugbara of Uganda).

[27] H. Fränkel, *Dichtung und Philosophie des frühen Griechentums* (New York, 1951), p. 77, on the dominance of a "polar mode of thought" after Homer, and pp. 341, 465; G. E. R. Lloyd, *Polarity and Analogy: Two Types of Argumentation in Early Greek Thought* (Cambridge, 1966), pp. 15-171, considers the appeal to pairs of opposites in modes of argument and forms of explanation down to Aristotle.

[28] Plato, *Phaedo*, 70-2; Aristotle, *Metaphysica*, 1069b, 1075a, 1087a-b; Aristotle, *Physica*, 188a-91a; and see J. P. Anton, *Aristotle's Theory of Contrariety* (London, 1957), pp. 31-49, 68-83.

evil. Augustine achieved this by comparing the course of world history with the forms of ancient rhetoric. The *civitas dei* and the *civitas terrena* symbolized an absolute dichotomy between the values and fortunes exhibited by communities in time, but this did not mean that they had independent origins or purposes. For God had composed history as the Romans wrote their poetry, gracing it with "antithetic figures". Just as the clash of opposites (*antitheta*) was the most effective form of verbal eloquence, "so is the world's beauty composed of contrarieties, not in figure, but in nature".[29] For Aquinas the problem of evil was solved by recourse to Aristotle's logic. His classification of the whole of human conduct under the opposites of specific virtues and vices was sustained by the rule that contrariety was the relationship of greatest difference. Likewise the key notion of evil as a deficiency of good was simply Aristotle's contrast between a positive condition and its privation. If there was no good in the world we could not speak of its privation; to the extent that we do speak of evil, good is presupposed. Conversely (in Augustine's formulation) "even that which is called evil, being properly ordered and put in its place, sets off the good to better advantage, adding to its attraction and excellence . . .". Without (say) injustice, "neither would avenging justice nor the patience of a sufferer be praised". The simple formal truth embodied in these arguments became the foundation of the Christian intellectual tradition; but the older cosmological doctrines were also readily assimilated both by philosophers like Boethius and later by Renaissance neo-Platonists.[30]

One way of examining the widespread influence of the language of contraries in the early modern period would be to consider its role in individual disciplines like physics, medicine, natural magic, astrology, psychology or ethics.[31] The point, however, is that since contrariety characterized the logic of the Creator's own thinking there was nothing to which it could not in principle be applied. This is illustrated by the extended discussion in the French classical scholar Loys Le Roy's *De la vicissitude ou variété des choses en l'univers* (1576). He begins with a statement of *concordia discors*; nature "desires" contraries

[29] Augustine, *De civitate dei*, xi. 18, trans. John Healey as *The Citie of God* (London, 1610, S.T.C. 916), p. 422.

[30] Augustine, *Enchiridion*, xi, xii-xv, trans. L. A. Arand in *St. Augustine: Faith, Hope and Charity* (Ancient Christian Writers ser., iii, London, 1947), p. 18; Aquinas, *Summa theologica*, i, q. 48, 1-2, in *Basic Writings of Saint Thomas Aquinas*, ed. A. C. Pegis, 2 vols. (New York, 1945), i, pp. 464-7; Boethius, *De consolatione philosophiae*, iv, carmina 6.

[31] See, for example, the medical controversy over the Galenic principle of *contraria curans contrariis*, or the "armies of contraries" in Baconian natural science: L. Thorndike, *History of Magic and Experimental Science*, 8 vols. (New York, 1923), ii, p. 887, iii, p. 220, vi, p. 231, viii, p. 134; Noah Biggs, *The Vanity of the Craft of Physick* (London, 1651), pp. 214-17; Francis Bacon, *De principiis atque originibus*, in *The Works of Francis Bacon*, ed. J. Spedding, R. L. Ellis and D. D. Heath, 14 vols. (London, 1857-74), v, p. 475.

because it is only in conjunction with its opposite that each entity or
quality can survive and contribute to the order and beauty of the
whole. The astronomical proximity of Venus and Mars is one instance;
the reciprocal action of the four elements in the generation, composition and preservation of sublunary bodies is another. To these Le Roy
adds logical, physiological and sociological examples. Painting, music
and grammar involve compositions of contrary elements and effects.
All sciences consist of the "comparing of contraries", such that physicians must relate health to sickness, and ethical and political philosophers "doe not onelie shew what is honest, just, and profitable; but also
that which is dishonest, unjust, and domageable". Thus are good and
evil both contrary and conjoined, "that in taking of one, both are tane
away". Finally Le Roy elaborates on the mutual antipathies which
keep all things within their bounds. These "contrarie affections" include rivalries among animals, plants and minerals, the struggle between reason and passion in human nature, the controversies of the
learned and, above all, the historical conflicts between classes and
nations. This enmity of peoples and the contrarieties of fortune which
result are God's way of recalling the world to a proper sense of moral
proportion.[32]

Le Roy's ideas about a substantive contrariety in all natural, intellectual and social phenomena were typical of sixteenth- and seventeenth-century accounts of universal order.[33] But his view that it could
best be captured by specific styles of discourse based on contrast reflected not only a patterning believed to be immanent in the Creation
itself but also contemporary theory in the arts of communication and
its influence on linguistic uniformity via countless school and university curricula. In dialectic textbooks, considering what was contrary to
a proposition was one of the topoi involved in devising arguments for
its defence or refutation. Its special appeal lay in opportunities for
striking and compelling antithesis between species at opposite ends of
the same genus; hence the aphorism *opposita iuxta se posita magis
elucescunt* which in Le Roy became the general principle of knowledge "that contraries when they are put neere, one to the other,

[32] Loys Le Roy, *De la vicissitude ou variété des choses en l'univers* (Paris, 1576),
trans. R. A[shley] as *Of the Interchangeable Course, or Variety of Things in the Whole
World* (London, 1594, S.T.C. 15488), pp. 5^v-7.

[33] See, for example, Lambert Daneau, *Physice christiana*, trans. T[homas]
T[wyne] as *The Wonderfull Woorkmanship of the World* (London, 1578, S.T.C.
6231), pp. 84^v-6; Jean Bodin, *Colloquium heptaplomeres*, trans. M. L. Daniels Kuntz
as *Colloquium of the Seven about Secrets of the Sublime* (Princeton, 1975), pp. 144-9;
Pierre De La Primaudaye, *L'académy françoise*, trans. T.B. as *The French Academie*
(London, 1589, S.T.C. 15234), p. 691; John Eliot, *The Monarchie of Man*, ed. A. B.
Grosart, 2 vols. (London, 1879), ii, pp. 131-5; Pontus De Tyard, *Deux discours de la
nature du monde, et de ses parties* (Paris, 1578), pp. 80^v-1^v; Nicolas Caussin, *La cour
sainte*, trans. T. H[awkins] as *The Holy Court* (London, 1634, S.T.C. 4874), pt. iii, pp.
30, 198. For other references, see E. Wasserman, *The Subtler Language: Critical
Readings of Neoclassic and Romantic Poems* (Baltimore, 1959), pp. 53-66.

they appeare the more cleerely".[34] Its popularity was therefore not restricted to the obvious applications in *encomium* or *vituperatio* but reflected the developing sixteenth-century fashion for rhetorical amplification as a strategy of argument. Quite apart from a multitude of occasional uses it sustained the meaning of whole treatises, ranging in size and seriousness from the *Paradossi* of Ortensio Landi to the Puritan William Gouge's thesaurus of family duties, in which each was matched with its contrary aberration.[35] Carried over from logical terminology, the argument *a contrariis* or "by antithesis" became conventional in a very wide range of contexts.

In addition, contrariety was the essence of several of the important figures or tropes for the "colouring" of discourse discussed by textbook rhetoricians under the heading of *elocutio*. The most influential of these was *contentio* (*antitheton*), the balancing of sentences, phrases or individual words with opposed meanings (and the figure chosen by Augustine to represent the character of metahistory). Other related devices were *contrapositum*, *contrarium*, litotes, oxymoron and *antiphrasis*. It would be impossible to indicate briefly all the literary conventions associated with these figural schemes, or the central importance of contrariety in creating such primary moods as irony or parody. But Henry Peacham thought that "antithesis"was one of the best methods of garnishing orations and said that none was more popular in his time, while George Puttenham agreed on the extent of usage but regarded it as excessive.[36] Among verse traditions alone, the idiom of contrariety was the basis of three forms of enormous influence, the Petrarchan love sonnet, the metaphysical conceit and the neo-classical loco-descriptive poem.[37] At the most general level of all, it

[34] Cicero, *Ad Herennium*, iv. 18, 25; Erasmus, *De duplici copia verborum ac rerum* (Strasbourg, 1516), fos. lxii[r-v]; Melancthon, *De rhetorica* (Basel, 1519), pp. 26-7; Thomas Wilson, *The Arte of Rhetorique* (London, 1553, S.T.C. 25799), p. 69[r]; Charles De Saint-Paul, *Tableau de l'éloquence françoise* (Paris, 1632), pp. 234-6.

[35] Ortensio Landi, *Paradossi*, trans. Charles Estienne as *Paradoxe qu'il vaut mieux estre pauvre que rich* (Caen, 1554), "Au lecteur", trans. Anthony Munday as *The Defense of Contraries* (London, 1593), quoted in B. Vickers, "*King Lear* and Renaissance Paradoxes", *Mod. Lang. Rev.*, lxiii (1968), pp. 308-9; William Gouge, *Of Domesticall Duties* (London, 1622, S.T.C. 12119), "Epistle dedicatory". Examples of other works arranged by contraries are Jean De Marconville, *De la bonté et mauvaistie des femmes* (Paris, 1571); Guillaume De La Perrière, *Le miroir politique*, trans. as *The Mirrour of Policie* (London, 1598, S.T.C. 15228).

[36] Henry Peacham, *The Garden of Eloquence* (London, 1577, S.T.C. 19497), Sigs. Ri[r-v]; George Puttenham, *The Arte of English Poesie* (London, 1589, S.T.C. 20519), ed. G. D. Willcock and A. Walker (Cambridge, 1936), pp. 210-11; cf. Saint-Paul, *Tableau de l'éloquence françoise*, pp. 251-2. Commentary in W. G. Crane, *Wit and Rhetoric in the Renaissance: The Formal Basis of Elizabethan Prose Style* (New York, 1937), *passim*; B. Vickers, *Classical Rhetoric in English Poetry* (London, 1970), pp. 68-121.

[37] L. Forster, *The Icy Fire: Five Studies in European Petrarchism* (Cambridge, 1969), pp. 1-60; E. Miner, *The Metaphysical Mode from Donne to Cowley* (Princeton, 1969), pp. 118-58; Wasserman, *The Subtler Language*, pp. 35-168.

is possible to argue that it played a vital part in sustaining that interest in paradox, contradiction and mutability which, it has so often been suggested, marked European literary sensibilities at the turn of the sixteenth century.[38]

Finally there were formative influences on the mentality we are considering which were peculiar to styles of religious discourse in the same period. There is scarcely any need to stress the significance of the Protestant doctrines of original sin and election, both of which demanded judgement by absolute extremes. But of equal importance was the pervasion of denominational polemic by an eschatology which radically altered the shape of Augustinian history.[39] The vision of a continuing struggle between antithetical communities or aspects of human nature was replaced by that of its rapid escalation, imminent climax and permanent resolution, whether millenarian or apocalyptic. The contrariety which marked the logic of all human actions was felt to be currently at its most uncompromising; the language describing the "last days" is accordingly full of images of the violent contrast of opposites. The key to the situation was thought by Protestant and Catholic alike to lie in the identification and analysis of Antichrist, a figure representing not merely enmity with Christ but the complete contradiction of Christianity by antithetical doctrines and false miracles.[40] The last chapters of the Book of Revelation spoke of the binding or destruction of Satan, the abolition of sin, darkness and death, and the reconciliation of Alpha and Omega. This, in effect, was to define the New Jerusalem as a state of affairs *without* privation in order to accentuate its difference in kind from the rest of human experience. It is clear that a new edge and urgency was added to the notion of contrariety by this dramatic foreshortening of historical perspectives and the acute anxiety to locate all things in either the Christian or Antichristian category.[41]

Running through these major influences on the character of early modern thought is the confusion between cosmology and the theory of knowledge common to all theodicy. For Pythagoreans and Platonists to conceive of the world as a musical composition described in terms of

---

[38] R. L. Colie, *Paradoxia epidemica: The Renaissance Tradition of Paradox* (Princeton, 1966), *passim*; J. Rousset, *La littérature de l'âge baroque en France* (Paris, 1954), *passim*; I. Buffum, *Studies in the Baroque from Montaigne to Rotrou* (New Haven, Conn., 1957), pp. 40-2.

[39] W. Haller, *Foxe's Book of Martyrs and the Elect Nation* (London, 1963), *passim*; P. Toon (ed.), *Puritans, the Millennium and the Future of Israel* (Cambridge, 1970), pp. 8-90; B. S. Capp, *The Fifth Monarchy Men* (London, 1972), pp. 13-45.

[40] See, for example, Lambert Daneau, *Traité de l'antechrist* (Geneva, 1577), pp. 64-5, 224-5; Florimond De Raemond, *L'antichrist* (Lyon, 1597), p. 52; George Pacard, *Description de l'antechrist* (Niort, 1604), pp. 1-10; and for England, C. Hill, *Antichrist in Seventeenth-Century England* (London, 1971), *passim*.

[41] For the related theme of contrariety and universal decay, see V. Harris, *All Coherence Gone: A Study of the Seventeenth-Century Controversy over Disorder and Decay in the Universe* (London, 1966), *passim*.

harmonic intervals was evidently to conflate substance and form. In Augustine, history was itself an utterance, literally a figure of God's speech. Contrariety was thus a universal principle of intelligibility as well as a statement about how the world was actually constituted. And men's ability to understand the moral language implanted in the Creation in the form of privations of good was a function of the way they ordered their own language by corresponding modes of antithesis in thinking and communicating. This was not a matter of mere heuristic convenience. For Aquinas it meant reducing all logical opposites to contraries, the juxtaposition of which enabled men to grasp moral, and by extension, all relations. In dialectical and rhetorical training it led to the use of specific forensic and literary strategies with which audiences could feel an especial affinity. In the heat of religious crisis casuists could think only in terms of *contraria immediata*, one of which had to be affirmed, there being no intervening species. Thus we find a manifest function insistently imparted to those contrary perspectives to which anthropologists studying non-European cultures have tended to attach only a latent meaning.[42] Whatever Christian men might meaningfully do or say presupposed the relation of contrariety.

IV

In 1604 the essayist William Cornwallis wrote that "man . . . cannot judge singlie, but by coupling contrarieties".[43] We might compare this with an epigraph of 1651 by the Spanish Jesuit Balthasar Gracian: "The things of this world can be truly perceived only by looking at them backwards".[44] For these were twin corollaries of the dominant intellectual assumptions of the age in which both festive misrule and conceptions of ritual witchcraft flourished. If the world was "composed of contraries" it was also a reversible world; indeed this was the only change to which it could conceivably be subject.[45] Moreover if such contrarieties were always relations of quality, that is, forms of privations of good, then to reverse the world was also to invert it, to turn what were in effect moral priorities upside-down. And since inversions were themselves contrary to the normal relations holding between phenomena, they were in turn assimilable to that same cosmological pattern of opposition which was God's way of expressing and men's way of grasping the intelligibility of things. That there was, once again, no limit to the application of this principle can be seen in a

[42] Needham (ed.), *Right and Left*, pp. xxv, xxxi-xxxii.
[43] William Cornwallis, *The Miraculous and Happie Union of England and Scotland* (London, 1604, S.T.C. 5782), Sig. Bi^r.
[44] Quoted by Rousset, *La littérature de l'âge baroque en France*, p. 24, and in translation by Babcock (ed.), *The Reversible World*, p. 13.
[45] Thomas, *Rule and Misrule in the Schools of Early Modern England*, p. 34.

remarkable treatise by Giacomo Affinati D'Acuto, *Il mondo al rover-sica e sossopra* (1602), where the turning upside-down of the pre-lapsarian world by sin is illustrated with reference not merely to man but relentlessly and exhaustively to every sublunary phenomenon, to the celestial spheres and to the angels and demons.[46]

Nevertheless, if we wish to go on to indicate the sorts of linguistic and symbolic conventions which governed the recognition of specific actions, including those attributed to witches, as inversions we can do this most effectively in the context of political writings and occasions. On the one hand, since the world of "agreeing discords" survived be-cause it conformed to divine laws of proportion, accounts of universal contrariety were invariably couched in the language of government. In England Bishop Godfrey Goodman traced the origin of all authority to God's insistence, in the cases of the first enmities of Genesis, that the body be subject to the soul, the flesh to the spirit, and women to men.[47] Likewise, at the opening of judicial sessions at Périgueux in 1583 Antoine Loisel suggested that it was a "more political" way of conceiv-ing of concord (in the seasons, the body and the arts) to attribute it to divine command than to the generative power of either contrariety or equality themselves.[48] Inversion in whatever context was thus neces-sarily a political act. On the other hand, in the life of actual societies and states it was resonant with special meaning; for these were institu-tions modelled on the divine paradigm, harmonizing contrarieties of status, interest and fortune by patriarchal and princely powers which were either historical derivations from or closely analogous with God's own rule.[49] Here the image of the world upside-down was peculiarly persuasive. By "correspondence" it endowed acts of social disorder with a significance far beyond their immediate character, attributing to them repercussions in every other plane of "government". And by antithesis it offered the opportunity of defending order *a contrariis* in relation to a situation in which all the normal patterns of authority were simply inverted. Like all knowledges, political theory depended for its cogency on the proximity of opposites, on what Le Roy in a work on how to study politics called "the method of teaching by con-

[46] Giacomo Affinati D'Acuto, *Il mondo al roversica e sossopra* (Venice, 1602); the work was translated into French by Gaspard Cornuère, *Le monde renversé san-dessus dessous* (Paris, 1610).

[47] Godfrey Goodman, *The Fall of Man* (London, 1616, S.T.C. 12023), p. 251; cf. La Perrière, *The Mirrour of Policie*, Sigs. Viv*ʳ⁻ᵛ*, on "agreeing discords" in marriage, the family and (by extension) the state.

[48] Antoine Loisel, *Homonoee, ou de l'accord et union des subjects du roy soubs son obeissance* (Paris, 1595), pp. 22-32; Loisel's address is a detailed application of Py-thagorean and neo-Platonist doctrines of *concordia discors* to the situation of con-temporary France.

[49] For a classic statement, see Jean Bodin, *Six livres de la république*, vi. 6, trans. R. Knolles as *The Six Bookes of a Commonweale* (London, 1606, S.T.C. 3193), p. 794; cf. Loisel, *Homonoee*, p. 35.

traries".[50] But in the case of order-disorder, with which, in one guise or another, sixteenth- and early seventeenth-century writers were pre-occupied, they were dealing not with a polarity like any other but with the primary polarity of Christian thought. The characterization of disorder by inversion, even in relatively minor texts or on ephemeral occasions, may therefore be taken to exemplify an entire metaphysic.

One obvious instance is that of comparisons between the prince and the tyrant, where the argument, both in logic and content, was in fact modelled directly on seminal accounts of monarchy given by Aristotle, Augustine and Aquinas. The qualities and duties of the prince, deduced from theological and moral postulates, were portrayed in terms of the perfectly virtuous man governing in an ideal situation. This paradigm ruler was to be contrasted with his opposite, whose government was in every respect contrary to the good; hence the emergence of a *speculum principum* tradition in political theory, history-writing and drama in which descriptions of tyranny rested on nothing more than a species of inversion.[51] In a typical discussion in his *Christiani principis institutio* (1516) Erasmus argued that the actions of the true monarch and of the tyrant were at opposite ends of every moral continuum and could not therefore be separately conceived or taught; a tyrant was simply one who turned every rule of political life upside-down.[52] James I too thought that understanding the "trew difference betwixt a lawfull good King, and an usurping Tyran" was a case of invoking the maxim *opposita iuxta se posita magis elucescunt* and setting out the "directly opposita" aims, policies and rewards of each.[53] However, the most sustained attempt to capture in language the inversions thought to constitute the actions of the tyrant is in a "set-piece" of antithetical contrasts repeated by at least three French authors, Jean Bodin, Pierre De La Primaudaye and Nicolas Barnaud, and one Englishman Charles Merbury. In Barnaud's *Le miroir des francois* (1581) this begins:

> the king conforms himself to the laws of nature, while the tyrant treads them under-foot; the one maintains religion, justice and faith, the other has neither God, faith nor law; the one does all that he thinks will serve the public good and safety of his subjects, the other does nothing except for his particular profit, revenge or pleasure; the one strives to enrich his subjects by all the means he can think of, the other

[50] Loys Le Roy, *De l'origine, antiquité, progres, excellence et utilité de l'art politique* (Paris, 1597), p. 14.

[51] Aquinas, *De regimine principum*, iii, in *Aquinas: Selected Political Writings*, ed. A. P. D'Entrèves (Oxford, 1948), p. 15; on the tradition in general, see A. H. Gilbert, *Machiavelli's "Prince" and Its Forerunners: "The Prince" as a Typical Book "de regimine principum"* (Durham, N. C., 1938), *passim*; G. Jondorf, *Robert Garnier and the Themes of Political Tragedy in the Sixteenth Century* (Cambridge, 1969), pp. 61-2; W. A. Armstrong, "The Elizabethan Conception of the Tyrant", *Rev. Eng. Studies*, xxii (1946), pp. 161-81.

[52] Erasmus, *Christiani principis institutio* (1516), trans. L. K. Born as *The Education of a Christian Prince* (New York, 1936, repr. New York, 1965), pp. 150, 156-65.

[53] James I, *Workes* (London, 1616, S.T.C. 14344), pp. 155-6.

improves his own fortune only at their expense; the one avenges the public injuries and pardons those against himself, the other cruelly avenges his own and pardons those against others; the one spares the honour of chaste women, the other triumphs in their shame . . .

There is scarcely any need to complete what is in fact a much longer passage to grasp the aptness of the rhetorical device and the conceptual language presupposed in writing about politics in this way.[54]

A second example is that of descriptions of disobedience itself. Often these were limited to the citing of commonplace parallels between the resistance of subjects to princes, children to parents, and servants to masters. But that this was a shorthand implying unspoken assumptions about a whole world upside-down can be seen from the elaborate account in which the Marian Catholic John Christopherson condemned the rebelliousness consequent upon liberty of conscience:

> dyd [not] children order their parentes, wyves their husbandes, and subjects their magystrates: So that the fete ruled the head and the cart was set before ye horse . . . was not al thinges through it brought so farre out of order, that vice ruled vertue, & folishnes ruled wisdome, lightnesse ruled gravitie, and youth ruled age? So that the olde mens saying was herein verified, that when Antichrist shulde come, the rootes of the trees shulde growe upwarde. Was there not beside, such deadly dissention for our diversitie in opinions, that even amonges those, that were mooste verye deare frendes, arose moste grevouse hatred. For the sonne hated hys owne father, the sister her brother, the wyfe her husband, the servaunte hys mayster, the subject the ruler.[55]

James I used the same idiom to describe the misrule which would result from papal claims to obedience; "the world itselfe must be turned upside downe, and the order of Nature inverted (making the left hand to have the place before the right, and the last named to bee first in honour) that this primacie may be maintained".[56] Another argument, typical in its verbal patterning, was Christopher Goodman's claim that when a man confuses obedience with its "playne contrarie", then "in place of justice, he receaveth injustice, for right wronge, for vertue vice, for lawe will, for love hatred, for trueth falshod, for playne dealing dissimulation, for religion superstition, for true worshippe detestable idolatrie: and to be shorte, for God Sathan, for Christ Antichrist".[57]

[54] Barnaud, *Le miroir des francois*, pp. 69-70; cf. Bodin, *Six livres de la république*, ii. 4, trans. Knolles, pp. 212-13; La Primaudaye, *The French Academie*, p. 601; Charles Merbury, *A Briefe Discourse of Royall Monarchie* (London, 1581, S.T.C. 17823), pp. 13-15. Other less elaborate contrasts are in La Perrière, *The Mirrour of Policie*, Sigs. Eiii^v-Fi^r; Jean Helüis De Thillard, *Le miroüer du prince chrétien* (Paris, 1566), Dedication; Jean De Marconville, *La maniere de bien policier la république chrestienne* (Paris, 1562), pp. 12^{r-v}.

[55] John Christopherson, *An Exhortation to All Menne to Take Hede of Rebellion* (London, 1554, S.T.C. 5207), Sigs. Ti^r-Tii^r, Tvi^v-Tvii^v.

[56] James I, "A Premonition to All Most Mightie Monarches", in *Workes*, p. 307.

[57] Christopher Goodman, *How Superior Powers Oght to be Obeyed of Their Subjects* (Geneva, 1558, S.T.C. 12020), pp. 9-10; cf. John Cheke, *The Hurt of Sedicion* (London, 1549, S.T.C. 5109), in *Holinshed's Chronicles*, ed. Sir H. Ellis, 6 vols. (London, 1807-8), iii, p. 1003; Anon., *A Remedy for Sedition* (London, 1536, S.T.C. 20877), Sigs. Aii^{r-v}.

Similar ways of thinking and writing marked the pamphlet literature of the French wars of religion. Artus Désiré went so far as to attribute all France's ills to a failure of patriarchal discipline which, apart from producing upside-down families, led, via providential punishment, to a society so corrupted:

> that today one takes the priest for adventurer and the adventurer for priest, the lord for villein and the villein for lord, the magistrate for constable and the constable for magistrate, the good woman for wanton and the wanton for good woman; in short, all is so turned upside-down that one can no longer tell the one from the other.[58]

Antoine Loisel matched Goodman's point exactly when he said that despite compelling reasons for order and obedience there were those "whose judgement is so inverted that they call war peace, disunity unity and discord concord".[59] Similar arguments came from antagonists on both sides. The Parisian magistrate Guillaume Aubert used stylistic antithesis to describe how sectarian militance had turned the principles of Christian pacifism upside-down. Pierre De Belloy, supporter of Henry of Navarre, associated rebellion with a universal overturning symbolized by the inversions which characterized Augustine's *civitas terrena*.[60] In such reactions to the disobedience thought to be inseparable from variety in religious or political allegiances we can distinguish a conventional rhetoric of disorder.

In a third context inversion was used to reinforce the same political point by its realization in the actions of symbolic personae. It no longer seems strange to read Renaissance court festivals for their sometimes esoteric political meanings. For they were conceived by the greatest artists of the period as statements about the power of royal authority to bring order and virtue to men's engagements. It was supposed that princes and courtiers who acted their ideal selves in suitable allegorical situations could, with a proper blending of artistic, poetic, musical and balletic resonances, actually draw down the principles of world harmony into the commonwealth. Thus the "device" would often move from a representation of civil or moral disorder to its transformation, and finally to scenes of homage to or apotheosis of royalty. This simple antithesis gave unity to the spectacle and since it was emphasized by contrasts in speech, dance, costume and even gesture, offered opportunities for extended experimentation with modes of inversion. In the major *ballets* at the French court, kings were seen to rescue the world

[58] Artus Désiré, *L'origine et source de tous les maux de ce monde par l'incorrection des peres et meres envers leurs enfans, et de l'inobedience d'iceux* (Paris, 1571), pp. 27ᵛ-36ᵛ; Désiré borrows inversions from Isaiah v. 20. For other biblical sources of the world upside-down, see Francois Le Jay, *De la dignité des rois et princes souverains* (Tours, 1589), pp. 34-56 (wrong pagination).

[59] Loisel, *Homonoee*, pp. 98, 103.

[60] Guillaume Aubert, *Oraison de la paix et les moyens de l'entretenir* (Paris, 1559), p. 11; Pierre De Belloy, *De l'authorité du roy* (Paris, 1587), pp. 6-7, 26ᵛ; cf. Affinati D'Acuto, *Il mondo al roversica e sossopra*, pp. 487-92.

from uncertainty, ambiguity and illusion and from threats of over-turning (*renversement*) by those wielding metamorphic powers. One such figure was Circé, who in the *Balet comique de la Royne* (1581) changed men into beasts, depriving them of their reason, and charmed popular opinion into confusing the benefits of peace with the perils of war. Another was Alcine, who in the *Ballet de Monsieur de Vendosme* (1610) turned men's faculties upside-down by an inordinate desire for pleasure, and their actual shapes into grotesqueries. Victims of such enchantments occur in several other *ballets* where they are also de-livered by agents of the counter-magic embodied in royal valour, wis-dom and beauty. There are complete entertainments where *le monde renversé* is not resolved; but in the context of the whole genre, a world peopled by figures, as Jean Rousset suggested, "always ready to turn themselves suddenly into their opposite", survived despite the inten-tions of kings.[61]

In the case of the Jacobean and Caroline masque this antipathy was always quite patent. Ben Jonson and his imitators deliberately empha-sized the contrariness of disorder by making it the subject of prefatory "anti-masques" in which the codes of political morality celebrated in the body of the masque were represented in antithesis. The logical mood of the whole entertainment was thus explicitly that of the argu-ment *a contrariis* that virtue was "More seen, more known when vice stands by";[62] while the highly elaborate inversions in anti-masque characterization and situation drew clearly on popular as well as learned conceptions of misrule. In *Time Vindicated to Himself* (1623) figures representing impertinent curiosity demand a saturnalian riot where slaves, servants and subjects "might do and talk all that they list"; "Let's have the giddy world turned the heels upward, And sing a rare black Sanctus, on his head, Of all things out of order".[63] The theme of giddiness is repeated in *Love's Triumph through Callipolis* (1631), a masque which praises perfect love in the guise of the queen but opens with depraved lovers whose lives are "a continued ver-tigo".[64] This is a world in which people not only act out opposites but also "know things the wrong way".[65] In *Salmacida spolia* (1640) the blessings of civil concord secured by Prince Philogenes cannot be truly perceived in an anti-masque society so corrupt that the nobility no longer protects, the poor no longer serve, and religion has become a

[61] M. M. McGowan, *L'art du ballet de cour en France, 1581-1643* (Paris, 1963), *passim*, esp. pp. 42-7, 69-84, 101-15, 133-53; J. Rousset, "Circé et le monde renversé: fêtes et ballets de cour à l'époque baroque", *Trivium* [Schweizerische Vierteljahres-schrift für Literaturwissenschaft und Stilkritik], iv (1946), pp. 31-53; cf. Rousset, *La littérature de l'âge baroque en France*, pp. 13-31.

[62] S. Orgel and R. Strong (eds.), *Inigo Jones: The Theatre of the Stuart Court*, 2 vols. (London, 1973), i, p. 288.

[63] *Ibid.*, pp. 350-2.

[64] *Ibid.*, p. 406.

[65] *Ibid.*, p. 366.

vice. Even the dreams of anti-masquers are appropriately disordered;
in *The Vision of Delight* (1617) Fant'sy asks:

> If a dream should come in now to make you afeard,
> With a windmill on his head and bells at his beard,
> Would you straight wear your spectacles here at your toes,
> And your boots o' your brows, and your spurs o' your nose?[66]

One surviving costume design by Inigo Jones strikingly captures these
visions; it depicts a "double woman" who is half a figure of beauty and
half a hag.[67]

With such creatures only symbolic confrontation was possible. In
Oberon (1611) moonlit obscurity, mischievous satyrs, irresponsible
hedonism and unchaste language represent an indecorum and unruliness which must vanish before the brilliance, propriety and solemnity
of Oberon's homage to the Arthurian king-emperor. And in *Pan's
Anniversary* (1620) it is the grossness and presumption of delinquent
Boeotians which bears no comparison, except one of antithesis, with
the world of the Arcadians, "persons so near deities . . . taught by Pan
the rites of true society".[68] Such contrasts were heightened in each
case by matching styles of expression in the language of music and
dance as well as in scenery and costume. One anti-masque measure
in *Coelum Britannicum* (1634) even consisted of "retrograde paces";
others were "distracted", "extravagant", "antic", and accompanied
by "contentious music" or "strange music of wild instruments". The
elaboration of an upside-down world was in fact complete, pointing up
with fullest possible effect a conception of kingship as the only power
capable of setting it to right.

However extravagant and stylized these various representations of
disorder may seem, it would be mistaken to think of them as less meaningful than those attempted from the vantage of (say) a tradition of
empiricism in political debate. For they were entailed by a metaphysical system with its own criteria of what was real. It was precisely
the ability of *ballets de cour* and masques (as spectacles inspired by a
neo-Platonic conception of art) to bridge the disjunction between the
ideal and the actual that made them so popular with their royal and
aristocratic patrons. Likewise the apparently purely literary devices of
verbal and syntactical antithesis employed in writings on tyranny were
those thought to be immanent in the language of all evil acts. These
necessarily manifested a divine logic and therefore could be properly

[66] *Ibid.*, p. 272.
[67] *Ibid.*, p. 390.
[68] *Ibid.*, p. 318. Especially helpful on the anti-masque are S. Orgel, *The Jonsonian Masque* (Cambridge, Mass., 1965), *passim*; W. Todd Furniss, "Ben Jonson's
Masques", in his *Three Studies in the Renaissance: Sidney, Jonson, Milton* (New
Haven, Conn., 1958), pp. 89-179. E. Welsford, *The Court Masque* (Cambridge,
1927), pp. 3-167, and P. Reyher, *Les masques anglais* (Paris, 1909, repr. New York,
1964), pp. 1-107, trace the origins of the court masque in traditions of misrule.

conceived of in no other way. To link disobedience with inversions of natural phenomena or with discordant music is assuredly not our way of talking about disorder in political arrangements; but these were inescapable corollaries of an organic view of a world made coherent not merely by analogous operations at each of its many levels but by actual chains of cause and effect. That trees might grow with their roots in the air, or left-handedness take priority, were not merely images of disorder but states of affairs that a man might expect to encounter. The visual symbolism of the court revel not only suggested moral and political truths, it really effected them in the manner of a talismanic magic.[69] Thus, while the world turned upside-down undoubtedly became a topos with a purely literary or iconographical reference, we should not underestimate its original appeal as a description of real events consequent upon acts of sin.

V

It was in a world accustomed to think in these ways about contrariety and disorder that the arguments of the demonologists made sense. In the face of Sadducism or qualms merely about publicizing witchcraft their whole intellectual engagement could be defended as an example, perhaps the paradigm case, of the principle that the appreciation of good consisted in the recognition and exploration of its privative opposite. In his *Daemonologie* (1597) King James claimed that:

> since the Devill is the verie contrarie opposite to God, there can be no better way to know God, then by the contrarie; ... by the falshood of the one to considder the trueth of the other, by the injustice of the one, to considder the Justice of the other: And by the cruelty of the one, to considder the mercifulnesse of the other: And so foorth in all the rest of the essence of God, and qualities of the Devill.

This applied to all specific offices and ordinances of divine origin, indeed to all features of a world imbued with an invertible morality. Thus James's own attempt in 1590-1 to write into the confessions of the North Berwick witches a special antipathy between demonic magic and godly magistracy had been a way of authenticating his own, as yet rather tentative initiatives as ruler of Scotland.[70] Similarly in Pierre De Lancre's *Du sortilège* (1627) it was the very fact that the Devil chose to mimic the Catholic liturgy which was said to be incontro-

---

[69] These are aspects of symbolism not sufficiently dealt with in M. Walzer, "On the Role of Symbolism in Political Thought", *Polit. Science Quart.*, lxxxii (1967), pp. 191-204.

[70] James I, *Daemonologie, in Forme of a Dialogue* (Edinburgh, 1597, S.T.C. 14364), p. 55; S. Clark, "King James's *Daemonologie*: Witchcraft and Kingship", in S. Anglo (ed.), *The Damned Art: Essays in the Literature of Witchcraft* (London, 1977), pp. 156-81. For the same point about the Devil made in a non-demonological context, see Thomas Starkey, *An Exhortation to the People, Instructynge Theym to Unitie and Obedience* (London, 1536, S.T.C. 23236), Sigs. Aii^v-Aiii^r.

vertible proof of its divinity.[71] The rationale of all such institutions would accordingly be seriously undermined without demonological science. Establishing in exact detail what occurred at a witches' sabbat was not arid pedantry or intellectual voyeurism but a (logically) necessary way of validating each corresponding contrary aspect of the orthodox world. And the full intelligibility of demonological literature was, in the end, dependent on success in reading into each individual facet of demonism an actual or symbolic inversion of a traditional form of life.

In this respect the most appropriate context of meanings was that of conceptions of disorder as a world turned upside-down by disobedience and tyranny. For demonic inversion was inseparable, in the first instance, from notions of archetypal rebellion and pseudo-monarchy. The Devil's original presumption prefigured every subsequent act of resistance, while the style of his rule in hell was, as Erasmus explained, a model for all those whose political and moral intentions were most unlike God's.[72] Although some sort of order could be discerned there, it was therefore fitting that it should comprise the opposite of perfect princely and paterfamilial government. Aquinas had established that demons only co-operated out of common hatred for mankind, not from mutual love or respect for magistracy. Though there were ranks among the fallen angels the criteria involved were those of greatness in malice and, consequently, anguish rather than worth and felicity. These principles became essential to all formal demonology and pneumatology.[73] Their relation to the wider context can be seen in a discussion such as D'Acuto's. Here the fact that demons had inverted the angelic nature is offered as one example, albeit historically prior, of a universal overturning wrought by the rebellion which constitutes sin. The contrarieties involved in the fall of Lucifer (for instance, from prince of heaven to tyrant of hell) and the qualities both of his subject devils and the corresponding moral faction of mankind are expressed in a series of the usual linguistic antitheses.[74] In effect, then, the Devil's regimen was a compendium of the paradoxes of misrule: a hierarchy governed from the lowest point of excellence, a society in which

---

[71] Pierre De Lancre, *Du sortilège, ou il est traicté s'il est plus expedient de supprimer et tenir soubs silence les abominations et maléfices des sorciers que les publier et manifester* (n.p., 1627), pp. 6-7; cf. Henri Boguet, *Discours des sorciers* (1590), in *An Examen of Witches*, ed. M. Summers (London, 1929), p. 61.

[72] Erasmus, *Christiani principis institutio*, trans. Born, p. 174.

[73] Aquinas, *Summa theologica*, i, q. 109, ed. Pegis, i, pp. 1012-16; Crespet, *Deux livres de la hayne de Sathan*, pp. 9ʳ⁻ᵛ; Pedro Valderrama, *Histoire générale du monde, et de la nature*, trans. from the Spanish by Sʳ· De La Richardier, 2nd edn., 2 pts. (Paris, 1619), bk. iii, 1, p. 6; Jean Maldonat, *Traicté des anges et démons*, trans. F. De La Borie (Paris, 1605), pp. 159ᵛ-69; Thomas Heywood, *The Hierarchie of the Blessed Angells* (London, 1634, S.T.C. 13327), p. 414. For use in general discourse, see John Pym's speech at the impeachment of the earl of Strafford, 25 November 1640: *Somers Tracts*, 2nd edn., 13 vols. (London, 1809-15), iv, p. 216.

[74] Affinati D'Acuto, *Il mondo al roversica e sossopra*, pp. 447-92.

dishonour was the badge of status and a *speculum* imitable only by the politically vicious. This was worse than simple anarchy.[75]

Moreover there was a specific sense in which demonic allegiance was necessarily associated with disobedience and its consequences. The voluntary contract with the Devil which was thought to be the essence of malevolent witchcraft could be seen, primarily, as spiritual apostasy, symbolized by rebaptism at the sabbat. But the non-sacramental significance of baptism and the insistence on both the physical corporeality of devils and their political organization inevitably brought it as close to an act of literal, if indirect, resistance. English Puritan demonologists argued that the proper spiritual response to the tribulations of Satan was that of Job, while using the language of politics to convey the essential rebelliousness of his agents the witches. William Perkins, for instance, recommended that the natural law enjoining the death penalty for all enemies of the state be extended to "the most notorious traytor and rebell that can be . . . For [the witch] renounceth God himselfe, the King of Kings, she leaves the societie of his Church and people, she bindeth herself in league with the devil".[76]   The text occasioning this argument, "For rebellion is as the sin of witchcraft" (I Samuel xv. 23), could be used to demonstrate the identity in substance as well as in seriousness of the two sins. Hence the sensitivity of French and English writers to the double meaning involved in the word "conjuration"; hence too the overtones in the claim made in the English *Homily against Disobedience* that rebels "most horribly prophane, and pollute the Sabbath day, serving Sathan, and by doing of his work, making it the devils day, instead of the Lords day".[77] While witchcraft was constituted by an act of revolt, rebels effectively promulgated the sabbat. Even the many commonplaces to the effect that civil rebellions could only result from bewitching or sorcery or from "the mixing of heaven and hell" take on an added meaning.

These associations of ideas must have influenced the understanding of *maleficium*. For it was to be expected that witches should intend not only outright confrontation with the godly prince (as Lambert Daneau warned in theory and as was actually alleged in Scotland in 1590-1)[78]

[75] A tract which brings together many of the features of the mentality of contrariety in an attack on the Devil's mockery is Artus Désiré, *La singerie des Huguenots, marmots et guenons de la nouvelle derrision Theodobeszienne* (Paris, 1574). The Huguenots, inspired by the Devil's desire to turn all things upside-down, have substituted for every true form of worship its exact opposite. This is said to bear witness to the "advancement of Antichrist" and is expressed in a series of linguistic antitheses; it is also called "witchcraft". *Ibid.*, pp. 7-8, 22-4, 40ᵛ.

[76] William Perkins, *Discourse of the Damned Art of Witchcraft*, in his *Works*, 3 vols. (London, 1616-18, S.T.C. 19651), iii, p. 651; cf. Henry Holland, *A Treatise against Witchcraft* (Cambridge, 1590, S.T.C. 13590), Sig. Aiiʳ.

[77] Anon., *The Seconde Tome of Homelyes* (London, 1563, S.T.C. 13663), pp. 292-3.

[78] Lambert Daneau, *Les sorciers*, trans. R.W. as *A Dialogue of Witches* (London, 1575, S.T.C. 6226), Sigs. Biiʳ⁻ᵛ; *Newes from Scotland* (1591), repr. in *Gentleman's Mag.*, xlix (1779), pp. 393-5, 449-52.

but the promotion of those other inversionary phenomena which were thought to be, or to symbolize, disorder. Thus it was widely accepted that they could destroy the marital hierarchy by using ligature to prevent consummation, by sowing dissension or by incitements to promiscuity. Pierre De Lancre and Sébastien Michaelis claimed specifically that witchcraft subverted familial authority by destroying filial love in its devotees and victims.[79] This echoed the earliest charges made against the alleged *maleficium* of the Vaudois by Johann Tinctor: "Friends and neighbours will become evil, children will rise up against the old and the wise, and villeins will engage against the nobles . . .".[80] In the Richard Brome and Thomas Heywood comedy *The Late Lancashire Witches* (1634) a well-ordered household is attacked (in a "retrograde and preposterous way") by such sorcery — the father kneels to the son, the wife obeys the daughter, and the children are overawed by the servants. The demonological point is hardly obscure but it is nevertheless underlined; a nephew comments that it is as if the house itself had been turned on its roof, while a neighbour protests that he might as well "stand upon my head, and kick my heels at the skies". Ligature and the symbolism of a charivari reinforce the same theme.[81]

The idea that witches could change themselves and others into animals is another instance of inversion. Although it became usual to argue that the transformations were illusory, the concept of metamorphosis itself, if it was entertained at all, suggested that instinct might replace reason and brutishness virtue. The further example of the natural disorders supposedly wrought by *maleficium* is perhaps the most explicit. Witches, with demonic aid, were assumed to interfere with elements and climate to achieve especially hurtful or unseasonable reversals. Their most powerful magic hardly knew these limits. Henry Holland thought that the notion "that witches have power to turne the world upside down at their pleasure" was mistaken, but only because it suggested that this was not, indirectly, God's work.[82] Nicolas Rémy listed the detailed wonders:

> there is nothing to hinder a Demon from raising up mountains to an enormous height in a moment, and then casting them down into the deepest abysses; from stopping the flow of rivers, or even causing them to go backwards; from drying up the very sea (if we may believe Apuleius); from bringing down the skies, holding the

[79] Pierre De Lancre, *Le tableau de l'inconstance des mauvais anges et demons* (Paris, 1612), p. 4; Sébastian Michaelis, *Histoire admirable de la possession et conversion d'une penitente, seduite par un magicien*, trans. W.B. as *The Admirable Historie* (London, 1613, S.T.C. 17854), p. 254.

[80] Johann Tinctor, *Tractatus de secta Vaudensium*, trans. as *De la secte qui s'appelle des Vaudois*, in J. Hansen (ed.), *Quellen und Untersuchungen zur Geschichte des Hexenwahns und der Hexenverfolgung im Mittelalter* (Bonn, 1901), pp. 186-7.

[81] *The Dramatic Works of Thomas Heywood*, ed. R. H. Shepherd, 6 vols. (London, 1874), iv, p. 178 (Act I, scene i). I. Donaldson, *The World Upside-Down: Comedy from Jonson to Fielding* (London, 1970), pp. 1-23, 37-45, 78-98, considers the play in a tradition of comic treatments of disorder as inversion, which drew on forms of ritual misrule and included festive drama such as the Jonsonian masque.

[82] Holland, *A Treatise against Witchcraft*, Sig. Giii'.

earth in suspension, making fountains solid, raising the shades of the dead, putting out the stars, lighting up the very darkness of Hell, and turning upside down the whole scheme of this universe.

These were extravagant claims, inspired by Ovid's Medea and Circe as well as Apuleius's Meroë and as popular with poets and dramatists as with demonologists like Rémy.[83] Nevertheless we recognize, with him, the familiar lineaments of the *mundus inversus*. Indeed an important part of the meaning of all these various types of *maleficium*, whether in the family, society, the body or the world, was that they were conventional manifestations of disorder.

Once descriptions of the diabolical polity and the alleged intentions of witches are seen in this context, it becomes possible to read related meanings into the symbolic actions of the sabbat itself. Here many contemporaries were forcibly struck by the systematic and detailed inversions of liturgical forms, by what they recognized as a specious religious observance. Yet since religiosity was not confined to church worship, elaborate ceremonies of homage, however perverted, did not preclude other interpretations. In fact they facilitated an understanding of sabbat rituals in terms of the forms of the Renaissance court festival. Thomas Heywood's own account of the induction of witches is couched in part in the language of formal patronage and clientage and tries to evoke a mood suitable to "the pompe of regalitie and state". The rubric is minutely observed, but the (unstated) intentions are there to remind us of the irony of the situation.[84] The most sustained of such descriptions is, however, in Pierre De Lancre's influential demonology *Le tableau de l'inconstance des mauvais anges et demons* (1612), where it is illustrated by an engraving by Jan Ziarnko. In form at least the occasion is unmistakably that of a court spectacle, organized by a "master of ceremonies and governor of the sabbat" before the thrones of Satan and a designated "queen of the sabbat". A new client is presented, courtiers engage in a feast and various *ballets*, and there is instrumental music. An audience of aristocratic figures includes a group of women "with masks for remaining always covered and disguised". There is the same emblematic quality here as in other court festivals of the period, the same attention to detail in the performance, the same use of symbol and imagery, and the purpose is equally didactic. "For an instant", it has been said, "one catches a glimpse of the magnificences at the late Valois Court".[85]

[83] Nicolas Rémy, *Daemonolatreiae libri tres* (1595), iii. 1, in *Demonolatry of Nicolas Rémy*, ed. M. Summers (London, 1948), p. 141. For a recent account of the classical sources of literary treatments of witchcraft, see G. J. Roberts, "Magic and Witchcraft in English Drama and Poetry from 1558 to 1634" (Univ. of London Ph.D. thesis, 1976), pp. 31 ff.

[84] Heywood, *The Hierarchie of the Blessed Angells*, p. 472.

[85] M. M. McGowan, "Pierre De Lancre's *Tableau de l'inconstance des mauvais anges et demons*: The Sabbat Sensationalised", in Anglo (ed.), *The Damned Art*, pp. 192-3; De Lancre, *Le tableau de l'inconstance des mauvais anges et demons*, bk. ii, 4, pp. 124-53. Ziarnko's engraving is found only in the 1613 edition, printed opposite p. 118.

This impression of a festive hell is, of course, confirmed and not weakened by an absolute antithesis of content. In place of godlike monarchy and perfect Platonic love, the sabbat celebrated the most extreme tyranny and the foulest sexual debasement, and its aim was not to bring moral order and civil peace through the acting out of ideal roles but to ensure chaos by dehumanization and atrocities. If Ziarn-ko's engraving shows a court, it is, then, an anti-court and De Lancre's impresario is not, as it were, a master of revels but a demonic lord of misrule. Certainly the symbolic inversions are not merely those of the world upside-down but specifically those of so many anti-masque *mises en scène*, albeit in more horrendous forms — the elevation of the passions over reason by ritual depravities, physical reversals involving the priority of left-handedness and backwardness and even complete bodily inversions, vertiginous dancing, discordant music and nauseating food. The mood is precisely that which Valois, Bourbon and Stuart court entertainments were intended to transcend, that of physical obscurity and illusion, moral dissimulation, the metamorphosis of shapes and the enchantment of understanding and saturnalian licence. The grotesque world of the sabbat was the logical and symbolic antithesis of the orderly world of *ballet de cour* and masque. According to Heywood, "the Divell doth th'Almighty zany. For in those great works which all wonder aske, he is still present with his Anti-maske".[86]

[86] Heywood, *The Hierarchie of the Blessed Angells*, p. 415. For other detailed accounts of the sabbat, see Francesco Maria Guazzo, *Compendium maleficarum* (1608), i. 12, in *Compendium maleficarum*, ed. M. Summers (London, 1929), pp. 33-50; Philip-Ludwig Elich, *Daemonomagia* (Frankfurt, 1607), q. 10, pp. 129-42; Rémy, *Daemonolatreiae libri tres*, i. 11-20, ed. Summers, pp. 40-66. Especially evocative of the mood of the anti-masque occasion is Francois Arnoux, *Les merveilles de l'autre monde* (Lyon, 1614), p. 5: "Hell is a palace of darkness, where the scorching fires serve as torches, the glimpses of devils as pictures and the shadows as tapestries". Examples of the many individual inversion-motifs associated with witchcraft are H. Baldung, *Hexenbilder* (Stuttgart, 1961), p. 16 (witch looking at the world upside-down through her legs); Gabriel Martin, *La religion enseignee par les demons aux Vaudois sorciers* (Paris, 1641), confession of Thomas Balbi of 1435 ("He turned a wooden chalice upside-down on the ground, as a sign of total aversion from God"); Thomas Dekker, John Ford and William Rowley, *The Witch of Edmonton* (1621), Act I, scene i, in *The Dramatic Works of Thomas Dekker*, ed. F. Bowers, 4 vols. (London, 1953-61), iii, p. 537, and George Gifford, *A Dialogue Concerning Witches and Witchcrafts* (London, 1603, S.T.C. 11851), Sig. Liv (man forced by sorcery to kiss the arse of his cow). These cases recall images of the world upside-down found in popular art and literature: see E. R. Curtius, *European Literature and the Latin Middle Ages*, trans. W. R. Trask (London, 1953), pp. 94-8; D. Kunzle, "World Upside Down: The Iconography of a European Broadsheet Type", in Babcock (ed.), *The Reversible World*, pp. 39-94. Common to popular, learned and demonological accounts is the image of bodily inversion: Donaldson, *The World Upside-Down*, Plate I (*l'homme renversé*); Affinati D'Acuto, *Il mondo al roversica e sossopra*, p. 235 (those who sin continuously "are without doubt turned upside-down, with the head planted in the earth and the feet standing in the sky"); De Lancre, *Le tableau de l'inconstance des mauvais anges et demons*, p. 75 ("at the sabbat ... everything is preposterous and done the wrong way; sometimes they worship him [the Devil] with backs towards him, sometimes with feet upwards"); cf. Heywood, *The Hierarchie of the Blessed Angells*, p. 473.

In these circumstances it is significant to find devisers of entertainments using the theme of the sabbat to reinforce the disorder which was so often their starting-point. The *Ballet de Tancrède* (1619) consisted of a confrontation typical of *ballet de cour* between the hero-warrior Godfrey De Bouillon and his knights and the besieged king of Jerusalem and the magician Ismen. The trees of a protective forest are guarded by demons and monsters summoned from hell by Ismen but the resolution of the Christian Tancred simply in entering its glades is enough to disarm the magic and force its disappearance. This does not sound like a sabbat occasion but the early stanzas in Canto XIII of Tasso's *La Gerusalemme liberata* which inspired the device spoke of the forest as a nocturnal meeting- and feasting-place for witches (*le streghe*) and De Lancre in his chapter on the sabbat singled out the same passage as evidence of a typical gathering.[87] Spectators must have been able to make the required associations, given the popularity of both source and episode. In any case the intentions were made clear in the dedication in the *livret* to the French "Tancred", the duc de Luynes: "It is you, Sire, who by your worth has courageously disarmed the monsters of wars and seditions which civil discord fetched from hell to impede the righteous designs of Louis the Just".[88] In this way the witchcraft of Tasso's sabbat was the symbolic clue to the disorder in the French state, while the magical powers of the depicted heroes *and* of the performance itself provided the appropriate remedies.

More extensive is Ben Jonson's use of the same theme in his first major excursion into the anti-masque form. In the *Masque of Queenes* (1609) twelve ancient queens, among whom Bel-Anna is the quintessence of virtue, are presented to Heroic Virtue, a monarch god, by Good Fame his daughter. They ride in a triumphal procession to pay their homage to him and decide to grace his court with their individual merits. The political allusions were not esoteric; only a truly exemplary prince such as King James could be rewarded with a reputation efficacious enough in itself to make his subjects want to imitate him in every respect. But to establish his point most effectively, that is *a contrariis*, Jonson needed not simply, as W. Todd Furniss suggested,[89] a spectacle

[87] De Lancre, *Le tableau de l'inconstance des mauvais anges et demons*, pp. 124-5: "In describing the enchantment made by the magician and sorcerer Ismen in the forest of Jerusalem, Tasso seems to speak of the sabbat exactly as our witches depict it to us".

[88] Scipion De Gramont, *Relation du grand ballet du roy, dancé en la salle du Louvre le 12 fevrier 1619 sur l'adventure de Tancrede en la forest enchantee* (Lyon, 1619), pp. 3-4, in P. Lacroix (ed.), *Ballets et mascarades de cour de Henri III à Louis XIV, 1581-1652*, 6 vols. (Geneva, 1868-70), ii, pp. 161-98; McGowan, *L'art du ballet de cour en France*, pp. 117-31. That Godfrey was regarded as an exemplary prince in *speculum principum* literature is also important to the meaning of this *ballet*, setting him in antithetical opposition to the tyrant Aladdin and underlining the antipathy between Christianity and demonic magic: Thillard, *Le miroüer du prince chrétien*, pp. 108-9.

[89] W. Todd Furniss, "The Annotation of Jonson's *Masque of Queens*", *Rev. Eng. Studies*, new ser., v (1954), pp. 344-60.

of false religious worship, but an antithetical conception of court life and values (even if this was not entirely secular) expressed in ritual form. He found it in the demonologies of Rémy, Johan Gödelmann, Martin Del Rio, Ludwig Elich, Bodin, Paolo Grillandi and James himself. The resulting anti-masque ("an ougly Hell") depicts in the persons of twelve hags and their minutely detailed witchcraft the "faythfull Opposites" of the "renowned Queenes" and their equally ritualistic but exactly contrary magic. Their homage is to the tyrant Devil-Goat and their aim is to profane the night's proceedings and subvert the royal virtues; as their leader proclaims:

> I hate to see these fruicts of a soft peace,
> And curse the piety gives it such increase.
> Let us disturbe it, then; and blast the light;
> Mixe Hell, with Heaven; and make Nature fight
> Within her selfe; loose the whole henge of Things;
> And cause the Endes runne back into theyr Springs.

Jonson explained that these powers of inverting Nature were frequently "ascrib'd to Witches, and challeng'd by them-selves" and that he had found them described in Rémy as well as Ovid, Apuleius and other authorities.[90]

The antithesis at which he aimed is symbolized most expressly in the dance, perhaps the focus of all masque meanings. The witches "vizarded, and masqu'd", accompanied by "a strange and sodayne Musique", fall:

> into a magicall Daunce, full of praeposterous change, and gesticulation, but most applying to theyr property: who, at theyr meetings, do all thinges contrary to the custome of Men, dauncing back to back, hip to hip, theyr handes joyn'd, and making theyr circles backward, to the left hand, with strange phantastique motions of theyr heads, and bodyes.

The measures of the noble queens, on the other hand, "were so even, & apt, and theyr expression so just; as if Mathematicians had lost proportion, they might there have found it".[91] So fundamental was this notion of proportion in neo-Platonic conceptions of order that we can readily see how Jonson and his audience could conceive of these two sets of dancers as emblems of contrary modes of ethical and political life. The *Masque of Queenes* is about the victory of one of these modes. At the height of the sabbat, the witches, their hell, and above all the

[90] Orgel and Strong (eds.), *Inigo Jones*, i, pp. 132-8; I have used the text of the *Masque of Queenes* with Jonson's annotations in *Ben Jonson* [Works], ed. C. H. Herford and P. and E. Simpson, 11 vols. (Oxford, 1925-52), vii, pp. 278-319, lines 6-7, 24-5, 132, 462, 431-4, 144-9 (and annotation), and the commentary in Orgel, *The Jonsonian Masque*, pp. 130-46. The "mixing of hell with heaven" suggests outright sedition; see p. 119 above, and Francis Bacon, "A Letter Written out of England" (1599), in *The Works of Francis Bacon*, ed. Spedding, Ellis and Heath, ix, p. 116.

[91] Jonson, *Masque of Queenes*, ed. Herford and Simpson, lines 45, 344-50, 753-6; on the significance of the dance, see J. C. Meagher, "The Dance and the Masques of Ben Jonson", *Jl. Warburg and Courtauld Inst.*, xxv (1962), pp. 258-77.

power of their *maleficium* are negated simply by the bruit of the royal reputation (a single blast of "loud Musique") and the sight of virtue; just as the valour of Tancred is enough in itself to dispel the demonism of Ismen. These magical knock-outs are in fact very striking, given the demonological belief that the efficacy of witchcraft waned in direct proportion to the legal and ethical bona fides of the prosecuting magistrate and his determination in rooting it out.[92] The argument about the ability of royal courts to bring order to the world could not have been put more effectively.[93]

VI

Given the enormity of their sins and a world in which all phenomena were subject to inversion there was in fact no limit to the disorder of which (with the Devil's aid and God's permission) witches were capable. Nevertheless it is clear that audiences and readers were able and expected to make sense of their activities in a number of conventional ways, anchoring the meaning of witchcraft in terms of styles of thinking and writing about the world upside-down. Each detailed manifestation of demonism presupposed the orderliness and legitimacy of its direct opposite, just as, conversely, the effectiveness of exorcism, judicial process and even a royal presence in actually nullifying magical powers confirmed the grounds of authority of the priest, judge or prince as well as the felicity of his ritual performance. But it also had indirect meaning in terms of the many relations, both of causal interdependence and of "correspondence", which interlaced the Christian and neo-Platonist universe. The Devil's tyranny was an affront to all well-governed commonwealths but also to every state of moral equipoise. The wider implications of attacks on the family, and of the fact that they were promoted largely by women, could hardly have been missed in a culture which accepted the patriarchal household as both the actual source and analogical representation of good government. The reversing of the human bodily hierarchies or of priorities in natural things had effects which could literally be felt throughout a world thought to be an organic unity of sentients. Especially resonant

---

[92] Jonson, *Masque of Queenes*, ed. Herford and Simpson, lines 354-9; cf. the counter-magical efficacy of the royal glance in the *Ballet de Monsieur de Vendosme* (1610): McGowan, *L'art du ballet de cour en France*, p. 75. The relevant demonological arguments are in Jakob Sprenger and Heinrich Kramer, *Malleus maleficarum* (1486-7), ii, q. 1, in *Malleus maleficarum*, ed. M. Summers (London, 1928), pp. 90-1; Jean Bodin, *De la démonomanie des sorciers* (Paris, 1580), bk. iii, 4, pp. 139-44; Rémy, *Daemonolatreiae libri tres*, i. 2, ed. Summers, pp. 4-5; James I, *Daemonologie*, pp. 50-1; see also Brome and Heywood, *The Late Lancashire Witches*, in *The Dramatic Works of Thomas Heywood*, ed. Shepherd, iv, pp. 255-7.

[93] In these circumstances there was a double irony in blaming a sorcerer for the disorders at the mock court of the Christmas "Prince of Purpoole" at Grays Inn in 1594; see "Gesta Grayorum", in J. Nichols (ed.), *The Progresses of Queen Elizabeth*, 3 vols. (London, 1823), iii, pp. 279-80.

297

were references to the dance; for dancing not only had its own powers to confer (or destroy) order and virtue but figured the harmonic relations to which every phenomenon was subject. A single ritual act such as the anal kiss perverted religious worship and secular fealty, dethroned reason from a sovereign position on which individual well-being and social relations (including political obligation) were thought to depend and symbolized in the most obvious manner the defiant character of demonic politics as well as its preposterousness.

In these ways demonology superimposed image upon image of disorder. This profusion of levels of meaning made witchcraft beliefs ideal material for the literary imagination; but that they should have been integrated in performances as carefully structured as the court *ballet* and masque, shows how naturally they cohered with men's general conception of things. The best example of a dramatic fusion of this sort is, of course, in Shakespeare's *Macbeth*. It is a critical commonplace that the pervasive disorder in the play is expressed in a series of multiple inversions of contraries in the personal, political and natural planes.[94] Especially striking in the present context are the substitution of tyranny for true magistracy, both in fact and in Malcolm's self-accusation to Macduff,[95] and the reiterated consequences of disobedience to anointed kings and fathers. Even without the explicit witchcraft it would have seemed quite appropriate that Macbeth should be prepared to turn the world upside-down,[96] that his castle and kingdom should become a hell and that his actions should be inspired by ultimately deceitful incantations. Nevertheless the witches' presence is vital, for it establishes the two crucial features of the play's atmosphere. One is the sense of obscurity, uncertainty and dissimulation which clouds the subsequent action and its physical location with the effect of claustrophobia. The other is the repeated expression in linguistic antitheses of the inversions which this action embodies and provokes. Both are fixed at the very outset, not only by the famous ritual utterance, "Fair is foul, and foul is fair", but also by the reference to a "hurlyburly" with its suggestion of misrule and topsy-turvydom.[97] We must suppose that the dramatic effectiveness of this opening scene presupposed the wider context in which demonism was traditionally understood.

VII

A contextual reading of Renaissance demonology may not help us to answer the major questions about the genesis or decline of the Euro-

[94] L. C. Knights, "How Many Children Had Lady Macbeth?", in his *Explorations* (London, 1946, repr. Harmondsworth, 1964), pp. 28-48; Shakespeare, *Macbeth*, ed. K. Muir (Arden edn., London, 1951), "Introduction"; G. I. Duthie, "Antithesis in *Macbeth*", *Shakespeare Survey*, xix (1966), pp. 25-33; K. Muir, "Image and Symbol in *Macbeth*", *Shakespeare Survey*, xix (1966), pp. 48-9.
[95] *Macbeth*, IV. iii. 45-139.
[96] *Ibid.*, IV. i. 50-61.
[97] *Ibid.*, I. i. 3-11.

pean "witch-craze", although it surely confirms the view that these were related to the fortunes of an entire world-view. My aim has been rather to sketch some of the conventions of discourse which governed the successful persuasion of audiences at the height of the persecutions — say, between 1580 and 1630. In fact these turn out to be so important that it becomes difficult to explain, not how men accepted the rationality of the arguments, but how, occasionally, sceptics doubted it. What it made sense for demonologists to say depended partly on traditional metaphysical notions about the logical shape and moral economy of the world and partly on shared linguistic patterns for describing its most disturbing aspects. The first entailed a conception of evil for the sake of structural coherence, linking demonism with all privations of good; the second required inversion (both in forms of thought and forms of words) to ensure linguistic felicity, linking demonology with the articulation of key political concepts. The idea of witchcraft was not then a bizarre incongruity in an otherwise normal world; like all manifestations of misrule it *was* that world mirrored in reverse, and the practices of the alleged witches were no less (and no more) meaningful than those of ordinary men and women. It may be true that the demonologists, like other late sixteenth-century writers, were preoccupied with a disorder which appeared to characterize all their affairs. Grounds for such apprehension have been found by historians in an acute instability wrought by inflation, social mobility, sectarian violence and warfare. But to attribute the belief in demonic witchcraft to some determining "social dysfunction" would not only beg philosophical questions about the way language gives such traumas the meaning they have but ignore the extent to which contemporaries found reassurance in demonological (and millenarian) explanations, even of chaos. In the same way the discovery of instances among believers of what we would today recognize as clinical insanity could never warrant the view that Europe was in the grip of a "collective psychosis". This would be to explain away what in effect was a constitutive assumption of its culture, whereas part of what we mean when we speak of a "world-view" at all is surely that its constituents need no other explanation than their coherence one with another. The primary characteristic of demonological texts as historical evidence is not their supposed unverifiability but their relationship to what J. L. Austin called a "total speech situation";[98] their meaning for the historian may be thought of as exactly symmetrical with their original meaning as linguistic performances.

University College, Swansea   *Stuart Clark*

---

[98] J. L. Austin, *How to do Things with Words*, ed. J. O. Urmson (London, 1962), p. 52.

Witchcraft and Religion in Sixteenth-Century Germany: The Formation and Consequences of an Orthodoxy

By H. C. Erik Midelfort

The relation of religion and witch hunting has never been clear. The most flamboyant interpretations have tried to link the most severe witchcraft trials with a particular religious point of view, such as Puritanism.[1] Careful scholars, however, have shown that Puritanism was badly split on the subject of witchcraft, and that no orthodoxy ever emerged.[2] The German historians of the last century also tried to associate witchcraft with religion. Protestants tried to prove that ideas of witchcraft emerged among the medieval scholastics and were formally approved by Pope Innocent VIII, in 1484.[3] Catholics objected, however, that the period of large witch hunts came after the Reformation and that Protestants depended not on the scholastics but on the Bible and on Luther for their witchcraft theories.[4] Rationalist historians have viewed this confused debate with

---

s'ensuit ..." etc. und die Schilderung der *Histoire des martyrs*, a.a.O., S. 562 ff. („Massacre à Carcassonne").

86. *Languet* 2,196 f. (Paris, 23. Januar 1562): „Decima huius mensis celebrata est caena Lugduni, et eo die communicarent ad decem millia hominum. Interea autem dum isti communicant, alia decem millia erant in armis, qui observarent, ne quid tumultus exoriretur. Postridie qui fuerant in armis communicarunt, et qui pridie communicarant, successerunt in eorum locum. Res est peracta sine ullo tumultu, et ipsi actioni interfuit gubernator urbis." Der Gouverneur ist wohl Francois d'Agoult, Graf de Sault, gewesen. Vgl. C.O. 19,409 ff. (Calvin – Pfarrer von Lyon, Mai 1562).

1. R. Trevor Davies: *Four Centuries of Witch Beliefs* (London, 1947).

2. John L. Teall: "Witchcraft and Calvinism in Elizabethan England: Divine Power and Human Agency," *Journal of the History of Ideas* 23 (1962), 21–36.

3. G. Längin: *Religion und Hexenprozess* (Leipzig, 1888); Soldan-Heppe: *Geschichte der Hexenprozesse*, ed. Max Bauer (2 vols., Munich, 1912).

4. Johann Diefenbach: *Der Hexenwahn vor und nach der Glaubensspaltung in*

266

disdain and have condemned religious fanaticism in both Protestant and Catholic camps for inspiring the witch panics.[5] Both Catholics and Protestants, it seemed, were equally to blame.

At the same time that this dispute over witchcraft theory was reaching stalemate, a body of evidence was accumulating to suggest that there were indeed large differences from region to region in the severity of witch hunting. It has been commonly accepted that Catholic regions of Germany, for example, conducted the worst witch hunts of all. The church lands of Bamberg, Würzburg, Trier, Fulda, and Ellwangen were famous as the worst examples of the witch craze. Catholics could only reply that whereas Catholic witchcraft trials were orgies of panic, Protestant trials were an everyday occurrence. Needless to say such assertions need testing. Regional comparative studies are still incomplete, but what data we do have tend to confirm the impression that, in general, Catholic regions were indeed more severe than Protestant ones. In the German Southwest, for example, a careful count of all known trials between 1560 and 1670 yields several interesting conclusions. We know that Protestant regions conducted at least 163 trials and executed at least 620 persons. At the same time, Catholic regions conducted some 317 trials and executed at least 2328 persons. In terms of severity, in other words, Protestant regions executed 3.9 persons per trial while Catholic regions were nearly twice as severe, executing 7.4 persons per panic.[6]

This conclusion is filled with problems, since as we already noted, scholars have spent the last one hundred years demonstrating that Catholics and Protestants did not differ in their beliefs regarding witchcraft. If no differences can be found in the idea structure, how can one explain the much more severe witch hunting of German Catholics when compared to their Protestant neighbours?

Closer scrutiny of the southwest-German data yields a clue. The difference between Catholic and Protestant regions becomes really clear only with the year 1600. Until the end of the sixteenth century Catholics conducted trials that were only 20 to 30 per cent more severe than Protestant trials of the same period. In the seventeenth century, however, the Catholic rate of executions per panic actually climbed from 6 to 8.6. At the same time, however, the Protestant rate dropped from 4.5/panic to 3.5/panic.

Deutschland (Mainz, 1886); Nikolaus Paulus: *Hexenwahn und Hexenprozess vornehmlich im 16. Jahrhundert* (Freiburg i. Br., 1910).

5. Cf. especially H. R. Trevor-Roper: *The Crisis of the Seventeenth Century. Religion, the Reformation and Social Change* (New York, 1968), pp. 90–192.

6. Details will be found in my dissertation for Yale University, "The Social and Intellectual Foundations of Witch Hunting in Southwestern Germany, 1562–1684."

	Protestants			Catholics		
	trials	exec.	exec./trial	trials	exec.	exec./trial
1560–1600	49	218	4.5	150	896	6.0
1601–1670	114	402	3.5	167	1432	8.6
Total	163	620	3.9	317	2328	7.4

This finding should lead us to reexamine the conclusion that Protestants and Catholics displayed no marked differences in witchcraft theory. That conclusion was largely based on sixteenth century writers, and especially on a comparison of Luther and Calvin with contemporary Catholic thinkers. We can see now that indeed few differences need to have existed in the sixteenth century, but that some sort of break around 1600 would be expected. This kind of analysis leads us on to a wholesale reconsideration of the entire concept of witchcraft in sixteenth-century Germany.

In general a good part of most scholars' difficulty with witchcraft theory has been their attempt to analyze that theory into its smallest composite elements. Following the monumental work of Joseph Hansen, historians have learned to view witchcraft as a conglomerate body of weird ideas.[7] Hansen argued that the medieval scholastics and the inquisition together fashioned a witchcraft theory that took final form in the *Malleus Maleficarum* of 1486. He asserted that by 1540 the entire machinery of law, scholastic theory, and a myriad of occult details had been so effectively assembled that the mechanism worked without essential change for a century after 1540. Hansen himself asserted that the outbreak of witchcraft trials after 1540 was "nothing but the natural dying out of the medieval spirit, which the Reformation only partially pushed aside and in this matter hardly even touched."[8] Viewed as a composite mechanism, it is indeed true that after 1540 few if any really new details were added to the concept of witchcraft. Men now knew of all of the major variants of the pact with the devil, the sabbath, the devil's mark, flight, copulation with demons, and the concoction of poisons and charms. Scholars have been so fascinated with this variety of elements that they have usually failed to recognize that witchcraft did not require a complex of elements at all, but really only three crucial ideas, namely the permission of God, the physical power of the devil, and the pact of the witch with the devil.[9] If God were willing and the devil able, witch-

---

7. Joseph Hansen: *Zauberwahn, Inquisition und Hexenprozess im Mittelalter* (Munich and Leipzig, 1900); *Quellen und Untersuchungen zur Geschichte des Hexenwahns und der Hexenverfolgungen im Mittelalter* (Bonn, 1901).

8. Hansen: *Zauberwahn*, p. 4.

9. Abraham Saur used this tripartite analysis explicitly in "Ein kurtze newe

268

craft came into existence every time a person abandoned his faith and gave himself to the devil. Granted these three ideas, sixteenth-century witchcraft theorists could deny at will such diverse elements as flight to the sabbath, familiar spirits, and storm raising, without for a moment denying the concept of witchcraft or rejecting its forcible eradication. Once we realize that witchcraft in the sixteenth century was not a composite of wild and disparate details jumbled together by "monkish logicians," the significance of 1540 as a watershed vanishes. We are left free to examine changes that emerged only after that date, and free also to sort out a series of competing traditions and attitudes in the sixteenth century in search of an explanation for the sharp increase in Catholic witch hunting after 1600.

In the field of law, both the *Malleus Maleficarum* and the imperial code of 1532 called the *Carolina* emphasized the genuine harm done by witchcraft. The *Carolina* even asserted that harmless witchcraft was to be less severely punished than true *maleficium*.[10] In line with this distinction, trial evidence always strenuously insisted that convicted witches were not merely apostates from the faith but murderers, thieves, and propagators of plague, frost, and hail.

On a theoretical level, however, the *Carolina's* distinction between harmful and harmless magic grew to seem less and less adequate. Could one seriously argue that the tiniest bit of harm done was worse than the most blasphemous devil worship? Legislators and theologians alike in sixteenth-century Germany were driven to conclude that the real distinction lay between diabolical and non-diabolical witchcraft. Such a distinction did not involve any gross distortion of the *Carolina* since that imperial code already punished blasphemy (Article 106) and theft of the eucharistic host (Article 172) with death. Law makers could argue that witchcraft was a form of blasphemy and could show that witches often stole the host for desecration or for use in magical ceremonies.

For reasons like these, Catholic and Protestant legists after 1540 came increasingly to view the essence of witchcraft as allegiance to the devil. The emergence of this kind of view in the *Saxon Constitutions* of 1572, and in most other German ordinances in the later sixteenth century, has often been taken as the high tide of witchcraft delusion and a departure from the sound principles of the *Carolina*. Actually it is more appropriate to say that this shift in theory was a logical, even sensible, extension of the *Carolina*. It would be inexact and

---

Warnung Anzeige und Underricht ob auch zu dieser Zeit under uns Christen Hexen Zäuberer und Unholden vorhanden. Und was sie aussrichten können," in *Theatrum de Veneficis* (Frankfurt a. M., 1586), pp. 202–214.

10. Gustav Radbruch, ed.: *Die peinliche Gerichtsordnung Kaiser Karls V. von 1532* (Carolina) (Stuttgart, 1962), Article 109, p. 76.

269

misleading to describe the sixteenth century in Germany as simply a transition from *maleficium* to heresy in the consideration of witchcraft. As noted already, trial material throughout Germany and to the end of the *seventeenth* century continued to emphasize *maleficium* as strongly as heresy or apostasy. Yet the later sixteenth century did see a growing group of thinkers who saw life, death, and even crime in spiritual terms. It was they who perceived the ambiguity of the *Carolina* and moved to correct it in regional codes in both Protestant and Catholic sectors of Germany.

Critics have long noticed in German literature and popular broadsides after 1540 the movement toward a more spiritual or moralizing view of the world.[11] It became more common, for example, to view bad weather and "natural" disasters as moral messages from God.[12]

Hans Sachs exemplified this movement in simple terms when he had God exclaim in a *Fastnachspiel* of 1554:

> "Since they all from my goodness flee
> I pull them by the hair to me,
> And give them plagues and dire need
> So they are forced to give me heed."[13]

It would be foolish to argue that such a providential view of life was an invention of the sixteenth century, but after 1540 it came to dominate the view of an exceedingly wide spectrum of public opinion.

The impact of such providential and moralizing views on witchcraft theory is not immediately apparent. Luther for one certainly viewed unusual phenomena as moral messages from God, but he refrained from organizing or altering his fairly commonplace jumble of ideas on witchcraft.[14] His disciple, Johann Brenz, presents a different picture. This reformer of Schwäbisch Hall and of Württemberg made a careful study of the Book of Job in 1526 which convinced him early in his career that the true source of disasters was God

---

11. Freiherr von Liliencron: "Mitteilungen aus dem Gebiete der öffentlichen Meinung in Deutschland während der 2. Hälfte des 16. Jahrhunderts," *Abhandlungen der Historischen Classe der Königlich Bayerischen Akademie der Wissenschaften* Vol. 12 (Munich, 1874), Part III, pp. 105–170, esp. p. 139.

12. Gustav Hellmann: "Meteorologie in deutschen Flugschriften des 16. Jahrhunderts," *Abhandlungen der preussischen Akademie der Wissenschaften: Physikalisch-mathematische Klasse*, Jahrgang 1921, Nr. 1, pp. 21–22.

13. Hans Sachs: "Ein spiel mit 4 person zw spielen: Sankt Petter leezet sich mit sein freunden unden auf erden," in *Zwölf Fastnachtspiele aus den Jahren 1554 bis 1556 von Hans Sachs*, ed. by Edmund Goetze, Neudrucke deutscher Literaturwerke des XVI. und XVII. Jahrhunderts, Nr. 60–61 (Halle, 1886), pp. 63–64; my translation.

14. Paulus: *Hexenwahn*, pp. 20–47, "Luthers Stellung zur Hexenfrage."

270

Himself.[15] They were God's way of chastising, warning, and testing His people; they called specifically for repentence. Such a view of hardship was growing in popularity in the first half of the sixteenth century, but it had no necessary impact on theories of witchcraft. Even Brenz, in 1535 and again in 1537, expressed the common notion that witchcraft was physically dangerous.[16]

Perhaps it took a concrete situation for Brenz to realize that this ordinary view of witchcraft encouraged moral lassitude. A hail storm in 1539 brought him to express an essentially different point of view – one whose foundation Ulric Molitor and Martin Plantsch had laid a generation or two before the Reformation.[17] Brenz considered hail storms to be tests or punishments from God, as we have noted. Yet his congregation laid the blame on witches. Brenz now saw that this was a dangerous evasion of the whole point. Job had never blamed his calamaties on magic. Brenz felt driven to insist that storms came directly from God and that witches could not be linked with them in any way.[18] How then was one to regard the witches who later admitted that they had indeed caused particular storms? With an argument that might have pleased David Hume, Brenz asserted that witches confused sequence with causal relationship. What actually happened was a complex deception. The devil could often tell when God was moving to chastise His people with a storm, or the devil might simply see the storm coming from afar. He could then rush to his faithful, the godless witches, and prompt them to work their magical rituals. When the storm finally came, of course the witches thought that they had *caused* it. With this theory, which he borrowed from Molitor, Brenz was able to have his cake and eat it too. He was able to stress the fact that storms were direct warnings from God. No witch should take the blame and relieve God's people of their moral duty to examine themselves and repent. On the other hand, Brenz had not denied the power of the devil to work evil; nor had he denied the existence of godless

---

15. *Hiob cum piis et eruditis Ioannis Brentii commentariis* (Hagenau, 1527); cf. Martin Brecht: *Die frühe Theologie des Johannes Brenz*, Beiträge zur historischen Theologie, Nr. 36 (Tübingen, 1966), pp. 153–167.

16. *Operum Reverendi et Clarissimi Theologi D. Ioannis Brentii ... Tomus Septimus* (Tübingen, 1588), p. 158; *Operum Reverendi ... Brentii ... Tomus Primus* (Tübingen, 1576), p. 496.

17. Molitor: *De laniis et phitonicis mulieribus Teutonice Unholden vel Hexen* (Constance, 1489); I have used the German version in the *Theatrum de Veneficis*. Plantsch, *Opusculum de sagis malefices* (Pforzheim, 1507).

18. Brenz: "Ein Predig von dem Hagel und Ungewitter," in *Evangelien der fürnembsten Fest und Feyertagen im Jar* (Frankfurt a. M., 1558), tr. by Jacob Gretter. A Latin version is easily accessible in Johann Weyer (Wierus), *Opera Omnia* (Amsterdam, 1660), pp. 575–581.

271

witches. These apostates were worthy of death in a way that simple heretics were not.[19]

In this way Brenz's views on witchcraft developed a more spiritual and moralizing tone with emphasis on God's providence. His development parallels the shift we saw earlier in the interpretation of the *Carolina*, but would not be of great interest had he not in fact founded a school of interpretation that was established orthodoxy in Württemberg for one hundred years and whose influence extended far beyond the borders of Württemberg.[20] Echos of Brenz appear even in his opponents.[21]

This foundation of what we can call the "providential" school of witchcraft had two far reaching implications which are worth brief examination here. Both involve questions which need more investigation. They are the interrelated problems of the essence of "crime" in the sixteenth century and the denominational differences between Catholics and Protestants regarding witchcraft.

One of the questions Brenz and his school raised was the extent to which a person was criminally responsible if he did not "do" anything harmful. Brenz had after all argued that witches could not really work magical effects, but that they were worthy of death anyway. When Brenz's sermon on hail storms reached Johann Weyer, the famous Rhineland defender of witches, it became clear that two philosophies of law were in conflict. Weyer's basic position was that the pact with the devil did not, and indeed could not, exist; the women who confessed their league with the devil were, therefore, poor deluded dreamers, led astray by hallucination or mental illness. In 1565 Weyer wrote to Brenz asking for support in the attack on witch hunting.[22] Weyer asked why the spiritual crime of witchcraft should merit capital punishment when even Brenz conceded

---

19. Brenz: "Ob ein Weltliche Obrigkeit in Gottlichen und billichen Rechten die Widertauffer durch Fewr oder Schwert vom Leben zum Tod richten lassen möge," in *Consiliorum Theologicorum Decas IV,* ed. Felix Bidembach (Lauingen, 1607), pp. 211–234; cf. translation in Roland Bainton: *Concerning Heretics, Whether they are to be persecuted ... An anonymus work attributed to Sebastian Castellio* (New York, 1935), pp. 154–169.

20. The list of thinkers in this Württemberg tradition includes Matthaeus Alber, Wilhelm Bidembach, Jacob Heerbrand, Conrad Wolfgang Platz, Johann Schopf, Johann Georg Sigwart, Lucas Osiander, Christoph Stähelin, Tobias Lotter, Thomas Birck, Felix Bidembach, Theodor Thumm, Johann Adam Osiander, Daniel Schrötlin, Johann Harpprecht, Heinrich Bocer, Erich Mauritius, and Georg Heinrich Häberlin. Details on them and on their views may be found in my dissertation, cited above in fn. 6.

21. Especially Johann Spreter, Jacob Gräter, and David Meder; for details consult my dissertation, cited above in fn. 6.

22. Cf. Paulus: *Hexenwahn,* pp. 115–117.

272

that heretics should not be burned. Why should not witches be treated with the Word of God like other sinners?[23]

In an exceedingly polite letter Brenz responded by praising Weyer's defense of innocent women in a time when the rabble, like the ancient Roman mob, clamored for their death.[24] Brenz was in basic agreement with Weyer that large witch hunts were wrong. Yet he reached that conclusion by a different chain of reasoning and felt compelled to repeat his conclusion that true witches were to be executed since "conatus perfectus habeatur pro facto & opere ipso"; *i.e.*, a full or complete attempt is considered equal to the deed itself.[25] In this way attempted murder and attempted adultery were punished as severely as the crimes themselves. The criminal's guilt was every bit as full whether he actually performed the crime or not. His will was corrupt and expressed itself in a "conatus perfectus"; nothing more was necessary for condemnation.

Weyer's second letter to Brenz pinpointed this issue with clarity. Although attempted murder was indeed a real crime, Weyer held that witches could not perform a "conatus perfectus" since the deed itself was impossible. If witches were not capable of causing storms, as Brenz conceded, then they could never make a complete attempt at causing storms.[26] Weyer rightly singled out Brenz's confusion of sin with crime – a confusion common in the sixteenth century – and noted that by the spiritual standard of the Bible, simple lust was as bad a sin as full-fledged adultery. Yet law was a human, not a spiritual, standard. Witches should be judged by their deeds, not by the corruption of their wills.[27]

Brenz did not respond to this thrust of Weyer. No doubt he remained unconvinced. But the suggestions implanted by Weyer were to flourish in the seventeenth century, when men once again tried to determine what it was that witches were really guilty of.[28] Whether guilt resides in the intention or in the act, and what to do about it in either case, remains a problem whose historical roots need much further study.[29] It may be suggested that Weyer's attempts to

---

23. Weyer, *Opera Omnia* (Amsterdam, 1660), p. 585. The correspondence was first printed in the Basel, 1577, edition of Weyer's *De Praestigiis Daemonum*, cols. 817–836.

24. Weyer, *Opera Omnia*, p. 588.

25. *Ibid.*, p. 590.

26. *Ibid.*, pp. 593–594.

27. *Ibid.*, p. 595.

28. The Württemberg (Lutheran) theologians Theodor Thumm, Johann Adam Osiander, and Georg Heinrich Häberlin, all of the seventeenth century, followed Weyer in denying capital punishment for supposed pacts with the devil.

29. Other students have focused on the distinction between the tragic hero and the villain in sixteenth-century literature and suggest the crucial difference between these two types to be the extent to which the human will is actually corrupt or merely

273

relieve witches of guilt involved him in an argument that could be extended to eliminate the category of responsibility altogether. When we attempt to explain why Weyer's school of thought was so generally ineffective despite the large band of followers that he attracted, we must see that Weyer's interpretation led him to oppose capital punishment merely for total corruption of the will. It seems that Weyer's analysis at this point was one of radical utility, rejecting all notions of crime and guilt until some actual harm became apparent. Regardless of the subtlety of his psychology and the long providential tradition on which his theology was grounded, Weyer's legal interpretations led him further than even the most celebrated skeptics of the seventeenth century were willing to go. Thomas Hobbes and Pierre Bayle, for example, both agreed with Brenz that witches must be punished not for the harm they do, but for their desire to do harm.[30] The controversy between Brenz and Weyer is symptomatic of the kind of dispute that emerged in the later sixteenth century, as witchcraft became more and more a spiritual affair, a matter of the will, a problem in psychology.

Despite their disagreements on the matter of responsibility, Weyer and Brenz both raised the question of God's action in the world and tended to exculpate the human actors in God's drama. By giving Weyer their general support, Brenz and his school laid the foundations for a shift in the Catholic doctrine of witchcraft. In short, by opposing Brenz and Weyer, Catholics came to define a specifically Catholic doctrine of witchcraft. When Brenz first put his thoughts

---

deluded by strong passions. Those who thought in terms of this dichotomy could easily sympathise with rash acts of passion while condemning the conscious and wilful opposition to moral law. Brenz seems to have held this view, and could see witches as morally corrupt and worthy of death because of their conscious choice of evil, regardless of their melancholy humors. On the other hand, Weyer may have intended a union of will and intellect, insisting that severe diseases of the intellect (e.g. hallucinations) rendered the will incapable of guilt. The most persistent student of this fascinating problem was Lily Bess Campbell, *Shakespeare's Tragic Heroes: Slaves of Passion* (New York, 1952), esp. p. 101; *Collected Papers of Lily B. Campbell*, ed. by Louis B. Wright (New York, 1968), pp. 385–388, 434–438.

30. Thomas Hobbes: *Leviathan* (New York, 1955), p. 31; Pierre Bayle: "Réponse aux questions d'un provincial," in *Œuvres diverses* avec une introduction par Elisabeth Labrousse (Hildesheim, 1966), Vol. 3, pp. 562–565. Such an explanation of Weyer's ineffectiveness seems to me more precise than H. R. Trevor-Roper's suggestion that Weyer's doctrine "could not be refuted. But equally it could not refute the witch craze," *The Crisis of the Seventeenth Century*, p. 149. Certainly it seems more accurate than the attempt to discredit Weyer's knowledge of psychology by E. William Monter: "Inflation and Witchcraft: The Case of Jean Bodin," in *Action and Conviction in Early Modern Europe,* ed. Theodore K. Rabb and Jerrold E. Seigel (Princeton, 1969), pp. 371–389, esp. 382.

274

concerning witchcraft on paper, he was not conscious of standing outside the traditional view of the Church. Indeed he relied heavily on two pre-Reformation Catholic writers, Molitor and Plantsch. As we have seen, most modern students of witchcraft theory in Germany have simply concluded that Protestants agreed generally with Catholics throughout the sixteenth and seventeenth centuries.

This view becomes even more plausible when we observe that each confession in Germany, Lutheran, Calvinist, and Catholic, had a wide spectrum of views on witchcraft. In each of the three groups we can find writers who agreed essentially with Brenz that witches were harmless blasphemers, justly put to death but never to be credited with causing hardship. This "providential" wing of all three denominations insisted that there was a moral meaning to catastrophe and urged men to repent their sins if they wanted plagues and storms to cease.[31] Scholars are well familiar with the opposite wing – of Luther, Erastus, and Bodin – men who feared the results of the dreadful blasphemies of the witches, and often the direct physical harm done by the witches. For this wing, man's response to catastrophe had to be to find its human cause and exterminate it. During the sixteenth century, these views were jumbled together in such confusion that scholars have concluded that Catholics did not seriously differ from Protestants on this score.

This is, however, a misleading conclusion. By the end of the sixteenth century we find indications that a specifically Catholic view had crystallized. Witchcraft theory changed, but not by the addition of some new element, as one would be forced to argue if one used Hansen's mechanical model of witchcraft discussed earlier. In large measure the process seems to have been a response to Protestant pressure. In the second half of the sixteenth century, as confessional differences became clear, each denomination worked at developing a position that excluded all the errors of its opponents. In the attempt to provide an unambiguous image, each denomination came to reject ideas which had been tolerable earlier. Much of this rejection followed no logical theory, but was a blind attempt to exclude ideas associated with the confessional enemy.[32] Protestants like Jacob Heerbrand of Tübingen condemned Catholic rites, blessings, and

31. Lutherans: Brenz's school (cf. fn. 20 above), J. G. Gödelmann, J. Ewich, etc. Calvinists: H. Witekind, A. Prätorius, R. Scot, G. Gifford. Catholics: J. Zink, J. Lorichius. Details will be found in my dissertation cited above in fn. 6.

32. For the whole idea of the construction of a confessional image, consult the seminal article by Ernst Walter Zeeden: "Grundlagen und Wege der Konfessionsbildung in Deutschland im Zeitalter der Glaubenskämpfe," *Historische Zeitschrift* 185 (1958), pp. 249–299.

275

paraphernalia as diabolical magic.[33] When one recognizes Heerbrand as one of Brenz's firmest supporters in the providential tradition regarding witchcraft, one can begin to imagine what the Catholic rebuttal would look like. Not only Heerbrand's Lutheranism, but also his witchcraft theory would come under attack. In other cases Catholic scholars themselves were singled out and attacked as magicians.[34] Other writers influenced by Brenz suggested that Catholic territories as a matter of course had more witchcraft than Protestant lands.[35] One preacher characterized Catholicism as superstitious and therefore naturally inclined to witchcraft. In contrast, he pompously maintained that "no truly Protestant woman could become a witch."[36]

In response, the Catholics could assert that the real source of witchcraft was the Reformation itself, a position held by the famous scholar Martin Del Rio.[37] Other Catholic preachers blamed storms and disasters not on witchcraft, but on the new heresy of Luther.[38] It is understandable that in times so filled with charge and counter-charge, the Catholic party might be led mistakenly to attack specific doctrines of witchcraft as if they were part of the Protestant threat. This would seem to explain why Cornelius Loos, a faithful Catholic priest, suffered savage repression in 1592 and was forced to recant the ideas he had learned from Weyer. The condemnation of Loos specifically attacked his assertions as heresy.[39] Before this judgment there had been no real Catholic orthodoxy on witchcraft. But now it seemed that Weyer was in league with the large Protestant tradition of Brenz, and that together these troublemakers were bent on denying human agency with regard to evil. In response to Weyer and the whole

---

33. "Mera verè Diabolica impia et blasphema magia," Jacob Heerbrand: *Disputationes Theologicae In Inclyta Tubingensia Academia Publice Discutiendae* (Tübingen, 1575), "Disputatio de Magia," p. 478.

34. E.g. Jacob Heilbronner: *Daemonomania Pistoriana Magica et cabalistica morborum curandorum ratio ...* (Lauingen, 1601), pp. 12–17.

35. Johann Georg Sigwart: *Ein Predigt vom Reiffen und Getröst* (Tübingen, 1602), fol. 3, verso.

36. Jacob Gräter: *Hexen oder Unholden Predigten* (Tübingen, 1589), sig. A2, verso, to B1, recto.

37. Längin: *Religion und Hexenprozess*, pp. 133–134.

38. Christoph Stähelin: *Brunstpredigt. Behalten zu Dornstetten am Schwarzwald* (Tübingen, 1607), p. 12; Conrad Wolfgang Platz: *Newe Zeitung und Busspiegel. Von dem Straal so zu Biberach ... eingeschlagen* (Tübingen, 1584), p. 14.

39. Johannes Janssen: *Geschichte des deutschen Volkes seit dem Ausgang des Mittelalters*, 15th edition, ed. by Ludwig von Pastor (Freiburg i. Br., 1924), Vol. 8, p. 632. This was the explicit view of Peter Binsfeld; cf. Henry Charles Lea: *Materials Toward a History of Witchcraft* (Philadelphia, 1939), Vol. 2, p. 578; Del Rio also supported this view, cf. Vol. 2, pp. 643–644.

276

Brenzian school, Catholics retaliated by expunging doctrines from their midst which had formerly belonged to the common domain. After 1600 we do not hear German Catholics proclaim the theory that witches could really do no harm, a theory that numerous Protestants continued to hold.[40]

In 1604 a Catholic legist of Freiburg im Breisgau condemned Weyer and his Lutheran cronies as patrons of the witches. For this writer it was now a specifically *Protestant* theory that witches were not to be executed for merely spiritual crimes.[41] In 1614 the Catholic jurist Leonhard Kager of Schwäbisch Gmund tried unsuccessfully to stop the raging witchcraft trials in that town. He was reminded that only "our Weyerian adversaries" made use of the argument that witches were mentally ill, and was scolded for drawing heavily on the "illusions of non-Catholic writers."[42] It is no wonder that subsequent Catholic opponents of witch trials confined themselves to legal abuses and avoided the pitfalls of witchcraft theory.[43] Lutherans even came to accept the over-simplified categories set up by the Catholics. In 1687 a Lutheran scholar at Tübingen accepted the idea of denominational orthodoxy in the field of witchcraft, and described a specifically *Lutheran* theory, one which he thought achieved a firm middle ground between the overly lenient views of Weyer's school and the overly strict school of both Catholics and Calvinists.[44] It seems clear that these attempts to describe witchcraft theory in terms of confessional differences did gross injustice to the common and complex sixteenth-century heritage. As we have seen, the sixteenth century did not have any orthodox interpretation of witchcraft at the start. Each of the three confessions remained split into at least two wings regarding witchcraft. And yet the growth of a spiritualizing tendency in literature and thought in the second half of the sixteenth century had produced a remarkable providential thrust that had shaped both Weyer's and Brenz's style of thought.

We noticed what this shift meant for the interpretation of the *Carolina* and explored the ambivalent relation between Brenz and Weyer. And finally we

---

40. In fact, important Catholic treatments of the theory of witchcraft virtually vanish in the seventeenth century.

41. Friedrich Martini: *De Ivre Censuum seu annorum redituum ... commentarius ... Cui, eodem authore, ad calcem adnexa est nova Carolin. Constitution 109 & 218 in praxi frequentissimarum Interpretatio* (Freiburg i. Br., 1604), p. 519.

42. Württemberg, Hauptstaatsarchiv Stuttgart, B117 (Reichsstadt Gmünd), Büschel 122 (untitled and unpaginated response to Kager's Consilium).

43. This is even the case with the most powerful denunciations of witch hunting, like that of Friedrich von Spee *(Cautio Criminalis)*. His work was a strictly legal, not a theological or psychological, attack.

44. Johann Adam Osiander: *Tractatus Theologicus de Magia* (Tübingen, 1687), p. 293.

277

have seen that Catholics probably identified Weyer with the Protestant cause and felt driven to eradicate this part of their own tradition to present a more united front against the Protestants. Their choice was unfortunate. I would suggest that the hard line they finally took against witchcraft led to disproportionately more witch hunting in Catholic parts of Germany than in Protestant parts. We began our survey of the problem of witchcraft and religion with the observation that Catholic witch hunting seems to have grown more severe in comparison to Protestant trials, and that the new severity dates from roughly 1600. I would argue that the greater severity of the Catholic approach was closely connected to the growth of a providential school of witchcraft and to the successful attack of Catholics on that school, even when found among their own ranks. The search for Catholic identity seems to have had sorry consequences.

The sixteenth century cannot any longer be viewed as merely static in the realm of witchcraft theory. Nor can witchcraft be understood as a mere composite of superstitious details. Witchcraft theory and religion intersected in a dynamic cooperation that had profound social and legal consequences throughout the sixteenth and seventeenth centuries.

Zusammenfassung

Aus einer Auszählung aller Hexenprozesse im deutschen Südwesten geht hervor, daß der auffallende Unterschied zwischen protestantischen und katholischen Herrschaften in bezug auf ihre Behandlung der Hexen erst nach 1600 zu bemerken ist. Nach 1600 waren die Katholiken etwa zweimal so streng wie vorher. Die Gründe dafür kann man in der Entwicklung der theologischen Äußerungen von Predigern und Schriftstellern finden. Um die Mitte des 16. Jahrhunderts gab es kaum einen Unterschied zwischen den Äußerungen über Hexen aus dem protestantischen oder dem katholischen Lager. Beide hatten einen „Flügel", der Gott als Quelle aller Not und Unglück ansah und Reue als einziges erlaubtes Verhalten verlangte. Theologen wie Johannes Brenz hielten es für Aberglaube, Hexen verantwortlich für Hagel und andere von Gott kommende Unfälle zu machen. Beide konfessionellen Lager hatten aber auch einen „Flügel", der die Hexen als die Urheber von Hagel, Frost und Unglück betrachtete. Für diese Gruppe war der Hexenprozeß ein logisches Abwehrmittel. Es stellt sich heraus, daß die Brenz'sche Schule so stark wurde, daß die Katholiken deren Position für die einzige echt protestantische Stellungnahme hielten. Um etwa 1600 versuchte die katholische Seite ihre Position zu stärken. Der intransingente (sogenannte Brenz'sche) Flügel wurde verworfen (z. B. Cornelius Loos). Die Gegenreformation hatte also die Wirkung, daß selbst in kleineren unwichtigen Fragen ein Unterschied zwischen Katholiken und Protestanten fixiert wurde. Diese katholische Orthodoxie hatte eine große Bedeutung für die besondere Härte der Katholiken in Hexenprozessen des 17. Jahrhunderts.

278

12

The scientific status of demonology

STUART CLARK

> We use the word "supernatural" when speaking of some native
> belief, because that is what it would mean for us, but far from in-
> creasing our understanding of it, we are likely by the use of this
> word to misunderstand it. We have the concept of natural law, and
> the word "supernatural" conveys to us something outside the ordi-
> nary operation of cause and effect, but it may not at all have that
> sense for primitive man. For instance, many peoples are convinced
> that deaths are caused by witchcraft. To speak of witchcraft being
> for these peoples a supernatural agency hardly reflects their own
> view of the matter, since from their point of view nothing could be
> more natural.[1]

In a treatise on witchcraft first published in Trier in 1589 a German
bishop explained that all apparently occult operations that were not in
fact miracles could be ascribed in principle to physical causes. For
whether or not any particular instance was actually demonic in inspiration, "magic" was simply the art of producing wonderful natural
effects outside the usual course of things and above the common understanding of men. It followed that "if this part of philosophy was
practised in the schools in the manner of the other ordinary sciences
. . . it would lose the name of 'magic' and would be assigned to physics
and natural science [*et Physicae naturalique scientiae asscriberetur*]."
Likewise, in a set of theses on magical operations and witchcraft published a year later in Helmstädt, a natural philosopher and physician
began by arguing that "magical actions and motions are reducible to
considerations of physics [*Ad Physicam considerationem reducuntur
motus et actiones magicae*]." We might be tempted to read into such
statements intimations of that scepticism which (it is said) ultimately
undermined the learned belief in the reality of demonic effects, espe-

351

cially those associated with witchcraft, by accounting for them just as adequately in natural scientific terms. But the bishop was in fact Peter Binsfeld, and the notable contribution of his *Tractatus de confessionibus maleficorum et sagarum* to classic demonology, as well as its association with vigorous witch hunting, make it inconceivable that he could have meant to convey any general form of doubt.[2] The more obscure proposer of theses, Martin Biermann, although anxious to refute some of the extreme demonological opinions of Bodin, was no less traditional in his belief in the possibility of limited demonic activity in the world and in the reality of pacts between demons and both magicians and witches.[3]

It seems that insofar as they depend on an assumed disjunction between the "occult" and the "scientific," our expectations about belief and disbelief in such texts may be misleading. Understanding what sort of scepticism was most threatening to orthodox demonology depends on grasping its central intellectual defenses. But since these appear to *include* the use of natural scientific explanations, we need to look again at our assumptions about what it made sense for demonologists to accept as an account of the natural world and its processes. There is still a tendency to think that the flourishing of the debate about demonism and witchcraft somehow contradicted the general cultural, and especially scientific, achievements of the sixteenth and seventeenth centuries. If, however, this debate was not isolated from, or even antagonistic to, other aspects of Renaissance thought, including its science, then the contradiction becomes artificial. It is this wider issue of rationality, as well as the question of what was meant by arguments such as those of Binsfeld and Biermann, that involve us in reconsidering the status of demonology as an attempt to offer an ordered construction of natural reality.

A beginning might be made with those individual scientists who concerned themselves with demonology without any sense of incongruity or of the compromising of their criteria of rational inquiry: from Agostino Nifo, Giovanni d'Anania, and Andrea Cesalpino in sixteenth-century Italy to Henry More, Joseph Glanvill, and Robert Boyle in later seventeenth-century England. Others not primarily concerned with natural philosophy nevertheless combined it with demonology without intellectual embarrassment: for example, Jean Bodin, Lambert Daneau, and the Dutchman Andrea Gerhard (Hyperius). In perhaps the largest group there were the many physicians who made special studies of demonic pathology: the Italian Giovanni Battista Codronchi, the Germans Wilhelm Schreiber and Johann Wier, the Swiss Thomas Erastus, the Englishman John Cotta, and the many French doctors involved in cases of possession, among them Jacques Fontaine, Michel Marescot, and Pierre Yvelin.[4]

Intellectual biography would, however, only drive us back to issues. Some of these were, of course, merely practical. Arguments about the etiology and treatment of the various conditions associated with melancholia provided a general context for many medical incursions into demonology.[5] In the further case of the investigation of demoniacs it has even been suggested that exorcists, possibly displaying an empiricism beyond that of their medical colleagues, carried out what amounted to controlled experiments in order to test for the marks of true possession.[6] Other issues brought theorizing about demons, along with narratives of witchcraft, indirectly into scientific debate, as in the arguments over incorporeal substance in Restoration England. If, for instance, we can now see that Glanvill's demonology was inseparable from his experimental philosophy, it is because behind both lay the perception of a threat to Anglican theology posed by the Sadducism of scientific "materialists" and others.[7] Glanvill thought that the study of spirits could be recommended to the Royal Society without contradicting its standards of inquiry. Nevertheless, in this context the spirits entered scientific investigation, as another natural philosopher and demonologist, George Sinclair, remarked, primarily as "one of the *Outworks of Religion*."[8] The resulting blend of the newest scientific ideals with the oldest witchcraft beliefs was achieved at a key moment in both their histories. Yet the understandable interest shown in this example should not obscure the real novelty involved. What had changed was not the idea that the devil could be retained in a perfectly natural account of the world; it was the view of nature presupposed by this enterprise.

This can be illustrated if we consider a further set of issues, certainly not unrelated to theological questions (or indeed to Baconian elements in the activities of the Royal Society), but generated directly by what was regarded as the central ontological characteristic of demonic phenomena: the fact that they were extraordinary. The principal themes of sixteenth- and seventeenth-century demonology were the qualities and powers of demonic agents and the effects produced by their activity in the world. These were not merely moral effects: They were either real, physical operations, or they appeared to be, for demons were consummate deceivers. Yet neither were they commonplace. At the very least they were, as Glanvill himself put it, "somewhat varying from the common *Road* of *Nature*."[9] In fact, for the most part they were prodigious in character and, therefore, often confused with other apparently aberrant phenomena. The key questions faced by demonologists were thus of a causal and criterial kind: What was the exact causal status of demonic effects? What laws did they obey or disobey?

What were the criteria for distinguishing between their true and illusory aspects? Along what point on the axis from miracles through natural wonders to ordinary natural contingencies were they to be placed? Tackling such questions involved making distinctions that were critical for any explanation of phenomena, whether demonic or not – distinctions between what was possible and impossible, or really and falsely perceived, and between both supernature and nature, and nature and artifice. It had to be decided what were the boundary conditions governing miracles, prodigies, marvels, and "prestiges"; how to define and use categories such as "magic" and "occult"; and how to relate the explanatory languages of theology and natural philosophy. However bizarre the resulting discussions may sometimes seem, they were genuine attempts to establish criteria of intelligibility for the understanding of a very wide range of what were taken to be puzzling events, that is, events which were said to have "no certain cause in nature."

This concentration on the interpretation of essentially perverse phenomena is not easily related to any narrowly conceived "scientific revolution" in the same period.[10] But this does not mean that it was peculiar to demonologists. What helped to give the debate about demonism and witchcraft such a general currency toward the end of the sixteenth century was the extent to which its interest in the eccentric in nature was a shared intellectual preoccupation. In his remarkable study, *La Nature et les prodiges: l'insolite au XVIᵉ siècle, en France*, Jean Céard has indicated both the range of the literature dealing with monsters, prodigies, and marvels (as well as with the more general features of "variety" and "vicissitude"), and the fundamental character of the conceptual problems it raised in the overlapping territories of philosophy, theology, and science. More recently the specific case of the monstrous has been canvassed as an important individual indicator of changes in explanatory models in early modern France and England.[11] Demonologists often considered an identical teratology – for example, the monsters generated by incubus or succubus devils – and they usually located demonic prodigies semiologically within a broadly apocalyptic account of God's intentions. On the other hand, their stress on demonic manipulation of the natural world was rather oblique to the theme of nature's own generosity or fecundity in producing forms, which emerges strongly from the literature of the "unusual." The important point, however, is not that they may have given different answers to those engaged in the wider enterprise, but that they confronted the same epistemological puzzles. Wherever and to what extent the devil and witches were actually situated in the causation of irregular events are less significant than the broader identity of purpose. It is in this sense that Céard's work enables us to think of demonology as continuous and not discontinuous with Renaissance natural philosophy.[12]

Moreover, the nature of this link does seem to have been recognized from within the "great tradition" of early modern scientific thought. Francis Bacon's proposal (in his *De augmentis scientiarum*) for a natural history of "pretergenerations" – "the Heteroclites or Irregulars of nature" – has often been cited in the context of prodigy literature, but the general relevance of Bacon's project for demonology is thought to have been negligible. In both its theoretical stance and its actual influence on the early program of the Royal Society, this proposal certainly made the marvelous a central rather than a peripheral category of investigation. Bacon's argument was partly technological – that rarities in nature would lead men to rarities in art – but it was also epistemological; hence, the repetition of the suggestion in Book 2 of the *Novum organum*, at the heart of what we have of his actual logic of inquiry. Singularities and aberrations in nature were not merely correctives to the partiality of generalizations built on commonplace examples; as deviations from the norm they were especially revealing of nature's ordinary forms and processes. This makes the example on which Bacon chose to concentrate in the *De augmentis scientiarum* all the more striking:

> Neither am I of opinion in this history of marvels, that superstitious narratives of sorceries, witchcrafts, charms, dreams, divinations, and the like, where there is an assurance and clear evidence of the fact, should be altogether excluded. For it is not yet known in what cases, and how far, effects attributed to superstition participate of natural causes; and therefore howsoever the use and practice of such arts is to be condemned, yet from the speculation and consideration of them (if they be diligently unravelled) a useful light may be gained, not only for the true judgment of the offences of persons charged with such practices, but likewise for the further disclosing of the secrets of nature.[13]

It would not be totally implausible to transpose even Bacon's point about the technological potential of knowledge of "erring" nature into a demonological context and to ask, for instance, whether the treatment of demoniacs was regarded as offering particularly decisive tests of the efficacy of medical (as well as exorcistic) practices. However, it is the fact that he thought of witchcraft narratives in connection with the epistemological benefits of this knowledge that is so suggestive. For in effect this not only made demonism and witchcraft fit subjects for natural philosophy, but elevated them to the rank of Baconian "prerogative instances," that is, areas of empirical inquiry especially privileged by their unusual capacity to disclose natural processes. This idea surely helps us to understand the role of European demonology in the wider setting. Its appeal in the scientific context was undoubtedly its ability, together with that of prodigy literature in general, to tackle one of the most intractable subject matters known to the period. Adapting Bacon's argument somewhat, we might say it was able to confront empirical and, more so, conceptual issues that, though fundamental to all systematic investigation, were laid bare in an especially illuminating manner by the very waywardness of the phenomena dealt with and the struggle to understand them. In this broader sense demonology was one of the "prerogative instances" of early modern science.

What matters here, again, is not that Bacon should eventually have arrived at the same interpretation of these phenomena as the demonologists. His principle that extraordinary events were worth more attention than ordinary ones had a formal truth, whether it was decided that they were all natural or all demonic. However, if, as we have seen, this was not in fact the nature of the choice that had to be made, then the real intellectual distance between a figure like Bacon and the world of demonology may not in any case be as great as it appears. In the *De augmentis* and the *Novum organum*, Bacon talked as though it was a personified nature itself which erred, not a nature acted on by demonic forces. In the *Sylva sylvarum* he also suggested that it was popular credulity which was responsible for the attribution of purely natural operations to some sort of efficacy in witchcraft. An example was the way the hallucinogenic effects of the "opiate and soporiferous" qualities of magical ointments were mistaken for the (supposedly real) transvections and metamorphoses that appeared in witches' confessions.[14] Above all, Bacon insisted that the only phenomena which were nonnatural were true miracles. It is not surprising that these views have been associated with outright naturalism and, therefore, with philosophical indifference to the problems raised by witchcraft beliefs. Yet all of them can be found in the writings of the demonologists, and the second and third might even be said to be presuppositions of their inquiry. The relative importance of demonically and nondemonically caused events remains the only really contentious issue, and here even Bacon allowed for the first when he remarked that "the experiments of witchcraft are no clear proofs [i.e., of the power of the imagination on other bodies]; for that they may be by a tacit operation of malign spirits."[15] Once again we are faced with the artificiality of bringing the modern notion that there is a difference of kind between the "scientific" and the "occult" to the investigation of what were simply differences of degree between varying conceptions of nature.

That the literature of demonology had any meaning at all in this wider context has been obscured by two misapprehensions about the inten-

tions of its authors. Because the sensational aspects of witchcraft belief
– the demonic pact, the sabbat, the reality of *maleficium*, and so on
– have caught the modern attention, this has suggested, first of all, that
the original texts concentrated narrowly and moralistically on the description of these particular crimes and the appropriate judicial and
penal response. Of course, these topics were important, and some –
notably the alleged transvection of witches to sabbats and their transmutation into animals – raised just those issues that demanded serious
epistemological consideration. But the intention was to examine any
phenomenon of sufficiently dubious credentials to warrant the suspicion that it was demonically caused. This led demonolgists way beyond
the range of topics and attitudes that have been traditionally associated
with witchcraft beliefs. Martin Del Rio defined *magia* as "an art or
technique which by using the power in creation rather than a supernatural power produces various things of a marvellous and unusual
kind, the reason for which escapes the senses and ordinary comprehension." Within literally a few pages we find him tackling the validity
of whole sciences such as natural magic, astrology, mathematics, and
alchemy, as well as such questions as whether there is any physical
efficacy in the innate qualities of magical practitioners, or in the imagination, or in the use of ritual touching, looking, speaking, breathing,
and kissing, and whether characters, sigils, arithmetical and musical
notation, words, charms, and amulets have any intrinsic powers.[16]

What is striking in his *Disquisitionum magicarum* and in other demonologies of similar scale, such as Francisco Torreblanca's *Daemonologia* and Giovanni Gastaldi's *De potestate angelica*, is the enormous variety of the subjects examined for their standing in reality and
knowledge as well as in morals. At the end of his second volume Gastaldi, having already considered natural and other forms of magic, the
traditional topics of witchcraft theory, the arts and prodigies of Antichrist, the healing power of the kings of France, the question of bodily
transmutation, and the power of demons over magicians, sorcerers,
and evil doers, adds a "Disputatio unica" in which he asks of particular
wonders whether they are "natural" or "superstitious." These include
the movements of the tides, the possibility of speaking statues, the
effects of words and music on animal behavior, the power of fascination, the extraction of solid objects from the human body, and the
proper cure for tarantism. Even modest monographs tried to cover the
same borderland between the naturally marvelous and the magically
specious. Thus, if we turn from Pierre de Lancre's best-known work
on the witch trials in Labourd, the *Tableau de l'inconstance des mauvais anges et demons*, to one of his other demonological writings, *L'Incredulité et mescreance du sortilege plainement convaincue*, we find
another typical range of topics: the reality of sorcery, fascination,

whether touching itself can harm or heal, divination, and how to distinguish between good and evil apparitions.[17]

The repetition of this pattern in many other texts rules out the view that it was random or haphazard; yet witchcraft itself was clearly not the only point of departure. Conversely, such topics and many of the same strategies of argument occur in accounts of curious natural and human behaviors that are not ostensibly demonological at all; for instance, in André du Laurens's treatise on the royal touch, where the idea that this form of ritual healing might be demonic has to be overcome,[18] or in more general surveys of the marvelous such as Claude Rapine (Caelestinus), *De his quae mundo mirabiliter eveniunt*; Scipion Dupleix, *La Curiosité naturelle*; and Gaspar Schott, *Physica curiosa*.[19] Demonology was not, then, anchored only to the question of witchcraft and witch trials. It meshed with other discussions with which it shared common intentions, whether or not its conclusions were the same. This enables us to see more easily how demonology could have been a genuine vehicle for what may be called a scientific debate – a debate concerning the exact status of a variety of extremely questionable phenomena. Indeed, it was this guiding issue that, despite the apparently disparate choice of themes, gave demonology real unity of purpose.

The second misapprehension has more seriously affected our understanding of the intentions behind this literature because it has prevented us from seeing the literature as a contribution to a debate at all, or at least to one of any complexity. This is the idea stemming from such early commentators as G. L. Burr and H. C. Lea, that (again on the issue of the reality of witchcraft) demonology could be divided into *either* belief *or* scepticism, with the assumption that belief was a cut-and-dried affair committing a writer to accepting the whole structure of what was alleged.[20] In fact, what is striking is how few examples there are at each end of the spectrum ranging from total acceptance of all demonic claims – where we find only Bodin and perhaps Rémy (in some passages from his *Daemonolatreiae*) – to total rejection – where we find only Reginald Scot and his English followers. This leaves a vast middle ground occupied by hundreds of texts where genuine attempts are made to discriminate between what is to be accepted and what rejected, where authors are familiar with a number of sceptical positions,[21] and where scepticism as well as belief is evident in their own views as demonologists. Repeatedly we are warned that the subject is controversial and obscure and that, faced with the question of the reality of demonic magic, no rational man would insist that it was all illusory or all true. This is the position adopted by Del Rio, Philipp Ludwig Elich, Francesco Maria Guazzo, Benito Pereira, James VI and I, John Cotta, Noël Taillepied (in the allied field of apparitions), and many others.[22] The example of Henri Boguet's *Discours des sorciers*, often singled out as an especially dogmatic work, shows just how carefully witchcraft confessions might be tested against assumptions about real and spurious causal efficacy. What governed his attitude was not any blanket credulity, but, as Lucien Febvre recognized, the application of standards of what was both possible *and impossible* for human and demonic agents to effect.[23]

Demonologists did not simply pile up the positive evidence for the guilt of demonic witchcraft. They tried to separate phenomena correctly attributed to demonic agency from phenomena incorrectly so attributed, and to both they applied a second set of criteria dealing with truth and illusion. They therefore had at their disposal four categories of explanation, or four explanatory languages, dealing, respectively, with real demonic effects, illusory demonic effects, real nondemonic effects, and illusory nondemonic effects. And they were well aware, without this compromising their general acceptance of demonic agency, of the category errors that could occur when (say) confessions contained nonetheless impossible feats, when the illusions of the devil were mistaken for reality, when unfamiliar but quite undemonic natural contingencies or startling technological achievements were blamed by the uninformed on demonism, or (above all) when hallucinatory experiences stemming from ordinary diseases or narcotic substances were attributed to witchcraft. This is clear, for instance, in Pierre Le Loyer's *Quatres Livres des spectres ou apparitions*, where in the context of a defense of the reality of demonism against the arguments of "naturalists," a variety of almost Pyrrhonist objections are marshaled against accepting either the evidence of the senses or the promptings of reason in cases of apparently aberrant phenomena.[24] Likewise, François Perrault's *Demonologie*, after typical emphasis on the dangers of both outright scepticism *and* outright credulity, consigns reputedly demonic effects such as *ignis fatuum* and *ephialtes* to the category of the purely natural.[25] We shall find the same features in discussions of natural magical instances in demonological contexts. The fact that a range of explanations was open to the great majority of writers enabled them to probe the conceptual puzzles of their subject matter to an extent that would have been impossible if, as is often assumed, their options had been limited to supporting or criticizing witchcraft trials.

This can be illustrated in more detail if we take the central topic of demonic power and consider the implications of the ways its effects could be explained. For despite their anxiety to warn readers of the threat of demonism and witchcraft in the world – and this is, of course, the tonality that we have tended to recognize most readily – demonologists were also, without exception, committed to exposing the limitations, weaknesses, and deceptions of the devil. In both a theologically and evangelically critical sense they were attempting to demystify and deflate demonic pretensions: theological, because of the paramount need (in the age of Reformation claims and counterclaims) to distinguish between the genuinely and the quasi miraculous; evangelical, because of an audience thought to be prone to believe anything about demonism and to overreact with "superstitious" countermeasures. It was always granted that demons had not lost their physical powers after their fall from grace and that their cumulative experience since the Creation, their subtle, airy, and refined quality, and their capacity for enormous speed, strength, and agility enabled them to achieve real effects beyond human ability. Nevertheless, it was also invariably insisted that such effects were within the boundaries of secondary or natural causation. They were either forms of local motion or alterations wrought by the application of actives on passives, even if both types of operation were (say) enormously accelerated. Explanations of this are found everywhere in demonology; here they are summarized by John Cotta:

> Though the divel indeed, as a Spirit, may do, and doth many
> things above and beyond the course of some particular na-
> tures: yet doth hee not, nor is able to rule or commaund
> over generall Nature, or infringe or alter her inviolable de-
> crees in the perpetuall and never-interrupted order of all
> generations; neither is he generally Master of universall Na-
> ture, but Nature Master and Commaunder of him. For Na-
> ture is nothing els but the ordinary power of God in al things
> created, among which the Divell being a creature, is con-
> tained, and therefore subject to that universall power.[26]

Satan might, of course, interfere with the initial specific conditions of natural events, but he could not dispense with the general laws governing their occurrence.[27]

This situation was not changed, only complicated, by the fact that where his power to produce real effects gave out, his ingenuity in camouflaging weaknesses by illusory phenomena took over. He could corrupt sensory perception, charm the internal faculties with "ecstasies" or "frenzies," use his extraordinary powers over local motion to displace one object with another so quickly that transmutation appeared to occur, present illusory objects to the senses by influencing the air or wrapping fantastic shapes around real bodies, and, finally, delude all the third parties involved so that no testimony damaging to his reputation as an agent was available. The devil was, therefore, severely limited in what he could really effect (for, as Boguet pointed out, even his delusions were species of natural action), but there was nothing that he might not *appear* to effect.[28] Demonologists consequently went to considerable lengths to expose such *glaucomata* or "lying wonders" in order to reveal the ontological and epistemological as well as the moral duplicity involved. The debate focused on the most spectacular claims – that witches could attend sabbats in noncorporeal form, that demonic sexuality could result in generation, and, above all, that humans could be changed into animals – for in these cases a manifest demonic incompetence to create the real effects that were claimed without breaking natural laws led to complicated strategies of deception on his part, none more involved than the last. Discussions of the possibility of lycanthropy in fact contain some of the most interesting examples of demonologists trying, in what I have suggested was a scientific way, to explain a particularly refractory set of claims.

In Jean de Nynauld's *De la Lycanthropy*, for example, we find the gamut of explanatory languages. He writes to disabuse the ignorant on a subject that surmounts the expectations of the senses but that nevertheless has its causes. Bound by the "divinely instituted course of nature," the devil cannot create fresh forms or change the essential character of existing forms. He can therefore only simulate transmutation of witches into wolves by troubling their imaginations, taking advantage of physiologically induced dream experiences, adding demonic efficacy to the ordinary strength of hallucinogenic unguents, and superimposing the required shapes and properties on their bodies in order to deceive any spectators. Thus while real transmutation cannot occur either nondemonically or demonically, there are real effects resulting from natural conditions and substances that lead to all the required sensory experiences, and that, because they are natural, the devil can manipulate. It might seem tempting to recruit Nynauld as a "sceptic." Yet he does not doubt the existence of witches or their use of potions made from slain infants. What he does is analyze all such phenomena on naturalistic lines in order to reveal the causal relationships between the chemical composition of the narcotic elements in such potions, the sensation of being "transmuted," and the psychosomatic effects of folly and credulity. Similarly, he argues that while no unguent can physically effect transvection to sabbats, this is not always an illusion either, since the devil can achieve it by means of local motion. None of this sets Nynauld apart from a supposed "believer" like Boguet, who accounted in exactly the same terms for the phenomena mistakenly thought to result from real lycanthropy and attendance at the sabbat in spirit only.[29]

This is only the briefest summary of a debate that appears in virtually every text. Although some of its features have attracted attention before, its implications for the scientific status of demonology have, I think, been neglected.[30] At the very least, we cannot go on ascribing to the category of the "supernatural" discussions whose purpose was to establish precisely what was supernatural and what was not. Demonism was said to be part of the realm of the natural, for it lacked just those powers to overrule the laws of nature that constituted truly miraculous agency. It must be stressed, therefore, that demonic intervention did not turn natural into supernatural causation. It is the case that its effects were sometimes labeled "nonnatural" or declared to be not attributable to natural causes. But in context this rarely meant more than either their going beyond what might normally have been expected from the ordinary "flow" of causes and effects, or their unfamiliarity or impossibility in relation to the nature known to and practiced upon by men or (less often) their reflection of the devil's desire to break the restraints he was under.[31] The distinguishing criterion of demonic, and indeed all forms of magic, was not that it was supernatural but that it was *unusual*. Even Nicolas Rémy's contradictory statements might be reconciled along these lines. While appearing to follow Bodin in his view that demonism was irreconcilable with any standard of what was natural, he nevertheless qualified this with several comparisons with what were merely the normal limitations and processes.[32] The danger in this situation of preempting meanings by thinking of the "supernatural" only in its modern sense is well shown by the case of John Cotta, who, after using the term several times in his *The Triall of Witch-Craft*, explained that

> although . . . the Divell as a Spirit doth many things, which in respect of our nature are supernaturall, yet in respect of the power of Nature in universall, they are but naturall unto himselfe and other Spirits, who also are a kinde of creature contained within the generall nature of things created: Opposite therefore, contrary, against or above the generall power of Nature, hee can do nothing.

Cotta's tract is of particular importance in this context because it is dominated by his awareness of the epistemological issue of how one could speak of acquiring "naturall knowledge" – by sense experience, reasoning, or conjecture – of such difficult and inaccessible phenomena. Yet William Perkins had also argued that demonic effects only seemed wonderful because they transcended both the "ordinarie bounds and precincts of nature" and the capacities of men, "especially such as are ignorant of Satans habilitie, and the hidden causes in nature, whereby things are brought to passe."[33]

Others reflected this relativism in preferring to use such terms as "quasi-natural"[34] or "hyperphysical."[35] And Del Rio captured it exactly when he proposed the category of the "preternatural" to describe prodigious effects that seemed miraculous only because they were "natural" in a wider than familiar sense.[36] But whatever terms were used, demonic effects were in principle part of natural processes, and in this sense demonology was from the outset a natural science: that is, a study of a natural order in which demonic actions and effects were presupposed. In fact, despite its reputation for intellectual confusion, demonology derived considerable coherence from a notion that there were limits to nature. As Perkins explained: "What strange workes and wonders may be truely effected by the power of nature, (though they be not ordinarily brought to passe in the course of nature) those the devill can do, and so farre forth as the power of nature will permit, he is able to worke true wonders."[37] This was also, necessarily, the standard in terms of which aspects of witchcraft beliefs could be rejected as illusory. The unity of Boguet's treatise and of his views about the inadmissibility of many demonic phenomena was a function of precisely this criterion. And the same intention in James VI and I's *Daemonologie* to link an account of what was possible in magic, sorcery, and witchcraft with the question "by what naturall causes they may be" drew a special commendation from Bacon.[38] The general application of this principle did not mean that demonologists always ended up locating the boundaries of nature in the same place. It was the fact that there was such uncertainty on this issue at the end of the sixteenth century that made demonology both a debate within itself and a contribution to a wider controversy among philosophers, theologians, and scientists. What is significant is the very adoption of the criterion itself. Beyond nature lay only miracles, which no one claimed devils could perform. The question we have to ask, therefore, is not the one prompted by rationalism (Why were intelligent men able to accept so much that was supernatural?), but simply the one prompted by the history of science (What concept of nature did they share?). And as Kuhn and others have shown, this is not something that can be settled in advance.

For these reasons P. H. Kocher was surely mistaken when he suggested that bringing Satan into nature was a prelude to exiling him from scientific inquiry altogether, and that in the English context it was in effect the first step toward the penetration of demonology by that rationalism which produced the radical scepticism of Reginald Scot. This was to prejudge just what was meant by "scientific" in sixteenth-century science. The reason why so many physicians, including Nynauld and, for that matter, a "sceptic" like Johann Wier himself, felt no incongruity in examining the demonic as well as the ordinary causes of lycanthropy and other aspects of witchcraft was because they were *both* natural forms of causation. Guazzo cited Codronchi, Cesalpino, Valesius, and Fernel in support of the view that a sickness could be both natural and instigated by the devil; to this list might be added Jean Taxil, Jourdain Guibelet, and Giano Matteo Durastante. In these circumstances any choice between one explanation and the other was a matter of emphasis, not of principle.[39]

Demonic effects were not, then, qualitatively different from natural effects, but their causation was obscure and hidden from men. They were, in a word, occult, and this alerts us to another important aspect of the relationship between demonology and science. This is the exactly analogous epistemological stance taken up by demonologists and natural magicians. It has been assumed that the subject of natural magic entered demonological discussions in only two guises. It could be totally assimilated to demonism and then cited in order to further blacken the moral reputation of all forms of magic. Here the literature of witchcraft simply added a further layer of denunciations to a very old tradition of Christian hostility to the magical arts.[40] More significantly, it existed as a threatening source of potentially corrosive scepticism because it could explain mysterious natural effects in a way that usurped the accounts given by demonologists. The suggestion is that, like the other sciences of the "occult" tradition, natural magic had greater explanatory power than Aristotelian natural philosophy in this area.[41] There is, of course, evidence for both these stances, but they were not the only ones, and they may not have been the most typical.[42] In the light of what has been said about the naturalism inherent in quite orthodox demonology, the distinction involved in the second may turn out to be rather overdrawn, at least before 1677 when John Webster made it the foundation of his *The Displaying of Supposed Witchcraft*. Most writers wished to downgrade demonic effects by insisting on their ultimately natural (or more strictly, preternatural) character, while at the same time recognizing their occult appearance to the layman. This suggests a much more positive role for the idea of natural magic in their arguments, one which, far from undermining their belief in demonism, actually enabled them to sustain it.

This is, in fact, just what we find. Natural and demonic magic were at opposite ends of the moral spectrum, but they were epistemologically indistinguishable. The devil was therefore portrayed as a supremely gifted natural magician, the ultimate natural scientist. Paolo Grillandi said that he knew "more of natural things and the secrets of nature than all the men in the world put together," including those of "the elements, metals, stones, herbs, plants, reptiles, birds, fish and the movements of the heavens." King James agreed that he was "farre cunningner [sic] then man in the knowledge of all the occult proprieties of nature." In Rémy's view, demons had "a perfect knowledge of the secret and hidden properties of natural things." To Perkins, the devil had "great understanding, knowledge, and capacitie in all naturall things, of what sort, qualitie, and condition soever, whether they be causes or effects, whether of a simple or mixt nature."[43] Such characterizations suggest that even the merely commonplace dismissal of natural magic as satanic was more than a chapter in the history of a reputation. When Benito Pereira explained that it was actually learned from incredibly well-informed demons, this tells us as much about assumptions concerning what devils could know as about any suspicion of the "occult."[44] Moreover, the repeatedly expressed idea that the devil was the most expert natural philosopher put the demonologist in much the same intellectual predicament as the natural magician, or indeed the Aristotelian, when he discussed occult (as opposed to manifest) qualities: that of coming to terms with effects which could be experienced but whose causes might be unknowable. A remark of Perkins puts the epistemological challenge posed by the devil rather effectively:

> Whereas in nature there be some properties, causes, and effects, which man never imagined to be; others, that men did once know, but are now forgot; some which men knewe not, but might know; and thousands which can hardly, or not at all be known: all these are most familiar unto him, because in themselvs they be no wonders, but only misteries and secrets, the vertue and effect whereof he hath sometime observed since his creation.[45]

In these circumstances the fact that demonologists often used the possibility of a natural magic to buttress some of their own central arguments becomes much less surprising than it seems at first. To begin with, there were occasions when writers who in no way doubted the general reality of witchcraft phenomena cited instances from natural magic to suggest that, nevertheless, there were many occult effects in nature which were wrongly confused with demonism simply because their causes were unknown or uncertain. We can see an example in the *De sagarum natura et potestate* of Wilhelm Schreiber (Scribonius), famous for his defense of the water ordeal in witch trials. Schreiber expressed plenty of the ordinary alarmism about witches and their guilt, but he took up a typical position between ascribing too little and too much to them, extremes which (he said) only a proper knowledge of natural philosophy could avoid. By this he meant knowledge both of the ability of unaided nature to generate its own marvels (here he used the play imagery – *lusus naturae* – common in the prodigy literature and in Bacon), and of the capacity of a mimetic and licit natural magic to repeat such marvels artificially. The latter he described traditionally as the most perfect philosophy in its knowledge of the mysteries and secrets of nature and as practiced by the Persian and Egyptian magi and by Moses, Solomon, and Daniel.[46]

A second case arose when demonologists, accepting without question that demonism and witchcraft had *some* sort of efficacy, wished to expose the claim that it lay in the actual means used, where this was (say) a ritual incantation or conjuration or some spurious physical means. This could be done by citing the natural but hidden causal links involved, recognizable only in terms of a knowledge of naturally magical effects. An example here would be De Lancre's attempt to discredit the idea that touching itself had an inherent efficacy. He argued that apparently supportive instances drawn from the unusual behavior of animals, plants, or metals – the torpedo fish, the *echeneis* or remora – or from natural magnetism could be explained in terms of various secret but perfectly natural properties and "antipathies." There were some such effects of which the causes were so hidden that they would never be known, and here men ought to be content with doubt and not strive, in the manner of "naturalists," for explanations at any risk to plausibility. But in other cases the reader might be referred to the works of the natural magicians, to Levinus Lemnius for the bleeding of corpses in the presence of the murderer, and to Jerome Fracastor for the *echeneis*.[47]

Third and most commonly, demonologists cited the science of the occult characteristics of natural things when they wished to reduce the status of demonic operations from the apparently miraculous to the merely wonderful. And this was in fact the context for Peter Binsfeld's remark that magic was just an esoteric form of physics. Because ordinary men were unaware of all nature's secrets, they attributed to the realm of the miraculous demonic effects that originated in natural powers, however elevated. And to this same distinction between popular superstition and learned science could be traced the reputation of natural magic, which appeared equally strange but was really only "a certain hidden and more secret part of Natural Philosophy teaching how to effect things worthy of the highest admiration . . . by the mutual application of natural actives and passives." Examining marvels from this source, such as the salamander, the volcano, and the magnet, would, Binsfeld thought, put the devil's works into proper focus.[48]

Fourth and finally, any remaining strangeness in the character of real demonic effects could be dissipated by the suggestion that they were in fact no more difficult to accept than the parallel claims made by natural magicians for what Boguet called "Nature . . . assisted and helped forward by Art." The speed to which demons accelerated ordinary processes like generation by corruption might (he admitted) invite scepticism. But if alchemists were to be believed, they too could "by a turn of the hand create gold, although in the process of Nature this takes a thousand years." Nor was there any reason to doubt that Satan could make a man appear like a wolf, for "naturalists" such as Albertus Magnus, Cardan, and Della Porta had shown how it was possible to effect similar "prestigitations." Somewhat similarly, Sébastien Michaelis compared demonic effects with the marvels described by Mercurius Trismegistus in his *Asclepius* to show that "there are many effects . . . against and above" the ordinary causation of things. For Rémy the yardstick offered by natural magic was what it revealed of nature itself rather than of art. When he came to consider the question of the reality of the objects supposedly ejected from the bodies of demoniacs, he cited the natural explanations for this being a true phenomenon given by Lemnius and Ambrose Paré (in his *Des Monstres et prodiges*), with the following comment: "If then Nature, without transgressing the limits which she has imposed upon herself can by her own working either generate or admit such objects, what must we think that the Demons will do."[49]

Naturally these arguments were often blended together. Elements of the second and third can be found in Lambert Daneau's dialogue, *De veneficis*, where the apparent (but spurious) efficacy of the forms of words and symbols used in witchcraft is explained away in terms of the natural means (like poisons) interpolated by demons. These are often very strange but never miraculous; instead, they are comparable with technical achievements like the flying wooden dove of Archytas. This reference to one of the classic marvels of the magical tradition (it is also discussed by Agrippa, Campanella, Dee, and Fludd) would not have been lost on Daneau's readers.[50] The idea of natural magic did not therefore always weaken demonology by implying some challenge to theories of demonic agency; on the contrary, it could provide important strengthening points of reference whenever there was a need to contrast or equate this agency with something comparably natural yet occult. Many repeated the standard indictment that the historical natural magic of the Persians and Egyptians had degenerated in time and was now indistinguishable from diabolism. Some, like Pereira and De Lancre, cautioned about the publication of natural magical works on the grounds that free access to such secrets was dangerous. But there was a sense in which the sort of scientific inquiry represented by them – that is, the concept itself of natural magic – remained an intrinsic part of their theories of knowledge. Given the frequency with which it is dealt with in the texts, it may even have been a necessary part of the intellectual structure of demonology.[51] From one direction this may still seem to constitute the debasement of what was undoubtedly a form of science by its association with satanism. The point to be reemphasized is that, considered from a different direction, it illustrates how closely demonological and scientific interests in certain interpretive issues can be identified with each other. Nor must it be forgotten that, conversely, natural magicians were led to a consideration of demonism by the questions raised in their discipline. Della Porta's examination of the powers of the witches' unguent, though excluded from later editions of his *Magiae naturalis*, was widely cited. Georg Pictor's *De illorum daemonum qui sub lunari collimitio versantur* was thought to be sufficiently cognate with the supposititious works of Agrippa for them to be published together in translation in England in 1665. Even Lemnius, who was reputed then and has been since as an outright "sceptic," did not exclude demons from the physical world. In his *De miraculis occultis naturae* they appear among the "accidents" of diseases, insinuating themselves "closely into men's bodies" and mingling with "food, humours, spirits, with the ayre and breath" as well as with violent and destructive tempests. They do not, of course, bulk large in Lemnius's natural philosophy; but neither are they ignored.[52]

This leads on to a final reflection on the entire range of attitudes to demonic magic and witchcraft phenomena in the Renaissance and Reformation period. By establishing that it was (in part) an epistemological debate – a debate about the grounds for ordered knowledge of nature and natural causation – which occupied the middle ground in demonology, we should be in a better position to interpret the views at the extremes. We can see, for instance, why Reginald Scot's radical scepticism stemmed not, as is sometimes suggested, from his espousal of the principles of natural magic, or in particular from the idea that, since miracles had ceased and all created things were left with only their natural capacities, all causation must also be natural. For this only begged the more fundamental question of what *counted* as a natural capacity; and since demonologists themselves endowed devils with such capacities, this was not a sceptical stance that posed any threat.[53] Scot's most telling argument was his reduction (in an Appendix to his *Discoverie of Witchcraft* of 1584) of all demonic agents to a noncorporeal condition, thus removing them from physical nature altogether. When demonologists attacked "naturalism," it was this step which they often had in mind – that is, not merely the commitment to a naturally caused world, but the denial of a devil capable of using such causation for evil ends. It was the fact that the principle of demonic agency's naturalness was not *itself* in doubt which, in other cases of supposedly damaging objections, enabled them to turn sceptical arguments to their own use. At the other extreme we can see that Bodin's reluctance to doubt anything in this area resulted from his view that it was impious to place any advance limits on what was possible in nature. To apply the language of physical events to metaphysical operations was a fundamental category error. Since aspects of magic and witchcraft belonged to this metaphysical reality, there was no criterion for accepting or rejecting them, other than trust. This obliterated the distinction that enabled most other demonologists to make sense of the world. But their case was the case of natural science as a whole. As Jean de Nynauld remarked, Bodin's position made all learning impossible, for "all the means for separating the false from the true would be taken away" if it was admitted that tomorrow the world might (with God's permission) be qualitatively different.[54]

Such issues were not, of course, discussed only at the time of the European "witch craze". Demonologists owed the foundations of their arguments to accounts of broadly the same range of phenomena given by Augustine and Aquinas. The question of what significance was to be given to the marvelous in nature had a very long history indeed. What may be suggested is that the need to reconsider the validity of these phenomena and of the criteria for understanding them was felt especially keenly in the sixteenth and seventeenth centuries, after which consensus was again established. No doubt the witchcraft trials themselves contributed to this. More importantly, the urgency stemmed from the unprecedented intensity of theological controversies concerned with the status and prevalence of miracles, the exact properties of religious objects and forms of words, the possibility of divination in a divinely ordained world, the apocalyptic meaning of prodigies, and so on. It may also be related to the fresh impetus given by disputes about the fundamentals of scientific and philosophical thought to the consideration of problems of epistemology – problems that came to be pursued with special vigor in the various parallel areas of the extraordinary in nature and art. The fact that they were also dealt with in discussions of incubus and succubus devils, flights to the sabbat, and werewolves should not deter us from accepting these, too, as contributions to scientific discourse.

Notes

1 E. E. Evans-Pritchard, *Theories of Primitive Religion* (Oxford, 1965), pp. 109–10.

2 Peter Binsfeld, *Tractatus de confessionibus maleficorum et sagarum*, 2nd ed. (Trier, 1591), pp. 174–6. In this argument Binsfeld follows Francisco Victoria, *Relectiones theologicae* (Lyons, 1587), relectio XII, "De arte magica," pp. 452–3.

3 Martin Biermann (propos.), *De magicis actionibus exetasis succincta* (Helmstädt, 1590), theorem I; cf. theorems XIII and LXXII, sigs. A3^{r-v}, D2^r.

4 Further details of medical interest in demonology, in the context of a supposed "slow progress to an enlightened attitude," are given by Oskar Diethelm, "The Medical Teaching of Demonology in the 17th and 18th Centuries," *Journal of the History of the Behavioural Sciences*, 6 (1970), pp. 3–15.

5 Sydney Anglo, "Melancholia and Witchcraft: The Debate between Wier, Bodin and Scot," and, emphasizing medical viewpoints, Jean Céard, "Folie et démonologie au XVIe siècle," both in *Folie et déraison à la Renaissance*, ed. A. Gerlo (Brussels, 1976), pp. 209–22, 129–43. Evidence of a general affinity of attitudes and methods between demonology and the "new

science" is offered by Irving Kirsch, "Demonology and Science During the Scientific Revolution," *Journal of the History of the Behavioural Sciences*, 16 (1980), pp. 359–68. The same author's "Demonology and the Rise of Science: An Example of the Misperception of Historical Data," *Journal of the History of the Behavioural Sciences*, 14 (1978), pp. 149–57, merely points to coincidences in the timing of new interests in both fields.

6 D. P. Walker, *Unclean Spirits: Possession and Exorcism in France and England in the Late Sixteenth and Early Seventeenth Centuries* (London, 1981), p. 13 and passim; he calls this "an aspect of early modern science that has not yet . . . been investigated." H. C. Erik Midelfort, "Sin, Folly, Madness, Obsession: The Social Distribution of Insanity in Sixteenth-Century Germany," in *Understanding Popular Culture: Europe from the Middle Ages to the Nineteenth Century*, ed. Steven L. Kaplan (forthcoming).

7 Moody E. Prior, "Joseph Glanvill, Witchcraft, and Seventeenth-Century Science," *Modern Philology*, 30 (1930), pp. 167–93; T. H. Jobe, "The Devil in Restoration Science: The Glanvill–Webster Witchcraft Debate," *Isis*, 72 (1981), pp. 343–56.

8 George Sinclair, *Satan's Invisible World Discovered* (Edinburgh, 1685), p. xv.

9 Joseph Glanvill, *Sadducismus triumphatus*, 4th ed. (London, 1726), p. 8.

10 Hence the somewhat artificial linking of the debates of the witch hunt with the classic "revolution" in science in Brian Easlea, *Witch-Hunting, Magic and the New Philosophy: An Introduction to Debates of the Scientific Revolution 1450–1750* (Brighton, 1980), pp. 1–44 and passim.

11 Katharine Park and Lorraine J. Daston, "Unnatural Conceptions: The Study of Monsters in Sixteenth- and Seventeenth-Century France and England," *Past and Present*, no. 92 (1981), pp. 20–54.

12 Jean Céard, *La Nature et les prodiges: l'insolite au XVIᵉ siècle, en France* (Geneva, 1977), passim, esp. pp. 352–64; cf. Lynn Thorndike, *A History of Magic and Experimental Science*, 8 vols. (New York, 1934–58), which, despite its astonishing range, is decidedly unsympathetic to the literature of witchcraft. For Thorndike's distaste for the subject, see V, 69–70; and for a characteristic judgment on a respectable Aristotelian whose demonology involves a "deluded mixture of theology and gross superstition," see his remarks on Cesalpino's *Daemonum investigatio peripatetica* (Florence, 1580), in VI, 325–8.

13 Francis Bacon, *De augmentis scientiarum*, bk. II, chap. 2, in *The Works of Francis Bacon*, ed. J. Spedding, R. L. Ellis, and D. D. Heath, 14 vols. (London, 1857–74), IV, 296; cited hereafter as *Works*. Cf. *Novum organum*, bk. II, aphorisms 28–9, in *Works*, IV, 168–9; *The Advancement of Learning*, bk. II, in *Works*, III, 330–2; *Parasceve ad historiam naturalem et experimentalem*, aphorisms 1–4, in *Works*, IV, 253–7 (all references are to the English trans.). Thomas Sprat, *The History of the Royal Society of London*, 3rd ed. (London, 1722), pp. 214–15, defends the study of "the most unusual and monstrous Forces and Motions of Matter," without mentioning witchcraft. For Boyle and Glanvill on witchcraft and marvels, see Prior, pp. 183–4.

14 Francis Bacon, *Sylva sylvarum: or a Natural History in Ten Centuries*, century X, no. 903; cf. no. 975; in *Works*, II, 642, 664.

15 Ibid., century X, no. 950, in *Works*, II, 658. For an "experiment solitary touching maleficiating," see century IX, no. 888, in *Works*, II, 634.

16 Martin Del Rio, *Disquisitionum magicarum* (Lyons, 1608), bk. I, chaps. 2–5.

17 Giovanni Tommaso Gastaldi, *De potestate angelica sive de potentia motrice, ac mirandis operibus angelorum atque daemonum*, 3 vols. (Rome, 1650–2); cf. Francesco Torreblanca (Villalpandus), *Daemonologia sive de magia naturali, daemoniaca, licita, et illicita, deque aperta et occulta, interventione et invocatione daemonis* (Mainz, 1623), bk. II, pp. 176–403; Pierre de Lancre, *L'Incredulité et mescreance du sortilege plainement convaincue* (Paris, 1622).

18 André du Laurens, *De mirabili strumas sanandi vi solis Galliae Regibus Christianissimus divinitus concessa* (Paris, 1609), chap. 9.

19 I have used the French trans.: Claude Rapine (Caelestinus), *Des Choses merveilleuses en la nature où est traicté des erreurs des sens, des puissances de l'âme, et des influences des cieux*, trans. Jacques Giraud (Lyons, 1557), chap. 8, pp. 113–30 ("On the Operation of Evil Spirits"); Scipion Dupleix, *La Curiosité naturelle rédigée en questions selon l'ordre alphabétique* (Rouen, 1635), pp. 393–4; Gaspar Schott, *Physica curiosa, sive mirabilia naturae et artis* (Würzburg, 1667), bk. I, pp. 1–195. Schott also deals with ghosts, miraculous races, demoniacs, monsters, portents, animal marvels, and meteors.

20 G. L. Burr, "The Literature of Witchcraft," in *George Lincoln Burr*, ed. R. H. Bainton and L. O. Gibbons (New York, 1943), pp. 166–89; H. C. Lea, *Materials Toward a History of Witchcraft*, ed. A. C. Howland, 3 vols. (Philadelphia, 1939; New York, 1957).

21 For a striking example of the presentation of sceptical arguments in a discussion nonetheless committed to the reality of demonism, see Loys le Caron (Charondas), *Questions divers et discours* (Paris, 1579), quest. VIII, ("Si par incantations, parolles ou autres semblables sortileges l'homme peult estre ensorcelé et offensé en ses actions et forces naturelles"), fols. 31ᵛ–43ᵛ; cf. the same author's *Responses du droict français* (Paris, 1579–82), bk. IX, response 43 ("Si les sorciers et sorcières sont dignes de dernier supplice"), pp. 445–50. For the flexibility and variety in theories of witchcraft, see H. C. Erik Midelfort, *Witch Hunting in Southwestern Germany, 1562–1684: The Social and Intellectual Foundations* (Stanford, 1972), pp. 10–29.

22 Del Rio, bk. II, quaest. 6, p. 61; Philipp Ludwig Elich, *Daemonomagia* (Frankfurt, 1607), chap. 5, pp. 60–1; Francesco Maria Guazzo, *Compendium maleficarum*, trans. and ed. Montague Summers (London, 1929), bk. I, chap. 3, p. 7; Benito Pereira, *De magia, de observatione somniorum, et de divinatione astrologia* (Cologne, 1598), bk. I, chap. 1, pp. 4–5; James VI and I, *Daemonologie, in the Forme of a Dialogue* (Edinburgh, 1597), p. 42; John Cotta, *The Triall of Witch-Craft* (London, 1616), dedicatory epistle, sigs. A2–A3ᵛ; Noël Taillepied, *Traité de l'apparition des esprits* (Rouen, 1600), trans. and ed. Montague Summers as *A Treatise of Ghosts* (London, 1933), pp. xvi–xvii, 39–40.

23 Lucien Febvre, "Sorcellerie: sottise ou révolution mentale?" *Annales E.S.C.*, 3 (1948); trans. K. Folca as "Witchcraft: Nonsense or a Mental Revolution?" in *A New Kind of History from the Writings of Febvre*, ed. Peter Burke (London, 1973), pp. 185–92.

24 Pierre Le Loyer, *IIII Livres des spectres, ou apparitions et visions d'esprits, anges et Démons se monstrans sensiblement aux hommes* (Angers, 1586), partly trans. Z. Jones as *A Treatise of Specters or Straunge*

Sights, Visions and Apparitions Appearing Sensibly Unto Men (London, 1605).

25 François Perrault, *Demonologie ou discours en general touchant l'existence puissance impuissance des demons et sorciers* (Geneva, 1656), chaps. 1–3, pp. 1–52.

26 Cotta, chap. 6, p. 34.

27 For standard accounts of demonic power and knowledge and their limitations, see Silvestro da Prierio (Mazzolini), *De strigimagarum daemonumque mirandis* (Rome, 1575), bk. I, chaps. 13–15, pp. 95–126; Otto Casmann, *Angelographia* (Frankfurt, 1597), pt. 2 ("De malis angelis"), chaps. 12–14, 18–20, pp. 428–57, 508–82; Johann Wier, *De praestigiis daemonum et incantationibus ac veneficiis* (Basel, 1568), bk. 1, chaps. 10–18; Torreblanca, bk. II, chaps. 5–10, pp. 191–220; Guazzo, bk. I, chaps. 3–4, 16, pp. 7–11, 57; Gervasio Pizzurini, *Enchiridion exorcisticum* (Lyons, 1668), praeludium, chap. 6, pp. 14–16. For a typical analysis of the devil's powers over local motion, see Leonardo Vairo, *De fascino* (Paris, 1583), bk. II, chap. 13. For a discussion of his interference in the conditions of natural combustion, see Adam Tanner, *De potentia loco motiva angelorum*, quaest. 6, in *Diversi tractatus* ed. Constantine Munich (Cologne, 1629), pp. 90–1.

28 Descriptions of the range of illusion techniques are again in most standard demonologies; e.g., Guazzo, bk. I, chap. 4, p. 9. But see full accounts in Anthoine de Morry, *Discours d'un miracle avenu en la Basse Normandie* (Paris, 1598), pp. 39–56; Andrea Gerhard (Hyperius), "Whether That the Devils Have Bene the Shewers of Magicall Artes," in *Two Commonplaces Taken Out of Andreas Hyperius*, trans. R. V. (London, 1581), pp. 47–81; and André Valladier, "Des Charmes et sortileges, ligatures, philtres d'amour, ecstases diaboliques, horribles, et extraordinaires tentations de Satan . . . ," sermon for Third Sunday in Advent 1612, in his *La Saincte Philosophie de l'ame* (Paris, 1614), pp. 619–41. For the fact that demonic delusions were also naturally caused, see Henri Boguet, *Discours des sorciers*, trans. and ed. Montague Summers and E. A. Ashwin as *An Examen of Witches* (London, 1929), p. xliii.

29 Jean de Nynauld, *De la Lycanthropie, transformation, et extase des sorciers* (Paris, 1615), passim; cf. Boguet, chaps. 17, 47, pp. 46–51, 145–8.

30 P. H. Kocher, *Science and Religion in Elizabethan England* (San Marino, Calif., 1953; New York, 1969), pp. 119–45; Wayne Shumaker, *The Occult Sciences in the Renaissance* (London, 1972), pp. 70–85.

31 This last idea is in Jacob Heerbrand (praeses.), *De magia dissertatio* (Tübingen, 1570), prop. 6, p. 2.

32 Nicolas Rémy, *Daemonolatreiae* (Lyons, 1595), bk. III, chap. 12; bk. I, chap. 6; bk. III, chap. 1; trans. and ed. E. A. Ashwin and Montague Summers as *Demonolatry* (London, 1930), pp. 181–2; cf. pp. xii, 11, 141.

33 Cotta, p. 34; William Perkins, *A Discourse of the Damned Art of Witchcraft* (Cambridge, 1610), epistle; cf. pp. 18–21, 27–8, 159.

34 Paolo Grillandi, *Tractatus de hereticis et sortilegiis* (Frankfurt, 1592), quaest. 7, p. 96.

35 Johann Georg Godelmann, *Tractatus de magis, veneficis et lamiis recte cognoscendis et puniendis* (Frankfurt, 1591), bk. I, chap. 8 ("De curatoribus morborum hyperphysicorum praestigiosis").

36 Del Rio, bk. I, chap. 4, quaest. 3, p. 25; cf. Rémy, bk. II, chap. 5, p. 113.

37 Perkins, p. 23.

38 James VI and I, "To the Reader," cf. p. 42; Bacon, *De augmentis scientiarum*, bk. II, chap. 2, in *Works*, IV, 296. See also Elich, chap. 6, pp. 75ff.

39 Guazzo, bk. II, chap. 8, p. 105; for Taxil and Guibelet, see Céard, "Folie et démonologie," pp. 129–43. Janus Matthaeus Durastantes, *Problemata . . . I, Daemones an sint, et an morborum sint causae* (Venice, 1567), fols. 1–83ᵛ.

40 For a recent survey of this tradition, see Edward Peters, *The Magician, the Witch, and the Law* (Brighton, 1978), passim.

41 H. R. Trevor-Roper, *The European Witch Craze of the Sixteenth and Seventeenth Centuries*, rev. ed. (London, 1978), pp. 58–9; K. V. Thomas, *Religion and the Decline of Magic* (London, 1971), pp. 579, 646; P. W. Elmer, "Medicine, Medical Reform and the Puritan Revolution," unpublished Ph.D. thesis, University of Wales, 1980, pp. 289–302; Jobe, pp. 343–4.

42 For entirely negative accounts of magic, see James VI and I, *Daemonologie*, and Niels Hemmingsen, *Admonitio de superstitionibus magicis vitandis* (Copenhagen, 1575). There is an excellent example of the fully sceptical use of natural magical evidence in Michel Marescot et al., *Discours véritable sur le faict de Marthe Brossier de Romorrantin prétendue démoniaque* (Paris, 1599), pp. 29–30; trans. A. Hartwell as *A True Discourse . . .* (London, 1599), pp. 22–3. The authors do not, however, rule out the possibility of demonic possession in principle. Nor was the argument that only extraordinary effects above the laws of nature could be attributed to the devil (those of the Brossier case not being of this sort) a very telling piece of antidemonology, for the devil was conventionally placed within such laws.

43 Grillandi, quaest. 6, pp. 59, 68–9; these remarks are found in many other texts. James VI and I, p. 44; Rémy, bk. II, chap. 4, p. 107; Perkins, p. 19.

44 Pereira, bk. I, chap. 3, pp. 21–2.

45 Perkins, p. 20; for the epistemological problems posed by occult qualities in the wider context of scientific and philosophical controversy, see Keith Hutchison, "What Happened to Occult Qualities in the Scientific Revolution?" *Isis*, 83 (1982), pp. 233–53.

46 Wilhelm Adolf Schreiber (Scribonius), *De sagarum natura et potestate* (Marburg, 1588), pp. 29–35; for the presence of demons in Schreiber's natural philosophy, see his *Rerum naturalium doctrina* (Basel, 1583).

47 Pierre de Lancre, disc. III ("De l'Attouchement"), fols. 113–77, esp. fols. 124–57. In the same way Boguet referred to Della Porta for the real natural effects of the witches' unguent, and Perkins discussed the well-known natural magical instance of the basilisk or cockatrice, concluding that fascination by breathing or looking alone was either fabulous or the indirect result of natural causes like contagion. There are arguments very similar to De Lancre's in Vairo, bk. II, chap. 10.

48 Binsfeld, pp. 173–8.

49 Boguet, pp. 64, 148–9; Sébastien Michaelis, *Pneumologie, ou discours des esprits*, 2nd ed. (Paris, 1613), trans. W. B. as *Pneumology or Discourse of Spirits* (London, 1613), pp. 5–6; Rémy, bk. III, chap. 1, pp. 139–41.

50 Lambert Daneau, *De veneficis* (Cologne, 1575), pp. 94–5, trans. R. W. as *A Dialogue of Witches* (London, 1575), sigs. H6ᵛ–16ᵛ. For the dove of Archytas, see Frances Yates, *Giordano Bruno and the Hermetic Tradition* (London, 1964), pp. 147–9, and *The Rosicrucian Enlightenment* (London, 1972), p. 76.

51 A point perhaps insufficiently realized by D. P. Walker, *Spiritual and Demonic Magic from Ficino to Campanella* (London, 1958), pp. 145–85, for even Del Rio thought that to avoid attributing all unusual effects to demonism one had to know of the many things surpassing ordinary scientific inquiry (bk. II, quaest. 5, pp. 60–1).

52 Giovanni della Porta, *Magiae naturalis, sive de miraculis rerum naturalium* (Naples, 1558), bk. II, chap. 26, p. 102; *Henry Cornelius Agrippa: His Fourth Book of Occult Philosophy*, trans. R. Turner (London, 1655), pp. 109–53; Levinus Lemnius, *Occulta naturae miracula* (Antwerp, 1561), fols. 83–87ᵛ, quotations from the English trans., *The Secret Miracles of Nature* (London, 1658), pp. 86–90, 385.

53 In this respect it is instructive to compare Reginald Scot, *The Discoverie of Witchcraft* (London, 1584), bk. I, chap. 7, pp. 14–15, with Le Caron, *Questions divers*, fol. 32ʳ, where the point is absorbed into conventional demonology.

54 Nynauld, p. 77; the argument is in fact identical to that of Rapine, p. 121. Cf. Jean Bodin, *De la Démonomanie des sorciers* (Paris, 1580), preface and "Refutation des opinions de Jean Wier," fols. 239ᵛ–40ʳ, 244ʳ, 247ᵛ, 251ʳ⁻ᵛ.

Acknowledgments

Anglo, Sydney. "Evident Authority and Authoritative Evidence: The *Malleus Maleficarum*." In Sydney Anglo, ed., *The Damned Art: Essays in the Literature of Witchcraft* (London: Routledge & Kegan Paul, 1977): 1–31. Reprinted with the permission of International Thomson Publishing Services Ltd. Courtesy of Yale University Sterling Memorial Library.

Withington, E.T. "Dr. John Weyer and the Witch Mania." In Charles Singer, ed., *Studies in the History and Method of Science* (Oxford: Clarendon Press, 1917–20, vol. I): 189–224. Courtesy of Yale University Medical Library.

Fatio, Olivier. "Lambert Daneau 1530–1595." In Jill Raitt, ed., *Shapers of Religious Traditions in Germany, Switzerland and Poland, 1560–1660* (New Haven: Yale University Press, 1981): 105–19. Reprinted with the permission of the Yale University Press. Copyright 1981. Courtesy of Yale University Sterling Memorial Library.

Monter, E. William. "Inflation and Witchcraft: The Case of Jean Bodin." In Theodore K. Rabb and Jerrold E. Siegel, eds., *Action and Conviction in Early Modern Europe* (Princeton: Princeton University Press, 1969): 371–89. Reprinted with the permission of the Princeton University Press. Courtesy of Yale University Cross Campus Library.

Pfister, Ch. "Nicolas Remy et la Sorcellerie en Lorraine a la fin du XVI Siècle." *Revue Historique* 93 (1907): 225–39, 28–44. Courtesy of Yale University Sterling Memorial Library.

Anglo, Sydney. "Melancholia and Witchcraft: The Debate between Wier, Bodin, and Scot." In Gerlo, ed., *Folie et Déraison à la Renaissance* (Brussels: Editions de l'Universite de Bruxelles, 1976): 209–28. Reprinted with the permission of Editions de l'Universite de Bruxelles. Courtesy of Yale University Sterling Memorial Library.

337

Clark, Stuart and P.T.J. Morgan. "Religion and Magic in Elizabethan Wales: Robert Holland's Dialogue on Witchcraft." *Journal of Ecclesiastical History* 27 (1976): 31–46. Copyright Cambridge University Press 1976. Reprinted with the permission of Cambridge University Press. Courtesy of Yale University Seeley G. Mudd Library.

Estes, Leland L. "Reginald Scot and His *Discoverie of Witchcraft*: Religion and Science in the Opposition to the European Witch Craze." *Church History* 52 (1983): 444–56. Reprinted with permission from *Church History*. Courtesy of Yale University Seeley G. Mudd Library.

Clark, Stuart. "King James's *Daemonologie*: Witchcraft and Kingship." In Sydney Anglo, ed., *The Damned Art: Essays in the Literature of Witchcraft* (London: Routledge & Kegan Paul, 1977): 156–81. Reprinted with the permission of International Thomson Publishing Services Ltd. Courtesy of Yale University Sterling Memorial Library.

Hitchcock, James. "George Gifford and Puritan Witch Beliefs." *Archiv für Reformationsgeschichte* 58 (1967): 90–9. Reprinted with the permission of the author. Courtesy of *Archiv für Reformationsgeschichte*.

Briggs, K.M. "Some Seventeenth-Century Books of Magic." *Folklore* 64 (1953): 445–62. Reprinted with the permission of The Folklore Society, University College London. Courtesy of Yale University Sterling Memorial Library.

Darst, David H. "Witchcraft in Spain: The Testimony of Martín De Castañega's Treatise on Superstition and Witchcraft (1529)." *Proceedings of the American Philosophical Society* 123 (1979): 298–322. Reprinted with the permission of the American Philosophical Society. Courtesy of Yale University Sterling Memorial Library.

Clark, Stuart. "Inversion, Misrule and the Meaning of Witchcraft." *Past and Present* 87 (1980): 98–127. World copyright: The Past and Present Society, 175 Banbury Road, Oxford, England. Reprinted with the permission of the Society and the author from *Past and Present*: A Journal of Historial Studies. Courtesy of Yale University Sterling Memorial Library.

Midelfort, H.C. Erik. "Witchcraft and Religion in Sixteenth-Century Germany: The Formation and Consequences of an Orthodoxy." *Archiv für Reformationsgeschichte* 62 (1971): 266–78. Reprinted with the permission of the author. Courtesy of Yale University Divinity Library.

Clark, Stuart. "The Scientific Status of Demonology." In Brian Vickers, ed., *Occult and Scientific Mentalities in the Renaissance* (Cambridge: Cambridge University Press, 1984): 351–74. Copyright Cambridge University Press 1984. Reprinted with the permission of Cambridge University Press. Courtesy of Yale University Cross Campus Library.